Civil Rights in the USA, 1863–1980

David Paterson and
Susan and Doug
Willoughby

Series Editors
Martin Collier
Erica Lewis
Rosemary Rees

D1424760

Heinemann

Heinemann is an imprint of Pearson Education Limited,
a company incorporated in England and Wales, having
its registered office at Edinburgh Gate, Harlow, Essex, CM20 2JE.
Registered company number: 872828

Heinemann is a registered trademark of Pearson Education Limited

First published 2001

ISBN: 978 0 435 32722 4

11
14

Designed and typeset by Wyvern 21 Ltd, Bristol
Printed and bound in China (CTPS/14)
Index compiled by Ian D. Crane
Picture research by Penni Bickle

Photographic acknowledgements
Associated Press: 59, 132, 142, 185, 255
Corbis: 92, 122, 129, 135, 145, 166, 213, 289
Hulton Getty: 23 (both), 27, 31, 66, 72, 83, 88, 101, 103, 115, 119,
136, 149, 159, 161, 168, 183, 236
Illustrated London News: 240
Peter Newark: 43

CONTENTS

HOW TO USE THIS BOOK

This book is divided into two parts. The AS part contains detailed accounts of the events and personalities of the period. Although it is written in a largely descriptive style, it also introduces some analysis of the social and political conflicts and changes that took place in the USA over this fairly lengthy period of time, and poses some of the questions that students of the period should be asking. The questions at the end of each chapter are intended to stimulate students to think analytically and to encourage a deeper understanding of the issues. They require them to select, sort, classify and deploy information to produce a supported and reasoned response to the question. For students studying the post-1945 Civil Rights Movement, the earlier chapters provide essential background for developing a deeper understanding of the origins and significance of the demand for civil rights and of the nature of the USA's multicultural society.

The A2 part of the book is more analytical in style and highlights some of the issues that have been the subject of varied interpretations and historical debate. It is important, however, that the relevant chapters of the AS part are read in conjunction with topics in the A2 part so that students develop the depth of understanding that comes from a detailed knowledge of the period. The A2 part is intended to stimulate reflection, appreciation of the complexity of the issues and to inspire further research and enquiry. Inevitably, parts of this book are, after all, the interpretations of the authors.

At the end of the AS and A2 parts there are Assessment sections. These have been based on the requirements of the new AS and A2 specifications provided by the three Awarding Bodies, AQA, Edexcel and OCR, as appropriate. There are exam-style source and essay questions for each relevant specification, together with advice on how to construct and express the answers.

The book covers the main features set out in the History specifications. The subject of Civil Rights in the USA has been approached by the Awarding Bodies with a different emphasis in each case. In line with the specifications the book deals primarily with the African-American struggle for civil rights, but does also discuss, to a lesser degree, the civil rights issues of other ethnic groups, women and other 'minority' groups. The authors have endeavoured to produce a study of the evolution of modern US society during this period with all its complexities, contradictions, conflicts and tensions. In so doing, it is hoped that the book will be of interest and value to all students following these courses.

AS SECTION: CIVIL RIGHTS IN THE USA, 1863–1968

Introduction

This part of the book traces the development of the Civil Rights Movement from its beginnings in slavery, emancipation and mass immigration.

In 1863, President Abraham Lincoln made the decision to emancipate the slaves. When the American Civil War ended in 1865, the issue of the extent to which freed slaves should be free and equal citizens of the USA became a matter of heated political debate, especially in the southern states. **Freedmen** were given the vote and briefly enjoyed some political status during this period, which was known as Reconstruction. This, however, was short-lived. By 1877, their earlier gains had been lost and they had become condemned to a life of poverty and discrimination as well as violence and prejudice, as white Americans asserted their superiority.

Throughout the nineteenth century, the ancestors of the original white settlers felt threatened, not only by the influx of freed slaves, but also by the thousands of immigrants who flooded into the USA in search of freedom and prosperity. Their arrival and heavy concentration in the big cities fanned the racist flame and they, too, experienced prejudice and violence. Consequently, as the population of the USA grew, it also became deeply divided. African-Americans, therefore, were not alone in attempting to gain recognition of their rights. Of all these groups, the saddest experience was that of the Native Americans (Indians) whose culture and way of life was completely destroyed during the second half of the nineteenth century, as white Americans moved and settled in the west, taking their land. During this time, in the face of adversity, African-Americans developed a strong sense of self-awareness and solidarity that would prove crucial in their struggle for civil rights.

It is important to understand, however, that the quest for these rights inevitably varied across the USA according to regional difference and variety. In those areas, especially the southern, former slave-owning states, where African-

Americans represented a significant percentage of the population, the issue of civil rights was paramount and highly controversial. There was also resistance here on the part of white Americans to reform. In the north, where slavery had been opposed but where there was still an African-American population, the struggle for recognition took a different form. People in regions of the USA where there were few, if any, ethnic minorities could be deprived of their rights by extreme poverty. These issues are approached in this book although the predominant focus is the struggle for black civil rights.

It was not until after the Second World War that the modern Civil Rights Movement really got under way. The more favourable verdicts of the US Supreme Court on the rights of *all* US citizens were coupled with a strong Black Civil Rights movement in the southern states of the USA, where white racist feelings were at their strongest and where racial segregation was legally enforced. Influential leaders such as Martin Luther King emerged during the 1950s to organise new and more militant forms of protest, as African-Americans were increasingly reluctant to accept the kind of treatment from most white Americans that the previous generation had endured. The movement captured the public imagination and much support from the more liberal white northerners who had become much better informed about the near-enslaved status of many African-Americans in 'the land of the free'.

During the early 1960s, campaigns for civil rights achieved notable successes and won the support of successive presidents Kennedy and Johnson, as a result of which, the US Congress passed substantial civil rights legislation that outlawed discrimination in many fields and guaranteed the vote for African-Americans. This inspired other ethnic minorities to renew their efforts to achieve real equality during the late 1960s. But while the campaign was a considerable success in the south (although some problems still existed), the social and economic problems of the African-American ghettos in the northern and western cities remained largely unresolved and had given rise to a more assertive form of campaigning, in the shape of Black Power.

In spite of the major gains of the fifties and sixties and although the battle for political and legal equality seemed to have been won, civil rights issues continued to be a focus as US politics moved to the right. This was especially so during the presidency of Richard Nixon, who was preoccupied with foreign affairs, in particular with the Vietnam War. Suspicion and rivalry in political circles also distracted politicians from ensuring that civil rights legislation was implemented, although some progress was made for African-Americans and the USA's other ethnic minorities. By this time, however, the social problems were massive. By 1970, the extension of equality to all US citizens still had some way to go.

CHAPTER 1

America – 'land of the free'?

INTRODUCTION

'We hold these truths to be self-evident, that all men are created equal, that they are endowed by their Creator with certain inalienable Rights, that among these are Life, Liberty and the Pursuit of Happiness.'

The American Declaration of Independence, written by Thomas Jefferson in 1776

The United States of America (USA) came into being as an independent state in 1783, after the **colonists** (originally British) fought for and won their freedom from British rule in the **American War of Independence**. Almost from the beginning, Jefferson's words helped to create an image of the USA as a land of freedom, opportunity and promise. In reality, it was far from being this. Even at that time, there were already around 500,000 men, women and children who were slaves. The property of their owners, they were either bought and sold in public auctions like cattle or born into captivity. These slaves were mostly in the cotton-growing **southern states**. Though some white people regarded the practice with distaste and disapproval, the institution of slavery remained largely unchallenged until the mid-nineteenth century. By this time, the small, fledgling state that originally occupied the eastern seaboard of the continent had expanded from coast to coast, and thousands of people of differing cultural origins were flooding into the USA, hoping to find the kind of freedom and happiness that Jefferson promised. He could not have known, of course, that they would come. His claim was made only in the name of the colonists, the descendants of the first British settlers. When confronted by these large numbers of people from different backgrounds and cultures, the colonists continued to hold the view that the 'new world' was only for them.

In claiming their right to freedom and equality as citizens of the USA, immigrants and freedmen alike arguably produced

KEY TERM

Colonists were the people who left Europe to set up new communities in America during the seventeenth century. Many of these were escaping from religious persecution. The lands on which they settled were subject to British law and government and so became British territories (colonies). There were originally thirteen of these stretching down the east coast (see the map on page 6).

KEY EVENT

American War of Independence. By the late eighteenth century, the American colonists were resentful of government from Britain. They were taxed by Britain and paid taxes on imported goods that had to come through Britain. They had no representation in parliament. Their protests were ignored so, from 1774, they planned open rebellion. This led to the American War of Independence (or Revolutionary War). The first shots were fired at Lexington on 19 April 1775.

the most dynamic feature of modern US history – the struggle for civil rights. This book is about that struggle.

Civil rights are those rights that citizens are entitled to expect in a free and democratic state. They include the right to vote and to be represented in government, the right to equality of opportunity (to education and work, for example), the right to receive the protection of the law and the right to be judged fairly before the law. Civil rights should guarantee the liberty of the individual, including the freedom to think, act and speak without fear. It is the duty and responsibility of government to create the environment where these rights can by enjoyed equally by creating and enforcing an effective legal framework. Much of the emphasis, therefore, of the movement for civil rights in the USA was on securing the necessary legislation to ensure that all American citizens enjoyed these rights.

Why was it such a struggle?

The answer to this question is partly political. Conflict arose when, in seeking to extend the rights of one individual or group of individuals, the rights and freedoms of others appeared to be being violated. The movement for civil rights sometimes challenged the fundamental philosophy of the American Constitution and the Bill of Rights (see page 18) but it also sought to uphold and implement them fairly. It was also a struggle because, in order to succeed, it was necessary to overcome racial prejudice on a huge scale. Ultimately, legislation can ensure some degree of change, but the battle to overcome the negative attitudes and perceptions of the mass of people is much harder to win. These are points that need to be considered when judging success and failure.

Nevertheless, the movement of African-Americans to win their civil rights, particularly in the second half of the twentieth century, inspired many other groups in the USA whose ancestors had gone in search of the American dream only to experience discrimination and prejudice. Their plight inspired the enthusiastic support of many white Americans, who enjoyed full civil rights.

Before we embark on the study of this remarkable movement, it is first essential to learn something about the earlier history of the USA – the land, its diverse peoples and, particularly, its form of government.

AMERICA – THE LAND

The frontier moves west

When the Americans won their independence, towards the end of the eighteenth century, their leaders were faced with a huge challenge. Freed from British control of government, trade and finance, and deprived of the protection of the British army, they now had to establish a practical and philosophical basis for the political, economic and social life of the new republic.

Security was a vital issue. Britain, France and Spain continued to have territorial possessions and economic interests on the North American continent. The undesirable presence of foreign interests created an impetus, in the minds of Americans, to expand, own and occupy the vast lands that lay to the west of the USA's initial frontier, removing these foreign interests in the process.

The growth of the USA, 1783–1853.

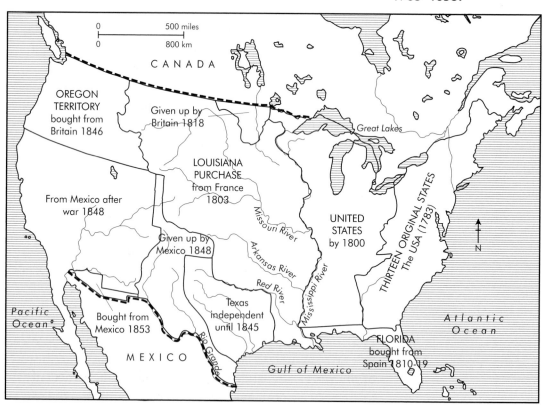

By 1800, migration of 'white' Americans into the Mississippi valley had displaced the Native American tribes who inhabited those lands and pushed the frontier of the USA westwards to the Mississippi River.

During the first half of the nineteenth century, the USA gradually extended its frontier, acquiring lands in the west by negotiated purchase or outright war. By 1853, the USA extended from the Atlantic Ocean in the east to the Pacific Ocean in the west.

Settlement of the new territories

The USA's newly acquired lands were vast and varied, and government-sponsored exploration revealed their extent and potential wealth. They were, however, devoid of white settlers. Consequently, their potential remained unexploited and, more seriously, they remained vulnerable to renewed interest from foreign powers.

The need to populate these newly acquired lands led to government-backed programmes to encourage people to 'go west'. Americans from the east responded, in increasing numbers, to the availability of land released by the government for settlement. After 1845, the lofty philosophy of **'Manifest Destiny'** – the belief that it was the destiny of Americans to populate the continent – added impetus to the significant movement to the Far and Midwest that had begun in 1843, when the first wagon train blazed the trail to Oregon.

Consequences of expansion

The extent and diversity of the land of the USA, the opportunities it offered and the challenge it presented of developing its potential, all contribute to an understanding of some of the issues associated with the struggle for civil rights.

When the government of the USA embraced all the land of the continent, in theory it also accepted responsibility for the future of its indigenous peoples. When it encouraged migration and immigration of peoples of differing beliefs and cultures from many parts of the world, it unwittingly set the scene for division and racism.

Expansion westwards brought to a head the differences of belief among politicians about slavery. Was the use of slave

'Manifest Destiny' was the belief, first expressed publicly in 1845, that white Americans were destined to occupy and govern all the territories of North America. This belief, coupled with concerns about security, justified the desire to gain land and, when the time came, the displacement of the Native Americans.

labour acceptable in the newly settled territories in the west? To those who wanted to put an end to slavery altogether, the idea that it might actually be expanded was particularly abhorrent. This was an issue that would sooner or later have to be confronted.

For those Americans who braved the hardships of the journey west and struggled with the land and the climate in order to settle and prosper, these experiences shaped the values and attitudes that were to influence their perceptions of people of other cultures and racial origins.

It is appropriate, therefore, to look more closely at all of these peoples.

AMERICA – THE PEOPLE

The 'melting pot'

In 1782, a Frenchman named Jean de Crèvcœur described America as being like a huge 'melting pot', into which people of differing origins and cultures were placed together and were transformed by the American experience into Americans. In reality, for a whole variety of reasons, this did not happen.

Today, the different cultures and origins of the American people are reflected by the term 'hyphenated Americans'. Hence, the ancestors of the original slave population or African immigrant peoples are referred to as 'African-Americans'. Those who migrated from Europe are called 'European-Americans'. Those from Mexico or southern US states who are of Spanish origin are known as '**Hispanic**-Americans'. The native Indians are commonly referred to as 'Native Americans'.

You will meet all of these terms in this book. In writing history, however, it is sometimes artificial to use current terms in past situations. For example, we will encounter a time when the ancestors of the original British settlers referred to themselves as 'Native Americans'. Similarly, there will be occasions when, for the purposes of clarity, the terms 'white' and 'black' will need to be used, but without any kind of racist or discriminatory intention.

Hispanic All those of Spanish origin. The word was used at this time to describe those of Puerto Rican as well as Mexican origin living in the USA.

The first Americans

Thousands of years before the first white settlers arrived on the North American continent, it was populated by tribes of Asian origin. These people had crossed the land bridge that existed over the Bering Straits from Siberia to Alaska and had settled in North America. It was Christopher Columbus who first named them 'Indians' in 1492.

By the end of the eighteenth century, many Indian tribes had encountered Europeans. Sometimes this brought diseases against which the Indian tribes had no immunity. Invariably, it deprived them of their land. However, they traded with the 'white men' and professed the desire to be 'brothers'. This desire was not recognised or incorporated into the independent USA. On the contrary, as settlers moved westwards in the nineteenth century, the government broke promises and treaties, and the Indians were systematically dispossessed of their lands.

Those Indians who remained in some of the eastern states were deprived of any protection and driven out. In Georgia, for example, laws were passed in the 1820s confiscating Indian property and prohibiting Indians from testifying against 'whites' in court. In the Midwest, the largely **nomadic tribes** who lived by hunting were forced to struggle for survival on smaller and smaller areas of land, before finally being virtually imprisoned on **reservations**, dependent on the government, their culture and traditional way of life destroyed.

The **Dawes Act** (1887) gave the Indians the rights of citizenship, including the protection of the law and the requirement to pay taxes. Some white Americans subsequently applied themselves to the tasks of educating the Indians and converting them to Christianity. Others considered them worthless and viewed their traditional culture with contempt. Both of these groups, in their different ways, contributed to the destruction of the Indians.

Native Americans remained the most neglected and impoverished of all the USA's ethnic minorities. During the twentieth century, they were deprived of vast areas of their reservation lands and offered financial inducements to leave what remained and move into urban areas. Undoubtedly, some benefited from education and entered the professions, but far

KEY TERMS

Nomadic tribes The Plains Indians had no settled communities. They roamed the Great Plains following the buffalo, living in villages of tipis that could be dismantled quickly.

Reservations were clearly defined lands that were allocated by the government to tribes of Native Americans, in order to remove them from lands that white settlers wished to occupy. At first, this was done with the apparent agreement of some of the Native Americans. Their traditional culture and way of life was destroyed by confinement to these limited areas. Plains tribes were unable to hunt buffalo and many tribes were dependent on food and clothing supplied by the US government through their appointed Indian Agents, who were frequently dishonest. Conditions were appalling and starvation was common.

The **Dawes Act** (1887) authorised the breaking-up of reservation lands into individual units. It was an attempt to destroy the tribal bonds that held Indians together and prevented them from becoming 'americanised'.

more found themselves living in appalling conditions in the cities and enduring discrimination and racial abuse. It is not surprising that, as the movement for black civil rights gained momentum in the second half of the twentieth century, articulate Indians joined the movement and demanded, among other things, the right to be called Native Americans, as well as compensation for the loss of their reservation land.

The original English settlers

The people who settled in what was to become the USA in 1783 were largely of English origin. By 1700, there were 200,000 settlers. They had first emigrated to the American continent during the seventeenth century, either to escape religious persecution or in search of economic security. The most famous are the Pilgrim Fathers – Puritans who set sail from England in the *Mayflower* and landed, in 1620, near Cape Cod, in what came to be known as New England.

Many more followed, establishing Puritan settlements in Massachusetts, Connecticut and Rhode Island, and destroying the Native Americans in the process. They often used merciless brutality, because the Native Americans would not give up their land or would not succumb to Christian conversion. The settlements they established were founded on religious bigotry, which is perhaps surprising given that they had themselves suffered persecution in England. Towards the end of the seventeenth century, the Quakers had established a settlement in Pennsylvania. This was one of the few places, along with Rhode Island, New Jersey and Delaware, where any kind of religious tolerance was practised.

After the initial struggle to survive, these early settlements prospered, due to the hard work and determination of their inhabitants. These characteristics, together with their narrow Protestant outlook, remained an intrinsic part of the make-up of these people for generations to come, and influenced their attitudes to others who would come after them. In particular, hostility to Roman Catholicism, which had been a feature of religious prejudice back in England, continued and remained deeply divisive wherever Catholicism was encountered, first in colonial and then in independent America.

Settlers of the southern colonies (Virginia, the Carolinas and Georgia) were distinctive from their northern counterparts. While society in the northern colonies represented a cross-

This cartoon depicts President Andrew Jackson in 1829, with the Native Americans shown as small children or dolls. In 1830, Jackson secured the passage through Congress of an Indian Removal Act, giving him the authority to remove Indians from the land by force, if necessary.

section of the social order, in the south, the colonists were more obviously from the gentry class, wishing to gain prosperity by the labour of others.

Initially, the labourers were white servants but, from the late seventeenth century, slaves were imported from the west coast of Africa. By the eighteenth and nineteenth centuries, the cotton and tobacco plantations of the south depended on the continuation of slavery. Religious beliefs were far less influential for southern than for northern settlers. Northern settlers were predominantly the ancestors of those of strict Protestant beliefs. These beliefs influenced their laws and determined their lifestyles more precisely than those in the south where religious beliefs were more varied. Religion provided southerners with neither a philosophical basis for their political convictions, nor an overriding work ethic.

African-Americans

The enslavement of African men and women in the USA dates from the seventeenth century. Laws passed in the 1660s defined the slave status of non-whites as hereditary, so their children also automatically became slaves. Even before independence, the **Triangular Trade** in human beings across the Atlantic Ocean had increased the African-American population to twenty per cent of the total population of the thirteen original states. As the cotton-based economy of the southern states grew during the nineteenth century, so did the states' dependence on slave labour. Although Congress banned the importation of slaves in 1808, slaves were encouraged by their owners to enter into a form of marriage and to reproduce, so causing the slave population to grow.

The morality of slavery was hotly debated. While its strongest advocates were in the south, many northerners were also sympathetic to pro-slavery arguments and certainly had little, if any, concept of racial equality. Hence, this institution, seen now as cruel and inhumane, was frequently projected as protective and providing the opportunity for the exercise of Christian charity and the extension of Christian virtues.

Ultimately, slavery played a significant role in bringing about the split between the northern and southern states that resulted in the American Civil War (1861–5) and led to the emancipation of the slaves in 1863. African-Americans were subsequently plunged into yet another phase of persecution

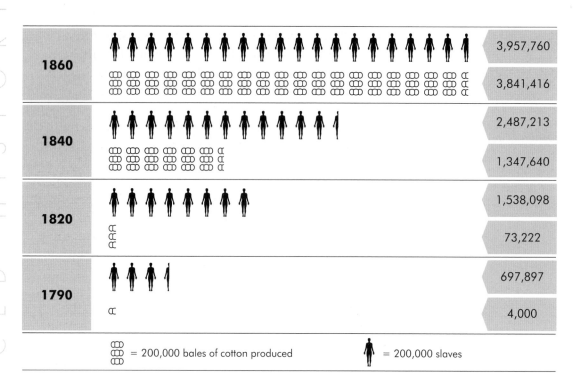

1860	3,957,760
	3,841,416
1840	2,487,213
	1,347,640
1820	1,538,098
	73,222
1790	697,897
	4,000

= 200,000 bales of cotton produced   = 200,000 slaves

and hardship. True freedom and equality were not so easily won. The struggle had only just begun.

Nevertheless, the shared experience of slavery united African peoples, whose cultural origins were diverse. In slavery, they developed a common form of language – **'pidgin'** English – and their own distinctive music and dance forms, which were frequently the means of expressing their sorrow and suffering. In addition, religion became increasingly important: by the nineteenth century, large numbers were being converted to Christianity. In their Methodist, Baptist or Presbyterian churches, they heard sermons that they would ultimately interpret as condemnation of their subjugation and that would fire them with enthusiasm to press for their rights to live as free and equal human beings. In slavery the foundations were laid for the eventual emergence of a sense of identity and cultural pride.

Hispanic-Americans

This term is used to describe, collectively, a variety of Spanish-speaking people. In the second half of the nineteenth century, these were largely Mexicans who had been forced off their land in California, Arizona and New Mexico, when these areas were absorbed into the USA. As more white Protestant Americans migrated west, the fact that these

The growth of cotton production and the slave population, 1790–1860.

KEY TERM

'Pidgin' was a dialect developed by slaves. It was a mixture of English and parts of the slaves' original African languages. Among other things, it enabled slaves with differing tribal origins to communicate. Also, it was probably almost totally incomprehensible to their owners!

KEY TERMS

Ghettos are, strictly speaking, parts of a city separated off by a wall or a fence. In black ghettos in the USA, African-Americans lived in a particular part of the city from which it was often difficult to move. Whites would frequently use clauses in property laws to prevent blacks moving to another district. Housing quality in the ghettos was generally very inadequate and there was serious overcrowding.

Aliens are foreign residents who have not usually been naturalised (i.e. made citizens of a country).

Prospector In 1848, gold was discovered in California. This led to an influx of men seeking to make a fortune by digging or panning (searching for gold in streams by sieving the silt on the bottom) for gold. They were called prospectors.

Irish potato famine
Potatoes were the staple diet of the poor in Ireland during the nineteenth century. The years 1845–6 were extremely wet and the potatoes rotted in the ground. The result was that the poor starved to death. Poor harvests made it hard for tenant farmers to pay their rents and they were evicted. Those who could manage to scrape together enough money to buy a passage, left their homeland for the USA and the hope of a better life.

people were not only Spanish speaking, but also Roman Catholic, led to conflict. Deprived of their land, the vast majority of Mexican Americans became labourers living in **ghetto** areas, called 'barrios', in cities such as Los Angeles.

By the mid-twentieth century, immigrants from Puerto Rico and Cuba who poured into the south-eastern states, had augmented the number of Hispanic-Americans. In the ghettos of San Francisco and Los Angeles, their lives were so appalling that, in the 1930s, about half a million returned to their homeland. In 1932, 200,000 Mexican **aliens** were expelled. Those who remained, however, campaigned to be treated fairly and with respect, and became actively involved in the movement for civil rights.

Immigration

In 1847, an enterprising young Jewish man arrived in the USA from Bavaria. He travelled to the west coast after hearing about the discovery of gold in California. He had no intention of becoming a **prospector**. He had obtained rolls of strong cloth and, when he arrived, he opened a factory making hard-wearing overalls and trousers for the gold diggers. His name was Levi Strauss, 'father' of the blue jeans that now bear his name. He is an example of at least one immigrant who gained fame and fortune. But his was not a success story shared by all.

Europeans had been attracted to the opportunities of the New World since the seventeenth century, but it was really from the beginning of the nineteenth century that mass immigration began to take place. Between 1815 and 1860, five million immigrants arrived in the USA from Europe, three million immigrating in only nine years (1845–54). These were predominantly from Ireland and Germany. Between 1845 and 1850, the **potato famine** in Ireland drove one million Irish settlers to undertake the difficult and dangerous voyage across the Atlantic Ocean to escape poverty and starvation.

Although some immigrants of German origin were farmers who moved further west, others, especially the Irish, settled in the eastern urban areas. There, they entered low-paid labouring work and the women became servants. In the latter decades of the nineteenth century, their numbers were swelled by another ten million, and by yet another eighteen million between 1890 and 1920. This latter wave included

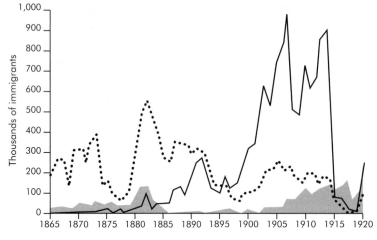

Changing patterns of immigration to the USA, 1865–1920.

Legend:
- •••••• Immigrants from northern and western Europe
- —— Immigrants from southern and eastern Europe
- ▓▓▓ Immigrants from Asia, North America and South America

Italians, English, Scottish and Welsh settlers, 200,000 Japanese and 40,000 Chinese, as well as several thousand Mexicans. Immigration continued until 1929, when restrictions were imposed by the government.

Nativism

Immigration made a massive impact on the lives of those white Americans who were born and bred in the USA and therefore considered themselves 'native'. They believed that the USA was their birthright and that white Protestant American ideals had to remain pure. They were strongly anti-immigrant and, in the 1850s, joined organisations such as the **Know Nothing Party**, whose purpose was clearly set out in its propaganda materials: 'Our mission is to restore America to the Americans, to purify and strengthen this nation . . . to keep it clean from corruption.' Other right-wing, nativist groups, such as the **Ku Klux Klan**, took up this cause and emerged during the struggle for civil rights. In the meantime, the influx of so many immigrants led to serious violent incidents during the late nineteenth and early twentieth centuries, especially in urban areas.

Why did immigration arouse such strong feelings?

A number of factors provide an answer to this question:

- The sheer number of immigrants was daunting, especially considering the narrow time span of their arrival and their

KEY TERM

The **Know Nothing Party** was a secret political society that grew up in the mid-nineteenth century in response to the influx of foreign immigrants. It was not opposed to immigration as such, but wanted to ensure that immigrants had no civil rights. Its slogan was 'Americans must rule America'. It wanted foreigners and Catholics banned from holding public office, stricter naturalisation laws and literacy tests for voting.

concentration in urban areas. It is claimed that the Irish population of New York City, for example, was twice as large as that of Dublin in 1890. By this time, four-fifths of the city's population was made up either of immigrants or of the descendants of immigrants.

- Religious antagonism was another major factor. A significant proportion of immigrants were Roman Catholic. This was especially true of the Irish, Italians and Hispanics. Anti-Catholicism ran deep in nativist US society. There were also many Jews. By 1913, the Jewish population of New York City's Lower East Side was 1.25 million.

- Immigrants tended to cluster in specific areas of the cities. In these ghettos, they maintained their own native culture – language, lifestyle and customs, as well as religion. They had their own shops selling their own food, their own forms of entertainment and, sometimes, their own schools. There was, therefore, little social or cultural integration.

- Immigrants were seen to threaten the job opportunities of these native-born Americans. During the latter part of the nineteenth century, the USA, particularly in the north-east, had undergone an 'industrial revolution'. During this time, unskilled Irish and Chinese labour built the first transcontinental railway and worked as cheap labour in the mines. Invariably, immigrant labour was in competition with that of white native Americans. The problem was exacerbated by the fact that peak periods of immigration often coincided with periods of economic depression in the USA, when unemployment was high.

- Groups of other racial origin were often in conflict with each other, especially when it came to jobs. After the emancipation of the slaves, for example, freed 'blacks' and poverty-stricken Irish labourers competed for low-paid work.

- The majority of immigrants came from countries where they had had no rights or freedom. The freedom to express views and opinions was welcomed, especially by Germans and Italians, who became active in left-wing organisations, seeking change and improvement. This kind of political activism was controversial and resented.

The struggle for civil rights by black Americans must, therefore, be set against this background of racial, cultural and regional diversity. However, as it was an essentially political struggle, it is helpful to know something of the structure and function of the government of the USA.

AMERICA – THE GOVERNMENT

The USA is governed according to the Constitution of the United States. This sets out the rules and regulations, and defines the extent and limits of the powers of the different parts of government. It incorporates checks and balances to prevent any one part becoming too powerful. Above all, it is intended to protect all of the American people and their property. It is **democratic**. Today, all the American people participate in the choice of their representatives at every level. This has not always been the case.

Origins

The Constitution was drawn up in 1787, four years after the USA came into being, and it became effective in 1789, after a long and difficult process. The fundamental issue was how to devise a system that would not compromise the independence of each individual state and would recognise and preserve the differences between them. After all, the thirteen original states had only come together to fight for their freedom from Britain. Beyond that, they had each operated independently since, in some cases, they had little in common. None wished to surrender this freedom, but they recognised that there were some situations in which it was essential that they act in unity. Therefore, there had to be a unifying authority – in foreign affairs, defence and overseas trade, for example.

A federal system of government

The solution was to adopt a federal system. This provided for a federal (national) government based in Washington, DC, and a state government based in the capital of each state. Thus power was shared. States retained extensive powers to organise their affairs as they wished. They had the power to pass laws relating to the policing of the state, education and most other internal matters. In some states these laws imposed the death penalty for certain crimes. After slavery had been abolished, individual states could decide whether white and black students could be educated in the same school, or whether people of all races could ride on the same bus.

Federal laws had to be ratified (accepted) by two-thirds of the states before they became the law of the land. This became an issue in the campaign for civil rights. Also, these laws were often framed in such a way that loopholes could be found for avoiding their implementation. On the other hand, for much

KEY TERM

Democratic A system where the government is elected by the people who have the right to vote.

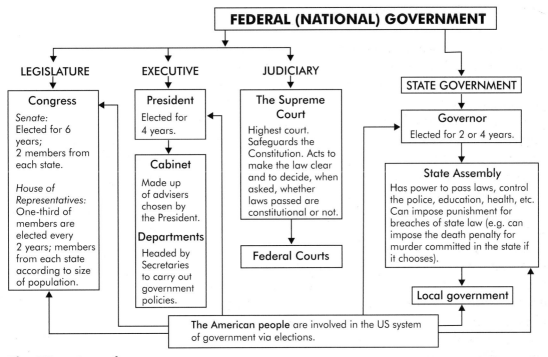

FEDERAL (NATIONAL) GOVERNMENT

LEGISLATURE

Congress

Senate:
Elected for 6 years;
2 members from each state.

House of Representatives:
One-third of members are elected every 2 years; members from each state according to size of population.

EXECUTIVE

President
Elected for 4 years.

Cabinet
Made up of advisers chosen by the President.

Departments
Headed by Secretaries to carry out government policies.

JUDICIARY

The Supreme Court
Highest court. Safeguards the Constitution. Acts to make the law clear and to decide, when asked, whether laws passed are constitutional or not.

Federal Courts

STATE GOVERNMENT

Governor
Elected for 2 or 4 years.

State Assembly
Has power to pass laws, control the police, education, health, etc. Can impose punishment for breaches of state law (e.g. can impose the death penalty for murder committed in the state if it chooses).

Local government

The American people are involved in the US system of government via elections.

The US system of government.

of the nineteenth century, after the westward expansion of the USA had begun, vast areas of the country that were beginning to be settled were insufficiently populated to become states. Until the population reached 60,000, these remained territories of the USA, governed directly from Washington, DC, and subject, therefore, to federal law.

A republic

There was no disagreement among those who drew up the Constitution that the USA should be a republic. They had had enough of monarchy! The head of state would be a president, who was responsible for proposing policies and ensuring that the country was governed effectively. There would also be a body to make laws and this body, called Congress, would be made up of the representatives of the people (see diagram above). This pattern was reflected at state level by the governor and state assembly.

The powers and control of the president were an issue. To preserve the freedom of the individual and control the power of the head of state, Americans arrived at a system that carefully regulated the process for electing a president and also made it possible for the president to belong to a different political party from the dominant group in Congress.

Although the position of President of the USA was (as it remains) a very powerful one, it was controlled. The president could propose laws, but only Congress could pass them. However, the president could exercise the right he was given by the Constitution to **veto** laws passed by Congress.

Amendments to the Constitution, the Bill of Rights and the Supreme Court

Any subsequent modifications that needed to be made were added as Amendments to the Constitution. These were introduced by the federal government and submitted to the state governments for ratification. The first ten amendments, ratified in December 1791, became known as the Bill of Rights. These established, in writing, the liberties of the individual that could not be infringed by interference from the government. They were protected by the Supreme Court (see diagram on page 17), whose role it was to scrutinise laws and ensure that they did not contravene the freedoms guaranteed by the Bill of Rights.

The American Constitution and the Bill of Rights provided the basis, at the end of the eighteenth century, for the claim that the USA was the shining example of freedom and democracy in the world. At this time, however, they protected and guaranteed these rights for what was to become a relatively small proportion of the country's future population. The challenge to the gleaming image would come when others, who regarded themselves as citizens of the USA, claimed the same rights and were denied them.

KEY TERM

Veto The act of rejecting or prohibiting a decision, action or law. It is a right of action vested in an individual or group. The US Constitution bestowed this right on the president, allowing him to veto legislation presented to him by Congress. Congress, however, can override any veto by a two-thirds majority.

SUMMARY QUESTIONS

1 Describe and explain the expansion of the USA by the end of the nineteenth century.

2 Describe and explain the main causes of tension in US society by the 1870s.

3 In your view, were any social groups in US society more disadvantaged than others? Explain your ideas.

4 How democratic was the USA by the end of the nineteenth century?

CHAPTER 2

Towards a kind of freedom, 1863–77

INTRODUCTION

On New Year's Day in 1863, President Abraham Lincoln signed the Emancipation Proclamation that bestowed freedom on well over three million of the slave population of the USA. By 1870, 700,000 freed slaves in the southern states had been given, with the Fifteenth Amendment, a fundamental civil right – the right to vote. In five of the southern states, black Americans were the majority of voters. Why, then, did civil rights become an issue?

Emancipation gave many former slaves only a brief glimpse of freedom and equality. As **W. E. B. Du Bois** wrote: 'the slave went free; stood a brief moment in the sun; then moved back again toward slavery'. In the search for the roots of the modern Civil Rights Movement, we need to begin with the end of slavery, examine its consequences and consider the progress made by freedmen in this period. That is the purpose of this chapter.

SLAVERY AND THE AMERICAN CIVIL WAR

Secession and civil war

In 1863, when Lincoln freed a significant proportion of the slave population, the USA was in the grip of the most terrible conflict in its history – the American Civil War. This began in 1861, following the **secession** from the USA of the slave-owning states, and lasted until 1865. In 1861, they had formed themselves into the **Confederacy** and drawn up their own constitution. This not only protected their right to own slaves in the eight existing states, but also made provision for the extension of slavery into new territories that the Confederacy might acquire at any future time.

This action could not be condoned in the northern states, where the anti-slavery movement was strong, but the south was prepared to fight for its right to be separate. It was a fierce and devastating war that divided families and left large numbers destitute. More importantly, it destroyed the unity of the USA. When the war ended, finding a basis on which unity and trust could be re-established was a major problem.

It is not necessary to discuss here all of the complex issues that led to the outbreak of the Civil War. However, the divergent attitudes to slavery in the northern and southern states were important.

Attitudes to slavery in the south before the Civil War

It would be simplistic to separate the north and the south on the basis of their attitudes to African-Americans. In the 1860s, approximately 90 per cent of African-Americans lived in the south and were mostly plantation slaves. In the southern states, the **plantation economy** made slaveholding an economic necessity. By the second half of the nineteenth century, owners claimed that it was impossible to run their cotton or tobacco plantations profitably without slave labour.

By 1860, 88 per cent of plantation owners farmed relatively small scale plantations, owning about 20 to 25 slaves. Owning slaves gave these people a sense of prestige and social position that they would not otherwise have had. Pro-slavery supporters called on biblical and historical precedents to support their claim that slavery was a normal and acceptable institution. After all, they said:

- in the Old Testament, Abraham had kept slaves
- at no time did Jesus Christ preach against slavery
- St Paul, in his letters, ordered slaves to obey their masters and actually returned a runaway slave to his master
- zealous supporters of slavery claimed that slaves were saved from devil worship and witchcraft by the institution and were then brought to Christianity
- there was a strong belief that God, who regarded negroes as an inferior or accursed race, had given slaves (like women) their station in life
- pro-slavery writers suggested that to free the slaves would lead to uprisings and bloodshed, and reminded their readers of the impact of mob rule during the French Revolution

Confederacy is the name given to the union of the southern (slave-owning) states that separated themselves from the Union in 1861. These were Virginia, North and South Carolina, Tennessee, Georgia, Alabama, Mississippi, Louisiana, Texas, Florida and Arkansas.

Plantation economy
Plantations were frequently very large, well-run farming units growing cotton or tobacco. They were almost exclusively worked by slave labour. The plantations invariably made their owners very wealthy, hence references to the 'planter aristocracy'. These owners built themselves huge mansions. However, the south was not exclusively organised into plantations. Many white farmers in the south were very poor and hostile to the rich planters, who enjoyed political influence as well as economic prosperity.

- if all of this was not sufficient justification, it was claimed that slaves were fed, clothed and treated with kindness by their benevolent masters.

This latter claim was not supported by the evidence of plantation slavery in action. In 1845, **Frederick Douglass**, a former slave, published his autobiography, the *Narrative of the Life of Frederick Douglass*. In his book he recounts the kind of incident that is more commonly associated with the institution.

> My first master's name was Captain Anthony . . . He was not considered a rich slaveholder. He owned two or three farms and about thirty slaves. His farms and slaves were under the care of an overseer. The overseer's name was Plummer. Mr Plummer was a miserable drunkard, a profane swearer, and a savage monster. He always went armed with a cowskin and a heavy cudgel. I have known him to cut and slash the women's heads so horribly, that even master would enrage at his cruelty . . . Master, however, was not a humane slaveholder. It required extraordinary barbarity on the part of an overseer to affect him . . . He would at times seem to take great pleasure in whipping a slave. I have often been awakened at the dawn of the day by the most heart-rending shrieks of an own aunt of mine, whom he used to tie up to a joist, and whip upon her back till she was literally covered with blood. No words, no tears, no prayers, from his gory victim, seemed to move his iron heart from its bloody purpose. The louder she screamed, the harder he whipped; and where the blood ran fastest, there he whipped longest.

While there were slave owners who were benevolent, it was the frequency of accounts such as this that fired the **Abolition Movement**, particularly in the north. Even so, it took a great deal of time and effort to convince people that slavery was an evil institution that had to be destroyed. If people in the south did believe it, they remained silent for fear of reprisals.

Attitudes to slavery in the north before the Civil War

Some religious groups in the north, especially the Quakers, had long been opposed to slavery. The earliest movement demanding its abolition dates from 1817, when the American Colonization Society was founded. It was a fairly moderate reform movement, demanding a gradual emancipation of the slaves with compensation for their owners. It also advocated repatriation to Africa for freed slaves. This was not well received by African-Americans themselves, who had been born in America and regarded it as their home. Consequently, the society was not really seen by all abolitionists as truly supportive of the American slaves. Nevertheless, white abolitionists such as **William Lloyd Garrison** campaigned not only for emancipation but also for full and equal civil and legal rights for African-Americans. Garrison was a member of the **Anti-Slavery Society** which was heavily involved in the campaign for **The Fourteenth Amendment**.

There was, of course, some slavery in the north, particularly in New York. Moreover, in spite of the support that abolitionist campaigners received in the north, there were significant proportions of the population who, even if they did not support slavery, were hostile towards any suggestion that African-Americans were equal to themselves or should have rights of citizenship. In 1845, a state legislative committee in Illinois pronounced: 'by nature, education, and association, it is believed that the Negro is inferior to the White man, physically, morally and intellectually . . . such is the opinion of the vast majority of our citizens'.

Political support for abolishing slavery

It required legislation to destroy slavery. Within the political system, the president did not have the power to do this alone. By the mid-nineteenth century, the federal system was still weak. The real power rested with the state governments. However, pro- and anti-slavery pressure groups could claim notable political support both on an individual and a party basis during the nineteenth century.

The traditional supporter of the anti-slavery cause was the **Whig Party**. This became absorbed into the **Republican Party**, formed in 1854. From its ranks came politicians who were to play a key role in reform, most notably **Thaddeus Stevens** and **Abraham Lincoln**. In contrast, the **Democratic Party** became split over the issue of slavery. By 1860 the Democrats had held power since 1828. However, their support came largely from the southern plantation owners, so many were reluctant to jeopardise their hold on power by espousing abolition. A leading pro-slavery Democrat was **Stephen A. Douglas**, who became the party's candidate in the presidential election of March 1860 that brought Abraham Lincoln to the White House.

Thaddeus Stevens (1792–1868) He joined the Whig Party and was elected to the House of Representatives in 1849. Here he fought to prevent the passing of the Fugitive Slave Act (1850), which ordered escaped slaves to be returned to their masters. He was a strong supporter of Abraham Lincoln

Abraham Lincoln (1809–65) took a keen interest in politics, supporting the Whig Party. He condemned slavery, but believed that the southern states had the right to maintain the plantation system. He was therefore critical of the Anti-Slavery Society. In 1856 he joined the Republican Party, standing against Steven A. Douglas for a seat in the Senate. He opposed Douglas's plan to allow people moving into the new territories in the west to own slaves. In 1860, Lincoln became the Republicans' candidate for President. The Democratic vote was split among three candidates and Lincoln was elected. He was inaugurated for a second term in March 1865, but on 14 April he was assassinated.

The **Democratic Party** began with Thomas Jefferson in the 1790s. It obtained its political support from the white southern planters, and farmers in the north. The Democrats lost political ground over the issue of slavery, many northern Democrats supporting its retention in the south.

Thaddeus Stevens.

Abraham Lincoln.

The political temperature began to rise significantly around the slavery question in the 1850s. By this time, abolition had become inextricably bound up with the preservation of the Union. The unity of the USA was threatened and Republican politicians, particularly, were faced with the challenge of maintaining it, but at what cost? The first price to be paid was the acceptance by anti-slavery politicians of the **Fugitive Slave Act** (1850). This was part of the **Compromise of 1850** accepted by northern Republicans in Congress to secure the agreement of the southern representatives to the admission of California to the USA as a free state and so prevent the extension of slavery (see page 26). Enforcement led to violent clashes between anti-slavery protesters, angered by the Compromise, and law enforcement officers.

Civil war on the horizon

The struggle between the north and the south reached a climax over the issue of extending slavery to the newly settled territories in the west. This was a key issue in the 1860 presidential election campaign. Lincoln and many of his Republican supporters clearly accepted the institution of slavery in the existing southern states, but were not prepared to countenance its extension into newly settled territories. Lincoln's view was that if it remained contained in the original southern states, it could eventually be ended. In his inaugural address on 4 March 1861, Lincoln said:

> Apprehension seems to exist among the people of the Southern States that by the accession of a Republican Administration their property and their peace and personal security are to be endangered. There has

never been any reasonable cause for such apprehension . . . I have no purpose, directly or indirectly, to interfere with the institution of slavery in the States where it exists. I believe I have no lawful right to do so, and I have no inclination to do so.

Lincoln, however, was seen in the south as the enemy of the plantation owners because of his apparent opposition to slavery. The states had already threatened secession in 1850 if the Fugitive Slave Act had not been passed. The election of Lincoln was the final straw. When seven of the southern states seceded in December 1860 and inaugurated their own President, Jefferson Davis, in February 1861, war became almost inevitable. It was a declaration of independence.

Davis subsequently claimed that federal forts in the territory of the new Confederacy now belonged to it and proceeded to lay claim to Fort Sumter in South Carolina. When the commanding officer refused to surrender immediately, the Confederate soldiers opened fire. At this point, Virginia, Arkansas, Tennessee and North Carolina joined the original seven 'rebel' states. The border slave states of Maryland, Delaware, Kentucky and Missouri remained part of the Union. Consequently, when Lincoln called for volunteers to fight in April 1861, it was not to further the cause of abolition. The slavery issue had severely weakened the bonds that held together the Union of all the states. As far as Lincoln was concerned, the war was intended to prevent them from being permanently broken.

Why did President Lincoln emancipate the slaves in 1863?

When the war began, Lincoln had no intention of liberating the slaves, even though many people in the anti-slavery movement urged him to turn the war into an emancipation crusade. Frederick Douglass claimed that 'to fight against slaveholders without fighting against slavery, is but a half-hearted business'. However, Lincoln did not want to lose the support of the slave-owning border states that had stayed loyal to the Union. He was also keen to keep pro-slavery Democrats in the north on his side.

When Union troops began to enter and capture Confederate territory, the issue of confiscated property arose. Slaves were seen as property. Lincoln was quick to argue that, as the southern states had illegally seceded, their property was still

Stephen A. Douglas (1813–61) became a Supreme Court judge in 1841. In 1854 he introduced the Kansas–Nebraska Bill to allow people moving into the newly opened territories of the west (Louisiana, Arkansas, Oklahoma, Kansas, Missouri, Nebraska, Iowa, North and South Dakota, Montana, parts of Minnesota, Colorado and Wyoming) to keep slaves. There followed a series of public debates with Abraham Lincoln, who opposed the extension of slavery.

KEY EVENTS

The **Fugitive Slave Act** (1850) allowed slave owners to arrest runaway slaves escaping to non-slave-owning states without a warrant. The Act made it possible for 'slave catchers' to come from the south and lay claim to free black people in the north, many of whom had been free for up to 30 years. In practice, it was virtually impossible to enforce.

The **Compromise of 1850** was drawn up to prevent the break-up of the Union. In 1849, the USA had acquired California, Utah Territory and New Mexico after a war with Mexico. The Republican Party wanted to prevent the extension of slavery to these territories, but the southern states wanted to allow slave owners who migrated or extended their businesses there to take their slaves. It was agreed that California would be a free state, but that the people of Utah Territory and New Mexico should decide the issue themselves.

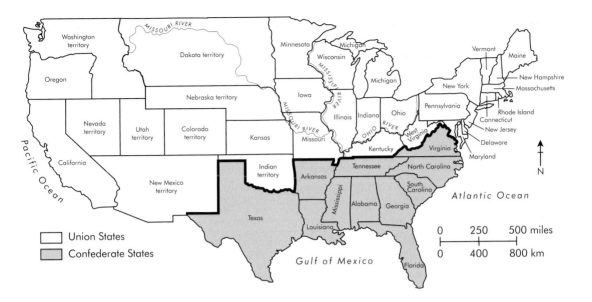

How the US states divided in the Civil War.

eligible for the protection that the Constitution afforded. He believed that to do otherwise would alienate southern rebels even further and reduce the possibility of the war coming to a satisfactory conclusion. The first Confiscation Act (1861), therefore, recognised slaves as property and did not give them their freedom. Instead, they were kept as contraband and put to work behind the lines until such time as the war came to an end. In this way, Lincoln hoped to encourage the southern rebels to return to the Union.

Lincoln revealed his attitude to emancipation in 1861 and 1862 when he sacked three of his commanding officers for trying to free slaves in order to recruit them into the Union army. However, as it became clear that the southern rebellion would not be easily suppressed, changing circumstances influenced Lincoln's perceptions of the war. A number of issues led him to change the focus of the war and, ultimately, to emancipate the slaves.

- Initially, the war did not go well for the north. Although immigration from Europe had swelled the population of the northern states and the Union armies were numerically greater, they were untrained and so gained little advantage. Losses were high on both sides and the fortunes of both fluctuated. There was concern in the north that slavery enabled the Confederate states to deploy more white men into their armies. Their wives and the slaves could run their plantations. This might give them an advantage.

- In July 1862, Congress passed a second Confiscation Act. This freed slaves who had been confiscated from rebellious masters or who had escaped and taken refuge behind Union lines. It also allowed former slaves to become soldiers. By linking emancipation to military necessity, Lincoln could be sure of maintaining the support of the pro-slavery lobby among northern politicians.

- There was a fear that an independent Confederacy might gain international recognition. Creating the semblance of the war as a battle against slavery was likely to focus foreign support on the emancipation issue and pre-empt formal recognition of the Confederacy.

- If Lincoln issued the Emancipation Proclamation himself he was likely to strengthen his personal position. Such a proclamation would almost certainly have come in time from the more **radical wing** of the Republican Party, whatever his objections.

The Emancipation Proclamation (1863)

In the end, the tide of events almost drove Lincoln to the position where he had little alternative but to grant freedom to African-Americans. In reality, he never lost sight of his original intention in fighting the war – to preserve the Union. He changed his position only when it became clear that the preservation of the Union depended on the emancipation of the slaves. He virtually admitted this, late in 1862, when he said:

> If I could save the Union without freeing **any** slave, I would do it, and if I could save it by freeing **all** the slaves, I would do it; and if I could save it by freeing some and leaving others alone, I would also do that.

In fact, he did the latter, since only the slaves in rebel states were freed by the proclamation. Moreover, he exempted slaves in the former rebel state of Tennessee from liberation. At the time, Tennessee was subject to the military government of Andrew Johnson, a pro-slavery former Democrat who was a loyal Lincoln supporter. Although Lincoln drew up the proclamation in July 1862, he waited until the military situation had improved before announcing it, so as to appear to be acting from a position of strength.

In September, following the Union army's success at the Battle of Antietam, he issued the Emancipation Proclamation, effective from 1 January 1863. Slaves in those

KEY TERM

The **radical wing** is the most fanatical section of a political party. In this case, it refers to those members of the Republican Party, led by Thaddeus Stevens, who campaigned not just for the emancipation of the slaves, but also for full rights of citizenship to be given to African-Americans.

Black Americans celebrating the Emancipation Proclamation in 1863.

states that remained loyal to the Union were not included, although in the wake of the proclamation, two of these – Maryland and Missouri – voluntarily liberated their slaves before the end of the war. By the time of his second inaugural address, in March 1865, Lincoln himself was depicting the war as a crusade to destroy slavery.

The immediate impact of emancipation

In many ways, the Emancipation Proclamation had little immediate effect, since it related to slaves in territories that the Union did not, at the time, control. It could be argued, however, that it gave added impetus to a movement that was already well under way by 1863 for, by this time, slavery was beginning to fall apart.

From the very beginning of the war, when Federal (Union) soldiers began to march into the south, slaves quickly got the message that they had come to destroy their oppressors, so they began to desert their plantations in increasing numbers. Alternatively, they simply refused to work. Reports coming from Louisiana also talked of gallows being erected by African-Americans from which to hang plantation owners. In November 1862, a report read: 'Slavery in southern Louisiana is forever destroyed and worthless, no matter what Mr Lincoln or anyone else may say on the subject.'

In many respects, then, the Emancipation Proclamation merely confirmed and added legality to a movement towards freedom that had already begun. Even so, it did not prevent the status of some slaves being affected by the fortunes of war, as the Union and Confederate armies struggled to gain the advantage. One former slave claimed to have been given his freedom fifteen times!

Reactions in the north

Emancipation received a mixed reception in the north. For those opposed to slavery, the Civil War now took on new meaning. While previously they may have been confused about the fundamental issues in the conflict, emancipation provided a purpose that, for them, it had previously lacked. They therefore fought on with renewed vigour. However, there were also pro-slavery supporters in the north who were angered by Lincoln's action. They incited anti-black protests in northern cities. The strongest response, however, came with the recruitment of African-Americans to the Union army. This began to happen in large numbers after the Emancipation Proclamation and was very significant.

African-American soldiers

Lincoln had issued the proclamation as a political reaction to the fluctuating fortunes of the war. However, the liberation of almost four million African-Americans (over one-third of the population of the southern states) was bound to have a profound effect on American society. After all, here was a huge section of humanity that had no social, political or economic status of its own. A declaration of freedom was only the beginning. What would follow? Lincoln's plans were unclear, but the leaders of the anti-slavery movement were determined to ensure that African-Americans were recognised as citizens of the USA. They believed that fighting in the Union army would secure this.

By the end of the Civil War, approximately 186,000 African-Americans had fought in the black regiments that were recruited in the north. They fought bravely, but this did not bring them recognition and respect. Instead, they faced discrimination and death.

- White soldiers would not fight alongside them, so they were formed into black regiments.

Frederick Douglass felt that fighting in the US army would allow African-Americans to gain citizenship:

Once let the black man get upon his person the brass letters, US; let him get an eagle on his button, and a musket on his shoulder and bullets in his pocket, and there is no power on earth which can deny that he has earned the right to citizenship.

- They were put into the front lines or into situations where large numbers were killed. Many languished in disease-ridden camps and died without seeing action.
- Until June 1864, they were paid about half as much as white soldiers.
- If the Confederate army captured them, they were sent back into slavery or executed. They were not treated as prisoners of war.
- Recruitment of former slaves was bitterly resented in the north, where immigrants from Europe and Ireland had swelled the urban population. Many of these immigrants were extremely poor and struggling to survive. Poverty drove them to volunteer for the Union army. African-Americans were, therefore, seen as unacceptable competition when they also volunteered. During the summer of 1863, riots broke out in which large numbers were killed. The worst was started by Irish immigrants in New York City. The army was sent in to re-establish order and opened fire on the rioters. By the end, over 1000 people had been killed or injured.

Assassination of Lincoln

The response to emancipation gave some clear indications of the crisis that loomed ahead. On 9 April 1865, the Confederate army surrendered at Appomattox. The Civil War was over. What did the future hold for the millions of freed slaves? By emancipating them, Lincoln had plunged them into the American 'melting pot'. Would they emerge as Americans? What was the next stage in Lincoln's plan for them? On 14 April 1865, Abraham Lincoln was **assassinated**.

POSTWAR RECONSTRUCTION, 1865–77

The impact of the war

By the time the war ended, the Confederate states were ruined. Buildings, roads and railways had been destroyed. The southern economy had collapsed and inflation had soared. Union soldiers occupied the south and the rebellious states came under military jurisdiction. The human tragedy was worse. Apart from the huge loss of life in the struggle, bitter and demoralised ex-soldiers, refugees from war-torn towns and cities and freed slaves roamed the countryside aimless and confused.

KEY EVENT

The assassination of Lincoln On 14 April, Lincoln went to Ford's Theater in Washington, DC, with his wife and friends. During the third act, an assassin, John Wilkes Booth, entered the President's box and shot him in the back of the head. Booth sympathised with the Confederate cause and resented Lincoln's policy towards Confederate rebels. Lincoln died in the White House the following morning. Booth was hunted down and probably shot by Union troops, although it has also been suggested he may have shot himself. Eight others were charged with plotting the President's death and four were hanged for the crime including Mary Surratt, the first woman in US history to be executed.

In contrast, the north was less adversely affected, at least economically. However, the loss of life was almost certainly as devastating to northern families as it was to those in the south. Some of the traditional industries that depended on raw materials from the south – cotton textiles, for example – slumped. But wartime industries producing arms, ammunition, military uniforms and clothing boomed. The government imposed **protective tariffs** on foreign imported goods to help domestic industry to prosper.

Immigrant labour filled the gap left by the native-born men and boys who went to fight, and so kept agriculture flourishing. More importantly, Congress passed a number of laws to extend the railway network, including the **Pacific Railroad Act**, and to open up the opportunities for further westward expansion. This legislation, introduced by the Republican Party, offered opportunities for self-improvement to all classes of people, but especially to the poor.

In the short term, the war particularly benefited wealthy businessmen and manufacturers who, besides taking advantage of the opportunities that the war offered to make a fortune, could offset some of their expenses by paying their workers low wages. While the men were away fighting, businesses could employ youths, women and girls at much lower rates. As a result, ordinary working people in industry suffered.

Future problems

Generally, the economy of the whole of the USA (north and south) was adversely affected by the war and this was certainly one problem that a post-war administration would have to resolve. However, there were two infinitely greater problems:

- How was the unity of the United States to be restored?
- What was to be the status and future of the several million slaves who had been freed?

To some extent, it was impossible to separate these two issues. On the morning of 15 April 1865, three hours after

KEY TERM

Protective tariffs were duties placed on goods being imported from abroad in order to protect home production of the same goods from foreign competition.

KEY EVENT

The **Pacific Railroad Act** (1862) authorised the building of a transcontinental railway linking the east and west coasts and gave impetus to the settlement of the west. The Union Pacific and Central Pacific companies were given land grants of 60 million acres (which they sold cheaply to would-be settlers to finance the building of the railway) and loans of $20 million.

Andrew Johnson.

Andrew Johnson (1808–75)
was apprenticed to a tailor in 1822 and soon owned his own business. He joined the Democratic Party and served for four years as governor of Tennessee (1853–7). In 1856 he was elected to the US Senate, where he opposed anti-slavery legislation. When Tennessee seceded from the Union in 1862, he refused to join the Confederacy and supported Lincoln throughout the war even though he still supported the retention of slavery. In May 1862, Lincoln made him military governor of Tennessee. He continued to support slavery after the Emancipation Proclamation. Lincoln's running mate in the presidential elections of 1864, he became President in 1865.

the death of Abraham Lincoln, **Andrew Johnson** was sworn in as the seventeenth President of the United States. One month later, without waiting for Congress to reconvene, he announced his plans for bringing the Confederate states back into the Union. So began the short period of **Presidential Reconstruction**.

Presidential Reconstruction – Johnson's plan

Johnson's plan shocked Republicans, not simply because the President had taken the initiative without consultation, but because of the nature of his proposals. The Republicans had hoped for a gradual readmission of the southern rebel states into the Union. The more radical wing of the Republican Party wanted to see ex-Confederates barred from political life. They also wanted to secure the vote for freed African-Americans. Johnson, on the other hand, followed a much more liberal course:

• Almost all southerners who were prepared to swear an oath of allegiance to the Union were to receive a pardon and **amnesty**. Once the oath had been taken, they could vote and stand for election to state assemblies. They were required to agree to the ratification of the Thirteenth Amendment (1865) to the Constitution that was about to be passed. This confirmed the illegality of slavery.
• All property was to be restored to them, except their slaves.
• Leaders – civil and military – were exempted from the offer of pardon, as were the wealthy plantation owners (i.e. anyone owning taxable property of $20,000 or more). Johnson was determined to punish these people for their 'treason'.

Johnson's plan in action

It soon became clear that Johnson was no enemy of the south. As one imprisoned southern senator wrote to him: 'By this wise and noble statesmanship you have become the benefactor of the Southern people in the hour of their direst extremity and entitled yourself to the gratitude of those living and those yet to live.' The plan had disastrous consequences for the freed slaves. In this respect, Johnson appeared in his true colours. During the war years, when he supported Lincoln, he never abandoned his support for slavery. 'I have lived among negroes all my life,' he said in a speech in 1863, 'and I am for this Government with slavery under the Constitution as it is.'

This was re-emphasised when, as President, he appointed advisers who were known to be unsympathetic to the concept of black civil rights and proceeded with his reconstruction plans. In practice, Johnson:

- pardoned southern rebels in far greater numbers than his plan had suggested (around 13,000 in total)
- abandoned the intention to charge with treason and punish southern politicians and army officers, and allowed them to resume their state offices
- failed to implement the policy of excluding rich planters from office in order to reduce their influence. Individuals could petition for pardon for supporting the rebel cause and, if successful, hold positions in state assemblies
- failed to enforce the requirement of newly elected state assemblies in the south to ratify the Thirteenth Amendment.

The reaction to Johnson's plan in the south

Here, there was little evidence of remorse on the part of southern politicians for their original act of secession. When the newly elected assemblies met, they reneged on most of Johnson's preconditions for re-entry to the Union. Most specifically, almost all refused to ratify the Thirteenth Amendment and ignored Johnson's request to give the vote to at least a proportion of the freed slaves. Radical Republicans in the north and others of the anti-slavery movement were horrified at the introduction by state legislatures of the **Black Codes**. These were justified in the south as guaranteeing protection for freed slaves and economic security for the plantation economy. However, in the north, they appeared racist and reactionary and attempted to replace one kind of slavery with another. Their intention was clearly to ensure that African-Americans never acquired land or political power.

There were other discriminatory aspects to the codes in some states:

- Heavier penalties were imposed on African-Americans who broke the law than on white Americans.
- In many states, African-Americans were banned from competing for jobs with white men. In some, they were restricted to specified jobs. Large numbers were forced to

enter into labour contracts with their former owners. This enabled plantation owners to continue to run their plantations. It effectively bound freed slaves to the land and their employers. It was simply another form of slavery.

• Former slaves who remained unemployed, if caught begging, were charged with vagrancy and fined. Those who were unable to pay the fine (the majority) could be hired out to plantation owners or other employers.

The Black Codes exposed the weakness of the federal government and the power of state government. Johnson had already made it clear that he did not necessarily support the extension of the franchise automatically to African-American men without any kind of voting qualification. They should be able to 'read the Constitution of the United States in English and write their names'. He also suggested the imposition of a property qualification, saying that the vote should only be given 'to all persons of colour who own real estate valued at not less than two hundred and fifty dollars'. The codes went further than severely limiting the extension of the franchise; they also prevented freed slaves from receiving their full rights as citizens of the USA. They were no longer slaves, but neither were they free and equal.

The reaction to Johnson's plan in the north

While there was limited recognition of the equality of African-Americans in the north, the unrepentant behaviour of the southerners in the post-war years did much to alienate northern people, whatever their political beliefs. The imposition of the Black Codes presented further evidence of defiance. Within the Republican Party, there were differing opinions about the extension of freedom and equality to former slaves and much confusion as to their future position in society.

Radical Republicans, led by Thaddeus Stevens, were pressing for the immediate extension of civil rights to African-Americans, whereas the more moderate wing of the party was inclined to favour a gradual programme of reform. For the more conservative Republicans, who had been closer to the pro-slavery stance of the Democratic Party, a comfortable compromise would have been to devise a definition of the permanent position of freed slaves in society that rested somewhere between slavery and full citizenship. Certainly, they favoured a role that confirmed the fundamental inferiority of African-Americans.

However, Johnson's high-handed approach and his obvious support of the south, as well as of the Black Codes, did much to unite the Republican radicals, moderates and conservatives against him. The effect was to put a fairly united Republican Party behind the cause of civil rights for former slaves and in opposition to the President. When Congress assembled in December 1865, it showed its disapproval of the actions of the southern states by refusing to allow southern delegates to take their seats. It then set about the work of destroying the Black Codes.

The Freedmen's Bureau

This was first set up by an Act of Congress in March 1865. It was a government body empowered to support freed slaves. It showed that the government was accepting some responsibility for the care of this large section of society. Somehow, freed slaves had to be helped and enabled to fend for themselves. Not all had been badly treated by their owners. Emancipation brought potential destitution to thousands.

The Bureau was intended to be only a temporary institution to ease the transition from slavery to freedom. However, early in 1866 a proposal was put before Congress to extend its powers – the Supplementary Freedmen's Bureau Act. In addition to extending its life for a further three years, it was suggested that the Bureau should set up military courts to deal with labour disputes between former slaves and their 'new' employers, and to protect African-Americans from those aspects of the Black Codes that forced labour contracts on former slaves. Johnson unsuccessfully attempted to veto the passing of the Act.

The Civil Rights Act (1866)

This Act was intended to establish unequivocally the equality of African-Americans with other American citizens. In particular, it asserted their right to equality before the law. Once again, Johnson attempted to veto the bill. His motives were blatantly racist. He argued that the extension of such rights would 'operate in favour of the colored and against the white'. He even endeavoured to arouse more latent racist

---

The work of the Freedmen's Bureau

The job of the Freedmen's Bureau was to support freed black slaves in the short term and provide a basis for their long-term security. This was to be achieved in a number of ways, namely:

- helping to find homes and employment for former slaves

- providing food, education and medical care for them – between 1865 and 1866, the Bureau spent $17 million on setting up 4000 schools and 100 hospitals

- allocating land – abandoned and confiscated land in the South was divided up into 40-acre plots and leased to former slaves; they had the option to buy the land after three years.

feelings of others by suggesting that equality would result in racial inter-marriage. Congress overrode his veto. However, passing the Act was one thing, securing its ratification and enforcement was another. Only an amendment to the Constitution could ensure success.

The Fourteenth Amendment to the Constitution (1866)

The Republicans in Congress followed up the Civil Rights Act with the proposal of a Fourteenth Amendment. The first two terms of the amendment were a virtual declaration of war on the Black Codes:

- All persons born or **naturalised** in the USA were citizens. No state, therefore, had the right to limit their right of citizenship unless this was authorised by law. All citizens were entitled to the protection of the law without discrimination.
- If any state denied the vote to any male citizen, its representation in Congress would be proportionately reduced. This clause was clearly aimed at the southern states with a high proportion of African-Americans. If the vote were withheld from them, the reduction in the number of southern representatives in Congress would seriously weaken their political power.

The Fourteenth Amendment was an important political landmark in that it began to change the balance of power between the state and federal governments, particularly in the definition and protection of the civil and political rights of all US citizens. It is not surprising that it produced a political furore. Southern politicians were outraged, as was President Johnson who refused to compromise. Only one of the eleven southern states (Tennessee) ratified the amendment. Consequently, when the elections to Congress were held in 1866, a united Republican Party went to the country, predominantly on the issue of the Fourteenth Amendment. Their landslide victory gave them a dominant position in both the Senate and the House of Representatives, and reflected support for the amendment.

From this point, Congress seized the initiative from President Johnson and carried through a programme of Reconstruction in the south that made ratification of the Fourteenth

Amendment by state governments a prerequisite to the readmission of each former rebel state to the Union. This was done by a series of **Reconstruction Acts** passed between 1867 and 1868. In every case, Johnson attempted to veto the passing of the Act, but he was repeatedly overruled by Congress.

The Fifteenth Amendment to the Constitution (1870)

Ironically, while the Republicans had used acceptance of the Fourteenth Amendment to bring the southern states into line and guarantee African-Americans in the south their rights, there were states in the north that refused to give them the vote. Hence, the Fifteenth Amendment was intended to ensure that African-Americans had the vote not only in the south, but also in the north. This was not, of course, altruistic on the part of the Republicans. It was intended to secure the black vote for the party and so keep it in power in both the north and the south. The amendment prohibited 'the denial of suffrage because of race, color, or previous condition of servitude.' There was opposition from the Democrats, but they were not powerful enough in state assemblies to prevent its ratification.

Unfortunately for the supporters of African-American suffrage, there were loopholes in the amendment that were particularly evident to the southern states. They had no problem in accepting the amendment because its terms still did not preclude the imposition of voting qualifications, at least to limit the number of African-American voters. Moreover, there was nothing in the amendment to guarantee that former slaves or their offspring could hold office. Hence, the Fifteenth Amendment was ratified in 1870. Andrew Johnson had retired from office the previous year, when **Ulysses S. Grant** was sworn in as the eighteenth President of the United States.

The Civil Rights Act (1875)

This second Civil Rights Act aimed to prohibit segregation in public places, except in schools. It appeared to be a further gesture by Congress of its desire to control southern politics and force its will on state assemblies. However, by the time it was passed, the Senate was no longer so preoccupied with punishing the southern states for their rebellion. President Grant was abandoning the repressive policies towards the South that had characterised the Reconstruction years.

The Reconstruction Acts (1867–8) The first Act invalidated the state governments set up by Lincoln and Johnson, except in Tennessee which had ratified the Fourteenth Amendment. The states were divided into five military districts. Former states wishing to regain their status had to draw up a new constitution giving the vote to African-Americans. This had to be submitted to Congress for approval prior to readmission. The Act also invalidated the pardons that Johnson had given to Confederates who had supported secession. This deprived them of their right to vote. Some states were so opposed to black male suffrage that they were prepared to live indefinitely under military rule. Johnson encouraged them by replacing military governors appointed by Congress with men sympathetic to the southern cause. Subsequent Acts therefore refined the proposals.

In the South, the Democratic Party was working to remove Republican control and take power. It did this by intimidating black voters. Some were prevented from voting altogether. Those who voted Republican were discriminated against in jobs, housing and land tenancies. A disputed presidential election in 1876 (see page 46) depended for its outcome on the votes of Louisiana, South Carolina and Florida. It is not surprising that, in this climate, the Act was never enforced. The Supreme Court eventually threw it out in 1883, on the basis that it contravened the rights of individual states to decide on issues of segregation for themselves.

African-Americans – the reality of freedom

While politicians and legislators argued the finer points of rights and status in the north, what were the realities of life for freed African-Americans in the south? Perhaps two incidents serve to illustrate at least part of the answer this question:

- At the beginning of May 1866, two horse-drawn carriages collided on a street in Memphis, Tennessee. One was driven by a white man. The other driver was black. The latter was subsequently arrested. A group of black war veterans, recently discharged from the army, came to support him and a white crowd soon gathered. Three days of racial violence followed. Mainly Irish police and firemen attacked the South Memphis shantytown where the former black soldiers lived. Black people were beaten up on the street. When the rioting ended, 46 of them were dead, 5 black women had been raped, and the houses, schools and churches in the black community had been robbed or burned.
- Three months later, there was similar violence in New Orleans when around 200 former African-American soldiers marched in an orderly procession to support the elected delegates who were going to draw up a new state constitution incorporating black suffrage. A riot broke out in which 34 black people were killed and over 100 people were injured.

Both of these incidents are indicative of the level of racial tension and abuse that had been unleashed by emancipation and the subsequent political moves to give African-Americans their civil rights. However, the most notorious example of racism in action in the south is the organisation and actions of the Ku Klux Klan.

The Ku Klux Klan and 'White Supremacy'

However ludicrous its titles may appear, in action the Klan was devastating. Its policies were supportive of the Democratic Party, the planters and all those who opposed any suggestion of rights and equality for former slaves. The violent atrocities that it committed were unprecedented and were directed not only against black people, but also at anyone who supported them or furthered their cause. Hence, Republican politicians and any white men who furthered the cause of equality for African-Americans felt the full force of their hatred and prejudice.

It is clear that much Klan activity was focused on keeping black people in subordination and on restoring the slave-based plantation economy. This is shown by the fact that Klan activity was almost exclusively located on the plantation belt in the south. Many other areas were totally unaffected by Klan activity. Anyone involved in helping former slaves to improve themselves was attacked. African-Americans who had been given the vote were threatened and intimated before elections. Any former slaves who showed signs of achieving economic independence were also attacked, as were local black political activists. Jack Dupree of Monroe County, Mississippi, was not only identified as a Republican, but was also known to be outspoken in his demands for equal rights. He was attacked by members of the Klan, who cut his throat and disembowelled him in front of his wife.

These attacks usually took place at night and were carried out by groups of Klansmen leaving behind a burning cross as their calling card. African-Americans were reluctant, perhaps even afraid, to resist these attacks because they wanted to be seen to be living in a peaceful and law-abiding way. They preferred, instead, to leave their homes and hide in wooded areas to avoid attack.

Ultimately, the activities of the Klan became so appalling that their leader, Nathan Forrest, actually disassociated himself from it after he had unsuccessfully ordered it to disband.

In her autobiography, *Song in a Weary Throat*, Pauli Murray recounts the experiences of her grandparents in the years just after the end of the Civil War:

> Grandmother often stayed alone in the farm near Chapel Hill . . . It was a time when the Ku Klux Klan in Orange County sought to run colored farmers off their land and Grandmother's isolated cabin in the woods was an easy target . . . Late at night she was awakened by the thudding of horses' hooves as night riders, brandishing torches and yelling like banshees, swept into the clearing and rode round and round her cabin, churning the earth outside her door. She never knew when they might set fire to the place, burning her to death inside, and some nights she was so terrified that she would get out of bed, creep through the woods to the roadway and trudge the twelve miles to Durham, preferring the dark, lonely but open road to the risk of being trapped in the farm.

The emergence of the Ku Klux Klan and other white supremacist organisations, such as the Knights of the White Camelia and the White Brotherhood, has been explained in terms of the fear and reaction of poor white people whose livelihoods were threatened by the sudden influx of cheap black labour. There is no doubt that, in some parts of the south where the African-American population outnumbered that of white Americans, the fear of black domination was very real. This interpretation, however, cannot be fully supported, since poor, young white people carried out the atrocities alongside lawyers, doctors, dentists and clergymen. They were also under the direction of rich, powerful and influential men.

Attempts by state administrations to end terrorism were ineffective. Finally, in 1870 and 1871, Congress passed a number of **Enforcement Acts** to deal with terrorist violence. The Ku Klux Klan Act (1871) brought crimes, such as violent intimidation to prevent people exercising their right to vote or hold office, within the jurisdiction of federal courts if the state authorities refused to take action. Prosecution of members of the Klan began in 1871. By 1872, the Ku Klux Klan had been suppressed, but it was revived again in the 1920s.

THE EXPERIENCE OF FREEDOM

What did freedom actually mean for the majority of African-Americans in the south? In spite of the dangers and difficulties, the experience of being free was initially exhilarating. It meant that they were now free, in theory, to travel wherever they wanted to go. Many used this newly acquired mobility to go in search of their children or other family members who had been sold to other plantation owners. The Freedmen's Bureau tried to assist in this process and to resolve other family difficulties. Families were reunited, often after a separation of many years. Informal plantation marriages were legalised so that, by 1870, 80 per cent of African-American families were strong, stable, family units.

Land ownership and sharecropping

Most liberated slaves hoped eventually to own their own land. However, while some eventually moved west and took advantage of the land offered under the terms of the **Homestead Act** or obtained some land in the south under the terms of the **Southern Homestead Act**, the majority never realised their dreams. There were several reasons for this:

- A thorough reform and reorganisation of land ownership in the south was essential to make the land available to freedmen. The majority could not afford to buy land anyway.
- Even if they acquired land, few established efficient, working farms, as they did not have the capital to buy seed, tools and other equipment.
- Former plantation owners still needed labourers. The labour contracts that impoverished freedmen entered into between 1865 and 1866 led them into another form of captivity. They were offered wages, food and housing in return for work. The wages quickly dwindled and many were paid with a small proportion of the crop. They were persuaded by the Freedmen's Bureau that wage labour initially would help them to better themselves eventually. The situation was aggravated by falling prices due to low productivity and poor harvests. Landowners blamed the unproductive workforce.

By 1870, **sharecropping** was the most common system in operation on former cotton plantations. Many freedmen and poorer white farmers were surviving in this way by the late 1870s. However, as prices fell, sharecroppers found themselves increasingly in debt and had to search for means of raising capital to support the shortfall from the sale of their crops. To overcome this problem, they entered into agreements with local merchants or businessmen, who provided them with the supplies they needed on credit. The security for these loans was a claim or 'lien' on their next crops. Interest rates were high – as much as 50 per cent. Many sharecroppers were soon permanently in debt. By the time they had given one half of their crop to the landowner in rent and the other half to the merchant, they had nothing for themselves.

So the downward spiral continued for, while in debt, the sharecropper was tied to his land. As cotton prices plummeted, he lacked the resources to diversify or change his crop. Illiterate freedmen were an easy prey for merchants who were only too pleased to dupe them. Poverty had huge implications for freedmen. Apart from the daily difficulties, it shattered their hopes and dreams of land ownership and independence. Moreover, in states that identified ownership of property as a voting qualification, it meant that they continued to be denied their political rights.

The growth of African-American solidarity

The modern Civil Rights Movement owed much to the assertiveness, self-awareness and organisation of African-Americans themselves. Under slavery, the experiences of shared adversity created a sense of community and common identity characterised by religious beliefs and practices, language and music. After liberation, African-American institutions began to develop and grow, particularly in the form of church and self-help organisations. From the closing decades of the nineteenth century, therefore, there was a clear recognition that true freedom and equality could come only from self-improvement. The results may have been limited, but the measures that were taken were remarkable for their vigour.

Education and self-help

Booker T. Washington described the post-emancipation period as a time that saw 'a whole race trying to go to school'. Education was quickly recognised as fundamental in the quest for equality. The work of the Freedmen's Bureau in establishing schools has been discussed above. The vital role of church organisations in supporting the development of schools is described below. Literacy was essential in many states to secure the vote. The process of learning was hard, especially for adults, and many gave up the struggle or attended school irregularly. Nevertheless, standards of literacy did improve, albeit very slowly.

In urban areas, black people seized the initiative themselves to set up schools for their children and often for themselves. They joined together to buy land or disused buildings (even slave markets) to build or create schools and employ teachers. Black tradesmen gave skill and labour free of charge. In rural areas, schools were set up in people's homes. Moreover, young people were able to take advantage of the founding of the black colleges of higher education in the north. Fisk

Booker T. Washington (1856–1915) was the son of a black slave woman and a white father whom he never knew. As a boy, he worked in menial jobs until he was given the chance to be educated by the wife of the mine owner who employed him as a houseboy. She took an interest in Washington's education, and in 1872 he became a student at Hampton Agricultural Institute. He became a teacher and gained national recognition when he founded the Tuskagee Negro National Institute to increase the prospects of his own race by providing academic and vocational education. He went on to become a presidential adviser on African-American affairs.

University, Howard University and Hampton Institute provided the quality of education that would eventually enable black people to become teachers and future political leaders.

Much else was done by African-Americans between 1865 and 1877 to help themselves. Sickness and funeral savings clubs helped poor black people to save for difficult times. These were particularly helpful to those who had only recently become wage-earners. However meagre this wage was, the clubs helped them to organise their money and plan for the future. Drama clubs and debating societies joined with a larger array of social activities to enhance the quality of life for freed slaves.

Black churches

Religion continued to play a vital part. In captivity, African-Americans had derived strength and comfort in their troubles from a profoundly held belief in Jesus Christ as their personal messiah. Their church services provided the only opportunity for them to meet together and, in the process, to share a growing sense of injustice as they contrasted Christian teaching with their own experience. This was also a strong unifying factor that continued into freedom. Hence, **independent black churches** grew rapidly during the period following the Civil War. Their contribution to the development of self-awareness among black communities was immense. The importance of their structure and organisation must not be underestimated, and their role in the history of civil rights is pivotal.

The collapse of plantation slavery removed from African-Americans a harsh system of discipline, but a system of discipline, nevertheless. What would replace it? While former slaves were subject to state and federal law, the churches filled a potentially dangerous vacuum by providing a moral code of behaviour that their members were expected to follow. Courts were also set up, especially in rural areas, to try to punish those who broke the rules. Church courts dealt with cases of immoral behaviour and settled arguments and disputes within the community. The minister in the church inevitably played a key role. He became the spokesperson for the community.

Politics

It is not surprising that, as African-Americans sought to gain a political voice, black ministers became politically active. Many of these were active not out of ambition, but because

Independent black churches
Many of these churches had already appeared in the north in the late eighteenth century, such as the African Methodist Episcopal Church. Southern converts now swelled their numbers. Others, such as the Negro Baptist Church, had their roots in plantation life. African-Americans who had previously attended predominantly white churches now flocked to those that were distinctively their own. Church organisations did not just minister to the spiritual needs of their members. The churches were also actively involved in every aspect of life. This combined to strengthen African-American communities in the decades after emancipation. The churches provided schools and social activities such as picnics, outings and gatherings.

Blanche K. Bruce.

they believed they had a responsibility to look after the political interests of their people. Over 100 black ministers, therefore, served on state legislatures between 1865 and 1877. Nevertheless, they remained significantly in the minority in most state assemblies. Only in South Carolina, where African-Americans formed 60 per cent of the electorate, did they command a majority vote. Two secured seats in the American Senate during this period.

Black politicians and, indeed, those African-Americans enfranchised by the Fourteenth and Fifteenth Amendments, were almost exclusively supporters of the Republican Party. They saw the party that had given them freedom as their saviour. This gave the Republicans a foothold in the south and an influence in its affairs that it had never had before – a position that was temporarily supported by many of the poorer, non-slave-owning white farmers in the south who were opposed to the richer plantation 'aristocracy'.

The welfare and progress of freedmen depended heavily on the Republicans maintaining this dominant position in the south. By 1877, however, their support had diminished. As the political situation in the north deteriorated for the Republicans, the focus of their attention moved from the south. The subsequent weakening of their hold in the southern state legislatures and the accompanying rise there in the fortunes of the Democrats spelt disaster for the African-American cause.

WHAT HAD BEEN ACHIEVED BETWEEN 1863 AND 1877?

Civil rights

The years from 1863 to 1870 had been remarkable for the Republican Party. It had emancipated the slaves and successfully introduced legislation to secure their rights of citizenship. Even so, there were limits to the success of enforcement. This is shown not only by the Black Codes, but also by the struggle between the federal and state governments to secure ratification of civil rights measures by the states. By the 1870s, the constitutional conflict that had arisen over the power of the federal government reached a climax. The Republican legislation of the Reconstruction period came under the scrutiny of the Supreme Court. Vital clauses of the Fourteenth and Fifteenth Amendments were interpreted in such a way as to effectively nullify all the rights that these had conferred on African-Americans.

- The 'Slaughterhouse' decision (1873) (see page 60) said that the Fourteenth Amendment protected an individual's national rights, but did not protect the civil rights that he or she derived from state citizenship. The decision destroyed the effectiveness of the amendment to protect the individual from the racist actions of the state authorities.
- The Court ruled that several aspects of the Enforcement Acts were invalid. In 1876 the Court also threw out the charges against thirteen white men from Louisiana, who had shot 30 black militiamen who had surrendered following a battle during the civil war.
- In 1883 the Court declared the Ku Klux Klan Act (1871) and the Civil Rights Act (1875) to be invalid.

The Reconstruction legislation had attempted to give to all African-Americans the right to vote and the right to equality before the law. By the time the Supreme Court had finished, there was little left of this programme. The situation was compounded by the fact that, after 1872, the legislation that had established the Freedmen's Bureau was not renewed. The Bureau therefore ceased to exist, and the provision it made went with it.

By the early 1870s, many white Americans in the north were becoming increasingly opposed to the extension of rights to African-Americans. They considered that the Republicans had gone too far, and support was therefore growing for the Democrats. The Republicans also lost control of the south. By 1875, Thaddeus Stevens and several other supporters of equality had died. The African-Americans in the south had lost their most influential political champions. States in the south were now able to modify their Black Codes even further in order to eliminate the black vote. In addition literacy tests and property requirements were used. **'Grandfather' clauses** were introduced by some states.

Education
The unquenchable thirst for knowledge displayed by freedmen began to be satisfied. By 1870, $1 million had been spent on education. By this time also, the number of trained

In 1874, Bruce was elected by the state of Mississippi to enter the Senate – the first African-American to do so. As a senator, he served on a number of key government committees and worked to secure improvements in many aspects of black life, including more generous land grants in the western territories for former slaves. He also campaigned for the rights of other ethnic minority groups – Native and Asian (Chinese) Americans. In 1888, he gained some support for his nomination to run for the vice-presidency. From then until his death in 1897, he continued to hold public offices, including that of trustee of public schools in Washington, DC.

KEY TERM

'Grandfather' clauses
These stated that African-Americans could have the right to vote provided that this right had been in the family for at least two generations. This excluded all who had been freed from slavery.

black teachers was increasing, a testimony to the success of the higher educational establishments that had been set up for African-Americans. During this period, however, teachers tended to come from northern families that were already free before emancipation.

Teachers, like the ministers of the church, became key figures in the black communities they served, generally giving advice and support as well as settling disputes. Between 1865 and 1877, approximately 70 black teachers entered politics, securing seats in state legislatures. In some areas of the south, however, there was strong white opposition to educating former slaves. In rural areas, where young people and adults had to travel long distances to reach a school, they were frequently intimidated by white vigilantes such as the Ku Klux Klan. Consequently, by 1877, 80 per cent of African-Americans were still illiterate, although standards of literacy were improving among children. (In some southern states it had been illegal to teach slaves to read and write.)

Politics

Freedmen were surprisingly knowledgeable about the legislation passed by the federal government during the post-emancipation period to secure their civil rights. They also appreciated that real equality and the end of prejudice and discrimination were well beyond their grasp. The degree to which ordinary African-Americans in the south were politically active varied from state to state. In some areas, they attended mass meetings. In others, they were ambivalent and showed little inclination to active involvement. They were frequently terrorised and intimidated at election time and effectively prevented from using their vote where it had been given.

By the 1870s, the African-American community was also beginning to show signs of fragmentation. In border regions, for example, and in the north, those who had never been in captivity showed strong inclinations to discriminate between themselves and former slaves. They did not want their children to be educated with them and they assumed leadership of political organisations. This may help to explain the inactivity of freedmen. Differences were also becoming evident in the interests of influential blacks and the mass of ordinary people. The former wanted equal rights; the latter wanted to own land.

For the mass of emancipated slaves, the end of slavery was only the beginning of the struggle to survive by themselves. The dream of owning land became a reality for relatively few. Labour contracts bound many to their bosses, as slavery had bound slaves to their owners. Sharecropping might have been a halfway house, but it still left the landowner effectively in control and, in times of economic hardship, the system tended to make sharecroppers the slaves of their crops. There were areas in the south where sharecroppers chose to grow food crops rather than cotton, so that they achieved at least some degree of self-sufficiency. Poverty, violence, racism and discrimination, however, were the everyday realities for the vast majority. Whippings, beatings and murder continued to be the experience of former slaves who attempted to take what had been offered to them – freedom and equality. In Texas, for example, during a three-year period, there were 1000 murders of blacks by whites for trivial reasons.

The Compromise of 1877

Interest within Congress in the African-Americans, their welfare and the extension of their civil rights was already receding by 1876. However, in the 1876 presidential election, there was a disputed outcome. The Democratic candidate, Samuel J. Tilden, had a majority of the people's votes, but he did not have a clear majority over his rival Republican candidate, Rutherford B. Hayes, in the **Electoral College**. A dispute arose over the votes from the three southern states of Louisiana, South Carolina and Florida. They had given in two sets of returns and both candidates claimed that the votes were theirs. The dispute was shrouded in dubious activities on all sides. Tilden needed only one vote in the college, whereas Hayes needed all nineteen votes.

In the end, an electoral commission set up by Congress decided to award all the votes to Hayes. The Democrats were furious. Further political uncertainty was threatened, so Hayes negotiated to get the support in Congress of the southern Democrats. The result came to be known as the Compromise of 1877. In return for the support of the southern Democrats in Congress, Hayes agreed to withdraw federal troops from the south and the policies of Reconstruction, already weakened, were finally abandoned. Abandoned also were the freed slaves who, deprived of the support of the anti-slavery Republicans in the north, were

KEY TERM

Electoral College This is the system, embodied in the American Constitution, whereby the American people are involved in the election of their President and Vice-President. They vote for members of an Electoral College depending on their own political views. Each state has its own Electoral College made up of individuals nominated by the political parties – mainly the Republicans and Democrats. Once elected, the college members meet to cast their votes for the candidates for the two offices. The successful candidate will usually have received the votes of the majority of members of the Electoral College.

now virtually at the mercy of southern state legislatures dominated by Democrats. These were allowed to pursue their policies of segregation and discrimination unimpeded by federal intervention.

By 1877, the slave had, as Du Bois suggested, stood for a brief moment in the sun. During that time, he had learned to stand up for himself and he had tasted the delights of freedom sufficiently to want more. One lasting benefit had been the discovery of lost family members and the re-establishment of the family unit. By 1877, when the period of Reconstruction ended, however, he had virtually to retrace his steps back into the shadows.

SUMMARY QUESTIONS

1 Which of the following were the most influential in securing the emancipation of the slaves:

- the Abolition movement
- the American Civil War
- the policies of Abraham Lincoln?

2 What was Reconstruction trying to achieve? Why did it fail?

3 How far were African-Americans responsible for securing their own freedom?

4 How important were each of the following in helping African-Americans to gain freedom and equality during the period from 1865 until 1877:

- the Freedman's Bureau
- the Republican Party
- the Presidents
- the federal government
- state assemblies?

5 Why did attempts to give freedmen their civil rights cause tension between the federal and state governments?

6 Is it a fair judgement to claim that African-Americans were little better off socially, economically and politically in 1877 than they had been in 1863?

CHAPTER 3

Race relations and civil rights, 1877–1917

INTRODUCTION

During the final decades of the nineteenth century and the first of the twentieth, US society became increasingly multi-cultural and deeply divided. While African-Americans continued their struggle for freedom and equality, other groups of different cultural origins also became the focus of prejudice and discrimination. These included approximately 240,000 Native Americans whose traditional way of life, mainly on the Great Plains, was destroyed. Forced to live in restricted areas called reservations, dependant on the white man's generosity, they were deprived of the rights and liberties of US citizens. Their story is one of human tragedy on a massive scale. The period also saw a massive influx of immigrants, mainly from Europe, lured by the promise of cheap land and prosperity as the US government encouraged westwards expansion by opening up land for settlement. This chapter will explore and measure the progress of African-Americans in their quest for civil rights. It will also consider the plight of the Native Americans and the impact of large-scale immigration.

THE PLIGHT OF THE NATIVE AMERICANS

Settlement of the Great Plains

The Native Americans had remained unmolested as long as white settlers did not want their land. However, wherever white people settled on the North American continent, Native Americans were uprooted and displaced. Invariably, this caused the kind of hardship that resulted in death and, therefore, in the depletion of the Native American population. For decades, the Native American tribes that occupied the Great Plains had been left to themselves. Until the 1840s, this area was known as the 'Great American Desert' to white Americans. They believed that it could not sustain life as they knew it. The Native Americans could have it! Here, these predominantly nomadic tribes roamed freely, hunting the buffalo on which they depended almost totally, living according to their tribal laws and customs, and practising their own religious beliefs.

The 1860s saw increasing westward migration and white settlement on the Great Plains. Former Native American territory was now in demand. A series of **Indian treaties** between the tribes and the federal government systematically reduced the lands that had once been promised to the Native Americans for ever. By 1867, for example, the Sioux tribes who were native to Minnesota had handed over 24 million acres of their land to the federal government. Their homelands now became confined to two clearly defined areas – reservations – from which it was impossible to sustain their traditional hunting and nomadic lifestyle. In return for their land, the US government promised them annual payments and support to develop an agricultural economy. Neither of these promises was fulfilled. This is only one example of many such broken treaties with the tribes.

The completion of the first transatlantic railroad across the continent in 1869 accelerated the influx of settlers and brought the two cultures increasingly into conflict. The buffalo, on which many tribes still depended, were randomly killed for amusement by bored travellers, who shot them from their train windows. By the early 1870s, buffalo skins were in fashion in the east and therefore in big demand. White buffalo hunters killed thousands of buffalo, stripping their skins and leaving the carcasses to rot. By 1875, the herds had been reduced by nine million and the animal so precious to the tribes was on its way to extinction. Native Americans found themselves dependent on the white man's promises and on his generosity. Both were unreliable.

Native Americans on the warpath

Forced on to ever-decreasing areas of the Plains, their lifestyle and culture destroyed, starving and abandoned, the tribes became increasingly hostile. During the 1860s, hunger was primarily responsible for the massacre of settlers in a series of clashes that came to be known as the **Plains Wars**. Suddenly, a solution to the 'Indian problem' became a high priority for the federal government. The projected solutions reflect the

KEY EVENTS

Indian treaties A series of treaties made between the federal government and the Native American tribes between 1851 and 1868. In each case, the federal government took more land from the Native Americans and reduced the areas in which they could live: Fort Laramie Treaty (1851), Fort Wise Treaty (1861), Medicine Creek Treaty (1867) and Fort Laramie Treaty (1868).

The Plains Wars The name given to a series of clashes between Native American tribes and the US army: Little Crow's War (Sioux, 1862), the Cheyenne Uprising (1863), Red Cloud's War (Sioux, 1867) and the 'Winter Campaign' against the Cheyenne (1868).

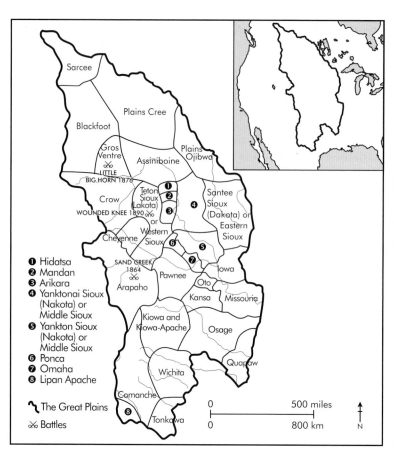

The Native American tribes of the Great Plains and battle locations.

- ❶ Hidatsa
- ❷ Mandan
- ❸ Arikara
- ❹ Yanktonai Sioux (Nakota) or Middle Sioux
- ❺ Yankton Sioux (Nakota) or Middle Sioux
- ❻ Ponca
- ❼ Omaha
- ❽ Lipan Apache

🔦 The Great Plains

✖ Battles

> It makes little difference where one opens the record of the history of the Indians; every page and every year has its dark stain. (Helen Hunt Jackson, *A Century of Dishonour*, 1881)

The Sand Creek Massacre (1864) In November, a troop of US cavalry under Colonel John M. Chivington attacked an undefended Cheyenne camp that was flying a white flag of peace and surrender. The cavalry rode through the camp, killing and mutilating women and children. By the end, 163 Cheyenne had been killed, of whom 110 were women and children. Some were taken into captivity and paraded before white American theatre audiences along with the scalps of their dead. Chivington left the army soon after when it became clear he might be court-martialled for inciting his men to commit these atrocities.

predominant attitudes of white Americans. With the exception of a very small number of artists, writers, travellers and explorers who had made the effort to learn about and understand the ways of the Plains Indians, the majority regarded them as worthless savages. Nevertheless, the search for a solution produced two conflicting schools of thought:

- The 'humanitarians' believed that the Native Americans needed to be 'saved' by the civilising power of the white man's culture. These views were strongly held by some politicians and some in government circles.
- The 'exterminators' were of the view that Native Americans were no better than vermin and should be wiped out once and for all. These beliefs were dominant among the officers and generals in the US army. They explain some of the acts of vicious cruelty, such as the **Sand Creek Massacre** (1864), inflicted by the army on Native American women and children during the Plains Wars.

KEY EVENTS

The Battle of the Little Bighorn (1876) General Custer and the Ninth Cavalry were part of an attack on a Sioux/Cheyenne encampment. The aim was to round up Native Americans who had left the reservation and were defying the authorities by refusing to return. Custer divided his men into 3 units in an attempt to surround the 'enemy', but he was vastly outnumbered. His unit of 200 men came under attack and all were killed, including Custer.

Massacre at Wounded Knee (1890) Wounded Knee is the site in South Dakota where the Sioux Indians were finally rounded up by the US army in 1890. This was the result of the growing popularity of a religious ritual called the 'Ghost Dance' – an attempt by a people living in misery on the reservations to regain their lost way of life. This frightened white settlers in the area who believed that an Indian uprising was imminent. The reservation police believed Chief Sitting Bull to be responsible and shot him when he tried to resist arrest. His followers fled to the camp of the elderly Chief Big Foot near Wounded Knee Creek. There they were surrounded by the army who fired on the Indians, killing 200 unarmed men, women and children.

The government retained control of Native American affairs until 1876, when they were handed over to the army following Custer's defeat at the **Battle of the Little Bighorn**. This final attempt by Crazy Horse and Sitting Bull to rescue the Native American tribes from destruction finally convinced the politicians that dealing with Native Americans was a job for the army. All remaining renegades were rounded up and placed on reservations. Inevitably, these were sited on poor-quality land that no one else wanted.

Civil rights for Native Americans?

Initially, Native Americans had no freedom or rights of citizenship. They were dependants of the state and were not taxed. They had no political representation other than the remnants of the humanitarian lobby in Congress. By the early 1880s, the thinking here was to introduce measures that would remove the last vestiges of tribal culture and so 'civilise' the Native Americans. The Dawes Act (1887) was the result. By this Act, reservation lands were divided up and allocated to the head of each Native American family – 160 acres for arable farming, 320 acres for pasture. In this way, the Native Americans could become farmers and landowners. They were also given certain rights of citizenship – in particular, the right to the full protection of federal law.

Although this may have looked quite promising in theory, the reality was more dismal. It took some years after the Act was passed for the reservation lands to be divided up. When this happened, Native Americans received the poorest land, white speculators having first picked off the best. Consequently, even when some Native Americans became landowners, their efforts were unsuccessful and were abandoned.

Large numbers of Native Americans continued to live on reservations, where they experienced hunger, disease and hardship. The late 1880s were particularly desperate years. The government cut its meat subsidies to the Sioux reservations, where disease had already killed off large numbers of cattle. Once again, starvation and desperation led to one final attempt by a small band of Sioux to escape and return to former days. It all ended shamefully at **Wounded Knee**.

The devastating effects of the government's policy towards the Native Americans of the Plains is reflected in their

Bodies being buried at Wounded Knee, 1890.

declining numbers. By 1900, of the estimated 240,000 who inhabited the Plains in the 1860s, only about 100,000 remained. But the picture was not entirely bleak. In some areas of the continent, some Native American tribes adapted to reservation life – the Navajos in Arizona and New Mexico, for example – and on the Plains, population figures began to rise again in the early decades of the twentieth century.

However, Native Americans were despised and treated with contempt by white Americans. By locating them on reservations, the government had physically segregated them from the rest of the American population and, although they were able to cling to some aspects of their ancient tribal culture, Native American children in particular were exposed to the white man's education. Some children were actually taken away to boarding school. Like their African-American counterparts, those who later gained rights of citizenship faced discrimination and intimidation in the exercise of their rights. They retained a sense of injustice and a profound belief that they had been cheated and robbed of their land. Yet they were unable to assert themselves, as they lacked leadership and unity. Tribal differences and hostilities remained, even in the face of adversity. However, Native Americans were ultimately attracted to the modern Civil Rights Movement as a vehicle for restitution.

IMMIGRATION IN THE USA

Westward expansion and racial tension in the late nineteenth century

The tragedy of the Plains Indians was not the sole outcome of the westward expansion that characterised the closing decades of the nineteenth century. Westward expansion was also partially responsible for drawing peoples of different national origins and cultures to the USA. It thus created, at an alarming speed, the cosmopolitan society that presented such a challenge to the thinking of the original white, Protestant Americans. The 'incomers' were lured by the promise of cheap land, 'buy now pay later' finance and the vast range of opportunities that seemed to offer instant prosperity to anyone who was prepared to take the risk.

The first discovery of gold at Sutter's Fort in California in 1848 led to a huge influx of fortune seekers. It also precipitated the growth and development of San Francisco, rapidly making it the most important financial and commercial centre in the USA. It was also one of the most racially and culturally mixed. Between 1850 and 1870, 50 per cent of the population of San Francisco had not been born in the USA. By 1900, 36 per cent had been born abroad, but a further 50 per cent of the native-born population were of immigrant parentage.

Who were these people, where did they come from and what was their experience? Many were European – English, Irish, German and Italian. A large number were Roman Catholics or Jews. There were also Chinese. Of all the peoples of the USA, with the possible exception of the African- and Native Americans, Chinese-Americans suffered vilification and discrimination on a significantly greater scale than others and were totally deprived of their civil rights.

Chinese-Americans

Initially, Chinese workers came to work in the gold mines. In the 1860s, they formed a large proportion of the gangs of navvies who built the Union Pacific Railway. They were characterised by their willingness to work extremely hard, to do the kind of work that no one else wanted to do, and by their resilience and resourcefulness. For example, in the 1850s, some Chinese-Americans bought smallholdings to grow vegetables. They had recognised that there was a demand for these in the Californian mining towns. They soon horrified their neighbours and customers when it became clear from the smell that they were using human waste, which they collected, as a fertiliser!

Chinese-Americans were hated in all US cities, where they formed a comparatively small, but easily recognised, ethnic minority. Hatred was especially strong in San Francisco, manifesting itself in a number of ways:

- As the English, German and Irish established themselves and came to dominate the industrial workforce of the city, the Chinese were excluded. They were driven into occupations that no one else wanted. Consequently, even though they represented only 4 per cent of the population by 1900, they provided the cigar makers (68% of the workforce in this industry), laundry workers (52%), textile workers (31%) and domestic servants (21%).
- They were obliged to cluster in their own area of the city – Chinatown – and frequently went in terror of leaving its confines. Even those Chinese merchants who managed to become quite wealthy could exercise influence only within the confines of the ghetto.
- They were frequently made scapegoats in times of unemployment or industrial unrest. They were accused of keeping wages low because they provided a ready source of cheap labour, and of taking jobs from other workers. In 1877, for example, when the Chinese totalled about ten per cent of the population, the Irish-born leader of the Working Man's Party, Denis Kearney, organised a march to support demands for an eight-hour working day. Although this was ostensibly an anti-management demonstration, Kearney managed to orchestrate the march to include demands for the removal of the Chinese. Whipped up into a frenzy of racial hatred, the marchers rampaged through Chinatown burning, looting and beating. Twenty-five Chinese laundries were destroyed and the population was terrorised. Many returned to China following this outrage.
- Chinese-Americans were not allowed to become naturalised, unlike other immigrants. They were, therefore, denied the rights of citizenship guaranteed by the Fifteenth Amendment.

Chinese immigrant labourers at the Deadwood mines in the Dakota Territory.

- In 1882, Congress passed the Chinese Exclusion Act, banning Chinese immigration for ten years. There was massive support for this ban in many quarters, but trade unions were particularly vocal.

Hispanic-Americans

Between 1846 and 1895, the US government pursued a policy of consolidating its lands in the west. In order to ensure their security and integrity, lands were acquired as a result of war with Mexico. These lands included California, Arizona, Texas and New Mexico. The acquisition of land, however, inevitably brought with it the land's indigenous people, who were of Spanish origin. Some of these were wealthy landowners, who were fairly readily accepted and assimilated into the social circles of white Americans. Hispanic-Americans from these classes took seats in the House of Representatives. On the other hand, the experience of the poorer, darker-skinned Hispanics, who were largely itinerant agricultural labourers, was more akin to that of the Chinese.

Later, migrant Hispanic workers crossed the Mexican border in search of work, and others from Puerto Rico (following its annexation by the USA in 1898) and Cuba also arrived. They ended up not only in San Francisco and the far west, but also in New York, Chicago and other large, eastern cities. In their case, however, the government was able to resolve fairly easily the racial conflict that their presence precipitated. Hispanics themselves did not all cross the US border with the intention of staying. Many were short-term, seasonal workers. On the other hand, they were also easily repatriated, and this was a course of action to which the US government frequently resorted when racial tension mounted.

European-Americans

Westward expansion undoubtedly increased the attraction of the USA to thousands of poor or persecuted people from Europe during the second half of the nineteenth century, although the vast majority of those who came continued to settle in the east. Between 1860 and 1900, the US population was swelled by around 26 million immigrants. Initially, they came from northern and western Europe. But from the 1880s onwards, they increasingly came from southern and eastern Europe – Italy, Russia, Poland, Czechoslovakia, Hungary, Ukraine, Finland, Greece, Turkey, Portugal, Syria, Armenia and Lebanon. The racial and religious mix was phenomenal.

Their arrival caused huge problems and created a great deal of social deprivation and poverty in urban areas. Invariably, immigrant groups settled in recognisable ghetto areas in big cities, where they retained their own language and cultural traditions. As time went by, they established their own shops, schools, banks and churches. Consequently, the big cities of the USA took on a multicultural flavour that many native-born white Americans found alienating.

Country	Total
Germany	5,500,000
Ireland	4,400,000
Italy	4,190,000
Austria-Hungary	3,700,000
Russia	3,250,000
England	2,500,000
Sweden	1,000,000
Norway	730,000
Scotland	570,000
France	530,000
Greece	350,000
Turkey	320,000
Denmark	300,000
Switzerland	258,000
Portugal	210,000
Holland	200,000
Belgium	140,000
Spain	130,000
Romania	80,000
Wales	75,000
Bulgaria	60,000

European immigration to the USA, 1820–1920.

CONSEQUENCES OF IMMIGRATION

Immigration and the industrial revolution

By the time of the arrival of people from China, Mexico, Europe and elsewhere, the USA was in the throes of its own industrial revolution. The social impact of this was huge in itself. Poor working conditions, poverty and laissez-faire policies that gave employers carte blanche to do as they pleased with their workforce, were all features of this change in the USA, as they had been in Britain in the first half of the nineteenth century. But in the USA, immigration accelerated urban growth and exacerbated an already tense situation, particularly as peak entry periods frequently coincided with spells of economic depression, high unemployment or strained industrial relations.

Immigrants, who were frequently illiterate, were prepared to take on the dirty and dangerous jobs in mines and factories that no one else wanted. Immigrant women were willing to endure some of the highest levels of exploitation – working in excess of sixteen hours a day in 'sweat shop' conditions in the textile industry, for example. They lived in the worst housing conditions and endured the lowest levels of poverty. Their acceptance of these conditions angered poor, native-born Americans, who believed that the abundance of immigrant labour kept wages low and condemned them also to poverty. They had no bargaining power when employers knew that they could always use cheap immigrants to break strikes.

Year of entry to the USA	Number illiterate (in any language)
1896	83,196
1897	44,580
1898	44,773
1899	61,468
1900	95,673
1901	120,645
1902	165,105
1903	189,008
1904	172,856
1905	239,091
1906	269,823
1907	343,402

Immigrant illiteracy, 1896–1907.

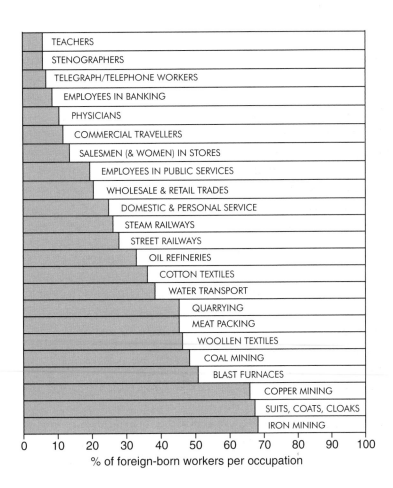

Percentage of foreign-born workers in different occupations, 1910.

Race relations and civil rights, 1877–1917   57

Trade unions struggled anyway to gain recognition and influence. Where they existed and had influence, they contributed to increasing tensions when they discriminated against certain groups of workers – Italians, Chinese and African-Americans, for example. Inter-racial hostility such as that between the Irish and African-Americans, who frequently competed for jobs in the northern industrial cities, increased the complexity of race relations.

Nativism

Racial and ethnic tension was, therefore, an increasingly dominant feature of urban life in the USA at the end of the nineteenth and the beginning of the twentieth century. The effect of high levels of immigration on the original white Protestant Americans increased their sense of innate superiority and their determination to maintain racial 'purity'. Were they not, after all, the original settlers and founders of the USA, whose destiny it was to populate the continent? Were they the real 'native' Americans?

They despised the lifestyle of certain immigrant groups – the Germans and Italians, for example, whose cultural traditions involved, by their standards, the heavy consumption of alcohol. This offended their puritanical sensitivities and they regarded the immigrants as lower class. They were suspicious of the political leanings and activities of Italian and German Americans. Unused to using democratic processes to achieve change in their old homelands, there was evidence that they were prepared to resort to violence and **anarchy** to achieve their ends in their new one. The **Haymarket Affair** of 1886 alarmed the public and the authorities, and alerted them to this real possibility.

Hence, white, Protestant Americans felt intimidated by the apparent influx of foreigners, even though these, at the highest point, represented only about 35 per cent of the total population. Their prejudiced fears were increased by the fact that significant numbers of these foreigners, who looked different and spoke a different language, were also Catholics and Jews. This kind of exclusive thinking, which was particularly dominant in small-town America, produced deepening racial prejudice and increased the determination to discriminate and segregate. It manifested itself in the emergence of anti-Catholic and anti-Jewish organisations,

	1860	1900
New York	1,000,000	3,500,000
Chicago	100,000	1,700,000
Philadelphia	560,000	1,300,000
Minneapolis	2,500	200,000
Los Angeles	5,000	100,000

Urban growth in the USA, 1860–1900.

KEY TERM

Anarchy describes the actions of those who use violence and disorder (e.g. the incitement of riots) to achieve their aims. In the USA at this time, this sometimes involved the use of bombs and explosives, as in the Haymarket Affair.

KEY EVENT

The Haymarket Affair (1886) In May, violence broke out between police and striking workers at the McCormick Harvester Plant in Chicago. Four workers were killed when the police opened fire. The following evening, a protest rally took place in Haymarket Square in the city. During the rally a bomb was thrown, killing seven policemen. The police retaliated by opening fire on the crowd. A further four workers were killed. The blame for this violence was placed on German anarchists led by Johann Most and August Spies.

An undated photograph of immigrants arriving at Ellis Island. The photograph has been staged to show the racial mix of immigants.

and in pressure groups campaigning for restrictions to immigration or at least for the imposition of a literacy test.

A kind of filtering process was established at Ellis Island to vet immigrants in an attempt to identify and reject potential anarchists and disruptive elements. Nevertheless, there were no barriers to European-Americans becoming naturalised and, therefore, American citizens, with all that this implied in terms of rights. They did, however, face discrimination and intimidation. Having their civil rights was one thing. Guaranteeing them in practice was another.

AFRICAN-AMERICANS IN THE LATE NINETEENTH CENTURY

African-Americans in the 'New' South

In Chapter 2, we traced the fortunes of African-Americans after emancipation and during the period known as the Reconstruction, after the end of the Civil War. Although the Fourteenth and Fifteenth Amendments had given African-Americans rights of citizenship that had been confirmed by the Civil Rights Acts of 1866 and 1875, the introduction of the Black Codes in many southern states had effectively excluded them from the exercise of their rights. During this period, the Republican Party dominated southern politics and, in some states, was maintained in this position by the black vote.

By 1877, however, the position of the Republican Party was weakening. State governments were increasingly challenging the provisions of civil rights legislation in the Supreme Court (e.g. the **Slaughterhouse case**) and introducing discriminatory laws against African-Americans. Added to this, the vicious and terrifying activities of the Ku Klux Klan were beginning to send some black people in search of a better life in the north. Nevertheless, the majority stayed in the south, where their experience of freedom and equality depended on where they lived. While voting qualifications based on literacy or property excluded them from voting in some states, in others the black vote was courted by politicians who were much more interested in excluding the old ruling planter elite.

In spite of this, earlier gains for African-Americans continued to be eroded:

- Test cases in 1883 resulted in a Supreme Court decision that the Civil Rights Act (1875) was unconstitutional. This Act had offered protection to African-Americans against discrimination and segregation. The principle was becoming established that state governments, not the federal government, should decide their own internal affairs. This became evident in 1890 when a bill was introduced in Congress to provide federal supervision of elections in the south to protect blacks from intimidation during voting. The bill was blocked by the representatives of the southern states in Congress, who described it as the

'Force Bill'. Southern politicians were under pressure from white voters to introduce harsh racial polices. In any case, southern politicians were frequently racist, particularly in the localities, and often took on political responsibilities to ensure white supremacy.

- During the 1890s, loopholes in the interpretation of the Fifteenth Amendment were exploited so that states could impose voting qualifications (e.g. payment of the poll tax, residency and literacy qualifications) and so prevent African-Americans from exercising their right to vote, while at the same time preserving, in principle, the right of all citizens to vote. For example, in 1898 the case of *Mississippi* v. *Williams* established that prospective voters must satisfy a board of registrars not only that they were literate and paid their taxes, but also that they understood the features of the American Constitution. Actions such as this led to a significant drop in the number of registered black voters. Of the 130,344 black voters registered in Louisiana in 1896, for example, only 5320 remained by 1900. This is not surprising since, in 1900, two and a half million African-Americans in the south were still illiterate. By 1915, almost every southern state had introduced voting qualifications.

- In 1892, African-Americans enjoyed a brief resurgence of political power as a result of the Populist movement. The Populist or People's Party in the south actually needed black votes and pressed for enfranchisement of black people in areas where they had previously been barred from voting. So, for a brief spell, the two races grew closer together in the south. However, this resurgence of black voting power created a reaction amongst the more conservative whites in the south. Violence and intimidation followed. The demise of the People's Party after 1896 produced a backlash amongst southern whites characterised by concerted action to disenfranchise blacks.

- During the last two decades of the nineteenth century, there was some industrialisation in the south. This was located in specific regions – cotton in the Carolinas, for example, and the iron industry in Tennessee and Alabama. White and black workers migrated to these areas in search of employment. Black workers were generally employed in the worst occupations. Those who moved to urban areas to provide services found themselves in competition with foreign-born immigrants and faced discrimination in urban employment.

- Black people continued to be affected by the existence of the 'grandfather' clauses that excluded them from voting (see page 44).
- Between 1887 and 1891, the introduction of **'Jim Crow' laws** in most southern states meant that segregation became firmly embedded. It remained a feature of everyday life for African-Americans until it became the focus of the Civil Rights Movement after 1945. The removal of segregation and discrimination became its biggest challenge.
- In 1896, the case of *Plessy* v. *Ferguson* established the principle of **separate but equal**. In this test case, the Supreme Court declared that segregation was not unconstitutional. Thus 'Jim Crow' laws in the south were upheld as lawful and as not contravening the rights of citizens, embodied in the Fourteenth Amendment. The fact that provision of education, medical care and services for African-Americans was far from equal did nothing to weaken its impact, especially in the south.
- In 1899, the case of *Cunningham* v. *The Board of Education* firmly established the principle of 'separate but equal' in education.

Other gains and losses

By 1910, nine out of every ten African-Americans still lived in the south and the vast majority of these were sharecroppers or part of the crop lien system. They were kept in a state of poverty by being either deliberately cheated or given low prices for their crops. Rents, services and, increasingly, rents and repayments of loans, all paid in kind to unscrupulous landlords and moneylenders, trapped sharecroppers and tied them to the land. Default in repaying loans also locked some blacks into labour contracts that tied them to the plantation almost as much as slavery had done.

The Ku Klux Klan had been outlawed, but racist violence was still rampant. Many black people suffered or died as a result of **lynching**, which, once again, the authorities did nothing about. In many instances, they either condoned or were part of it. Dreadful 'executions', which included burning alive as well as hanging, were carried out as punishments for alleged rape and infringement of any racial order. They were often preceded by viciously cruel torture of the victim. Rape was rarely the true cause. Sometimes, simply looking or whistling at a white woman was sufficient to arouse the wrath of the white population.

KEY EVENT

'Jim Crow' laws These were the laws passed in the south during the years following the Civil War to segregate African-Americans from white Americans. They provided for separate schools and hospitals, and separate areas on buses and trains. In some states, laws banned mixed marriages. Black people were also prohibited from using the same theatres, restaurants, hotels and public baths as white people.

KEY TERMS

Separate but equal describes the principle that was accepted that separate services and facilities, of an equal quality and standard, were acceptable for African-Americans

Lynching was mob action to execute people being held on suspicion of a crime but who were waiting trial. It became very common in the USA in areas where the maintenance of law and order was weak. However, in the years after Emancipation (freeing of the slaves), victims of lynching were predominantly negroes, whose alleged crimes were often based on flimsy or non-existent evidence.

In the 1890s, incidents of lynching in the USA as a whole reached 1,875, the majority of which were in the south, and they continued to escalate. In 1909, 88.6 per cent of victims were black. At least 50 victims during the period up to 1918 were women, some of whom were pregnant. No one was convicted for these illegal executions until 1918. It was to be some time before lynching was outlawed by the federal government. Lynching was a reflection of the frightening depth of racial hatred of white Americans. It was directed at all non-white people, but especially at African-Americans, who were still regarded as being at an earlier, and therefore lower, stage of human development.

While there were separate schools for black children, two and a half million remained illiterate in 1900. Besides excluding them from voting, illiteracy meant that African-Americans who became tenants, landowners or small businessmen could be easily tricked, especially by unscrupulous white people from whom they sometimes had to borrow money to keep afloat.

Poverty in the south

There is no doubt that black people in the south were most universally deprived of their civil rights, but it is important to appreciate that a significant number of white people in the south were also deprived of their rights as a result of poverty. Discriminatory laws that identified property and literacy as qualifications for voting were clearly intended to deny black people their right to vote. But, given the weak economic situation in the south, they also excluded a number of white people.

Even though the south had industrialised and the cotton and tobacco industries were thriving, factory employees (predominantly white women and children) were exploited, working very long hours for low wages. By 1900, the average wage in the south was only $509, compared with $1165 nationally. These white workers lived in poor-quality housing provided by factory owners, and their children received an inadequate education in schools provided by the firms they worked for, hence their low levels of literacy. While in the north only 1.6 per cent of the white population was illiterate (and these were mainly European immigrants), in the south 12 per cent of white people could neither read nor write.

Writing in *American Magazine* in 1908, Ray Stannard Baker described segregation on streetcars in Atlanta:

Over the door of each car, I found the sign, 'White people will seat from front of car toward the back and colored people from back toward front'. Sure enough, I found the white people in front and the Negroes behind.

As the sign indicates, there is no definite line of division between the white seats and the black seats, as in many other Southern cities . . . The colour line is drawn, but neither race knows just where it is . . . This uncertainty is a fertile source of friction and bitterness.

The very first time I was on a car in Atlanta, I saw the conductor – all conductors are white – ask a Negro woman to get up and take a seat farther back in order to make a place for a white man. I have also seen white men requested to leave the Negro section of the car.

Black people in the north

The drift of African-Americans from the south did not really become significant until the first decade of the twentieth century. However, those who did migrate north were little better off than they had been in the south.

- They had rights of citizenship, but faced threats and discrimination when they tried to exercise them. However, the increasing number of enfranchised black people in urban areas was a cause for concern among white voters. Certainly, their combined votes were capable of determining the outcome of elections at the local level – mayoral elections, for example. African-Americans had traditionally given their votes (when they had been allowed to use them) to the party that gave them their freedom – the Republicans.
- They were excluded from skilled work by trade unions, racially prejudiced employers and some groups of immigrant workers, especially the Irish. Menial work was all that was available. Black women, however, were in demand as domestic servants.
- While there was no legally determined segregation in the north, black people frequently experienced discrimination in practice in public places.
- In the big cities, they were marginalised and forced, through poverty and discrimination, to live in defined areas. By 1914 all cities had a black ghetto. These ghettos were unhealthy and overcrowded. Infant mortality rates were particularly high and violent crime became a common feature of these unsanitary and poorly policed areas.
- Interracial violence remained a prominent feature of their lives. In 1908, in Springfield, Illinois, violent clashes resulted in the deaths of four white people. Two black men were lynched and about 100 people were injured. Undoubtedly, much of this tension arose not simply as a result of prejudice but also from fear, as African-Americans came to outnumber whites in some of the smaller cities and towns in the north. By 1910, there were around 90,000 African-Americans living in cities such as New York and Washington, and over 80,000 in New Orleans and Philadelphia.

By the time the USA became involved in the First World War (1917), there is no doubt that American society was overtly racist. The depth of racial hatred among white

Americans was so great that it took a brave politician to fight for the cause of civil rights for African-Americans, in particular. This is not to say, however, that nothing was achieved. In the face of discrimination and segregation, African-Americans developed many of their own organisations and support systems. From their ranks emerged a number of prominent people who were the forebears of modern civil rights activists such as Martin Luther King (see pages 122–3) and Malcolm X (see pages 163–4). However, these early leaders were then, as later, divided in their aspirations for the future of African-Americans.

How did African-Americans try to improve their quality of life?

Excluded in practice from white institutions and organisations, African-Americans organised themselves into self-help groups and set up their own businesses. Black churches and religious organisations continued to have a huge influence. Black-run shops, barbers, banks, funeral directors and insurance companies began to spring up. These sometimes struggled to survive, but they were, nevertheless, a testimony to the determination of African-Americans to better themselves. The best route to this end was, however, a debatable point among those who emerged as potential leaders of black movements. The outstanding men of the early twentieth century were Booker T. Washington and W.E.B. Du Bois.

Booker T. Washington

Washington's career is a testimony to what former slaves could achieve. In 1880, plans were approved to build a Negro school in Macon County. Eight years later, the Tuskegee Negro Normal Institute was opened and Booker T. Washington was put in charge. This institution provided an academic education, but was really committed to giving young negro boys practical skills in farming, carpentry, brickmaking, etc. This is significant because it illustrates Washington's aspirations for his race. He raised money to improve and expand the original poor-quality buildings and attracted good teachers. Tuskegee gained a national reputation and attracted the support of a number of white benefactors, who approved of Washington's beliefs and vision. He also founded the National Negro Business League to help and support the setting up and running of black businesses.

Vice-President William Taft, Booker T. Washington and Andrew Carnegie outside the Tuskegee Institute during the Institute's 25th anniversary celebrations in 1906.

Washington's source of inspiration was his teacher at the Hampton Agricultural Institute, Samuel Armstrong. Armstrong believed that African-Americans should concentrate on developing their practical skills because, by providing these services, they would come to play their part and be accepted by white Americans. Washington took up this idea rather than pursing the political rights of black people. It seems likely that he believed that African-Americans would gain respect and, ultimately, their civil rights if they showed themselves to be responsible and reliable American citizens.

White politicians and businessmen applauded Washington's views. He seemed to be quite clearly accepting segregation and the idea that black people were inferior and had an identifiably non-political role in society.

Washington's approach brought him considerable support from white Americans, but disapproval from some

In his autobiography, *Up from Slavery* (1901), Washington wrote:

> I believe it is the duty of the Negro – as the greater part of the race is already doing – to deport himself modestly in regard to political claims, depending upon the slow but sure influences that proceed from the possessions of property, intelligence, and high character for the full recognition of his political rights. I think that the according of the full exercise of political rights is going to be a matter of natural, slow growth, not an overnight gourdvine affair.

African-Americans. It is clear from his autobiography that his ideas were not necessarily so simplistic. However, when he expressed his views publicly, they appeared to be those of the white people who backed the Tuskegee Institute. His black critics consequently came to the conclusion that he was much more interested in attracting white money for his educational establishment than in supporting the cause of civil rights.

Certainly, Washington was highly regarded by Presidents Theodore Roosevelt (1901–9) and William Taft (1909–13), who consulted him on African-American issues. The former attracted the wrath of southern politicians by inviting Washington to eat with him at the White House in 1901. But even though some politicians paid lip service to the principle of improvement for African-Americans, little progress was made in the effort to stop lynching or to enable African-Americans in the south to exercise their right to vote. Washington's appeal to Theodore Roosevelt fell on deaf ears. Undoubtedly, public support for black civil rights was politically contentious, and was guaranteed to diminish support for any politician brave enough to take it up.

Washington had many critics, but he also had many followers. Evidence suggests that a large number of African-Americans were satisfied by the role that Washington envisaged for them and accepted what came to be known as the 'Atlanta Compromise'. In November 1915, Washington died at Tuskegee, where about 8000 mourners attended his funeral.

William Edward Burghardt (W.E.B.) Du Bois

Of all Washington's critics, Du Bois was the most influential. His vision for the future of the African-American race was clearly influenced by his own experiences, which were, in several respects, different from those of Washington. After graduating from Fisk University in 1885, he spent two years at the University of Berlin and then returned to the USA to study African-American history at Harvard University. In 1895, he became the first African-American to receive a Ph.D. from Harvard. He then moved on to teach economics and history at Atlanta University.

Du Bois' vision for the future of his people appeared in a book written in 1903, *The Souls of Black Folk.* In his

Du Bois was overtly critical of Washington's 'Atlanta Compromise'. When Washington died in 1915, Du Bois wrote of him:

Booker T. Washington was the greatest Negro leader since Frederick Douglass, and the most distinguished man, white or black who has come out of the South since the Civil War. On the other hand, in stern justice, we must lay on the soul of this man, a heavy responsibility for the consummation of Negro disfranchisement, the decline of the Negro college and the firmer establishment of color caste in this land.

aspirations, Du Bois, along with others, undoubtedly began what can be described as the first Civil Rights Movement. He demanded full civil rights, the end of segregation, the extension of the franchise and equality of opportunity in all aspects of life and work. Moreover, he was clear about how this should be achieved.

Du Bois began his active campaign in 1905 with the setting up of the Niagara Movement. At the centre of this was the recognition that African-Americans were entitled to the rights and freedoms that every American citizen enjoyed. Support for the movement, however, was lukewarm. Washington's popularity and appeal, at that time, was clearly greater than that of Du Bois. Consequently, Du Bois joined forces with other like-minded activists in the National Association for the Advancement of Colored People (NAACP), founded by **Oswald Garrison Villard** in 1909. Its purpose, outlined by Villard at the inaugural conference was:

- the abolition of segregation
- equal voting rights
- educational opportunities for black people
- the enforcement of the Fourteenth and Fifteenth Amendments.

The white and black membership of the NAACP included some notable reformers who made their mark in many areas of social and political reform. Many of them were women, such as **Jane Addams** and **Mary McLeod Bethune**, who identified the cause of black civil rights with the **campaign for women's rights**. Membership of the NAACP grew quite rapidly. By 1918, there were about 43,994 members divided between 165 local branches across the country.

W.E.B. Du Bois' major contribution to the NAACP was to edit its magazine, *The Crisis*, established in 1910. It contained reviews and articles written by NAACP members and aimed itself at anyone interested in true democracy and the rights of all Americans irrespective of colour, race or creed. Consequently, it came to enjoy a wide readership. By 1917, its circulation had risen to 50,000 and this had doubled by 1919. Through the pages of *The Crisis*, Du Bois campaigned against:

Oswald Garrison Villard (1872–1949) His mother was the daughter of William Lloyd Garrison, the anti-slavery campaigner. He was educated at Harvard University and became a journalist, eventually owning the *New York Evening Post*. He supported radical reform, including the extension of the franchise to women and civil rights for African-Americans. Villard and his mother, Helen Francis Garrison, became founder members of the NAACP. He was a pacifist and opposed US involvement in both World Wars.

Jane Addams (1860–1935) became president of the Women's International League for Peace and Freedom, speaking at conferences all over Europe in the 1920s. She won the Nobel Peace Prize in 1931 for her work for peace and her books on the subject.

Mary McLeod Bethune (1875–1955) Both of her parents had been slaves. She was the fifteenth of sixteen children and remained uneducated until 1885 when she attended a mission school. She later trained to be a missionary to Africa, but was rejected because the missionary society did not accept African-Americans as missionaries. She became a teacher, eventually starting her own school for African-American girls. It was a great success and by 1922 had 300 students. She was active in the campaign for civil rights, opposing 'Jim Crow' laws and demanding federal action on lynching. She always voted, despite threats and intimidation from the Ku Klux Klan when it reappeared in the 1920s. She served in the administration of Franklin D. Roosevelt in 1936 and became vice-president of the NAACP in 1940.

- lynching
- 'Jim Crow' laws
- sexual inequality – 'every argument for Negro suffrage is an argument for women's suffrage'.

Du Bois' ideas and political leanings later aroused criticism (his support for the USA's entry into the First World War, for example) and, by the 1930s, his more extreme views led to accusations of Marxist sympathies. However, in the short term the NAACP had some notable successes:

- In 1915, the organisation campaigned against the film *Birth of a Nation* because of its portrayal of the Ku Klux Klan and African-Americans. The director of the film, D.W. Griffiths, was accused of racism. Although the protest failed to prevent the film becoming a box-office success, some cities did respond to the campaign and refused to allow the film to be shown.
- The NAACP successfully appealed to the Supreme Court to declare discriminatory laws in the south unconstitutional. In 1915 the Court declared 'grandfather' clauses to be unconstitutional, and in 1917 a local law in Louisville ordering residential segregation was declared invalid.

WHAT HAD BEEN ACHIEVED BY 1917?

On the eve of the USA's entry into the First World War, interracial violence and hostility remained acute. Race relations were complex and exacerbated by high levels of internal migration and immigration. All ethnic minorities endured poverty and discrimination, and race riots were becoming a feature of life across the USA. Some European immigrants, notably German-Americans and German-Jews, were achieving success, and the Irish and Italians were beginning to achieve political and economic status in some cities. The vast majority, however, remained poor and exploited, discriminated against in jobs by either the trade unions or employers. Housing and standards of education remained poor for the majority.

Although the Fourteenth and Fifteenth Amendments remained intact, 'Jim Crow' laws in the south were upheld, in principle and practice, by Supreme Court decisions, and they continued to segregate African-Americans in particular. Segregation in the south continued to be supported or condoned in political circles. However, the successes of the NAACP in 1915 and 1917 saw the beginning of change, albeit on a limited scale. The existence of the NAACP meant that civil rights now had an organised pressure group to ensure that it became a political issue.

Some African-Americans were receiving better standards of education, particularly in the north, and were improving themselves. This education was strongly biased towards vocational competencies. Nevertheless, there were notable achievements – Booker T. Washington and W.E.B. Du Bois were, irrespective of their beliefs, outstanding examples of what African-Americans could achieve. That organisations such as the NAACP could be founded as pressure groups for reform and command a wealth of talent and ability – black as well as white – is a testimony to achievement. The establishment of the NAACP during this period was an important development for the future of black civil rights.

While some African-Americans were securing recognition nationally, there was a trend away from the promotion of black politicians to important positions. During the presidency of William McKinley (1897–1901), black people were appointed to government positions and Booker T. Washington became his official adviser on African-American issues. However, he was severely criticised by southern politicians and subsequent presidents distanced themselves. Presidents Theodore Roosevelt and William Taft both consulted Washington unofficially and reduced the number of black appointments. There was no political will to address issues of civil rights. The election of Woodrow Wilson in 1912 was a further setback. Coming from the south, he supported segregation and removed African-Americans from government positions.

There was an improvement, during this period, in the standard of living of some African-Americans, particularly in the south. There, approximately 20 per cent of black farmers owned their own land by 1910 and their income from farming was rising. A reduction in the rate of mortality also indicates a rising standard of living, even though this was not universally enjoyed by urban black communities inhabiting the ghettos.

There was an increase in the number of black professionals, particularly teachers, and businesses serving black communities. Although these were fragile, they nevertheless represented initiative and achievement. They were also a gesture of defiance to those who sought to marginalise African-Americans by segregation.

Migration to the north increased the number of African-American voters but, in the south, the Black Codes continued to exclude significant numbers from voting. These laws applied equally to Chinese- and Hispanic-Americans (in Texas, for example).

SUMMARY QUESTIONS

1 What does the treatment of the Native Americans (Indians) reveal about attitudes of white Americans to people of other ethnic origins?

2 Compared with other ethnic groups who settled in the USA, the Native Americans received the worst treatment. Do you agree?

3 Were all immigrant groups unsuccessful in their efforts to settle in the USA? Explain your answer carefully.

4 Did the conditions for African-Americans deteriorate during the period covered by this chapter?

5 In what ways was this a very positive period for the growth of self-awareness of African-Americans?

CHAPTER 4

The inter-war years, 1920–41

INTRODUCTION

The 1920s and 1930s were some of the most exciting and challenging in the history of the USA. The 1920s were boom years when the USA stunned and fascinated the rest of the world with its affluence and dynamism. In the 1930s, however, it plunged into the deepest economic depression and took most of the rest of the world with it. It was on the road to at least partial recovery as a result of President **Franklin D. Roosevelt's** New Deal, when the Japanese attack on Pearl Harbor in 1941 plunged the USA into the Second World War. These were significant years for all Americans, but not least for its ethnic minorities. In this chapter we examine the impact of the boom, the Depression and the New Deal years on these groups and their continuing quest for freedom and the rights of citizenship.

THE IMPACT OF THE FIRST WORLD WAR

Isolationism

When the First World War broke out in 1914, the USA was pursuing a policy of **isolationism** in foreign affairs. Consequently, the US government, led by President **Woodrow Wilson**, adopted a policy of neutrality with the overwhelming support of Americans. Privately, given the multicultural origins of US society, it is not surprising that leanings and sympathies were mixed. Some supported Britain, while those of Italian and German origin were sympathetic to Germany and its allies. Most Americans, however, appreciated that neutrality made sense. The USA would undoubtedly benefit financially by lending money to all the belligerents and selling weapons and essential supplies. US industry was certainly poised to fill the gap that would be created when war interrupted the development, in particular, of some German industries, such as chemicals.

KEY PERSON

Franklin D. Roosevelt (1882–1945) was a Democrat and president from 1933 until his death. He was very popular with the people, who believed that he could bring the USA out of the Depression. He was born into a rich family and educated at Harvard. He became Governor of New York State in 1928, in spite of being left crippled by polio in 1921. As president, he initiated a set of 'relief, recovery and reform' policies that came to be called the 'New Deal'. Their purpose was to bring the USA out of the Depression by getting people back to work and restoring prosperity.

KEY TERM

Isolationism was the belief that the USA should turn its back on problems and events in Europe and concentrate on its own internal affairs.

Woodrow Wilson.

HEINEMANN ADVANCED HISTORY

Woodrow Wilson (1856–1924) was the Democrat President between 1913 and 1921. He believed that government should have the power to intervene to defend ordinary people from unscrupulous employers. As president, he was determined to work in the public interest. This marked the end of laissez-faire politics (see page 80) and the beginning of limited government intervention to bring about reform. It became known as the New Freedom programme. However, nothing was done to improve the position of African-Americans or to introduce welfare benefits for the desperately poor.

The Espionage Act was passed to limit the freedom of Americans to express their views about the government during wartime. An example of this in action was the government's successful move to suppress the magazine *The Masses* because it was critical of the government's conduct of the war. Attempts to uphold the freedom of the press through the courts failed and the ban on the paper was upheld.

The Selective Service Act conscripted four million men into the army. A significant number of these went into action in France, near the fortress town of Verdun.

The USA enters the war

By 1917, it had become almost impossible for the USA to sustain its neutral position, even though farming and industry had enjoyed an unprecedented boom from the production of arms, ammunition and food for the warring countries of Europe. Wage rates rose by 25 per cent between 1914 and 1917. When Wilson and Congress made the decision to support the Allied cause and entered the war, Americans greeted it with a mixture of resigned acceptance and outright opposition. The government dealt with the latter by passing the **Espionage Act** and the **Selective Service Act**, both of which, in their own way, effectively limited the individual freedom of all Americans. The war proved to be short but destructive for the USA and it embittered the families of the men who had gone to fight.

How the First World War affected race relations

As you read in the previous chapter, by the first decade of the twentieth century, race relations were extremely tense and interracial violence was becoming a common feature of life, especially in urban areas. President Wilson supported segregation laws in the south and rejected the efforts of activists such as Booker T. Washington to create more equal opportunities for black people to improve themselves – by giving them responsible jobs in the civil service, for example. He actually began to remove them from government positions. The war exacerbated these tensions in a number of ways:

- The expansion of the manufacturing industry, in response to the demand created by the war, dramatically increased the influx of African-Americans into the cities. During the war years, an estimated 500,000 moved into the cities of New York, Philadelphia, Boston, Chicago, Detroit and St Louis. Here they satisfied the demand for labour created by the wartime boom in production. They also replaced the men who had been called up to fight, and benefited from the reduction in the availability of cheap labour as immigration was drastically reduced in the war years. Areas of cities that had once been fashionable, such as Harlem and Manhattan in New York, were transformed into poverty-stricken ghettos that remained once the war had ended.

- African and Native Americans joined the US army and served with distinction in France. The experience of serving abroad in a less racist society increased their awareness of the extent of the discrimination that they endured at home. Many were increasingly prepared to demand what they were not freely given.

- When the war ended and white American soldiers returned home, they found that African-Americans had taken their jobs and apparently overrun parts of their cities. The subsequent competition for jobs and housing led to hostility and violence. This is often referred to as the 'Red Summer'. The **Chicago race riots** of July 1919 were one of the worst examples of this post-war violence.

- African-Americans who moved north during the war years did, however, gain the voting rights they had been denied in the south. While this was a positive gain in terms of civil rights, it also increased white hostility and resentment, as the increasing number of African-American voters proved significant, particularly in local elections. They also began to get their own representatives on city councils.

- In the post-war years, there was an increase in black newspapers which represented an increased assertiveness among African-Americans.

- Suspicion of certain European-Americans also grew. Not surprisingly, German-Americans faced hostility that lasted for some time after the war ended. German businesses were boycotted. Anti-German feeling undoubtedly accounted for much of the support for **prohibition** in 1919, as a large proportion of the USA's breweries were owned by Germans.

- Much of the opposition to the war emanated from some immigrant minorities. Italian-Americans were particularly hostile. Anarchist organisations that had been active in organising strikes in support of better wages now turned their attention to criticising the war, although the existence of the Espionage (1917) and Sedition (1918) Acts made this difficult. However, one Italian publication, *Cronaca Sovversiva* caused so much concern that its editor, Luigi Galleani, and his associates were arrested and deported at the end of the war.

In spite of all this, by 1920 the USA was poised to enter one of the most colourful and fascinating periods of its history.

KEY EVENTS

The **Chicago race riots**, July 1919 Tension in the city was increased by the wartime increase in the African-American population by 50,000. The riots started following an incident on the beach. A teenage black boy had accidentally drifted towards a 'whites only' beach. White people on the beach stoned him until he disappeared under the water. His death sparked thirteen days of sporadic violence when Irish and Polish workers attacked the city's black ghettos. This left 23 black and 15 white people dead, 537 injured and 1000, mainly black, families homeless.

Prohibition In 1919, the American Congress passed the Eighteenth Amendment to the Constitution. Sometimes known as the Volstead Act, this measure prohibited the production, sale and transportation of alcoholic beverages throughout the USA. This legislation was controversial and had dramatic consequences. It led to the illegal distillation of alcohol and an escalation of organised crime.

Cronaca Sovversiva was an anarchist journal that particularly alarmed the authorities because it advocated violence and revolution to achieve its aims. When it aggressively criticised the war, its production was banned under the Sedition Act.

THE 'ROARING TWENTIES'

Post-war USA – prosperity, poverty and prejudice

Between 1921 and 1929 Americans enjoyed unprecedented prosperity. By this time, the USA was the world's leading industrial nation. Based on the boost given to the US manufacturing industry by First World War demand and the wealth that this created, the economy took off in the post-war years. The boom that followed was produced by a combination of:

- the development of methods of mass production
- the growth of the mass media and the availability of radios
- the expansion of the manufacturing industry, mass producing cars, telephones, vacuum cleaners, washing machines, etc.
- the availability of credit, which facilitated consumer spending on a massive scale
- large-scale investment and stock market speculation, which provided the capital for industrial expansion, while making a small number of people extremely rich.

The USA appeared to the rest of the world, but especially to war-weary Europe, as ostentatiously affluent. It was almost a wonderland. Items that were luxury goods elsewhere were owned by the mass of the people there. This affluence must also be seen against the background of Hollywood cinema, daring styles of dress, parties and the sound of jazz. These were the sights and sounds of what came to be known as the 'roaring twenties'.

Yet, in many ways, this was a deceptive veneer. Beneath it all, the USA remained a deeply divided society and many people did not benefit from this boom (see pages 79–82). In spite of the claims of President **Herbert Hoover** in 1928 that 'The poor are vanishing from among us', levels of poverty remained startlingly high in some quarters. This poverty was not restricted to black people and immigrants. Moreover, at the very time when the USA was presenting itself as liberated and permissive, it also appeared narrow and reactionary. It could be argued that discrimination, prejudice and racism reached a peak during these years. Much of this was a continuation of the conflict that came as a result of the migration of African-Americans into the cities during the First World War and, to a lesser extent, the influx of

Hispanics and Chinese. It was also a reaction to the increasing influence of European-Americans on the culture of the eastern cities. Prejudice manifested itself in a number of ways.

The re-emergence of the Ku Klux Klan

The outlawed Klan had re-formed in 1915 in Georgia. By the mid-1920s, it claimed a membership (which included women) of between two and five million. Its hooded figures paraded openly in the streets of Washington, DC, and other cities. Burning crosses reappeared in the night to terrify potential victims. Beatings, mutilation, murder and intimidation once more became the norm in some communities. This time, however, the victims were not only African-Americans, but also immigrants who were Catholics and Jews, trade union members and anyone suspected of subversion. The Klan upheld the superiority of white, Protestant America. It enjoyed widespread support and, in states such as Oklahoma and Oregon, it exercised enormous political influence. Its activities were curtailed in the second half of the decade when allegations of corruption led to inquiries and a subsequent depletion in membership.

Anti-immigration laws

The **Quota Act** (1921) and the **National Origins Act** (1924) both targeted specific racial groups, banning or limiting their entry into the USA. Trained and talented people – artists, actors, singers, academics, nurses and all professional people – were allowed to enter the USA irrespective of their country of origin. Limitations were placed on the numbers of Italians and Poles (Catholics) and Russian Jews who were allowed to enter the country. Illiterate and unskilled Europeans were clearly unwelcome. After 1924 Asian immigrants, mainly Chinese and Japanese, were excluded completely. These are clear examples of institutional racism in operation. Conversely, however, at the same time, immigrants from French Canada and Latin America continued to pour into the USA. The Mexican (Hispanic) population of California rose from 90,000 to 360,000 during the 1920s, and by 1930 there were 2 million Mexicans in the USA.

The case of Sacco and Vanzetti

Sacco and Vanzetti were two Italian-Americans, known anarchists and associates of **Luigi Galleani**. They had opposed US entry into the First World War, avoided military

KEY TERM

KEY TERM

A **'cause célèbre'** is a test case or issue that attracts a great deal of discussion across a very wide area. In the case of Sacco and Vanzetti, there is an implication that the issues were exaggerated in order to attract international attention to the racial discrimination and denial of equal rights that existed in the USA at that time. In this case, it was argued that Sacco and Vanzetti suffered discrimination because they were of Italian origin and because of their political views, which, in a democracy, they had the right to hold.

KEY EVENT

The Bolshevik Revolution (1917) The Bolsheviks, led by Lenin, successfully took power in Russia in October/November 1917. The Tsar and his family were murdered in 1918 and Lenin set about the task of destroying capitalism and replacing it with a socialist system, where the huge gap between rich and poor would be closed. The wealth of the nation would be fairly distributed so that workers would share in the wealth that was being created by their labour. It is not surprising that these ideas terrified many influential people in the USA in the 1920s! In practice, communism led to persecution, repression and a denial of fundamental rights and freedoms.

service and supported workers' strikes. In 1920 they were charged with the murder and robbery of two men carrying a $15,776 payroll to the Slater and Morrill Shoe Factory in South Braintree, Massachusetts. At the time of their arrest, the USA was in the grip of a witch-hunt of alleged communists and anarchists (the Palmer Raids; see below).

When Sacco and Vanzetti stood trial, the judge, Webster Thayer, was clearly prejudiced against the two men because they were Italian immigrants and political activists. For this reason, their trial attracted huge, international media interest. When they were finally sent to the electric chair in 1927, there were riots in Paris, Geneva, Berlin, Bremen, Hamburg and Stuttgart. The case became an international **cause célèbre**. It is still hotly debated, but what is clear is that they were victims of ethnic discrimination and of the political mood of the day. It is claimed that they were denied the rights to which they were entitled – freedom of speech and a fair trial – and that they were condemned on the basis of highly circumstantial evidence. Vital evidence in their defence had been ignored.

The 'Red Scare' and the Palmer Raids

In the USA following the First World War, there was an almost irrational fear of communism. The results of this further reflect the intolerance and suspicion of the authorities towards immigrants. In 1917, the revolution in Russia had brought to power the **Bolsheviks** under the leadership of Lenin. The reports of the actions of the communists in Russia convinced the US Attorney-General, Mitchell Palmer, that the same things might well happen in the USA unless he purged the land of what he called 'foreign-born subversives and agitators'. His attitude was influenced by the fact that an attempt had been made on his life by anarchists in 1919.

On 1 January 1920, 6000 'aliens' were rounded up by the Justice Department and imprisoned or expelled from the country. Five elected members of the New York State assembly were prevented from taking their seats. Palmer's obsessive behaviour was infectious. Other state authorities carried out similar purging activities, spurred on by the explosion of an anarchist bomb in Wall Street on 16 September 1920. Thirty-eight people were killed. Although the purges subsequently subsided, prejudice remained and influenced the trials of known anarchists, who were, in some cases, denied their rights as citizens as a result of the prevailing attitudes of the time.

Prohibition

The ban on the production, transportation and consumption of alcoholic beverages that came into force nationally in 1920 is, in itself, an amazing piece of legislation. It represents one significant section of American society imposing its standards on the rest – hardly something that might be expected in an allegedly free society! Opponents of prohibition argued powerfully that it represented an infringement of civil rights, but they were unable to stop its implementation.

The intention was to make the USA 'dry' and so remove the social evils that were perceived to emanate from liquor. The pressure for this came predominantly from small-town USA, dominated by white, Protestant, church-going Americans. These were the descendants of the original Puritan settlers, many of whom held **fundamentalist beliefs**. They were able to impose their standards of morality on others because they were powerfully represented politically, both in Congress and in state assemblies. In the context of this study, however, of particular interest are the racist motives behind the pressure for the ban on alcohol:

* The successful brewers were German. Reference has already been made to anti-German feeling during the First World War. However, many of these brewers had also become wealthy and their wealth gave them political influence. This was resented.
* White, Protestant inhabitants of small-town USA were particularly critical of life in the big cities. Nativism flourished in what is referred to as the 'Bible belt'. Vice, crime and drunkenness were blamed on the foreign, immigrant populations of cities such as New York and Chicago. It could be argued, therefore, that prohibition was fundamentally racist.

If prohibition was intended to control these 'disreputable' elements, it failed rather miserably. The ban led to an increase in drink-related crime in these cities and the emergence of organised crime, involving the illegal distillation and sale of liquor and the escalation of gambling, prostitution and drug trafficking. The main beneficiaries were the men, often of Italian origin, who became legendary gangland bosses, such as **Al Capone**.

Poverty in the 1920s

While the 1920s were certainly 'roaring' for some, there were large sections of the population who were condemned to live in poverty. It is difficult to imagine how a country enjoying so much affluence could have accepted the levels of poverty that existed. Research carried out for the period between 1900 and 1930 showed that 16 million families (60 per cent of the total number) received less that $2000 a year – the figure recognised as being necessary to obtain basic necessities. This meant that 70 million people were living below this poverty line. Poverty discriminated and disadvantaged. It denied people the right to equality of opportunity, to better themselves by education, to live in decent housing and to have the dignity of a reasonable standard of living. In the southern states particularly, where literacy and property qualifications were imposed, poverty deprived people – white and black – of their right to vote. So, who were the poor in this age of national affluence? They were certainly not all African-Americans or immigrants, although a large number were.

Farmers. Farmers were among the poorest. The boom in consumer spending had passed them by. During the First World War, when the demand for food was high, farmers had borrowed heavily to expand their businesses. The post-war retraction left them with huge debts and unwanted crops. In the early 1920s, farm incomes ranged from $1240 to $460 a year. Of the USA's 5.8 million farming families, 54 per cent (about 17 million people) survived on an income of less than $1000 a year.

The distress of farming families was acute, but the government did little to help. There was legislation in 1922 to allow farmers to form cooperatives to help each other and another Act in 1923 to set up banks to give loans to groups of farmers. But the potential effectiveness of this was limited because, in 1922, the government had also imposed high tariffs on imported goods to protect US industry. This meant that other countries retaliated by putting high taxes on imported US goods, making them expensive. This did not help farmers, who really depended on being able to sell their food abroad, as they had done during the war. In 1927 and 1928, President Coolidge blocked a bill that would have helped to cushion farmers against sharply falling prices. The failure of the federal government deepened the divisions that already existed between rural and urban communities.

African-Americans. African-Americans in the south continued to struggle against poverty. In the 1920s, incomes fell below $200 a year. During the Depression years of the 1930s, one African-American commented: 'the reason why the Depression didn't have the impact on the Negro that it had on whites was that Negroes had been in the Depression all the time'. In the northern cities, soldiers returning from the war in 1918–19 wanted back the jobs that the African-Americans, who had migrated to the cities during the war, had filled. The return of the soldiers brought greater poverty to the black inhabitants of city ghettos such as Harlem and Manhattan in New York. Poverty deprived them of decent schools and proper food. The appalling living conditions seriously affected their health. In Harlem, for example, the death rate among African-Americans was 42 per cent higher than in other parts of New York. This was due to very high incidences of childbirth and infant mortality, tuberculosis, pneumonia and heart disease, aggravated by the lack of medical care.

Other groups. People living in poverty also included the elderly (there were no state pensions), the disabled and infirm, and families headed by females. Thousands of immigrants also found themselves living in poverty. This was largely because of continuing discrimination in jobs, especially skilled jobs, but also because, in spite of the boom, some industries were permanently in a state of slump – textile towns in New England, for example, and coalmining areas in Kentucky and Illinois. Both of these industries had attracted unskilled, immigrant labour. The **laissez-faire** policies of the state and federal governments offered no protection to workers, whoever they were. When they were driven by desperation to strike for higher wages, they were treated unsympathetically and repressively. Trade unions were handicapped by restrictive laws. Some unions did find money to help support needy members, but these were usually skilled workers.

KEY TERM

Laissez-faire was the idea adopted by many politicians that it was not the responsibility of government to be involved in economic issues. This allowed businesses to expand without restriction. There were also no legal restrictions to the way they treated their workers. Workers themselves had no rights and trade unions were either banned by employers or treated with hostility.

Attitudes to poverty. Some people living in extreme poverty were helped by private charities. The failure of the federal and state governments to help, stemmed mainly from the commonly held view that it was not the role of government to take care of the needy. There was a belief that poverty was part of the economic cycle and that it was, therefore, only temporary. Much of the explanation lies in widely held attitudes and values of the better off and the poor themselves. The views of the better off are reminiscent of those held in Victorian Britain – the poor were idle and feckless. Among the poor themselves, there was almost an acceptance that it was their lot in life to be poor and, therefore, their poverty was inevitable.

White civil rights activists were also drawn to social issues. The 1920s saw a massive expansion of the media and, particularly, of newspapers and magazines. Investigative journalism was revealing not only the extent and impact of poverty, but also its true causes. The same people who were supporting the NAACP (see pages 68–70) in its demands for an end to discrimination and segregation were also campaigning on issues such as working conditions and child labour. For them, it all came under the umbrella of the campaign for social justice. Their purpose was to achieve a fundamental change of attitude and purpose that would be reflected in effective legislation to secure civil rights and social reform. Many of these reformers were also involved in the campaign to secure full civil rights for another disadvantaged group, not hitherto mentioned – women.

Civil rights for women

Traditionally, the 1920s are seen as the time when young women in the USA flung off the values and inhibitions of their mothers and grandmothers. These 'flappers' had bobbed hair, wore loose, shorter-length dresses, allegedly had sexually permissive attitudes, and enjoyed partying and smoking. Nevertheless, these young, liberated feminists were a minority. Campaigners for women's civil rights came from a slightly older generation.

During the 1920s, groups of women continued a quest for emancipation that had begun in the nineteenth century. Before 1900, women had succeeded in their demands for rights to higher education and for access to the professions and, by 1900, they were accepted as doctors and lawyers. The focus of the campaign now switched to equality in wage and labour rights. Women had campaigned successfully for the vote in some states in the latter part of the nineteenth century. In 1917, Jeanette Rankin of Montana became the first woman elected to Congress. By the eve of the First World War, the national campaign was gaining momentum. Finally, in 1919, Congress passed the **Nineteenth Amendment to the Constitution** by a narrow majority. This became law on 26 August 1920 and women were allowed to vote in the presidential election of that year. However, African-American women in the south continued to experience discrimination when they tried to register to vote, as did African-American men.

In reality, having the vote made little difference to the majority of American women.

- Women in the western states had already been given the vote before 1920.
- Many campaigners for women's rights focused on specific issues such as equal pay. They did not see the vote as a means to this end.
- Jim Crow laws discriminated against black women voters as they did against black male voters.

There were one or two notable exceptions. In 1924, Nellie Taylor Ross of Wyoming became the first woman to be elected as state governor, while in 1926, Bertha Knight Landes became the first female mayor of a city (Seattle). On the whole, there was a lack of unity among female activists from different cultural groups, who tended to have different 'causes' that they wanted to pursue – the campaign against child labour, for example, and for some black and white women's groups, the campaign against lynching. So the next stage – the campaign to achieve equal rights – remained to be pursued.

'The Jazz Age'

The 1920s was not an entirely negative time for all African-Americans, for their music gave this period its distinctive sounds – jazz, rag and 'boogie-woogie'. This was the new and exciting music that rang out from nightclubs and speakeasies. It is ironic that white people, who regarded black people with

KEY TERM

The **Nineteenth Amendment to the Constitution** prohibited sex discrimination in voting. It also gave Congress the power to enforce this by legislation.

KEY PEOPLE

Louis Armstrong (1900–71) He became famous as a trumpeter, making his debut in 1917 in a New Orleans jazz band. He moved to Chicago, in 1922 and remained there until 1929, except for one year spent in New York. By 1925, he had his own band and was soon enjoying a national reputation as a jazz trumpeter and singer. He is now regarded as one of the greatest jazz artists of all time. His recordings, such as 'Ain't Misbehavin' and 'Tiger Rag', are jazz classics.

'Duke' Ellington (1899–1974) became a composer, conductor and pianist. In 1923, he moved to New York, where he assembled a ten-piece band. By the time of his death, he had come to be regarded, along with Louis Armstrong, as one of the most highly respected jazz musicians of the twentieth century.

hatred and contempt, were the very ones who were thrilled by their loud and **syncopated** rhythms. These came to typify the rebellious spirit of the times and gave the twenties its name – the Jazz Age.

In its original form, jazz was the casual and spontaneous music of the negro slaves who were encouraged to sing at work. In those days, improvised instruments – cans, pickaxes, and washboards – made the sounds that would delight white audiences during the 1920s. When jazz came into its own, it was performed by black artists who became legends in their own lifetime. **Louis Armstrong** was soon an international star. **'Duke' Ellington** moved from Washington, DC, to New York, where he performed in the Harlem Cotton Club.

The growth of the new radio technology ensured that the music of African-Americans, performed by them, was carried into millions of American homes – and they loved it! African-Americans, living in poverty and squalor, must have gained some pride from hearing their music and seeing some of their own receive such acclamation, especially from the 'white folks'. This could not, however, have compensated for the fact that, when black musicians entertained white audiences, fellow black people were banned.

A jazz group of the 1920s.

The 'Harlem Renaissance'

A further irony is that many of the talented black musicians and entertainers who were 'discovered' during this period emerged from the poverty and squalor of Harlem and other impoverished black areas. By the 1920s, the 87,417 African-Americans who lived there had been joined by 45,000 Hispanics (Puerto Ricans) and immigrants from the West Indies. From among the African-Americans came poets and writers as well as musicians. Writers such as **Langston Hughes** and **James Baldwin** were deeply influenced by the painful experiences of their race. They challenged the racism of white Americans through their writing and stood for real freedom and equality for African-Americans. They particularly made white readers aware of the thoughts and feelings of their people. Musicians drew the attention of white 'patrons', who managed to be attracted by the talents of the few while ignoring the poverty of the masses.

Divisions among African-Americans

While the achievements of writers and musicians are encouraging signs, they are also indicative of the divisions that were beginning to appear within the African-American population. Educational and business opportunities, as well as the chance to achieve stardom, were separating the 'haves' from the 'have nots'. The emerging black middle class had differing perceptions of what was needed and were not always sympathetic to the suffering and needs of the black masses.

The NAACP continued to fight against disfranchisement and lynching throughout the 1920s. Its leaders publicised details of lynchings between 1889 and 1918, and paid for large adverts to be put in national newspapers. It defied the intimidation of the Ku Klux Klan by holding its annual conference in 1920 in Atlanta, one of the Klan's capitals. However, the NAACP was predominantly middle class. While its members engaged in legal battles for the right of all African-Americans to vote and for better standards of education, black people in the south were reluctant to assert their rights because of threats and intimidation. In the north, where they already had the vote, they were much more interested in improving their everyday conditions.

In the 1920s, there were unsuccessful efforts to encourage black workers to form their own trade union. Community

**Marcus Garvey
(1887–1940)** worked as a printer in Jamaica and became active in the trade union movement there. He was inspired by the work of Booker T. Washington at the Tuskegee Institute and by black people whom he met while studying in England in 1911, who were active in the struggle for independence from British rule. When he returned to Jamaica, he wrote a book called *The Negro Race and Its Problems*. In 1916, he moved to the USA and founded the Universal Negro Improvement Association (UNIA) the following year. Garvey campaigned against lynching, 'Jim Crow' laws and the denial of the vote to African-Americans. Sometimes he differed from the NAACP about the means of solving the problems.

life did flourish in the ghettos, particularly as a result of the black churches and their social organisations. Ordinary African-Americans were drawn more readily to Marcus Garvey and his 'black is beautiful' philosophy.

Marcus Garvey and the Universal Negro Improvement Association

Marcus Garvey's impact on ordinary black people was very significant. Perhaps his greatest contribution to their development was his encouragement of them to have pride in themselves and in their culture and heritage. It certainly did much for his appeal to the masses of black ghetto dwellers. He argued that they were never going to be accepted in such a racist nation and that the only way to improve themselves, grow and prosper was to return to the land of their ancestors – Africa. In his book *School of African Philosophy* (1937), he wrote:

> It is the mission of all Negroes to have pride in their race. To think of the race in the highest terms of human living. To think that God made the race perfect, that there is no-one better than you, that you have elements of human perfection and as such you must love yourselves. Love yourselves better than anyone else. All beauty is in you and not outside you, for God made you beautiful. Confine your affection, therefore, to your own race and God will bless you and men will honour you.

He started the weekly newspaper *Negro World* to publicise his ideas, but he was not good at organising his finances. He set up the Black Star Steamship Company to help people return to Africa, but some who joined were obviously corrupt. Garvey was blamed for financial irregularities. In 1925 he was arrested for fraud, and after serving half of his five-year sentence he was deported to Jamaica. He remained active in the cause of civil rights for black people and toured the world making speeches. His attempt to create job opportunities was unsuccessful, but to the masses he was a hero. They were able to relate to Garvey, his approach and ideas much more readily than to the academic, legalistic thinking of the NAACP. Certainly, some of his ideas lived on and influenced civil rights activists in the 1960s.

By the end of the 1920s, then, it may appear that very little had been gained, in real terms, to advance the cause of civil rights. The NAACP had won some victories, but the period saw some of the worst examples of reactionary and racist behaviour and attitudes. There was, however, an increased awareness of cultural identity, particularly among the mass of

African-Americans, and of the rights to which they were entitled. This was accompanied by a growing expression of the determination to gain improvement.

THE DEPRESSION, 1929–32

On 24 October 1929, the bubble burst. The USA went bust. On that day, shares on the New York Stock Exchange plummeted to an all-time low. The panic that ensued had a spiral effect, resulting in the closure of banks and the bankruptcy of businesses. Wealthy men were ruined and ordinary people became unemployed in unprecedented numbers. The USA was plunged into a huge economic and social crisis that dominated at least the first half of the 1930s.

How did the Depression affect African-Americans and other minority groups?

The dramatic fall in production and the consequent rise in unemployment were the most significant factors affecting all minority groups during the Depression. By 1933:

- gross national product (i.e. the value of goods produced plus income from abroad) had fallen (since 1929) from $104 billion to $59 billion
- 24.9 per cent of the labour force was unemployed
- average earnings had dropped from $25 to $17 a week for those still in work
- industrial and agricultural production had more than halved
- massive cutbacks had been made in public spending, particularly on such things as education.

It is not surprising that, in these circumstances, the people who were most adversely affected in the inevitable competition for jobs were African, Hispanic and European Americans in unskilled work, who were often replaced by white 'native' labour. The big cities, where African-Americans and immigrants formed a large percentage of the population, were very badly hit. In Chicago, for example, 40 per cent of the population was unemployed. Voluntary groups tried to provide relief for the destitute, but their intervention did little to relieve the suffering of African-Americans and immigrant groups. In some cities, the rate of black unemployment reached 60 per cent.

The effect on education

A reduction in spending on education hit racial and ethnic minorities harder than white communities. This was especially true in the south, where states cut back on spending on black schools. In the north, only New York State refused to accept segregated schools. Often the segregation arose naturally from the fact that African-Americans clustered in ghetto areas. Spending on black education was considerably less than on white, even in the more prosperous years. On the other hand, the number of black students entering higher education grew steadily throughout the period after 1918. By 1933, there were 38,000 black students in colleges. The majority of these (97 per cent) were in the south.

Competition for work

By the end of the 1920s, legal limitations on immigration had significantly reduced the number of people arriving in the USA. In any case, the USA was less attractive in an economic depression than in an economic boom. However, the black population of the cities increased even more during the Depression, as more and more moved away from the agricultural south, where the cotton economy had collapsed, in search of jobs. Competition for work remained desperate, as unemployed white people were now prepared to do any job, including those that previously only black people had done. Large sections of the American population suffered as a result of hunger and disease, particularly between 1929 and 1933 when it was claimed that about 20 million people were starving. A significant proportion of these were African-Americans.

At the same time as competition for work was increasing in the cities, rural areas were being devastated by the Depression. Farmers were already struggling desperately even before the crash. Cotton planters in the south were some of the worst hit. The presence of Hispanic (Mexican) Americans as relief agricultural labour in rural areas increased tension between them and the White Americans at this time.

Native Americans

Native Americans struggled to farm at the best of times on their impoverished, reservation land. Few had succeeded in becoming independent, land-owning farmers, in spite of the Dawes Act (1887) (see page 9), and although the Native American population had increased since 1900, diseases such as tuberculosis were rife. The death rate was outstripping the birth rate by the early 1930s. Some moderate improvements were made. In recognition of the fact that many of them had fought bravely during the First World War, they were given rights of citizenship in 1924. However, this brought little obvious benefit or improvement.

President Herbert Hoover whose apparent failure to deal effectively with the devastating impact of the Depression was severely criticised, had an interest in and sympathy for the Native Americans. This may have been engendered by a report on the condition of the Native Americans published in 1928, which revealed the extent of the poverty and disease that they suffered. While the mass of Americans received totally inadequate aid during the Hoover years, federal spending was increased to improve the quality of life for the Native Americans. Quakers, like Hoover, were made responsible for Native American affairs and the provision of financial support, education and medical care were expanded. Franklin D. Roosevelt continued this approach when he became President in 1933 and introduced his New Deal.

A 'NEW DEAL' FOR ALL?

On 4 March 1933, Franklin Delano Roosevelt, a Democrat,

Franklin D. Roosevelt.

KEY TERM

'Alphabet agencies' The name commonly given to the government organisations set up by Roosevelt's New Deal, which were known largely by their acronyms, for example, AAA (Agricultural Adjustment Agency), CCC (Civilian Conservation Corps), PWA (Public Works Administration and TVA (Tennessee Valley Authority).

KEY EVENT

The **Agricultural Adjustment Agency** aimed to raise the price of farm produce in order to help farmers out of the Depression. This was done by paying farmers compensation or subsidies either to change their crop or to reduce the amount of produce actually going to market. This frequently meant that large amounts of produce were destroyed to keep prices higher. Cotton farmers and sharecroppers in the south were encouraged to plough ten million acres of their crop back into the ground! This also happened to tobacco crops. Six million piglets were also slaughtered to boost the price of pork. This work was supplemented by agencies providing credit to farmers at low rates of interest and another that helped tenant farmers to own their own land.

was sworn in as US President. In his inaugural speech, he made it clear that he intended to wage war against unemployment and poverty. Congress granted him unprecedented powers, for 100 days, to take control of the economy. His 'New Deal' was a series of measures to bring about relief, recovery and reform. These included the setting up, by legislation, of a number of organisations known as the '**alphabet agencies**', with policies to bring the USA out of the Depression. They were intended to create jobs and rebuild industry, agriculture and commerce. Roosevelt's powers entitled him to spend taxation revenue on job-creating schemes to get the USA back to work.

What did the New Deal do for minorities?

The answer to this question is debatable. The New Deal was not really about righting wrongs or establishing rights and freedoms. Its purpose was to stimulate the economy and create jobs. Hence, the plight of African-Americans and Hispanic-Americans remained acute throughout the 1930s in spite of Roosevelt's package.

Job-creation schemes

These continued to be discriminatory in practice. The preferential treatment of white workers in the allocation of jobs disadvantaged African-Americans and Hispanics. Some African-Americans must have benefited from the one million jobs that were created and from new housing provision by the end of the 1930s. In theory, provision was made under these schemes for all the USA's unemployed. However, in practice, aid to minorities was diluted by the racist attitudes of the administrators. Minimum wage rates, for example, were set at a lower level for black than for white workers. This situation was upheld by the major trade unions, which discriminated against black workers in every respect.

Agricultural policies

The agricultural policies of the New Deal enabled some African-American sharecroppers to own their own land through its compensation and credit schemes. But many illiterate black people were easily cheated and tricked when it came to allocating funds. The policies also led to the eviction of large numbers of African-Americans and to the unemployment of Hispanic-American labourers. Roosevelt's **Agricultural Adjustment Agency** (AAA) attempted to resolve the problem of plummeting agricultural prices by cutting production, destroying crops where there had been some degree of overproduction and putting areas of land out of use. As more acres were taken out of production, the need for farm labour fell. This trend adversely affected Hispanic-Americans. The compulsory reduction of cultivated acreage hit sharecroppers in the south very hard. Over half of these were black. So the trend to migrate into the towns of the north continued, increasing racial tension. In one city, notices appeared saying, 'No niggers, Mexicans or dogs allowed.'

Lynching and serious miscarriages of justice

Crimes such as these continued and increased. Even by the end of the 1930s, lynching was still not regarded as a crime and its perpetrators went unpunished. Suffering, however, increased the determination among African-Americans to resist persecution and to bring about change. Anti-lynching measures were high on the agenda of the NAACP and the UNIA (see page 85). Now, black women became active in the campaign to stop lynching. They formed the Association of Southern Women for the Prevention of Lynching and received support from **Eleanor Roosevelt**, the First Lady (president's wife), who demonstrated her strong opposition to racism very publicly on several occasions. Other similar women's groups were set up to oppose lynching, rape and racism.

However, attempts to make lynching a federal crime failed to be passed by Congress in 1935 and again in 1938. These would have punished sheriffs who failed to protect their prisoners from lynch mobs. Roosevelt did nothing to intervene in this process, even though he had the power to do so – an indication, perhaps, of the extent to which issues of race were crucial in determining political fortunes. When the government did have the opportunity to advance the cause of equality and civil rights, it failed to do so.

The case of Rubin Stacy

Rubin Stacy was a homeless tenant farmer in Florida, who had gone to the house of a white woman, Marion Jones, to ask for food. When she saw his face, she was frightened and screamed. He was arrested, but while being escorted by six deputies he was taken by a white mob and hanged at the side of his alleged victim's house. The deeply disturbing feature of

KEY PERSON

Eleanor Roosevelt (1884–1962) was the wife of Franklin D. Roosevelt. Although the mother of six children and a supportive First Lady, she was determined to pursue her own career. She actively supported organisations attempting to improve the position of women, such as the Women's Trade Union League, and to obtain the vote for women. She also supported groups opposed to racism and the demand for legislation to make lynching a federal offence, even though her husband distanced himself from this.

this incident is not just that people were able to convince themselves and others that this was the right thing to do, but that photographs of the hanging clearly show the presence of young children in the crowd. These had obviously been taken along by their parents to enjoy the spectacle. Roosevelt was unmoved by the case of Rubin Stacy, or by the fact that, in 1935 alone, twenty other people were lynched in the south. Two of these were women.

Self-help and social welfare

Some black women formed self-help groups for African-American families who were struggling to survive. The Alpha Kappa Alpha's Mississippi Health Project, for example, provided health care each summer from 1935 until 1942 for poor black communities. During Roosevelt's second term of office, the New Deal began to incorporate welfare issues, the care of the unemployed, and elderly and young families being predominant. However, African-Americans and other minority groups often faced discrimination or rejection when they tried to claim benefits.

Women's rights

The New Deal did little to advance the cause of women's rights. While there were notable exceptions, such as **Frances Perkins**, who became the first female member of the Cabinet, and Mary McLeod Bethune (see page 68), educated women generally found themselves condemned to menial work. Job-creation schemes were targeted at the male breadwinner. Minimum wages were established by the Fair Standards Act (1938), but wage differentials were maintained. Welfare provision helped young mothers, but the process of application for support was humiliating. Some states retained legal restrictions on the employment of married women.

It would be wrong, however, to paint a totally gloomy picture of the benefits of the New Deal for ethnic minorities. Although such benefits were limited, there were some.

Works Progress Administration (WPA)

This was established to provide work for unemployed writers, artists and actors, and it did benefit some individual writers and artists from minority groups. A number of public works schemes were set up during its eight-year existence, some

Eleanor Roosevelt with Mary McLeod Bethune (centre).

KEY EVENTS

The **Federal Writers' Project** was a government-sponsored project to employ writers in the production of such things as guidebooks, local history and folklore books. They carried out oral history projects, gathering together and publishing the memories of elderly, former slaves.

The **Federal Artists' Project** employed out-of-work artists to paint public buildings, such as schools, libraries, and courthouses, with murals. These often depicted working-class life. Sponsored artists were also able to develop their talent in portrait and landscape painting.

The **Federal Music Project** sponsored musicians to perform, especially in orchestral concerts. Money was provided to encourage young people to develop their musical abilities. Huge numbers of people had the opportunity to develop their talent under this scheme. A similar theatre project employed around 12,500 actors and theatre technicians to take drama, ballet and puppet productions around the USA. Some of these specially written productions were controversial and therefore brought the project criticism.

more dubious than others. However, the **Federal Writers' Project, the Federal Artists' Project** and the **Federal Music Project** were particularly successful in helping the few.

Native Americans

Native Americans seemed to benefit more obviously from the New Deal, perhaps because Roosevelt took an interest in their plight. Native American men had fought bravely in the First World War and, in recognition, had been guaranteed their rights of citizenship in 1924. However, during the 1920s there had been several attempts to deprive Native Americans of the reservation lands that had been allocated to them, especially if they were likely to be on oil fields. A senate inquiry of 1928 shocked the nation with its descriptions of dire poverty and disease.

In 1934, Roosevelt appointed **John Collier** as Commissioner for Indian Affairs, and he persuaded Congress to pass the **Indian Reorganisation Act** (1934). The Act and Collier's subsequent actions recognised and preserved traditional Native American culture and the right of the Native Americans to control their reservation lands. This was difficult, however, because in their struggle to survive they had leased areas of their lands to white farmers. Native Americans were increasingly involved in the work of the Indian Bureau, even though they did not take over the

HEINEMANN ADVANCED HISTORY

KEY PERSON

John Collier (1884–1968)
Before his appointment as Commissioner for Indian Affairs, Collier had been the secretary of the Indian Defence League and had worked with other reformers to secure the right of Native Americans to their religious and cultural life. He opposed the imposition of white culture on the tribes and provided the rationale for the Indian Reorganisation Act of 1934.

KEY EVENT

Indian Reorganisation Act 1934 (the Wheeler-Howard Act) is sometimes referred to as the Indian New Deal. It restored the right of the Native Americans to communal ownership of their land and therefore their tribal community life that had been destroyed by the Dawes Severalty Act (see page 9). It gave them back their right to govern themselves. Loans were provided to encourage Native American business development and to increase educational opportunities. It was, however, only partially successful. The break-up of tribal life was already well under way and the attempt to restore it caused confusion. However, millions of acres of Native American land were recultivated. The decline in the Native American population was arrested and it began to rise.

running of their own affairs as had been envisaged, partly because they were heavily dependent on federal aid.

The Indian Reorganisation Act gave Native American women formal political rights and provided them with opportunities to train for domestic work. It also stimulated interest in native arts and crafts. A small number of Indian women had the opportunity of higher education. Gladys Tantaquidgeon, for example, became an anthropologist and worked for the Indian Bureau, where she specialised in promoting and encouraging traditional Indian arts and crafts.

African-Americans and trade unions

The New Deal era gave a boost to the trade union movement generally and to the unionisation of African-Americans in particular. During the 1930s, black workers were persuaded by organisations such as the NAACP and the National Urban League to join trade unions. They were seen as the means not only to improve their immediate economic situation, but also, in the longer term, to further the cause of civil rights. Two main developments contributed to break down the prejudice of existing trade unions, such as the American Federation of Labor (AFL), and to encourage black people to become involved in union organisation:

- The National Recovery Administration (NRA) was set up in 1933 under the auspices of Frances Perkins (see page 91). Its responsibility was to produce job-creation schemes and establish regulations to address working hours and conditions, such as sweatshops and the use of child labour. Many of these schemes were beneficial to exploited immigrant labour. The National Industrial Recovery Act (NIRA) was passed with the purpose of fostering cooperation between both sides of industry. It gave employees the right to collective bargaining. The National Labor Board was established to enforce this provision. In 1935, this system was made permanent. It established clear rules for collective bargaining and set up regional boards to identify groups of workers who were entitled to bargain with their employers. This gave African-Americans the opportunity they needed. All that was now required was the courage to become involved.
- By the mid-1930s, some trade union activists clearly recognised that, to be successful, it was necessary for all

workers within an industry to be organised. This was particularly the case in mass-production industries with large labour forces. In 1935 the unions set up the Committee of Industrial Organisation (CIO). Its aim was to organise all workers in mass-production industries and, in the process, to abolish racial discrimination. It was a kind of umbrella organisation under which a number of unions gathered. One was the United Mine Workers' Union, which had never discriminated since it was founded at the end of the nineteenth century. Steel, clothing, textile and meat-packing unions – industries that all employed large numbers of black workers – joined. In the south, unions accepted black members but organised their black and white members in separate organisations.

The organisation of black workers, in itself, was not new. In 1925, for example, A. Philip Randolph had established the Brotherhood of Sleeping Car Porters and Maids to obtain better working conditions and higher wages from the Pullman Company. Such organisations, however, were unsuccessful because they had no legal foundation. The NIRA was an important turning point because it established the rights of black workers in law and, in so doing, recognised that the safeguard of rights was a political issue.

African-Americans were initially reluctant to use this opportunity to negotiate for improvement, but trade union membership was an important step in the quest for civil rights. It not only gave black people an enhanced awareness of the rights to which they were entitled; it also gave them, eventually, increased confidence in pursuing them. Some African-Americans, mainly from the working class, were also drawn to the more left-wing trade unions that were emerging. These were fundamentally influenced by communist ideology, but their egalitarianism and, therefore, their support for equal rights were understandably attractive. In fact, the American Communist Party (CPUSA) clearly saw black people, as well as other ethnic minorities suffering discrimination, as a promising source of recruitment.

Political influence and Roosevelt's 'Black Cabinet'

During the 1930s, the African-American vote became increasingly influential, especially in the north. Moreover, black voters themselves were becoming increasingly aware that the vote potentially empowered them. This growing awareness coincided with the increasing sense of self-awareness and of community that ghetto dwelling engendered. In some cities, such as Chicago, the black vote was deciding the outcome of local elections. African-Americans were also beginning to appreciate that the vote could be used to register protest as well as support. In spite of the criticisms of the New Deal, African-Americans were overwhelmingly supporters of Roosevelt. Like millions of white Americans, they believed and trusted him. His dynamism and enthusiasm also excited them. Perhaps unintentionally, he inspired them to go forward with their cause.

Roosevelt's decision to assemble a 'cabinet' of African-Americans is interesting in two respects:

• Although they were not politicians, they were highly educated and highly trained people. This is indicative of the educational opportunities that were arising for at least some black people.
• It was not unprecedented for the President to turn to black advisers (Booker T. Washington had advised his grandfather, Theodore Roosevelt), but the members of Roosevelt's 'Black Cabinet' are unusual in their number and the breadth of their involvement.

This was probably not an initiative that came solely from Roosevelt himself. Eleanor Roosevelt was almost certainly influential in their appointment, as were others surrounding the President. Their real influence is difficult to determine, since the men and women in Roosevelt's administration who drove the actual policies forward were all white. However, they did use their positions to press for social and economic improvement, and some of their efforts must have been successful. Their presence and increasing numbers must also have contributed to raising the self-esteem of African-Americans and to convincing them that Roosevelt was *their* President. Certainly, the numbers of black people in federal employment increased from 50,000 in 1933 to 200,000 in 1946, although the majority of these were in low-level, unskilled occupations.

The work of the NAACP goes on

In 1930, Walter Francis White replaced W.E.B. Du Bois as leader of the NAACP. During the 1930s, the NAACP worked hard to obtain the support of the mass of black people. It continued its campaign against lynching and influenced the two ultimately unsuccessful attempts to pass laws against it. Under the influence of White, the organisation:

- continued to encourage ordinary African-Americans to organise and assert themselves
- used the courts to challenge specific incidences of discrimination against black people – cases in which they were increasingly successful
- battled in the courts to challenge discrimination and denial of the exercise of civil rights in some of the southern states (these cases were not always successful)
- fought more successfully against the unequal funding and provision of education in some states.

War on the horizon

On 7 December 1941, Japanese planes carried out a surprise attack on the US naval base at Pearl Harbor, Hawaii. The war in Europe had been raging since 1939. As in 1914, the USA initially maintained a position of neutrality. During that time, US industry once again received a huge boost from the needs of war. It resolved, at least temporarily, the problem of unemployment and gave a fresh stimulus to the US manufacturing industry and to farming.

On 11 December 1941, Germany and Italy declared war on the USA. It came as no surprise. As in 1917, US troops prepared to join the war in Europe. African- and Hispanic-Americans, Native Americans, Catholics and Jews of immigrant stock were recruited along with white, Protestant Americans to be thrown into another kind of melting pot. At home, they filled the gaps in industry and essential services along with the previously homebound women of the USA. How would they all emerge from the war? The experience of the Second World War would prove to be a major turning point in the struggle for civil rights.

SUMMARY QUESTIONS

1 What factors led to increased racial tension in the inter-war years?

2 Which minority groups, if any, made the most progress during this period?

3 What were the major setbacks to the progress of civil rights during the 1920s and 1930s?

4 To what extent were the 1920s and 1930s years of achievement for African-Americans?

5 What significant changes and developments were taking place among African-Americans during these years?

CHAPTER 5

The Second World War and civil rights

INTRODUCTION

US military involvement in the Second World War was to
have a number of effects on civil rights and race relations.
Politically, this was not the best time for reform. If a
democratic country goes on a full-scale war footing, freedoms
can easily be eroded. Consequently, this was not a time when
civil rights for racial minorities advanced.

The context of the war meant that Japanese-Americans
suffered particularly badly. But in the black community, the
social and economic changes brought about by the conflict
would highlight their civil rights issues and show the future
direction of their activity. The war also brought about changes
for the Native American and Mexican communities. All in all,
the momentum of the Civil Rights Movement went up several
gears. This chapter looks at how this came about.

HOW DID THE WAR AFFECT AFRICAN-AMERICANS?

Segregation in the army

The presence of black people in the US army brought its own
tensions. Black people were not treated well, despite a higher
enlistment rate. They were seen as equal when it came to
being out in the front line, but other features of military life
reinforced segregation. At military parades, in church services,
when being transported and in the canteens, the races were
kept apart. Little had changed since the First World War.
The prediction made by Frederick Douglass during the Civil
War (see page 21) had been correct about the end of slavery,
but had not yet come about in terms of full citizenship.

More significantly, what was the point of fighting the racism of
the Nazis if African-Americans were to suffer similar treatment
at the hands of 'Hitlers' back in Alabama, Georgia or
Mississippi? The idea of southern racists being compared to

Hitler came first from journalists in 1941, wondering if the USA should enter the war at all. The starkest illustration of the comparison came in a lunchroom in Salinas, Kansas. German prisoners of war (few and far between in the USA at this time) were served in the whites-only area, whereas black people had to eat elsewhere. And when it came to treatment for injuries, the Red Cross was forced to segregate the blood of black and white people. James McGill, the General Surgeon to the Assistant Secretary of War, claimed it was inadvisable 'to collect and mix **Caucasian** and Negro blood'. Many white southerners argued that any change in policy would help, in their words, 'to Mongrelise' the nation. The treatment of black servicemen gave rise to the black press campaign for 'Double V' – victory against racism abroad and at home

Segregation in the air force and navy

In the other services, segregation was more artificial. Separate training for black pilots in the air force was made possible by providing a separate training ground at Tuskagee, Alabama, but on ships it proved particularly difficult. At first, black people were given only the dirtiest jobs, but the need for more sailors meant that some began to gain promotion, and segregation became harder to maintain. It is not surprising that the navy was the first branch of the services to desegregate in 1946.

Migration

Before the war, the 1920s and 1930s had already seen a substantial shift of black people to northern and western industrial areas, but when the conflict began it meant the creation of more new jobs, not least in the defence industries. Black people now moved north in even greater numbers to meet the labour demand. In 1940, over three-quarters of the 13.5 million black people still lived in the rural south, but the three and a half years of war saw a further 500,000 on the move. This involved travelling west to cities such as Los Angeles and San Francisco – where they joined Mexican immigrants – or, even more frequently, north to Detroit,

Black population in selected cities, 1940–5.

	1940	1945
San Francisco	4,800	32,000
Chicago	277,000	491,000
Detroit	149,000	209,000

Chicago or Washington. After the war, the trend continued at a similar rate. For black women it meant a greater variety of economic opportunities. Before 1941, three-quarters of them had worked in domestic service; by 1945 it was less than half.

Employment chances

But how fulfilling would these jobs actually be? Black people would often find they were discriminated against when applying for employment, and even if they were successful, they would not usually receive equal pay. They were often 'the last to be hired, the first to be fired' – a principle less frequently applied to white people. However, this was not just the prejudice of middle-class employers. The trade union bosses were not pleased to see them come and feared that they, like other migrants, would depress wages. Since they were used to low earnings in the south, it was believed that black people would be prepared to settle for less money than white people thought reasonable. When black people were promoted to positions of authority, white workers frequently walked out, as at Mobile, Alabama, in May 1943 when twelve black welders were promoted at a shipping company. Fifty people were seriously injured in the riots that followed.

The March on Washington Movement

The war speeded up developments that were already occurring before 1941. In that year, **A. Philip Randolph** suggested a march on Washington by thousands of black people. The purpose was to challenge the employment policies of the federal government. Only ten per cent of defence contractors employed black people in 1940. Randolph's proposal was abandoned when President Roosevelt agreed to make concessions. He ordered the setting-up of an organisation that would try to gain **equality of opportunity** for black people when it came to defence industry jobs in the federal government. This organization created in 1943 was called the Fair Employment Practices Commission (FEPC).

KEY PERSON

A. Philip Randolph (1889–1979) He was the founder and organiser of the Brotherhood of Sleeping Car Porters, an all-black union. He became President of the National Negro Congress in the 1930s. A socialist, Randolph sought to achieve better economic conditions for black workers by co-operating with the white labour movement. In the 1950s and 1960s he supported the Civil Rights Movement. His idea of a march on Washington was taken up again in 1963 when he worked with Martin Luther King and others on this major event (see page 143).

KEY THEME

Equality of opportunity One consistent thread throughout the Civil Rights Movement was the demand that black people should have equal opportunity with white people when it came to applying for jobs. This has proved very hard to achieve completely, even to this day. In the 1940s and 1950s, many states copied Roosevelt's federal idea and set up Fair Employment Practices Commissions of their own.

	1940	1945
Black unemployment (no.)	937,000	151,000
% employed in agriculture (men)	42	31
% employed in agriculture (women)	21	11

Black employment and, unemployment, 1940–5.

It had some effect. Black people were employed in aircraft factories for the first time; there was a 25 per cent increase in those working in the iron and steel industry. Their numbers employed in government service increased from 50,000 to 200,000. Other organisations were less responsive. For instance, the railroads normally refused to hire black people. In the Deep South, prejudice against hiring black people for the better-paid jobs remained as strong as ever.

Were black and white people treated equally in the north?

In theory, African-Americans would not expect to meet as much prejudice outside the workplace as they encountered inside. There were a number of reasons for this:

- They would be able to share transport and eating facilities with white people in ways not allowed in the south.
- Some northern white people who were not prejudiced could show their friendship more easily than southern white people. The latter would often be under pressure to conform to the general mood of segregation – or else be seen to be letting their race down.
- Black people were able to cast their vote much more freely in northern states. This meant that in a few places this vote could be really valuable. In Chicago, the Democratic Party

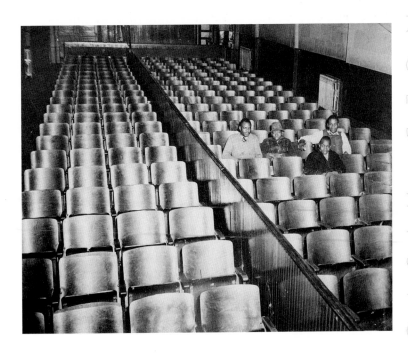

A cinema in 1943, showing the split seating sections for black and white audiences.

wooed the black vote with supposedly equal employment policies.

How much social integration was there in the north?

In practice, there was only limited mixing of the races. Black and white people were not happily living next door to each other, nor were their children attending the same schools.

- Black people tended to congregate in the same area of the town. The black district of Harlem in New York was now repeated in many other cities. There was the Watts district in Los Angeles, Philadelphia's Seventh Ward, Detroit's Paradise Valley and the South Side in Chicago.
- Often housing conditions were poor and black areas were seen as ghettos. This meant that many failed to break out of the **cycle of poverty**.
- As in the south, predominantly black schools usually had facilities considerably inferior to the white ones.
- In short, African-Americans would be subject to discrimination that was **de facto** rather than **de jure**.

Increased racial tension

All this led to considerable racial tension in the north, where black people were without great hope of regular employment and frequently at the poorest end of the community. Sometimes they resorted to violence and crime, as did Malcolm Little in New York, later to become famous in the early 1960s as Malcolm X (see page 163). In Detroit, tensions were particularly high and serious race rioting occurred in 1943. White workers were traditionally hostile to black workers in the city and the riot was sparked off by an argument between two motorists, one black and one white. Hours later, twenty-five black and nine white people were dead. Fifteen of the black people died at police hands.

In 1942, **James Farmer** set up a new organisation to seek equality for blacks. It was called the Congress of Racial Equality (CORE). Sit-in protests were organised against segregation in areas such as shops, hairdressing salons and swimming pools. This idea was to become very important nearly twenty years later.

KEY TERMS

A **cycle of poverty** is poverty that successive generations of the same family have found hard to avoid. In the case of the black American ghettos, poor education led to low-paid jobs or unemployment, which meant living in the most run-down areas of town, which in turn led to children attending the poorest schools, and so the cycle began again.

De facto means the actual position in reality. **De jure** means the official position in law.

KEY PERSON

James Farmer (1920–99) was the son of a Methodist minister. He was brought up in Mississippi before studying theology in Chicago, where he became interested in non-violent methods of resistance. He was the chairman of CORE between 1942 and 1950. He became a race relations officer with the Fellowship of Reconciliation, set up to monitor Roosevelt's Fair Employment Practices Committee, and in the 1950s became a trade union official. In 1961, he helped organise the dramatic and successful Freedom Rides (see page 131), during which he was badly beaten. He resigned from CORE in 1965 when it was being taken over by Black Power elements (see page 163). In the 1970s and 1980s he taught at various universities, writing his autobiography, *Lay Bare the Heart*, in 1985.

A commercial street in Harlem in the 1950s.

EFFECT OF THE WAR ON OTHER MINORITY GROUPS

With a population of over ten million, African-Americans were by far the largest ethnic minority group in the USA. At the outbreak of the Second World War, there were fewer than a million Native Americans, Puerto Ricans, Mexicans and Asian-Americans.

Japanese–American

What happened to the civil rights of the Japanese-Americans during the Second World War? For most, their lives were directly affected. At once, all Japanese assets on the US mainland were frozen, and those living in California – the majority – were viewed with great suspicion. Initially, a **curfew** was imposed against them; then, in March 1942, the process began of moving well over 100,000 Japanese from the coast to 'relocation camps' in the interior, where they were **interned**. Conditions were overcrowded – in Wyoming, for instance, 11,000 Japanese were crammed into one-room barracks intended for far fewer.

Asian-Americans (mainly Japanese, with some Chinese)	150,000
Native American Indians	345,000
Mexican-Americans	377,000*

*This figure is almost certainly an underestimate because of illegal immigration.

Ethnic minority populations in the USA, 1940

West Coast military commander John de Witt insisted that all the Japanese were a strategic danger. Public opinion appeared to agree with him. Racist rhymes began to circulate – 'slap the Jap right off the map' – and Japanese were alleged to have attempted to make American soldiers drunk. Japanese fishing trawlers were accused of mining harbours and Japanese farmers of poisoning vegetables, but hard evidence was lacking. The Californian Attorney-General, Earl Warren (see page 112) had no legal reservations about their treatment and the Supreme Court backed the measures taken against them in two separate judgments:

- In *Hirabayashi* v. *US* (1943), the Court upheld the West Coast curfew law.
- In *Koreamatsu* v. *US* (1944), the Court upheld the relocation programme.

Native Americans

With African-Americans becoming more conscious of the need to campaign for fairer treatment, and with evidence that Roosevelt might respond with positive action when under pressure, the Native Americans took a significant step, during wartime, to try to improve their lot. In 1944, they formed the National Congress of American Indians (NCAI). This organisation was clearly influenced by the style of campaigning undertaken by the NAACP, and it intended to launch a series of legal cases to establish rights such as equal educational opportunity. Vine Deloria Jr, a Sioux who wished to go to Law School, commented that Native Americans would bring case after case, if necessary, in order to effect a change.

But it would be a mistake to assume the Native American racial consciousness needed reawakening by civil rights activities elsewhere: it had been present for many years. Even before the Second World War began, members of the Iroquois tribe and four others had gone to jail rather than be drafted into the armed forces. In 1942, the Iroquois tribe had independently declared war on Germany and Japan.

A determination to attack the negative 'Cowboy and Indian' stereotype was apparent. But little progress was made at this stage. The low view of their culture among many Americans clearly remained. In truth, the Native Americans had neither prospered as independent farmers of the land nor become integrated into the mainstream of American society. They still occupied infertile land on isolated reservations in Alaska, Arizona, California, Mississippi, Montana, New Mexico, North and South Dakota, and Oklahoma. Alcoholism and illiteracy were both major problems. They did not desire integration, as black people did at this stage, but wished only to improve their standard of living and maintain their distinctive identity. Little progress was made on these issues until the 1960s.

Mexican-Americans

The war encouraged an increase in Mexican immigration into California, which had come to a halt during the Depression years. Indeed, during the 1930s nearly half a million Mexicans had been **repatriated**. Those remaining still lived mainly in California and the Lower Rio Grande Valley of Texas. However, there were also considerable numbers in Arizona, Colorado, Michigan and New Mexico. Agricultural work was the most common occupation: growing lettuces, sugar beet and cotton. Wartime conditions produced a renewed labour demand to fill vacancies caused by the recruitment of the armed forces.

With Mexico entering the war against Japan and Germany on the side of the USA in June 1942, the **Bracero Agreement** was signed between Mexico and the USA in the following month. However, when the war ended in 1945, Bracero continued. Californian growers liked the cheap labour and their influence in high places prevented Congress from repealing the agreement until 1964. But with competition from returning troops and a large number of Mexican immigrants – far outnumbering predicted figures – unemployment soon became an issue.

During the war, the Mexican influx had mainly been adult male, but now whole families were arriving. Like the Native Americans, not only were their unemployment rates high, but also their life expectancy was low and disease was a major threat to all. Often treated as aliens, the **Chicanos** lacked normal civil rights and many did not get on to voting registers through lack of understanding or outright hostility. But with the growing prosperity of the USA and the comparatively backward status of the Mexican economy, many illegal immigrants were tempted to make the trip.

KEY TERMS

Repatriated Returned to their country of origin. In this case it would mean the loss of their American citizenship.

Bracero Agreement Under the agreement, Mexico allowed its inhabitants to come and work in the USA for a temporary period with guaranteed conditions of employment.

Chicanos A word increasingly used in the 1960s by the Mexicans themselves to describe those who were now living in the USA. Originally a term of abuse, it was taken up by the Mexicans to signify pride in their ancient civilisation.

At this stage, there was no sign of a Mexican Civil Rights Movement. It was to take the more questioning atmosphere of the mid-1960s to produce a Hispanic campaign for improvements in their condition. Until the 1960s, moreover, there was no labour equivalent to the blacks' A. Philip Randolph. The trade unions for Mexican workers, active in the 1930s, disappeared in the war. Attempts at strikes during the late 1940s and 1950s were unsuccessful and usually crushed by employers. The most prolonged, in Kern County, California, from late 1947 to early 1949, ended in failure and large employers such as the Di Georgio Corporation refused to recognise trade unions.

HOW SIGNIFICANT WAS THIS PERIOD IN LAYING THE FOUNDATION FOR FUTURE PROGRESS?

There is no doubt that the period of the Second World War speeded up some significant developments in the black and other communities, namely:

- the move to work in industry in northern and western cities
- the issues of employment opportunities, housing and other social problems in the ghettos
- racial tension in northern areas as well as in the south
- the widening of horizons for many black people, who now became more impatient with 'Jim Crow' in the south
- activity in civil rights organisations like NAACP and CORE
- civil rights issues raised in the case of a number of racial minorities.

SUMMARY QUESTIONS

1 What were the main effects of the Second World War on the black community in the USA?

2 How were the fortunes of the other racial minorities affected by the war?

3 What civil rights issues became prominent as a result of the war?

CHAPTER 6

Post-war changes and the Civil Rights Movement

KEY TERMS

Cold War The term used to describe the period after 1945 when there were tense relations between capitalist and communist states (e.g. the USA and the USSR). Although no formal war was declared (hence the term 'cold'), the threat of a nuclear explosion was very real until as late as the 1980s.

The Secretary of State is a senior minister in the US federal government, helping the President to run the USA's foreign policy. Dean Acheson was the nearest US equivalent to a British Foreign Secretary.

KEY THEME

Anti-communism In the late 1940s and early 1950s, a number of east European states, as well as China, acquired communist governments. Many Americans were fiercely anti-communist, fearing that communism would undermine their capitalist system and traditions of freedom. Those merely suspected of having communist sympathies were frequently smeared and removed from public positions. The anti-communist mood continued into following decades and helps to account for the American determination to stay in Vietnam.

INTRODUCTION

Changing black attitudes

After the war, social developments at home helped the issue of black civil rights to come to the forefront. Some black people enjoyed a taste of racial integration during the war, such as those who went to the UK and other European countries. Many black people returned home at the end of the fighting looking for similar integration there. Those who stayed at home often felt the same way. The membership of NAACP had increased during the war from 50,000 to 200,000. It now had over 1500 branches and was represented in nearly every state of the Union. The National Urban League was also growing at this time, if on a more modest scale.

Changing white attitudes

Liberal white people, especially in the north, were also conscious of the US role in the **Cold War** against the Soviet Union. How could the USA champion individual freedom in the world generally while denying it to an important minority in its own country? As **Secretary of State,** Dean Acheson put it in 1946: 'The existence of discrimination against minority groups in this country has an adverse effect on our relations with other countries'. However, this could also have a downside. The strong **anti-communism** of post-war and Cold War USA meant that campaigning groups and individuals could be accused of communism by leading figures such as Senator **Joseph McCarthy**; hence the NAACP was banned in Alabama in 1956 and even felt obliged to organise a 'purge' of its supposedly communist members.

White Americans were now becoming more aware of just how black people were treated in the south, where violence against them was greater and where discrimination was more systematic. The spread of the motor car and the television set aided this awareness. In the following years, civil rights campaigners moved with ease around the whole of the USA to organise their various campaigns: they used the fact that transport was still segregated in the south as part of their campaign. They came to rely on the publicity of the television screen, as horrified northern white liberals saw racist southern police at work. Here, the 1950s were crucial. In 1949, 1 million American families had a television set; in 1960, it was 45 million. This proved very significant during the 1960s, when millions in a shocked nation watched the horrific treatment of civil rights protesters by racist police.

HOW DID BLACK PEOPLE CAMPAIGN FOR CHANGE?

Faced with accusations of communism after 1945, the NAACP was involved less with direct protest than it had been in the war. However, it continued to mount legal challenges to the system of segregation and discrimination, particularly with regard to education, voter registration and fair employment.

Education

In education, the NAACP attempted to challenge the 'separate but equal' doctrine of *Plessy* v. *Ferguson* (see page 62). Education was an area where inequality of treatment could be easily challenged: you could compare how much was spent on black schools and how much on white. For instance, research showed that in 1949 in Clarendon County, South Carolina, an average of $179 was spent on each white child in their schools, but only $43 on each black one. The pupil–teacher ratio was 20 per cent better in white schools than black; in addition, black teachers generally received about half the salary of white ones. As a result, the NAACP sued on behalf of the black children. Various other law suits followed (see page 180) and out of this would eventually come the important legal case of *Brown* v. *Board of Education, Topeka* (see page 112).

One of the most skilful of civil rights lawyers, **Thurgood Marshall**, put forward a series of powerful reasons why the legal system should acknowledge and tackle the lack of equality in the education system. The legal process moved slowly, however, as a number of similar cases gradually worked their way up to Supreme Court level. The efforts

Joseph R. McCarthy (1908–57) became a lawyer. A Republican Senator from 1946, he came to prominence in 1950 when he charged over 200 people in the State Department (federal government) in Washington, DC, with being communists. By 1954 his accusations were becoming wider and wilder, even touching upon President Eisenhower, and evidence to back up his claims was badly lacking. His allegations became discredited, he drank increasingly heavily and he died a disgraced and broken man in 1957. However, for a short time during the early 1950s, his views were widely accepted.

Thurgood Marshall (1908–93) was a leading black lawyer. He took cases regarding segregation to the Supreme Court on behalf of the NAACP and won nearly all of them (e.g. *Smith* v. *Allright* and *Brown* v. *Board of Education, Topeka*). In 1967, Marshall became the first black Justice of the Supreme Court.

were financed by the NAACP's Legal Defence and Educational Fund and eventually bore fruit.

Voter registration

In the field of voter registration there was more measurable, if limited, progress. In 1944, the Supreme Court decision in *Smith* v. *Allright* outlawed the **white primary** in Texas. As a result of the decision, the number of black people who were registered voters in the USA rose from two per cent in 1940 to twelve per cent in 1947. A few black people actually managed to get elected for state legislatures – about 25 – though none in the Deep South. In New York, Adam Clayton Powell went further and was elected to the Federal House of Representatives.

Employment

There was also progress in the taking-up of fair employment practices begun by Roosevelt's initiative in 1941. By 1953, 20 states and 30 cities had adopted these laws. But their effectiveness in both north and south can be questioned and enforcement was difficult. Nonetheless, black people were beginning to benefit from the general mood of post-war prosperity that was apparent throughout the states.

WHITE RESISTANCE IN THE SOUTH

Segregation and racism

It was clear that black people were making modest progress in the educational and economic fields. Perhaps because of this, white southern racist resistance to demands for equality became even more apparent in the post-war years. All the old Confederate states were involved, but the Deep South, Mississippi, Alabama, Georgia and South Carolina maintained segregation the most rigidly. With still only a few black Americans voting in these areas and the peristence of prejudice, many southern politicians would often increase their racist comments when it came to election time.

The strong anti-communist feeling of the Cold War period complicated matters further. Civil rights protests were linked, often unfairly, to communist activities. NAACP voter registration drives were met with heavy resistance in Mississippi and Alabama. In Mississippi, 95 per cent of black

KEY TERM

The white primary was where only white people had been allowed a preliminary vote to choose the Democratic Party candidates who would stand in the general election.

workers were employed by white people, and sharecroppers (see page 40) could easily be evicted and jobs lost if they were brave enough to attempt to register. In Alabama, a leading white lawyer asserted that **'negroes' would never be good enough to vote**. Few black people could take legal action against white people, still less hope for a favourable verdict. Governors and state officials, including the police, were generally racist in these states.

The Ku Klux Klan

Though it had not grown, the Klan was still present in those areas of the Deep South where it had traditionally operated. In 1946, 15,000 people marched to the **Lincoln Memorial** in Washington, demanding that the Klan be made illegal under federal law. Lynching was not as common or as public as it had been in the 1930s, but it still occurred. One of the most notorious cases was that of Emmet Till as late as 1955. He was fourteen years old and had allegedly whistled at a white woman. Though a trial took place of those accused of his murder, it was an astonishingly light-hearted affair with the jury drinking in the witness box. The defendants were found not guilty.

States' rights

Many southerners still used the old argument that imposing civil rights upon them was an unacceptable breach of their freedom: they wished to determine their own policies at state level, rather than have them imposed by the federal government. This was a favourite theme of figures such as Theodore Bilbo in Mississippi and Strom Thurmond in South Carolina. So strongly did Thurmond feel about this that he deserted the Democratic Party at the time of the presidential election in 1948 and ran as a Third Party candidate against the Democratic President, **Harry Truman**. Over a million people voted for his 'states' rights' campaign but, compared to 24 million votes for Truman and 22 million for Dewey, the Republican candidate, Thurmond's support was small.

The 1948 election reminds us of the minority that the Deep South was now in: the call of states' rights was less powerful now than it had been in the nineteenth century. Especially since the Roosevelt presidency and the New Deal, federal power was much greater and was likely to be used more frequently. States were increasingly dependent on grants from the federal government, and they were finding it hard to resist its demands. It was now more difficult to oppose a President – but not yet impossible, as Harry Truman was to find out.

Name	Dates	Party
Harry S. Truman	1945–53	Democrat
Dwight D. Eisenhower	1953–61	Republican
John F. Kennedy	1961–63	Democrat
Lyndon B. Johnson	1963–69	Democrat
Richard M. Nixon	1969–74	Republican
Gerald Ford	1974–77	Republican
Jimmy Carter	1977–81	Democrat
Ronald Reagan	1981–89	Republican
George Bush	1989–93	Republican
Bill Clinton	1993–2001	Democrat
George W. Bush	2001–	Republican

Post-war presidents of the USA.

Presidential dates can cause some confusion. Presidents are elected near the end of one year (November), but take office in the next year (now January, formerly March). Below are the serving dates rather than the election dates.

POLICIES OF PRESIDENT TRUMAN

Truman's attitudes

Harry Truman, became President on the death of Franklin Roosevelt in 1945.

In a 1947 report called *To Secure These Rights* the President's Committee on Civil Rights recommended:

- a permanent Civil Rights Division of the Federal Justice Department

- a permanent Commission on Civil Rights

- federal anti-lynching legislation;

- abolition of the Poll Tax

- laws to protect qualified voters

- a legal attack on segregated housing.

- In principle, he was not racist himself and personally favoured a better deal for black Americans.
- He was aware that the black vote in the northern cities and towns like Kansas City and St Louis, in his own home state of Missouri, could be very useful to the Democrats.

But:

- He was aware of the need to keep the southern white Democrat vote. Southerners would clearly oppose too much interference from the federal government.
- He appears to have been genuinely shocked when seeing racist violence in Texas in 1946, saying: 'My God, I'd no idea it was as bad as that; we will have to do something.' This was a revealingly ignorant comment coming from someone normally so well-informed.

The President's Committee on Civil Rights

Truman set up this commission, which in 1946 recommended action on civil rights. Truman outlined the basic requirements of all American citizens: homes, jobs, education and the vote. In none of these could black people be seen as equal to white people. However, no legislation followed, since the President could not persuade the Congress to pass it. So, by the end of his presidency in 1953, Truman's civil rights achievements were limited. However, he had at least identified civil rights as a moral issue. Moreover, in 1948, he used his authority as Commander-in-Chief of the Armed Forces and issued an executive order to end discrimination in the US military. Shortly after Truman left office, further changes occurred. The legal efforts of Thurgood Marshall and the NAACP came to fruition.

THE BROWN CASE: A LANDMARK VERDICT

Origins of the case

This crucial legal case regarding segregation in education reached the Supreme Court in 1954. It concerned Linda Brown, in an appeal brought by her father, Oliver. An all-white school was just around the corner from the Browns' home in Topeka, Kansas. But Linda had to attend an all-black school over a mile away. Efforts to obtain legal authority for her to go to her local school had not yet succeeded. So the case went, with a group of others, for consideration by the highest court in the land. It was known as *Brown* v. *Board of Education, Topeka*.

Thurgood Marshall and the case for Linda

Thurgood Marshall argued powerfully against the constitutional legality of segregated education. He was not merely asserting that black education should be given an equal status to white education. Education should be integrated. As witnesses, he produced educationalists, psychologists and other professionals to argue that segregation itself created low self-esteem among black people and made them feel they were being treated less than worthily.

The decision

The new **Chief Justice of the Supreme Court, Earl Warren**, agreed with this analysis and gave a verdict in the

Browns' favour. But he went further than merely saying that black people had not had an equal educational chance. He accepted the whole of Marshall's argument that segregation was not acceptable at all. Segregation, argued Warren, 'generates a feeling of inferiority as to their [blacks peoples'] status in the community . . . in a way unlikely ever to be undone'. The Fourteenth Amendment could be clearly interpreted. It required admission of all children on equal terms to public (state) schools. By the time the case was resolved it was too late for Linda to go to the elementary school her father wanted her to attend, but she did eventually manage to receive an academic education.

Result of the verdict

This was a landmark verdict that created an important **precedent** and was expected to produce major change. It did so in a number of places outside the Deep South where segregation still prevailed up to this point. Washington DC, Baltimore, St Louis and many other towns and cities now began to integrate. But progress was not quick. By 1957 less than 12 per cent of the 6300 school districts in the south had been integrated. Why was this?

There was considerable resistance in the south to the whole principle of integration. The argument used most often was states' rights. The federal government was seen as acting dictatorially in seeking to impose its values and opinions on those elsewhere. White Citizens' Councils were formed to protest. Senator Sam Ervin of North Carolina drafted the 'Southern Manifesto', which promised to fight the Brown verdict 'by all legal means'. This was an odd choice of phrase in view of the nature of the institution that had made the decision in the first place.

The Supreme Court itself had not been altogether clear about the timetable for change. After all, changing the nature of schools was going to be a more costly and complicated business than, say, enforcing the abolition of restrictions on the right to vote. In 1955 the Court issued a further statement, which became known as *Brown 2,* on the matter. Aware of the lack of action in many places on even beginning to comply with its verdict, Warren urged proceed 'with all deliberate speed'.

> ### KEY TERM
>
> **Precedent** is when the principles created by an important legal decision are followed in subsequent cases.

President Eisenhower failed to take substantial action to enforce the verdict. This was not because he was an out-and-out racist. In the District of Columbia he outlawed any forms of racial discrimination. His reluctance to take action elsewhere was because he was afraid of stirring up opposition, resentment and disorder in the south. Eisenhower made little comment on the Brown verdict. What he did say was negative.

- He regretted making Earl Warren Chief Justice of the Supreme Court – 'the biggest damn fool mistake I ever made'.
- He doubted the ability of legislation to change minds and hearts in this area – 'I don't believe you can change the hearts of men by laws and decisions.'
- As Commander-in-Chief of the armed forces, Eisenhower could use his power to enforce the Court's verdict. But again he felt using force to solve the problem was 'just plain nuts'.

RESISTANCE AT LITTLE ROCK

Events at Central High School

Events in the town of Little Rock in the state of Arkansas reveal an example of southern resistance to integrated education – but not an entirely typical one. Its Central High School was regarded as the premier high school in the south. Demand for places was high and the school achieved great academic success. In 1957, in the aftermath of the Brown verdict, 75 black children had applied to enter the school, but 50 had been rejected. A further 16 changed their minds when the white community made it clear that they were very hostile to the idea. This left just 9 children who were to run the gauntlet of white hatred.

On 3 September 1957 a hostile crowd gathered to watch the children attempt to enter the school. 'Niggers get back to the jungle,' they cried. The black children were to arrive together on the principle of safety in numbers. However one girl, Elizabeth Eckford, did not receive the message and had to walk up the street alone. 'Lynch her' and 'Tie her to the tree' were two of the more repeatable comments she received. But it was clear that the children could not enter the school,

Dwight D. Eisenhower (1890–1969) was Supreme Commander of the Allied Forces in the Second World War. He served two full terms as Republican President of the USA, 1953–61. 'Ike' was a popular figure because of his successful military past. He did not have strong party views. His conception of the presidency was passive rather than active; he did not favour aggressive action except as a last resort. His failure to take the presidential initiative after the Brown case is now seen as one of the weaker points of his presidency.

Federal troops confront a racist student from Little Rock Central High School, 1957

KEY PERSON

Orval E. Faubus was Governor of Arkansas in the 1950s. He was coming up for re-election and wanted to give the impression of standing firm on the issue of segregated schooling.

KEY TERM

The National Guard are local troopers in each state who would be called out to restore order when the occasion required. As Commander-in-Chief of the army, President Eisenhower had the power to bring them under his federal control rather than that of the state governor. This he did in the case of Little Rock.

however brave they were. The Governor of Arkansas, **Orval E. Faubus**, had no intention of complying with the Brown verdict. On Faubus's instructions the Arkansas **National Guard** barred the way. The previous night, the Governor had gone on television to predict that if the nine entered the school, 'blood would run in the streets'.

Why Eisenhower intervened

Eventually, President Eisenhower felt compelled to intervene because of the following sequence of events:

- Originally, Faubus had insisted that law and order could not be maintained if the black children entered the school.
- A Federal District Court then insisted that the school must be desegregated.
- Faubus again refused and troops barred the way again.
- Eisenhower and Faubus met to discuss the situation. Eisenhower got the mistaken impression that Faubus would no longer obstruct the court order.
- After the Federal Court repeated its order for the black children to enter the school, Faubus yet again refused. This time, however, he withdrew the state troopers and left Arkansas to attend a meeting of southern governors in Florida.
- Now that the white racists had the streets to themselves, violence broke out when the children entered the school, and they were forced to leave suddenly to avoid serious injury.

- Eisenhower was furious that the Governor had misled him and had seemingly deserted his post. He now decided to intervene.

Using his authority as Commander-in-Chief, he announced that the 10,000 troopers of the Arkansas National Guard were to be put under federal control. The same soldiers who had barred the way now kept white protesters back and escorted the children into the school.

Significance of Little Rock

Little Rock was not typical in one sense. It was the only occasion in the 1950s when President Eisenhower used his federal authority to intervene and enforce the Brown legal ruling. He felt that he had little option but to do so in the circumstances. It was almost as if Faubus regarded the entry of the black children into the school as inevitable, but did not want to be seen as the person allowing it. However, Little Rock was typical of the lengths to which southern white people would go to retain segregation. To see the film of respectable, well-dressed, middle-aged ladies push down barriers in anger when news came that the children had finally entered the school was to see real hatred in action.

Faubus was not finished. He later used his authority as Governor to close all the schools in Little Rock and so prevent integrated education for a further period. The school was not reopened until 1959, but then both black and white people could attend. In the meantime, the education of all children had been affected. By this time, however, considerable change had come on the civil rights front. Black people were becoming much more willing to protest and not just rely on federal protection.

HOW DID CIVIL RIGHTS EVOLVE IN THE EARLY POST-WAR YEARS?

There were a number of developments during this period:

- After 1945, the anti-communist mood of the Cold War made militant campaigning more difficult, although it did raise the issue of racist attitudes in the 'land of the free'.
- The NAACP concentrated on legal campaigns and

eventually achieved success in 1954, although a white backlash to its success led to the destruction of many southern branches, and it was even outlawed in Alabama in 1956.

- The Brown case was a major breakthrough for the Civil Rights Movement, even though it did not bring about the degree of immediate change that was anticipated at first.
- Little Rock is an important event in the history of civil rights in the 1950s, although not entirely a typical one.
- There was some presidential interest in civil rights, but it had limited effect.

SUMMARY QUESTIONS

1 What were the main post-war social changes that affected civil rights?

2 What were the effects of the Cold War atmosphere on civil rights?

3 Why was the Brown case of 1954 such an important legal breakthrough?

4 What forms did southern resistance to civil rights take?

CHAPTER 7

The Montgomery Bus Boycott and the emergence of Martin Luther King, 1955–6

INTRODUCTION

In the mid-1950s, two events of major importance signalled the future direction of the Civil Rights Movement: one was the Brown case (see Chapter 6) and the other was the Montgomery Bus Boycott of 1955–6, started by **Rosa Parks**. This event was inspired by the grass roots of the movement rather than being a concession from above. As such, it had a dramatic impact and influenced the subsequent development of demands for civil rights.

SEGREGATION ON PUBLIC TRANSPORT

Bus regulations

Segregation of the races on public transport, especially buses, was particularly humiliating for the black population. In Montgomery, Alabama, bus regulations were especially strict:

- The first ten rows were always reserved for white passengers.
- Black passengers could not sit next to white passengers and might therefore have to stand if only places next to white passengers were available.
- No black passenger was allowed to sit parallel to a white passenger.
- Black passengers had to move to the back of the bus if more white passengers got on and the bus was getting full.
- If it was full, the black passengers stood or were not allowed on. Sometimes they would have to buy a ticket at the front and then get off and walk to the back to get on.
- At all times, black passengers had to take orders from the white bus drivers, who were often rude to them. No black drivers were employed.

KEY PERSON

Rosa Parks was born in 1914. She was a Methodist and a member of the NAACP, and she worked as a seamstress. Mrs Parks was highly regarded in the local community as a woman of impeccable character. Her main claim to fame was as the woman who refused to get off the bus and so sparked the Montgomery Bus Boycott. Others had been arrested for similar reasons, but they were not thought respectable enough: they included, for example, unmarried mother Claudette Colvin. After the boycott, harassment by angry whites in Montgomery forced the Parks family to move to Detroit in 1957. She later set up the Rosa and Raymond Parks institute for self-development, giving career training to black youths. She was awarded the Presidential Medal of Freedom in 1996 and the Congressional Gold Award in 1999.

Rosa Parks

Bus transport was essential for large sections of the population, especially for the poorer classes, who could not, in the 1950s, afford to own the private motor cars that were becoming more common among the better off. Moreover, with housing patterns as they were, black people would frequently live in areas away from their place of work, so they needed public transport to get them there. Not surprisingly, 75 per cent of the local bus company's revenue was from black people.

Protests against segregation

As with the Linda Brown school case, this issue was an important one in many states and a number of towns had seen major protests against segregation on buses. For instance, Baton Rouge in Louisiana was the subject of a boycott of buses by black people in 1953. Led by a local Baptist minister, Rev. Theodore Jemison, the boycott showed how a community could organise a peaceful protest and gain widespread attention.

THE BOYCOTT IN MONTGOMERY

The start of the boycott

The boycott commenced in Montgomery, Alabama, in the final month of 1955. On 1 December, a former NAACP local secretary, Rosa Parks, refused to move when the bus driver demanded that she give up her seat for a white man. Thrown off the bus and prosecuted, her defence was taken up by the local black community. **Edgar D. Nixon**, a past president of the Alabama NAACP, had previously talked to Rosa Parks about the possibility of a major protest about segregation on buses if a suitable incident could be found. The case of the eminently respectable and respected Rosa seemed to provide the opportunity. With one of the local Baptist churches acting as a base, black people in Montgomery organised a boycott of buses.

Martin Luther King, whose reputation was made at this time, describes how on the first morning of the boycott, when it was still dark, his wife Coretta drew back the curtains in their front room early to see the first bus of the day come past. Seeing its headlights on the dark early December morning, she called out to her husband to come and look. The Kings waited tensely as the bus drew nearer and then they rejoiced. It was empty. But important as this moment seemed to be – for it indicated that the boycott was likely to work – King could hardly have appreciated the full significance of its potential impact in the years to come.

How did the protest progress?

It was a success from the first. Beginning on Monday 5 December, the boycott was designed to coincide with the commencement of the trial of Rosa Parks (she was fined $10). It was to last for almost a year and, remarkably, it held firm. This required great determination and perseverance from the local black community, considerable organisation and no little bravery. The Montgomery Improvement Association (MIA) was set up to co-ordinate activities.

At first, the demands of the boycotters were very modest. The protest was not expected to last long and a repeat of the campaign in Baton Rouge seemed likely. This had ended swiftly after a compromise agreement. But in Montgomery, in the heart of the Deep South, the authorities were less willing to make any concessions. The principal demands of the boycott leaders were:

- a more polite service from the white bus drivers
- the employment of black drivers
- the end of black passengers standing when the bus was not full.

Montgomery's all-white officials would have none of it. In refusing these moderate requests, they made a fatal tactical error. The stakes were then raised: within a few weeks the demand had become one for complete desegregation on Montgomery's buses. The boycott was to continue indefinitely and a series of legal appeals launched.

Volunteers were found to distribute leaflets publicising the activities of the protesters. Taxis were organised to help those who had too far to walk to work. The white authorities made this difficult by threatening to arrest taxi drivers who charged less than the standard fare. So a private car pool came into being. Many, however, were happy to walk for the cause and morale remained high. 'My feets is tired but my soul is rested,' said Mother Pollard, a 70-year-old, on refusing a lift.

Legal and constitutional challenge The Civil Rights Movement, especially in the 1950s and early 1960s, stressed the legality of what they were doing. In their view, the amendments to the American Constitution after the Civil War made segregation and discrimination illegal. The Supreme Court and the federal government should be able to overrule the southern state laws that did not treat black people as equal.

US federal court and federal district panel The Supreme Court in Washington, DC, was the final federal court, to which appeals eventually went. Lower federal courts or smaller panels would sit in relevant areas and be the first to judge cases that had a federal connection.

It summed up the determination and religious fervour with which this stage of the civil rights struggle was carried on.

Legal success

But what must not be forgotten in the excitement is that running parallel with the boycott was a **legal and constitutional challenge** that eventually found its way to an appeal hearing in the Supreme Court.

In view of the ruling on education in the Brown case, could segregation in another field – Montgomery's buses – still be allowed? In April 1955, well before the boycott began, a lower **US federal court** had given its opinion that the Brown verdict probably applied to buses as well as schools. In June 1956 a **federal district panel** decreed that bus segregation was indeed unconstitutional. The boycott, however, continued until the Supreme Court's confirmation of this decision on 13 November 1956, in a case entitled *Browder* v. *Gayle*. The former was a black woman who wished to ride on integrated buses, the latter was the Mayor of Montgomery, who did not. The following day, plans were made to end the boycott. It had lasted 381 days.

LEADERSHIP OF THE BOYCOTT

The boycott organisers

Ralph Abernathy, a black Baptist minister, had the idea that Martin Luther King should become involved. Jo Ann Robinson, a member of the Women's Political Council, thought up the double strategy of a boycott and a full-scale legal appeal; this idea came to be generally accepted. There were white sympathisers in the form of Virginia and Clifford Durr, and the help of eminent NAACP lawyers such as Thurgood Marshall and Robert Carter. Experts from the north were also drafted in during the campaign to give advice. These included the black organiser **Bayard Rustin** and a white minister, Glenn Smiley.

At the start of the campaign, Martin Luther King seemed very much a junior partner in the dramatic unfolding of events. How did King's fame come to outstrip that of the other eminent people helping with the protest? Here, it is necessary to look at a little of his background.

Why did Martin Luther King emerge?

Martin Luther King was from the top section of black society. Within the small but significant black professional class, providing services for their own community, ministers of religion were still among the most educated and most respected. King was born into this class in 1929, on 15 January, now a national holiday in the USA. His father was a Baptist minister in Atlanta, Georgia, and the young Martin Luther King was educated in the town at Morehouse College. He then studied for the Baptist ministry at Crozer Seminary, Chester, Pennsylvania. A successful student academically, he moved to Boston University where he received his Ph.D. in 1955. Shortly before the bus boycott began, he had taken up his first major church post as minister of Dexter Avenue Baptist Church, Montgomery.

King was not present at the meetings that began the boycott, but this lack of involvement was not to last. King was asked to chair the important meeting of Montgomery's black community that took place on the evening of the first day of the boycott. He was selected as a recent arrival in the town and was therefore relatively neutral when it came to the different groups, cliques and opinions that had developed over the years. From this humble beginning, he exerted outstanding leadership over the movement in a remarkably short space of time.

King's speaking ability

King's first main quality was his speaking ability. That first evening he gripped his audience with a powerfully delivered speech in the finest tradition of black southern oratory:

> We are tired – tired of being segregated and humiliated, tired by being kicked about by the brutal feet of oppression . . . There comes a time . . . when people get tired of being thrown across the abyss of humiliation . . . we are determined here in Montgomery to work and fight until justice runs down like water and righteousness like a mighty stream.

It reads impressively enough now, but imagine the atmosphere in which it was delivered. The chanting of the crowd of 5000, with their 'oohs' and 'ahs', 'yeses' and 'amens' that emotionally identified with the speaker, made it a dramatic and powerful experience. King had accurately

Summary of Martin Luther King's Life

1929	Born in Atlanta, Georgia on 15 January, now a national holiday in the USA
1944	Educated at Morehouse College
1948	Studied for the Baptist Ministry at Crozer Seminary (training ground for Ministers), Pennsylvania
1951	Began Doctor of Philosophy (PhD) studies at Boston University
1953	Married Coretta Scott
1954	Appointed Minister of Dexter Avenue Baptist Church, Montgomery
1955	Obtained a doctorate in theology from Boston University
1955/6	Took the leading part in the Montgomery Bus Boycott

Martin Luther King addressing a congregation in 1955.

KEY IDEA

Car pools Three hundred cars took workers to 42 different drop-off points and, despite the obvious complexities of such a scheme, it was a great success.

articulated the feelings of his audience and was to do so on many future occasions in the next twelve and a half years.

King's organising role

His role in helping to organise the boycott was also important. He was president of the Montgomery Improvement Association. After consulting his friend Jemison in Baton Rouge for advice, King decided that no charge was to be made for the **car pool** lifts, but donations were to be given to the MIA. By travelling around different states appealing for funds, King managed to get financial help from a variety of sources. These included the NAACP, which had been sceptical at first. He also organised prayer meetings at his and others' churches to maintain the spiritual strength of those involved, and he negotiated skilfully with the white leaders of Montgomery, such as City Police Commissioner Clyde Sellers.

Sometimes his organisational and speaking abilities were combined. Whenever morale seemed to be weakening and the soul as well as the feet was getting tired, a further meeting would be held and King would deliver another rousing speech. The campaigners would draw inspiration and renewed spirit, vowing to continue their protest. King also delivered Sunday sermons in the style of the old preachers who, as we have seen, could inspire black people to fight for their rights.

King's inspirational courage

King's third major contribution was his greatest. It was his reaction to attempts to frighten him and his community into ceasing the struggle. These efforts ranged from the stupid to the terrifying. In January 1956, he was arrested for speeding at 30 m.p.h. in a 25 m.p.h. zone, a rate that would cause 99 per cent of current drivers under 30 in the UK, and many older ones, to infringe the rules almost instantly. (King was 26 years old.) When his house was firebombed later in the same month, King showed impressive presence of mind. In a crucial move, he ordered those who planned retaliation to cease at once. The lack of hatred in his genuinely non-violent policy was there for all to see. He later admitted to receiving 30 to 40 threatening letters a day during the boycott.

In March 1956, King was put on trial for organising an illegal boycott, and was sentenced to a fine of $500 or just over a year in prison. However, he appealed and was released on bail, and the case never developed. White racist perceptions that he had become the key figure in the protest were correct, although he was not the only one to be charged – Nixon and Abernathy were as well, under a dubious law that stated boycotts could not be held without good cause. But in believing that they could distract King from the task in hand, the authorities in Montgomery showed a lack of judgement that was all too common in their ranks at this time and, in the end, worked against their own interests.

What was the King philosophy?

Behind these dramatic actions lay a strong-minded religious belief. King was brought up as an orthodox **Baptist**. There are three connected points to make here about the beliefs of King and his leading followers:

- They believed that it was God's will that they campaign for justice. The core of King's faith had not dimmed; it had broadened. He had become convinced that those of true belief must not simply affirm their faith, but act upon it. It was clear to him that he had been called by God to take a major role in the true emancipation of the African-American, and this might involve wider campaigns, leading to a hard and even dangerous time. If need be, he would devote his life to it. Black men and women must not simply accept their lot as ordained by God and resign themselves to rewards merely in a future life.
- They believed that justice could be achieved within the American system. The American tradition of freedom was associated with important measures such as the **Bill of Rights** that outlined many different liberties, the constitutional amendments guaranteeing equality, the right to vote for all and the recent signs of hope in verdicts like the case of Linda Brown. These all combined to give King and many of his followers the belief that, with federal help, they could triumph in their campaign. Their cause was just and would be seen as such by all fair-minded people in the USA. King believed in the 'land of freedom and promise' that had developed in the eighteenth century. But the promise of freedom needed to be extended to the black community.
- They believed that **non-violence** must be strictly maintained. In common with the aims of other similar movements (see Gandhi on page 126), no retaliation must

(see Gandhi on page 126)

KEY TERMS

Baptist A Protestant Church denomination believing in adult rather than infant baptism. In the USA, the southern Baptists were (and still are) an influential group. In King's time, the black and white congregations were normally separate. They put great emphasis on the individual's conversion and biblical authority. King retained the core of these beliefs but, under the influence of teachers like Benjamin Mays at Crozer Seminary, he came to believe in a more liberal Protestantism, stressing the importance of converting society as well as the individual. He was keen to emphasise the centrality of social concern in any genuine religious belief.

Bill of Rights The first ten amendments to the American Constitution, outlining rights such as freedom of speech and press, religious toleration, a fair trial and 'no cruel and unusual punishments'.

KEY THEME

Non-violence was a fundamental plank in King's philosophy, stemming originally from his Christian beliefs. It meant that protesters must be faithful to their belief in disciplined non-violent direct action. King regularly included explanations of these non-violent beliefs in his evening lectures and speeches at the time of the boycott.

be made, even in the face of the worst possible provocation. Fair-minded people were more likely to support the cause if the campaign could show that the argument was a simple one between good and evil, justice and injustice, love and hate. So the protesters must retain the moral high ground. Though they were prepared to break what they believed were grossly unjust and unconstitutional laws, this must only be done non-violently. This tactic was an ambitious one and called for solidarity. It was a message that King outlined repeatedly at his evening meetings:

> If cursed, do not curse back. If struck, do not strike back but evidence love and goodwill at all times. If another person is being molested, do not arise to go to his defense, but pray for the oppressor. (From a circular distributed by the bus boycott's organisers)

SIGNIFICANCE OF THE BOYCOTT

The Montgomery Bus Boycott was clearly an event of major importance in the civil rights campaign; yet it did not immediately produce other dramatic protests and events. It was to be 1960 before further drama occurred and 1961 before King himself led another major campaign. So why does Montgomery remain significant?

- It showed that the black community could be encouraged to take action themselves. Feelings of hopelessness and despair, that nothing could be done to break the vice of segregation and white control, were common in black communities. While lynching was not as common or as public, it still went on. The fear of giving evidence against white people and then being attacked for your pains was still very real. The solidarity and discipline shown was likely to be repeated, if not sooner then later.
- It achieved a success beyond the bounds of the wildest optimist. At first, the demands of the boycotters were modest. But as circumstances developed, they demanded more and got it. King took the view that, since the Montgomery authorities were not prepared to move one inch, neither would his side. This made the Montgomery boycott more significant than others that went on at a similar time, such as at Tallahassee in Florida.

- Another important civil rights organisation came into being – the **Southern Christian Leadership Conference** (SCLC).

Broadening horizons

After the SCLC was formed, Martin Luther King's horizons broadened. He became one of the acknowledged leaders of the southern Civil Rights Movement. But it was some time before he made an impact on a similar scale to Montgomery and, by the time he did, the campaign had moved on. In March 1957, King paid a visit to Africa and was present at the independence celebrations for the British colony of the Gold Coast, which was now to assume the name of Ghana. This was the first in a line of African colonies to receive its independence. The idea of expanding black freedom internationally, and the obvious parallels with the struggle for better treatment in the USA, was not lost on King.

In September 1958 in Harlem, King suffered a setback when signing copies of his book *Stride Towards Freedom*. A deranged black woman stabbed him, and the knife nearly penetrated his heart. The wound was so close to being fatal that it was said that if King had sneezed soon after the stabbing he might well have died. One young admirer's comment summed up the feelings of many black (and also white) Americans: 'I'm so glad you didn't sneeze.'

King visited other countries. In 1959 these included India, which signified his growing interest in the work of **Gandhi**. King was very interested in Gandhi's non-violent methods of protest. He attempted to find links between Gandhi's principles and beliefs (Hindu) and his own approach from a Christian base. In the UK, King appeared on an important television programme, *Face to Face*, where he had the opportunity to outline his philosophy to an increasingly wide and increasingly interested audience. He talked about the power of non-violent direct action. It had been difficult to persuade all his followers of this, but he had 'got the message across'.

Martin Luther King began to develop ideas in the direction of more confrontational non-violent protest. The bus boycott had been essentially non-confrontational. Now, at the end of the 1950s, he was moving towards more vigorous and organised but still peaceful protests – protests that would force a reaction and maintain the moral high ground for the Civil Rights Movement. Yet the first significant achievement in this direction came from North Carolina, an area less familiar to King.

Conclusion

The Montgomery Bus Boycott was a vital event in the progress of the Civil Rights Movement:

- It was a mass protest, involving all social groups in the black community.
- It lasted for a long time and showed what could be achieved by disciplined non-violence.
- It produced an outstanding leader, an important new organisation and a new philosophy.
- It drew the attention of the north to the system of segregation in the south, and exposed the unreasonable behaviour of many southern white people. This was helped by the growing influence of television in the 1960s.
- In company with the recent Brown decision, it raised the question of federal response to illegal acts of segregation and discrimination in the south.

SUMMARY QUESTIONS

1 Why could the Montgomery Bus Boycott be regarded as a great victory for the Civil Rights Movement?

2 What were the most important contributions of Martin Luther King to the boycott?

3 What were the most important beliefs of Martin Luther King?

CHAPTER 8

Further protests in the south

INTRODUCTION

After the 'fallow years' of the late 1950s, the Civil Rights Movement took off dramatically at the start of the 1960s. This development was not expected and owed much to a new generation of black students who were no longer prepared to accept segregation: thanks to the broader social changes that were taking place they were also in a better position to act. As a result, new organisations were formed and new styles of protest developed. The geographical range of the activity widened, and many people who were previously uninvolved became loyal, dedicated and very brave supporters. This included many white people and many students, both black and white. In particular, there was a major attack on the old 'Jim Crow' system of segregation in the south in the next few years.

THE SIT-INS, 1960

The Greensboro sit-in

The new phase in the Civil Rights Movement began on 1 February 1960. In Greensboro, North Carolina, **four students** from the local Agricultural and Technical College entered a branch of Woolworths and ordered food and drink at the 'whites-only' counter. This was not the first protest of its kind, just as Montgomery had not been the first bus boycott. In fact there had been sixteen similar **sit-ins** over the previous three years.

The result was that the students remained all day, returned with 23 others the following day (including three white students) then over 80 by the end of the third day, until Woolworths was forced to close on 6 February. The initiative had been seized and an important phase in the Civil Rights Movement had begun.

Why was the Greensboro sit-in so successful?

• The protesters were college students – idealistic,

KEY PEOPLE

The **four students** who began the sit-ins were Joseph McNeill, Ezell Blair, Franklin McCain and David Richmond. They were all first-year students at the college. The previous day, McNeill had been refused service at the Greensboro bus terminal because he was black. His complaint to his friends that evening led them to discuss how they could protest against the whole system of segregation. They decided to make the protest as public as possible in the centre of a busy high street store.

KEY TERM

The **sit-in** is a method of non-violent protest whereby protesters occupy an area normally forbidden to them and refuse to move. It was partly influenced by Gandhi's style of protest in India. Sit-ins had occurred in the 1940s outside the south, in large cities like Chicago and Washington, and even earlier. But in the 1960s they occurred widely and fairly suddenly. Other groups in the USA, the UK, France and elsewhere used sit-ins for a variety of protests in the coming years. They were particularly associated with students.

Civil rights demonstrators being attacked by the police in Birmingham, Alabama, 1964.

determined, spontaneous, with no jobs to lose and finding the best excuse yet for not handing in a piece of work.

- The Woolworth staff did not know how to react and did not call the police for some time. This allowed the protest to gather momentum.
- North Carolina was not as racist as some other parts of the south. There was some support for the students from prominent white people such as Terry Sandford, who was soon to be elected Governor. This was a very different reaction from that in Mississippi or Alabama, or even South Carolina.

What was the significance of the Greensboro sit-in?

- The sit-ins spread very widely and very quickly: by April, 78 different places were involved, such as: Raleigh, North Carolina; Jacksonville, Florida; Baltimore, Maryland; Chattanooga, Tennessee; and Richmond, Virginia. The biggest was in Nashville, Tennessee, the home of country and western music, where there were over 500 student protesters from four mainly black colleges. Altogether, over 100 cities were affected and nearly 50,000 people were actively involved in demonstrations.
- The sit-ins gained the support of a number of important

civil rights leaders: **James Lawson** in Nashville; **Floyd McKissick**, NAACP Youth Council leader in Georgia; **Fred Shuttlesworth**, a black clergyman from Birmingham, Alabama, and friend of Martin Luther King; and **Ella Baker**, a leading SCLC official from Atlanta.

The Student Non-violent Coordinating Committee

Fred Shuttlesworth realised the potential of the sit-in protests and phoned Ella Baker, urging her to 'tell Martin [Luther King] we must get with this'. King immediately pledged his support for the students. Three weeks later, Ella Baker arranged for King to speak to the protesters in North Carolina in the town of Durham. Baker, perhaps most importantly of all, took the view that the protest was 'bigger than a hamburger'. She set up a meeting at Shaw University in Raleigh, North Carolina, out of which came a new student organisation to co-ordinate protests, the Student Non-violent Coordinating Committee or SNCC (pronounced 'Snick').

SNCC was to confront a wide range of issues concerning equality and discrimination. What was desired was freedom from squalor, educational deprivation and inhuman treatment. Segregation at the lunch counter was just a symptom of a much wider set of attitudes towards black people that were being challenged. Peaceful protest had moved into a more organised and vigorous form of direct action. The tactic was to create a crisis and establish a tension out of which action would occur. The southern white community that had done nothing and ignored the issue would then be forced to confront it.

Reactions to the sit-ins

The reaction of the police was revealing. There were over 2000 arrests in all the sit-ins in 1960. Police frequently arrested the protesters for breaking the law, but ignored the white people who attacked them. Television cameras showed the rest of the USA the well-dressed, peaceful, book-reading, mainly black students and the loud-mouthed, uncouth whites swearing and frequently attacking them. US citizens could draw their own conclusions.

The bitterness of the white southern reaction to the protests began to play into the hands of the demonstrators. At first the abuse was verbal. Bernard Lafayette, a student protester

Ella Baker (1903–86)
attended Shaw University in Raleigh, North Carolina. She ran a black voters' registration campaign as early as the 1930s, and was active in the NAACP during the 1940s. She moved to Atlanta in 1957 to assist King and the SCLC. However, she disliked King's leadership style, saying 'Strong people don't need strong leaders.' Very importantly, she urged students, both black and white, to set up a separate organisation from the SCLC to avoid too much control from their elders. She was active in the Student Non-violent Coordinating Committee in the 1960s, but tended to take a background role, encouraging the young.

at the time, described how young men would shout insulting remarks such as 'What are you doing here, jungle bunnies?' But not just men: Frankie Henry, a young black female student sit-in protester from Tennessee, recalled years later how one white woman had stubbed her cigarette out on Frankie's arm – she still had the burn mark to prove it.

Non-violence

These protests were clearly linked with the King philosophy. The protesters were non-violent, merely covering their heads when they were beaten, and not striking back. Moreover, they were merely insisting on their rights under the existing law and looking to gain sympathy from liberal white people, especially in the north. Above all, they hoped to get the attention of the federal government, where the eight-year presidency of Dwight Eisenhower was in its last months.

How successful were they?

The sit-ins succeeded in getting a number of public facilities desegregated, especially lunch counters: for example, in San Antonio, Texas, in March, and Nashville, Tennessee, in May. Segregation in public areas such as parks was largely abandoned where it existed in southern Florida, Texas and towns such as Nashville and, in August 1960, Greensboro itself. Stores like Woolworths found their profits down by one-third while the protests were going on. By the end of 1961, 810 towns and cities had desegregated public areas.

In many different parts of the USA, black and white students were inspired to copy not just the sit-ins, but a whole range of protests to desegregate all kinds of facilities. But the Deep South remained largely unaffected. Here attitudes were hardening rather than softening, as the freedom rides would show.

Examples of protests:
swim-ins (pools), read-ins (libraries), watch-ins (cinemas) and even shoe-ins at shoeshine bars. There was even a sit-out in New Haven, Connecticut, where students blocked the pavement to protest about squalid housing conditions.

THE FREEDOM RIDES, 1961

What were the freedom rides?

One of the areas where federal regulations might be involved was inter-state transport. Suppose you boarded a bus in the north, but it then entered southern, segregated territory? Could black and white passengers still sit together or use the same eating and toilet facilities at the terminals? This was an issue that interested James Farmer, who had revitalised CORE. After

CORE's progress during the war years, it had lapsed into inactivity. Now, inspired by the progress made elsewhere, it was reviving. It also provided the opportunity for more idealistic students, white as well as black, to get involved with the campaigns. White sympathisers grew in number. Again, a Supreme Court decision sparked off the activity. The case of *Boynton* v. *Virginia* in 1960 had ruled against southern states being allowed to impose segregation in inter-state bus terminals. CORE set out to test whether this could be enforced.

The plan was to travel the whole distance between Washington, DC, and New Orleans. The idea behind it was that there would be a benefit to the movement whatever happened. If the mixed race team was allowed to stay together on the bus and in the waiting rooms, then segregation had received a blow. However, if they were set on, then their racist attackers would be seen to be aggressive, bigoted, unreasonable and acting illegally. In addition, media publicity would spread the message and expose the offensive behaviour of southern white people. The federal authorities, moreover, were expected to enforce the law and so this action would also force their hands.

Reaction to the rides

Those carefully selected for the task knew there might be trouble; they got it. They were attacked in Rock Hill, South Carolina, and then in **Anniston, Alabama**. But, as usually happened, the white police force made little attempt to find, let alone punish, the offenders.

A bus in flames after a firebomb was thrown in through the window while the bus was stationary due to a flat tyre. The bus was testing bus segregation in Anniston, Alabama, in May 1961.

The worst treatment, however, was reserved for Birmingham, Alabama. Driving through Alabama, the buses were escorted by over 30 state trooper cars and police helicopters circling overhead. However, when they crossed the Birmingham City boundary, all protection disappeared: they were now under the jurisdiction of the dreaded Birmingham police chief, **Eugene 'Bull' Connor**, who had failed to organise protection for them. The riders were subject to a vicious attack.

White protesters, considered 'race traitors' by other white people, were the focus of particular hatred. Jim Zwerg, a white student from Fisk University, Nashville, was kicked and punched until his teeth were knocked out. Then he was punched to the ground time and time again. His back was severely injured and he was temporarily disfigured. But in a television interview from his hospital bed he showed remarkable courage and bravery: 'We are dedicated to this . . . we are willing to accept beatings . . . we are willing to accept death . . . segregation must be broken down.'

When Ralph Abernathy's church held a rally of support for the riders in Montgomery, the building was surrounded and disaster was prevented only by the protection of federal marshals. These men, employed by the federal government in Washington, DC, would protect people regardless of race, unlike state or city police, who could not be guaranteed to do so.

Federal government action

One object of the freedom rides – showing up the viciousness of racism – had been achieved. Would the other aim, getting the federal authorities to act, also succeed? The chances of this occurring were higher than the year before, the year of the sit-ins. This was because of the new figure in the White House. **John F. Kennedy**, a younger and more liberal figure than Eisenhower, was now President. His brother, **Robert Kennedy**, held the office of **US Attorney-General**. An injunction was brought out against the Ku Klux Klan, who had been attacking freedom riders. Federal marshals were sent near to Montgomery and Robert Kennedy organised the desegregation of all inter-state travel.

There was, however, a limit to federal government action. They wanted to prevent violent disturbances at all costs, so it

KEY PEOPLE

John F. Kennedy (1917–63) was elected a Congressman in 1945 and a Senator in 1952. In 1961, he became President of the USA, the youngest ever elected. Great reforms were anticipated when he talked of a 'New Frontier'. He was slow to take up the cause of civil rights, but became determined to introduce a Civil Rights Bill early in 1963 after the troubles on the Freedom Rides and the protests in Birmingham, Alabama. He was prevented from seeing the final result by his assassination in Dallas, Texas, on 22 November 1963.

Robert Kennedy (1925–68) the younger brother of John, had a distinguished legal career and was US Attorney-General from 1961 to 1964, doing a lot to enforce civil rights legal rulings. He was elected Senator in 1964 but was assassinated in Los Angeles in 1968 while on a political tour to seek the Democratic Party nomination for President.

KEY TERM

The **US Attorney-General** is the chief legal officer in the federal government, responsible for seeing that federal law and the provisions of the American Constitution were kept to in the states.

would allow southern state governments to arrest demonstrators as long as the state officials also prevented white attacks on the protesters. When the freedom riders got to Jackson, Mississippi, for example, the police controlled the white people who were planning to attack them, but proceeded to arrest the riders and imprison them. The Kennedys had done a deal with Mississippi Senator James O. Eastland that the federal government would not intervene if order could be maintained. However, this was not good for the Civil Rights Movement, which wanted either a change in the law, or to appear martyrs in order to provoke such a change. The publicity generated from arrest and imprisonment was limited; television pictures of white people attacking peaceful black demonstrators would have had much more impact.

CHALLENGING EDUCATIONAL SEGREGATION

The case of James Meredith

Transport was not the only area where segregation was being challenged in the southern heartlands. Up until 1961, no black person had ever been admitted to the University of Mississippi (known as 'Ole Miss'). In that year, the Governor of Mississippi had physically barred an able black student, **James Meredith**, from entry. In June 1962, however, a federal court ruled that he was entitled to attend. This showed how much legal progress had been made with regard to educational integration. What was needed was a person bold enough to want to be the first to break the race barrier, with all the risks that this might imply. Meredith proved to be the man.

Mississippi Governor Ross Barnett and US Attorney-General Robert Kennedy disagreed about whether Meredith should be allowed to take his place. In the end, Barnett secretly agreed with Kennedy that Meredith should be admitted as long as he, the Governor, could make a public protest. But Barnett did not keep his word to provide protection. Meredith arrived at the university to be registered the following day. Angry mobs assembled and there was a delay in sending federal troops to protect the young black student. By the time they arrived, violence had erupted as 170 federal marshals desperately tried to keep order. Meredith survived, but two

James Meredith was born in 1933 and served in the air force before attending Ole Miss. An exceptionally brave and determined man, he was also something of a loner. However, this made him determined to fulfil single-handedly what he saw as a mission from God: to integrate a university where few black people had applied and none had previously been accepted. He went on a solo 'March Against Fear' in 1966 (see page 161). Though he was shot and injured on the march, it was carried on for him and he rejoined before the end, less than three weeks later. He became a stockbroker in the 1970s, supported the Republicans and voted against making Martin Luther King's birthday a public holiday in the 1980s.

James Meredith entering the University of Mississippi, 1962.

onlookers, including a French journalist, were killed. Petrol bombs were thrown at officials and a lead pipe felled one marshal. A television reporter was brutally attacked inside his car. Meredith's brave achievement was an inspiration to others, but he himself had to endure the humiliation of being segregated on campus, eating alone.

Educational segregation in Alabama

Mississippi was not the only state to attempt to bar black students. In Alabama, Governor **George Wallace** personally barred two black students from entering the University of Alabama at Tuscaloosa in June 1963. However, this was largely a complaint against what Wallace considered an infringement of state liberties. After making his protest, he accepted federal authority and the students were subsequently allowed in. Wallace's stand against black entry was popular among white people in Alabama. But there was less physical resistance than in the case of Meredith to what was now seen as the students' inevitable entry, given the support of federal authorities.

THE ALBANY CAMPAIGN

Martin Luther King had not been directly involved in the Meredith case and the disputes involving Wallace, but he had spoken to the sit-in demonstrators several times and made a major speech at Shaw University in April 1960. He also supported the freedom riders, but declined a request to join

---

KEY PERSON

George Wallace first stood for Governor of Alabama in 1958, but was defeated by John Patterson, a more hard-line segregationist. Wallace took a harder line in 1962 and was elected. In January 1963, he promised 'segregation today, segregation tomorrow and segregation for ever'. Originally a Democrat, he stood as an Independent candidate in the 1968 presidential election and won 13.5 per cent of the total vote. When the rules did not allow him to stand again for Governor of Alabama in 1966, his wife stood and was elected, effectively on his behalf. He was paralysed after an assassination attempt in 1973 and repented of his racist views towards the end of his life. He was elected Governor again in 1982 with black support, and finally retired in 1987.

Governor George Wallace of Alabama.

them. An admirer of Meredith, King nonetheless felt that his success smacked of **tokenism**, and more protests were needed.

These protests would increasingly include campaigns to get black people to register their names to vote, as well as calls for desegregation in public places. King was involved in a long campaign in Georgia during 1961–2. The origins of this movement came from the freedom riders of SNCC. When they were arrested in the town of Albany in December 1961, a local boycott began, backed up with rallies and protest meetings. King and Ralph Abernathy were invited to come and speak by Martin's old school friend William Anderson. They addressed meetings in the town. The next day, King and other campaigners staged a protest about segregation. They were ordered to disperse and, when they refused, were arrested and fined. King, to draw attention to the whole issue, refused to pay and was jailed. This was typical of many occasions when King found himself in prison, though nearly always for brief periods.

The police response

The tactic of provoking a violent response did not work this time. Local police chief, Laurie Pritchett, was tactically shrewd and knew how to prevent violence from breaking out:

- He prevented white demonstrators from being violent.
- He told the police to treat the demonstrators gently when arresting them.
- He promised to discuss segregation questions later. In fact, this did not happen and transport facilities were not integrated despite federal rulings on the matter.
- When King visited Albany a second time to protest about the lack of action, he was arrested again. But this time his fine was paid anonymously, so that he was released without being allowed to register his protest. It is thought that the anonymous donor was Pritchett himself.

The campaign ends in failure

King left Albany for good in August 1962. The campaign had not produced local change. Rather than being desegregated, the parks were closed and all the chairs were removed from the 'desegregated' library. The campaign had also failed to create a situation where the federal authorities felt obliged to act. It showed the need for cooperation between the different civil rights groups – the NAACP had been suspicious of SNCC interference in what it regarded as its patch. In turn, some radicals in the SNCC were becoming impatient with King and what they saw as too gentle a policy. A less shrewd police chief than Laurie Pritchett was needed to highlight the brutality of segregation, and a more united front from the civil rights organisations. Two important events in 1963 were to provide these ingredients, as we shall see in Chapter 9.

HOW FAR WAS RESISTANCE TO CIVIL EQUALITY OVERCOME IN THIS PERIOD?

- The sit-ins and freedom rides played a major part in bringing down some aspects of the 'Jim Crow' system in the south. Outside the Deep South they had a number of successes, especially in states like North Carolina, Texas and Tennessee.
- In Mississippi, Alabama, Georgia and South Carolina, they made less impression. Many white people in these states were determined to resist the demands of both the protesters and the federal government.
- The movement's tactics had not always been successful in getting change. Its support from the federal government,

though increasing, was still patchy. The Kennedy administration was reluctant to intervene unless law and order was breaking down.

- However, the movement learnt from its errors and now planned to target areas that would bring favourable results.

SUMMARY QUESTIONS

1 How large an impact did the sit-ins and freedom rides have on the system of racial segregation in the south?

2 What was the significance of James Meredith's attempts to enter the University of Mississippi?

3 Why was Martin Luther King's campaign in Albany less successful?

CHAPTER 9

Success for the Civil Rights Movement, 1963–5

INTRODUCTION

The campaigning, marches and speeches of the years 1963–5 saw the Civil Rights Movement at its high point. Militant non-violent campaigns such as the ones in Birmingham and Selma, Alabama were successful. The March on Washington emphasised the peaceful and multi-racial nature of the movement. But the passing of civil rights legislation also made it a time of concrete success.

CONFLICT IN BIRMINGHAM, ALABAMA

What was the aim of the campaigners?

The SCLC campaign (see page 126) in Birmingham, Alabama, during the spring of 1963 was one of its most dramatic and successful. Here was an attempt to achieve desegregation in one of the toughest possible areas. In Birmingham, segregation was practised on a large scale – not least because it was a large town by the standards of the south, with about 350,000 people, 140,000 of whom were black. Racial separation was extremely rigid. The baseball team had been forced to drop out of its league, so that any mixing of black and white in the town could be avoided. If there was success in such an area, surely it could happen in many other places too.

There was, for the campaigners, one hopeful sign. The police chief, 'Bull' Connor, was not likely to be as subtle as Laurie Pritchett in Albany. The SCLC actively sought to confront segregation and its brutal enforcement in the city head on. The result was a stand-off that provided favourable publicity and the retention of the moral high ground for the SCLC. He did not disappoint them.

Starting in early April, sit-in demonstrators demanded an end to segregation in the town. They also wanted an end to discrimination in employment and organised boycotts of shops that refused to serve black people.

The events of Birmingham in the spring of 1963

3 April	King and the SCLC arrive in the town. They demand desegregation, an end to racism in employment, and the establishment of a biracial committee. Segregated facilities are boycotted.
3–6 April	Sit-in demonstrators are arrested.
6–9 April	Marchers are arrested.
10 April	All marches are banned.
12 April	King is arrested for defying the ban.
20 April	King is released.
21 April	William Moore is murdered.
2 May	Young children are included in the protest for the first time.
3 May	'Bull' Connor sets dogs and fire hoses on the demonstrators; 1300 children are arrested in two days.
4 May	Presidential representative Burke Marshall is sent to negotiate a settlement.
5 May	Further demonstrations follow the arrival of 200 more students.
7 May	Demonstrations hit their peak, as onlookers in the park are fire-hosed. The Senior Citizens' Committee accepts the gradual introduction of desegregated facilities and the start of a biracial committee to discuss further changes.
10 May	King's press conference pleads for brotherhood and reconciliation.
11 May	Bombs damage the house of King's brother, A. D. King, and the SCLC's headquarters. There is a night of rioting by black people.

The murder of William Moore William Moore was a white man from Tennessee who set off on a 'freedom walk' to Mississippi, but was shot and killed (almost certainly by white racists, angry at white support for a black cause) near Gadsden, Alabama. The news added to the tense situation in Birmingham. SNCC worker, Diane Nash, led a group that continued the walk as far as Birmingham. When they arrived, the police arrested them for illegal marching and they were all jailed.

How did the crisis develop?

Police reaction was moderate at first and, for a time, 'Bull' Connor kept calm. But King defied a ban on further marches. Along with many others, he was imprisoned. For a while no concessions would be made, and after **the murder of William Moore** the atmosphere became very tense.

The breakthrough came at the beginning of May. With a shortage of volunteers to continue the protest, and King only just out of jail and attending an SCLC meeting in Memphis, an SCLC member, James Bevel, decided to recruit teenagers and sometimes even younger children to continue the protests.

This was a very controversial, but ultimately effective move. 'Bull' Connor lost his cool and within 24 hours of the change of tactic, he ordered fire hoses to be used against the protesters and police dogs to be set on them. The subsequent media pictures provided important publicity for the civil rights cause. It did not look good to the outside world to be fire-hosing children, some as young as eight or nine years old, as they came out of a church to begin a demonstration. Whether children should have been used at all was now forgotten. 'Bull' Connor apparently enjoyed seeing the 'niggers run', as he put it.

- The Civil Rights Movement now received even more support from those outside the Deep South, who increasingly saw the battle as a simple one of freedom versus bigotry. Just two examples from many: in Greenwich, Connecticut, white clergymen united to fight segregation on hearing of the dogs and fire hoses; and at Duke University, North Carolina, the university authorities chose this moment to announce that admissions would now be for both black and white.
- Many inhabitants of Birmingham itself now moved in the direction of desegregation. Even those not appalled by Connor's tactics and hesitant about the wisdom of integration were deciding that the economic disruption of the demonstrations outweighed the possible drawbacks of a more equal policy towards the black minority. This was the view, for example, of Sidney Smyer, president of the Birmingham Chamber of Commerce.
- Above all, the highly publicised scenes at Birmingham

Police dogs attacking a seventeen-year-old civil rights demonstrator in Birmingham, Alabama, 3 May 1963.

persuaded the federal government in general, and President Kennedy in particular, to take action. Kennedy remarked that 'Bull Connor has done more for civil rights than anyone else'. It was at this time that the federal government took a more purposeful stand for civil rights by planning a Civil Rights Bill to go before the US Congress.

What agreement was reached?

When King came back to Birmingham from Memphis, he found the **Senior Citizens' Committee** ready to negotiate a settlement in return for ending boycotts, marches and demonstrations. Birmingham's stores were to be desegregated and discrimination against black people in employment was to be ended. However, this was not a total victory: the desegregation was not immediate but in stages, and equal opportunities in employment would be difficult to monitor properly. Desegregation of schools and public areas was not mentioned. Bitterness and the scars of violence remained. But it was enough for King to claim success. Moreover, the President had been converted to the idea of a Civil Rights Bill sooner rather than later. This was seen as a vital gain for the movement.

The 'Letter from Birmingham Jail'

King's time in jail at Birmingham produced another very significant effect. While there, he wrote one of the most

KEY TERM

The **Senior Citizens' Committee** was senior in terms of experience and position rather than age. It included the business leaders of Birmingham, who became increasingly concerned with the economic effect of the disturbances in the area.

important documents in modern history ever written on scraps of paper: the 'Letter from Birmingham Jail'. Although this did not contain any new ideas, it became the classic justification of **civil disobedience**.

King wrote his letter in response to a group of eight white Birmingham clergy, who had written a public letter of their own entitled 'An Appeal for Law and Order and Common Sense'. Their letter urged black protesters not to demonstrate on the streets, but to confine their search for justice to the courts. In an important statement, King showed up the hypocrisy of those who did nothing to stop southern state governments ignoring justifiable Supreme Court Orders, but expected black people to obey unconstitutional laws. If black people were denied their legal right to vote, why should they be obliged to obey unjust edicts? And how much longer did they have to wait for justice? As King said in his letter: 'Perhaps it is easy for those who have never felt the stinging darts of segregation to say, "Wait".'

King had attempted to shame the clergymen into supporting his and, he believed, God's cause. Many other church leaders, especially those away from the Deep South, identified more with King's views. The March on Washington made this particularly apparent.

THE MARCH ON WASHINGTON, 1963

Why was the March on Washington so important?

It was not only the federal government and many church leaders that now wanted more joint action. The civil rights organisations themselves now looked to stage a large united demonstration. This was to involve reviving an old idea of A. Philip Randolph back in 1941 (see page 100); it again originated in the mind of Randolph, who suggested another March on Washington, DC. King's adviser at the time of the Montgomery Bus Boycott, Bayard Rustin, was also closely involved with the idea. The summer of 1963 would be an appropriate time for such an event, commemorating the centenary of the Emancipation Proclamation by President Abraham Lincoln. This had promised the abolition of slavery once the northern states had won the Civil War. The rally at the end of the march would take place at the Lincoln

Memorial. The event was significant in a number of ways:

- It was 'for jobs and freedom', indicating concern for black economic conditions as well as issues concerning segregation, and the radical, if not socialist, views of men like Randolph and Rustin. However, King moved the emphasis away from what Rustin wanted, towards freedom rather than jobs.
- It was to involve a very wide range of civil rights groups, including the NAACP (pages 68–70), whose leader **Roy Wilkins** doubted the more confrontational style of protest promoted by the SCLC and SNCC (page 130). The price paid for this show of unity was a toning down of the more radical economic messages. These were to emerge later.
- It would include white people as well as black people, who would march together in a thoroughly desegregated show of unity. About a third of the marchers were white.

The march was not opposed by the Kennedy administration, once it had received assurances about the moderate and peaceful nature of the march. This revealed a growing sympathy with the aims of the Civil Rights Movement, but also practical common sense: the President was persuaded by the argument that, since civil rights protesters were already on the streets, it was preferable that they were on them in a peaceful and orderly fashion.

King, who had led a small-scale Prayer Pilgrimage to Washington back in 1957, was to be the final speaker and bring the event to a fitting climax. At first hoping, ambitiously, for 100,000 marchers, the organisers found themselves with a crowd of nearly a quarter of a million. The Christian churches were prominent in the event and stood, over this issue, in a unity that had not been common among them on previous occasions. Other faiths also took part. One of the marchers was Jewish Democratic vice-presidential nominee in 2000, Joseph Liebermann.

It proved to be an impressive occasion, which succeeded in getting across a positive image of the Civil Rights Movement. Few listening could have been left unmoved by King's 'I have a dream' speech. His 'dream' included many eloquent visions and much effective imagery, and he used his skills as a preacher to tie in biblical quotations with his own text. He

The Civil Rights March on Washington, 1963.

was conscious of the Christian unity expressed at the meeting, but went even further down the road of religious solidarity. The dream became prophetic and wide ranging:

> On the red hills of Georgia sons of slaves and former slave owners will be able to sit down together at the table of brotherhood. I have a dream today . . . My four little children will one day live in a nation where they will not be judged by the colour of their skin but by the content of their character . . . We allow freedom to ring from every state and every city. I have a dream today . . . Every valley shall be exalted and every mountain and hill laid low, the rough places made plain and the crooked places made straight . . . All of God's children, black men and white men, Jews and Gentiles, Catholics and Protestants, will be able to join hands. I have a dream today . . .

Effect on the federal government

The event was regarded as a great success, well organised, peaceful and clearly demonstrating the degree of white support for the cause. The Kennedy administration had already considered civil rights legislation after the troubles at Birmingham, but the march gave the President extra leverage to urge support for the reform. He referred to it as 'a moral issue' and quoted from the American Declaration of Independence (1776) about all men being created equal.

The climate of opinion now prevailing made it possible to consider real change. Kennedy signalled his intentions by meeting over 1500 leaders from religious, labour and business groups, discussing the implications of civil rights. However, the possibility of the end of segregation produced still more extreme resistance from the south. In September 1963, three weeks after the Washington march, four black children in Sunday school were killed in a bomb attack on a black Baptist church in Birmingham.

THE CIVIL RIGHTS ACT OF 1964

The passage of the Civil Rights Bill

It is uncertain how **the attempt to pass the Civil Rights Bill** would have fared if Kennedy had remained President. In September, his proposed bill got through its first hurdle, the Judiciary Committee. In November 1963, it was ready to come before Congress. However, that month, J. F. Kennedy was assassinated in Dallas, Texas. If civil rights campaigners thought this would result in a long delay to the legislation, they were mistaken. Under the Constitution, the Vice-President automatically succeeded if the President died in office. This meant that the new occupant of the White House was **Lyndon B. Johnson**, who was particularly well equipped to get the legislation through Congress. For instance, he had much more experience of the workings of Congress than Kennedy.

- Johnson exploited the shocked mood of the American people after the death of Kennedy. He was prepared to milk the emotion that derived from the former President's death. 'No memorial ovation or eulogy could more eloquently honor President Kennedy's memory than the earliest possible passage of the Civil Rights Bill for which he fought so long,' asserted Johnson.
- He possessed the great powers of persuasion that were needed to get the bill through Congress. Johnson used his long experience as a Senator to pursue the right tactical mixture of forceful argument and sweet talk.
- Though himself a Democrat, he persuaded some Republicans to vote for the bill. This was crucial, as Johnson knew that many southern Democrats (unlike himself) could never bring themselves to vote for black civil rights. In particular, he got the Republican leader of the Senate, Everett Dirkson, on his side.
- He also managed to achieve a statement issued by all living

The attempt to pass the Civil Rights Bill The US system of government splits the powers into legislature (law making), executive (policy making) and Judiciary (law enforcing). The President, as head of the executive, can propose a bill to Congress (the legislature), but lacks power to ensure that his wishes become law. In this respect, he has less influence over passing legislation than the British Prime Minister. There is much less party discipline in the USA than in the UK.

Lyndon B. Johnson (1908–73) was a member of the House of Representatives 1938–47, a Senator 1948–60, Vice-President 1961–3 and President 1963–9, having been re-elected in 1964 with a landslide victory. Though not always entirely consistent, he was one of the few southern Senators to give general support to civil rights in the 1950s. He used his congressional experience to get the Civil Rights and Voting Rights Acts through both Houses. His 'Great Society' (see page 158) was a general attack on poverty and deprivation in the USA. He became increasingly sucked into the Vietnam conflict during the mid-1960s, which drained away his popularity. He decided not to stand for re-election in 1968.

ex-Presidents (Truman, Eisenhower and Hoover) in support of the principle of civil rights.

Johnson's strong support for the bill was a brave option. It meant going against many of his friends and colleagues. But he felt that the bill was necessary to ensure the south's place at the heart of the Union and to ensure the USA's continued social progress.

There were southern attempts to block the bill by a **filibuster**. In the end, however, it passed through both the House of Representatives and the Senate. In the House of Representatives there were 152 Democrats in favour and 96 (mainly southerners) against. The crucial factor was that Johnson had persuaded 138 Republicans to support the measure with only 34 against. There was similar success in the Senate, which voted 73–27 for the bill. For Johnson, it was a political triumph; for the Civil Rights Movement, it was an even greater success, for the tactic of working through the existing US political system rather than against it had succeeded.

Provisions of the Act

The 1964 Civil Rights Act contained the following provisions:

- There was a ban on exclusion from restaurants, stores and other public places.
- The Attorney-General could file law suits to speed up desegregation, mixed education and voting rights.
- The Fair Employment Practices Commission was now set up on a permanent legal basis. No racial, sexual or religious discrimination would be lawful.
- There was to be no discrimination on any federally aided programmes.
- A Community Relations Service was set up to deal with remaining disputes.

THE VOTING RIGHTS CAMPAIGN

Why was Selma selected?

It was yet to be established whether the provisions of the 1964 Civil Rights Act would operate in the south, since the state authorities might refuse to apply the law properly. The Act clearly needed to be tested and voting rights was seen as the area to try. Its impact was easily measurable by the number of black people in an area who had got on to the voting rolls. There were areas where little progress on this issue had been made. King and the SCLC decided to make an example of Selma, Alabama. The figures were stark. In Dallas County, which included Selma, 57 per cent of the population was black, but only 335 out of over 15,000 black people were registered to vote, as compared to over 9500 white people. This was a far worse state of affairs than under the Black Codes of the late nineteenth century. It seemed to go back almost 100 years to the trouble in New Orleans in 1866 over the legitimacy of black suffrage.

King partly picked the town for a campaign because it would be so tough. Over 3000 black people had recently been arrested for protesting about the lack of black voter registration, but Selma was not unique. It was also selected because it was felt that Sheriff **Jim Clark** would, if sufficiently provoked, lose his cool in the same way as 'Bull' Connor. Again, a correct assumption had been made.

How did the authorities act in Selma?

The authorities in Selma made it as difficult as possible for black people to vote. The courthouse was frequently not in session for registrations, and when it was, every excuse would be found to prevent black people from voting. Whereas white people would be registered without fuss, black people were asked qualifying questions before they were allowed to vote. There may no longer have been a 'grandfather clause', but electoral officials had found other ways of preventing the black vote. If they did not give the right answer, they would not be registered. An articulate Baptist minister, **C. T. Vivian**, later recalled how silly questions were asked of the potential black voters, such as 'How many bubbles are there in a bar of soap?'

Clark's treatment of black people had excited anger for some time. In particular, his treatment of a much-respected black woman, Amelia Boynton, whom he pushed over, brought a special protest. At first, Clark restrained himself, but then, like 'Bull' Connor before him, his temper snapped. On the television cameras he was seen poking orderly black citizens in the stomach. They were merely queuing to register. His attempts to provoke them into a violent reaction failed and

Martin Luther King and his wife Coretta Scott King at a black voting rights march from Selma, Alabama, to the state capital Montgomery, 1965.

his use of electric cattle prods on students only confirmed his reputation as a provocative racist with a short fuse. In a memorable confrontation with Clark, Vivian shouted at him as he moved away, unprepared for a discussion: 'You can turn your back on me, but you cannot turn your back on the idea of justice.' All this, in full view of the cameras, had a similar effect to 'Bull' Connor's antics in Birmingham two years previously. Just as this had pushed the Kennedy administration towards a Civil Rights Bill, so the voting rights campaign in Selma made President Johnson more likely to consider a separate Voting Rights Bill.

The treatment of the demonstrators in nearby Marion was even worse. But Marion received less immediate publicity because the press were also hit and injured on this occasion. The troubles in Marion ended tragically with the murder, by police, of Jimmie Lee Jackson, a black man trying to prevent his mother from being attacked. It was after this that the campaigners produced their next plan. This was to organise a civil rights march for the vote from Selma to the state capital of Alabama, Montgomery. However, only on the third attempt was the march successful.

Selma to Montgomery march

The first march was met by the police on the outskirts of Selma at the Edmund Pettus Bridge. The police violently forced the marchers back, again in full view of the cameras.

> ## Conflict in Selma: the main events of the early months of 1965
>
> | | |
> |---|---|
> | 2 January | King announces a new campaign in Selma. |
> | 18 January | 400 black people apply to register to vote. |
> | 22 January | 100 black schoolteachers protest at the courthouse at the treatment of Amelia Boynton. |
> | 1 February | King is arrested with over 700 others for taking part in an illegal parade. More are arrested the following day. |
> | 3 February | 300 students are arrested. |
> | 6 February | King is released and goes to talk to President Johnson. |
> | 7 February | 165 demonstrating students are sent on a forced 3-mile run by Clark and are poked by electric cattle prods. |
> | 10 February | 200 students refuse to leave the courthouse. |
> | 17 February | Night march in Marion from the church to the jail. Death of Jimmie Lee Jackson. |
> | 7 March | First attempted march to Montgomery. Police attack marchers by the Edmund Pettus Bridge. |
> | 9 March | Second attempted march is turned back by King at the bridge. Death of James Reeb. |
> | 21 March | Successful march to Montgomery begins. |
> | 26 March | Marchers arrive at Montgomery; speech by King. |

Martin Luther King arranged another march for two days later, inviting those from far and near to take part. However, because of legal doubts over whether Governor George Wallace of Alabama could stop the march, a federal court judge asked that any march be delayed until he had ruled on the matter. Unwilling either to disappoint his supporters or to disobey a federal court order, King decided on an uneasy compromise. He began the march, but everyone stopped and prayed at the bridge when requested to turn back. King then abandoned the march.

At the end of the month, once demonstrators knew that the march was legal and there was federal support, a third, and this time triumphant, march took place. With 25,000 people joining in, it was the biggest march ever seen in the south. To arrive in Montgomery, where so much had happened nearly ten years before, must have been an emotional experience for many of the marchers and, in addition to this, they were greeted by a rousing speech from King.

THE 1965 VOTING RIGHTS ACT

The reaction of Jim Clark, the violence of the police and the violent hostility of many southern white people to equal rights had an effect similar to that in Birmingham, two years previously. This time it was President Johnson who determined to act and introduce a Voting Rights Bill to Congress. Public opinion was now such that its success was always likely and it became law in August 1965. Once again, we see King and the SCLC appearing to have triumphed in one of the toughest areas to overcome. Desegregation seemed to be on the way out, and legal and political equality were apparently on the way to completion.

Provisions of the Act

The 1965 Voting Rights Act abolished literary tests and made illegal the kind of manoeuvres that had prevented black people from voting in large numbers in Selma.

The Voting Rights Act made the following illegal:

- demonstration of educational achievement
- knowledge of any subject
- ability to interpret material
- proof of moral character.

To some, this seemed to be the high water mark of the Civil Rights Movement. Yet in reality, Selma shows signs of the difficulties into which the movement was running. Some SCLC and SNCC members were showing signs of impatience with non-violence. They were mystified by King's apparently weak surrender on the second attempt at a Selma–Montgomery march. They were also increasingly pessimistic about whether southern white people would ever accept them as equals. They were incensed by the violence shown against them at the time of the marches. Reverend James Reeb, a white Unitarian minister, suffered an exceptionally vicious attack and died from his injuries. Because he was white, his murder particularly angered northern white opinion, although black people also lost their lives at this time, including Jimmie Lee Jackson. King was never to experience the same degree of success again. The Civil Rights Movement was about to enter a much tougher period.

HOW SUCCESSFUL WAS THE CIVIL RIGHTS MOVEMENT BETWEEN 1963 AND 1965?

In terms of high drama and achievement, the years 1963 to 1965 could be seen as the most successful for the Civil Rights Movement:

- Two successive US Presidents were committed to supporting the movement's demands.
- Public opinion in the USA was swinging even further towards racial equality.
- Martin Luther King's reputation was at its height.
- Two important acts were passed: the 1964 Civil Rights Act and the 1965 Voting Rights Act.

However:

- There were signs of tension and potential division in the movement that were to become increasingly apparent in the next three years.
- Only very limited progress had been made in improving the economic and social conditions of black Americans, especially in the north.

SUMMARY QUESTIONS

1 Why might the SCLC campaign in Birmingham be regarded as a success?

2 What does the march on Washington tell us about the nature of the Civil Rights Movement?

3 How did the terms of the Civil Rights Act and the Voting Rights Act benefit black people?

CHAPTER 10

Changes in the Civil Rights Movement, 1965–6

INTRODUCTION

In 1965 and 1966, the Civil Rights Movement met more difficulties than before and the nature of the movement broadened and changed. The SCLC and Martin Luther King were no longer so dominant, as other groups such as the SNCC began to challenge their approach. In fact, there were signs of some of these changes before 1965.

TENSION IN MISSISSIPPI

What did the Mississippi Freedom Summer do?

The tensions between SNCC and the SCLC that surfaced at Selma were not new. Since the end of the freedom rides, it had been decided to focus part of the campaigning attention on voter registration. During the winter of 1962–3, Mississippi in particular was targeted and, although progress was limited, the movement did recruit some new figures, such as **Fannie Lou Hamer**.

In 1964, SNCC member Robert Moses organised a Mississippi Freedom Summer movement to focus attention on the state that had the lowest proportion of black registered voters – under five per cent. One of the main aims was to gain more publicity all over the USA for this state of affairs. The tactics included welcoming white students: if these students were treated badly, it would gain more attention from the US media than would a similar fate for black people.

The Mississippi Freedom Democratic Party

At the same time, another development indicated a new direction for the movement. As well as encouraging the registration of blacks voters, the Freedom Summer looked for their involvement in a political organisation. The Mississippi Freedom Democratic Party was set up as an alternative to the

KEY PERSON

Fannie Lou Hamer (1917–77) had no political experience until she was recruited by SNCC in 1962 as part of their voter registration drive. She worked as a Field Secretary for SNCC and soon made a favourable impression. An active member of the Mississippi Freedom Democratic Party, she rejected the offered compromise on democratic representation, saying 'We didn't come all this way for no two votes'. She was a highly respected person in the movement, and many were appalled when Black Power extremists in SNCC sacked her for wanting to continue working with supportive white people.

official Democrats, to give black people proper representation. This would be in contrast to the **lily-whites** in the mainstream party. The aim was to gain official recognition of the group at the Democratic Party Convention in the autumn of 1964.

The party convention was a large annual meeting of the Democrats, and the convention in 1964, in Atlantic City, confirmed its support for Johnson's presidential campaign. The Mississippi Freedom Democratic Party claimed equal representation in the party because it had widespread black support. Eighty thousand black people had cast votes for its candidates in unofficial elections, yet a majority of these were not allowed to register or were too scared to because of threats.

However, the move met with a lot of resistance from official Democrats. Johnson was anxious for re-election in November 1964, and to prevent southern Democrats from turning Republican, he wanted to keep them happy by rejecting the claim of the Mississippi Freedom Democratic Party for equal representation. Consequently, its claim was disallowed.

After complaints, small concessions were made. The representatives could speak but not vote, and they could have two token representatives. Greater representation was offered in the following years, but Robert P. Moses of SNCC regarded these concessions as totally inadequate and rejected them. This was despite the pleadings of Martin Luther King who, aware of the paltry nature of the offer, was anxious to keep on good terms with Johnson. One result of these events was that many civil rights campaigners became disillusioned with white reformers such as President Johnson.

SOCIAL AND ECONOMIC PROBLEMS

The need for social and economic reform

Despite these difficulties with the Democratic Party, the achievement of political and legal equality, in theory at least, had been a victory for the Civil Rights Movement. But it was one thing to persuade the federal government of the need for changes in these areas, and quite another to achieve similar reform in the area of social and economic policy. Political

Lily-whites was a nickname for the white southern Democrats who opposed civil rights. Although northern Democrats and a few southern ones, such as Johnson, favoured civil rights, southern Democrats, mainly elected by white voters, were generally opposed.

and legal reforms did not need a large financial outlay by federal or state governments, and they could be achieved quite quickly and monitored relatively easily, especially if all the relevant authorities agreed.

However, there was much greater difficulty with social and economic reform:

- The problems often required a lot more cash to solve properly.
- They were very deep-seated and would take a long time to solve completely.
- They were often as acute in the north as the south, and sometimes worse.
- They involved racism that was hidden and/or informal, but no less significant for that and more difficult to identify and deal with.

It was easier, quicker and cheaper to grant black people the vote and the right to use the same restaurant than it was to ensure that they all had adequate social and economic facilities. For instance, they would have liked:

- adequate housing
- a decent school with adequate facilities
- an equal chance of satisfactory employment.

The Moynihan Report, 1965

At least the federal government was now actively concerned with these problems. **Daniel Moynihan** was asked by President Johnson to examine the whole question in detail. His **report** on black social conditions in 1965 revealed some statistics that caused much discussion.

Fifty per cent of black males between the ages of 16 and 25 were found to have criminal records. However, people in the liberal north did not conclude from this that black people were naturally more wicked than white people – a southern racist view. Rather, the statistics made it all the more urgent to deal with the social problems that were believed to have contributed in a major way to the high crime rates. The report concluded that legislation had emphasised problems of discrimination, but now black people needed to make further gains by self-improvement.

Education

Some progress had been made towards educational integration during the early 1960s, and the position was now certainly different from the time of Little Rock. But the number of black children in schools with white pupils was still only 15.9 per cent, and black educational achievement remained well below white levels. Because people naturally preferred their neighbourhood school, segregated schooling effectively reflected housing patterns. Since black people tended to live in one area and white people in another, they would rarely meet in whatever was their local school. There was a poverty trap: lack of schooling, lack of training, slum living and unemployment. This was especially true in the large northern and western cities, such as Washington, New York, Detroit, Chicago and Los Angeles.

President Johnson himself remarked it was not enough to 'open the gates of opportunity'. Positive steps needed to be taken to ensure that all black people had sufficiently good social and economic conditions to take advantage of opportunities.

Unemployment and poverty

Unemployment was a major problem. Black teenagers were nearly twice as likely to be out of work as white teenagers were, yet, as the table shows, it had not always been so. In 1965, a year of relatively low unemployment, the average figure for all white males was 4.9 per cent and for black 7.3 per cent. In the country as a whole, about one person in ten had an income under $5000 a year, but for black people alone it was one in three. Average black income, always much lower than white, was now only 53 per cent of the national average. Clearly these problems were not merely the problems of first-generation immigrants: there seemed no likelihood of improvement in the black condition, especially in the northern industrial areas.

Year	Black	White
1948	8	8
1965	23	13

Teenage unemployment rates in the USA, 1948 and 1965 (%).

THE CIVIL RIGHTS MOVEMENT LOOKS TO THE NORTH

The challenge of northern conditions

King and his supporters were becoming increasingly concerned with the particularly severe problems for black people in the northern states. The SCLC was alarmed by black rejection of non-violent methods outside the South. In these circumstances, it is perhaps not surprising that the Civil Rights Movement should expand from south to north. This would be a real challenge for King and the SCLC, who were less familiar with northern conditions.

- Black people in the north were more concerned with the economic and social problems outlined above, which showed little sign of going away, than with formal desegregation or the right to vote.
- They knew comparatively little of King's exploits and achievements in the south.
- They shared his Christian faith much less than their southern counterparts.
- And, partly as a result of all the above, they were less convinced by the idea of non-violent protest.

Housing in Chicago

King was now firmly established as a national and not merely a southern civil rights leader. In 1966 he decided to attack the question of segregation in housing. It was the obvious challenge once the decision had been made to move north. Disturbances in some of the large industrial cities the previous year had convinced King and some of his colleagues that they should go, and they went to Chicago in January 1966.

By focusing on Chicago, King and the SCLC adopted the same tactic as at Birmingham and Selma. Yet the problem was severe: the rapidly increasing black population now exceeded 800,000 in a city of 4 million, but they were almost entirely confined to the ghettos on the south and west sides.

King, living in a poor black area of the city, targeted segregated housing, but he was less familiar with conditions and outlooks in the north, and lacked a coherent strategy. The method of provoking short-tempered southern police chiefs in places like Birmingham and Selma would not work here. **Richard Daley**, Mayor of Chicago, was an enormously powerful city boss who had kept up the tradition of not discriminating against black people in employment, but he had done little about their appalling housing conditions.

HEINEMANN ADVANCED HISTORY

Daley had no intention of being helpful to King, other than making vague promises about improving the housing situation, but he hinted that he did not require outside help to do it.

Under attack at Marquette Park

King's worst moment came when he and other protesters marched into the all-white housing areas near Marquette Park. The ferocity of the attack on him and the naked hatred displayed by white people living there were even worse than those he had found among southerners. For one thing, the numbers were greater than most crowds in the south. For another, they more than matched southerners for racial viciousness, shouting 'Martin Luther Coon', waving Nazi flags and throwing bottles, bricks and rocks. One of the bricks hit King on the head, but he was not severely hurt and insisted on continuing with the walk. Some white people set off 'cherry bombs', a kind of firecracker.

The reception the campaigners received was a revelation to King and the SCLC, and indicated just how prejudiced and violent northern white people could be. In the end, a rather vague agreement was patched up with Daley, containing unkept promises about introducing open housing legislation and improving housing conditions in the city. It had been a learning experience for King, but not a success for the SCLC as a whole.

THE EFFECT OF THE VIETNAM WAR

The end of the 'Great Society' programme

For a time during the middle of the 1960s, it really seemed as if President Johnson was going to make major inroads into black poverty. His **'Great Society'** programme of reforms particularly targeted this area. His relationship with King was seen as the key to successes so far, such as the Education Act passed by Congress in 1965, which aimed to speed up desegregation in schools. More reforms were expected and further progress depended on a good relationship being maintained between the Johnson administration and civil rights leaders such as King. However, the escalation of the **Vietnam War** made this impossible.

The dilemma for King

US involvement in south-east Asia went back to the 1950s. But, under Johnson, the USA had become committed on a massive scale. This presented a dilemma for Martin Luther King. Morally he felt compelled to speak out against the war, for several reasons:

- The scale of the fighting and consequent suffering was something he believed should be condemned outright.
- When it came to the recruitment papers and the firing line, black soldiers were suddenly equal to white soldiers again, as they had been during the Second World War.
- The war was taking attention and money away from social

Black protesters speaking out against the Vietnam War, 1967.

problems at home, and the chance of further social improvement, especially for black people, was slipping by.

However, if King was to speak out against the war, he risked destroying the movement's relationship with Johnson and losing the reforms he was so anxious to see. For a time he remained silent. Then he became concerned by the US bombing raids of the spring and summer of 1965, and he called for a negotiated settlement that August. For the next eighteen months, though he said little, he was in an agony of indecision about the issue.

King criticises the war

In April 1967, he broke his silence with a powerful address at New York's Riverside Church. In this speech, King made it crystal clear that he regarded the war as uncivilised and wicked. He pulled no punches, asserting that the USA was 'standing before the world gutted by our own barbarity'. Not for the first time he had used a strong but apt phrase (it could also have been used to describe the actions of the more bigoted white southerners over civil rights). But this time the language, although it benefited his moral standing in the eyes of many, was not to his political advantage. Relations with President Johnson now took a downturn.

The whole issue affected King personally. He regarded all the expenditure on Vietnam as wasteful. Futhermore, he hoped desperately that another summer's rioting could be avoided. 'We can't live with another summer like the last,' he said.

The Poor People's Campaign

Late in 1967, King had the idea of another march on Washington, but this time of a rather different kind. It would be a march of the poor – of all races – the Poor People's Campaign. They would camp out within sight of the White House, their city of paper and cardboard being a visual reminder to the rich and powerful of how the other half lived. As King put it, he wanted to 'confront the power structure'. He planned that this march would begin from Marks, Mississippi, which was arguably the poorest town in the entire USA (and still is). It would recall other civil rights marches on Washington but, in having a camp, it would also imitate the **camp in Washington**. But King's proposed

KEY EVENT

1918 Camp in Washington
This is a famous event in US history at the end of the First World War. It was organised by unemployed ex-soldiers to draw attention to their plight.

Stokeley Carmichael

march was postponed until the summer of 1968 and by that time he was not around to lead it (see Chapter 11).

THE RADICALISM OF SNCC

The 'March Against Fear'

Not least among the young, many people in the Civil Rights Movement now had doubts about keeping the movement non-violent. This was apparent before 1966. But it was in that year that an incident occurred that seems to describe most clearly the prevailing mood of disillusion with non-violence. In June 1966, James Meredith decided to go on a one-man 350-km 'March Against Fear' through the southern states from Memphis, Tennessee, to Jackson, Mississippi. At first the walk went without incident but, when he was near Hernando, Mississippi, he was shot by an unknown sniper. Although his injuries were not life threatening, he was clearly not well enough to continue the march immediately, so plans were made by the SCLC, CORE and SNCC to complete it for him. The new chair of SNCC was **Stokeley Carmichael**, who pursued a particularly militant line.

Black Power

On this march, some of the attributes appeared of what became known as Black Power – the clenched fist and the slogan 'Black Power! Black Power!' The non-violent 'N' in SNCC was becoming more and more strained, and some of the slogans on the walk were distinctly aggressive, 'Burn baby burn' and 'Get Whitey' among them. This was a world away from the disciplined non-violence of a march organised by the SCLC, and King was appalled.

A new emphasis on black consciousness and racial pride was appearing. King was not against this as such. Indeed, he was putting greater emphasis on it in his own speeches. In Chicago, he had talked with approval of the need to be proud to be black and even of the necessity of more militant activity. But he did not approve of a policy of attacking white people and discouraging support even from sympathetic ones. This was both morally repugnant to his own philosophy and, he felt, tactically unwise.

A younger generation of black students was emerging who

KEY PERSON

Stokeley Carmichael (1941–98) was born in Trinidad and died in Guinea, West Africa, but he spent the years 1952–69 in the USA. He attended the mainly black Howard University in Washington. He was an organiser for SNCC between 1964 and 1966, when he became chair of the organisation. In 1967, he co-wrote *Black Power*, outlining his vision of the role for blacks in the USA. Some of the language in his speeches was extreme, such as 'smashing everything that white civilisation has created'. He left SNCC to join the Black Panthers in 1967. He left the USA in 1969 to live in Guinea, changing his name to Kwame Ture.

were impatient for more reform. The youngest could barely remember the days before the Brown verdict of 1954, yet they were only too well aware of the continuing discrimination against them, both formally and informally, in the south and the north.

Moreover, there was an alternative philosophy to embrace. The idea of Black Power was becoming increasingly accepted in many parts of the black community. Although it had been overshadowed by King and the SCLC, its time had now come.

CHANGES IN THE CIVIL RIGHTS MOVEMENT, 1965–6

During these years, the Civil Rights Movement underwent the following important changes:

- There was a shift in emphasis from south to north.
- Concern focused increasingly on social and economic questions rather than legal and political ones.
- A serious challenge was mounted to the non-violent and Christian-based beliefs of the movement.
- New leaders emerged who would challenge the dominance of Martin Luther King.
- Some of the hard-won sympathy that the movement had received from the federal government ended.

SUMMARY QUESTIONS

1 Why would the Civil Rights Movement find economic and social problems more difficult to deal with than legal and political issues?

2 What problems did King encounter in his campaigns in Chicago?

3 What difficulties did the Vietnam War cause for the Civil Rights Movement?

CHAPTER 11

The origins, nature and effects of Black Power

Summary of Malcolm X's life

- He was born in 1925 into a poor family in Omaha, Nebraska. He was named Malcolm Little.
- The family moved around a great deal, often after white attacks.
- In 1929 the family was forced to move after unknowingly living in a house with a 'whites-only' lease clause.
- In 1931 his father disappeared and was later found murdered.
- In 1937 his mother was committed to a mental institution.
- In 1938 he was expelled from school and sent to a Juvenile Detention Center in Michigan.
- In 1940 he moved to Boston, and then in 1941 to Harlem, New York. He became involved in drugs, gambling and burglary, and became addicted to cocaine. He was arrested and imprisoned for theft in 1945 and sentenced to eight years' hard labour.
- He spent 1946–52 in jail, where he converted to the Nation of Islam in 1949.

INTRODUCTION

By 1966, the idea of Black Power was an alternative philosophy to non-violent protest that civil rights activists could embrace. For some time it had been in the shadow of Martin Luther King and the SCLC, but it was now becoming increasingly accepted in many parts of the black community. Intriguingly, its greatest exponent, Malcolm X, died early in 1965, just as his ideas were becoming more popular.

WHAT WAS BLACK POWER?

Black Power included a number of different, loosely-defined ideas, but some central tenets could be identified in the mid to late 1960s. These included:

- rejection of non-violence
- Martin Luther King being regarded as the 'tool of the white man'
- white people not being wanted in the Civil Rights Movement
- Black Supremacy – the idea that black people should be in complete control of their own destiny
- demands for more effective and fair implementation of the law
- radical social change, especially in housing and education.

Many of these ideas had been outlined by Malcolm X during the 1950s. At that time he was the most articulate person putting forward these thoughts.

The background of Malcolm X

It is essential to be aware of Malcolm X's background if we are to understand him and his views. To white European readers, they might seem distasteful, and even racist. They are certainly a long way from the views of the Christian Martin Luther King. But the way Malcolm X had been treated by whites in his youth, in stark contrast to the relatively privileged upbringing of King, helped to give him a very different set of attitudes.

- Malcolm X was brought up in a family who were constantly harassed by white racists.
- He was deprived of his father, who was found dead, probably murdered by white people. His father had been a strong supporter of Marcus Garvey.
- He was forced to cope with a mother who was gradually losing her mind after her husband's death.
- He was the victim of white teachers talking down his ambitions when at school; in his autobiography, Malcolm X recalls a teacher telling him to forget about ambitious job applications because he was black.
- He was unable to get good educational opportunities, despite showing ability in his early school days.
- He mixed in criminal company in New York, so turning to a life of crime and drugs.

Conversion to Islam

While in jail between 1946 and 1952, he underwent a conversion to the Islamic faith that completely transformed his life. But it was not to mainstream Islam that he gave his allegiance; rather, it was to the fringe sect known as the **Nation of Islam** (or Black Muslims) and particularly to its leader, **Elijah Muhammad**.

Malcolm X discarded their unorthodox ideas towards the end of his life and embraced the mainstream Sunni Muslim faith. But, during the early 1950s, the theories of the Black Muslims, as they came to be popularly known, gave him a belief by which he could regain faith and respect in both himself and his race. At this time he **changed his name** from Malcolm Little to Malcolm X.

During the 1950s, he made a considerable reputation in two main directions:

- as a successful minister for the Nation of Islam
- as a prominent speaker, putting forward ideas about black pride and black power.

- In 1952 he came out of jail and rose rapidly up the ranks of the Nation of Islam. He dropped the name Little and became Malcolm X.
- In 1953–4 he was acting minister of the Nation of Islam's temples in Philadelphia and Detroit, and then was put in command of New York's temple.
- In 1962 he was made national minister of the Nation of Islam.
- In 1964 he was expelled from the Nation of Islam and travelled widely in African, Asian and European countries where there were many Muslims. This greatly broadened his horizons and made him realise that many Muslims were white (for example, in Bosnia).
- In 1965 he was assassinated by members of his old group.

KEY TERM

The **Nation of Islam (Black Muslims)** was a group founded by Wallace Fard, who led it until his disappearance in 1934, when Elijah Muhammad became leader. According to the racial theories of the Nation of Islam, all people had been originally coloured black until an evil scientist, Jacoub, had inbred the palest faces to produce a different and inferior race. Since Elijah's death, Louis Farrakhan has led the movement.

KEY THEME

Change of name to a letter
Under slavery, many black people had no surname. If they did, it was often the surname of their master's family. Black Power supporters felt this name to be invalid and a reminder of the oppression of slavery. They hoped to research into their real black name, but until they found this out they would merely take on a letter of the alphabet as their second name. So, Malcolm felt that the name 'Little' was not his. His own background was complex and it is likely that he had a white grandfather who had had an affair with (or raped) a slave girl.

The first began when he was made assistant minister of the Black Muslims' Temple Number One in Detroit in 1953. Immediately effective, he was asked to organise other temples as the movement grew in size from just a few hundred members to several thousand. Within a year, he was in charge of the important New York Temple and emerged as Elijah Muhammad's deputy.

The American 'nightmare'

Although barred by Elijah Muhammad from making specifically political statements, Malcolm X had a good deal to say about the nature of white American society and the status of African-Americans within the country. In the tradition of Marcus Garvey (see page 85), he saw black people as Africans rather than Americans. There was little point trying to integrate into white society, which was uniformly corrupt and racist. Malcolm X had no interest in sitting down to a meal or a coffee with white people, or as he graphically put it, 'Who wants to sit on the next toilet seat to a white?' Instead of King's American 'dream' he saw only an American 'nightmare'. The African-American was in a state of mental slavery towards white people and needed to be shaken out of it.

Rejection of accommodation with white people

Malcolm X rejected the idea of integration with the white community that King and others favoured. He believed that black development needed to be separate. Whether this would involve a separate state of the Union, total independence or a move back to Africa was never entirely clear. It certainly involved a rejection of American democratic values as a sham: white people would never apply these values to the black community. Unlike King, Malcolm had lived in the north, among working-class black people and had assessed the attitude of northern whites towards black people. They were no better than southern racists and in some senses worse. At least white southerners were open in their racism. In the north, racism was sometimes more disguised. Worst of all, in Malcolm X's eyes, were northern white liberals, who were hypocrites and 'wolves in sheep's clothing'. Black people needed to work out their own salvation and did not need the assistance of friendly white people to do it.

The threat of violence

Malcolm X also rejected the non-violent emphasis of the mainstream Civil Rights Movement. He saw self-defence against white aggression and oppression as a legitimate weapon and said so frequently. Above everything else, this made him a figure of suspicion both with the white authorities and with supporters of the King philosophy. Few even of the most militant civil rights protesters in the SCLC or NAACP wished to discuss issues with him. This was not merely because his views were regarded as unacceptable: Malcolm X also had a reputation as a formidable debater and a mesmerising speaker.

It could be argued that his violent posturing was merely aimed at frightening the authorities into action. He never undertook violent action himself and sometimes prevented it. The Black Muslims now became an established force to be reckoned with.

Political statements

In 1959, Malcolm X came to national prominence when he and the Black Muslims were the subject of a television programme, *The Hate that Hate Produced*. Malcolm X was seen expressing his views in his usual forthright style. He managed to get across the true extent of racist feeling in the USA, which many had assumed was confined to certain quarters of the south. The urban ghettos of the USA were full of the most serious social problems imaginable: crime, prostitution, drugs and unemployment. It was Malcolm X who drew attention to this and who warned that, if nothing was done, violence on a grand scale would erupt. Indeed it did, but ironically it happened just after his death.

Malcolm X could be withering in his attacks on the civil rights campaigners, calling the march on Washington 'the farce on Washington'. But his most controversial comment was saved for the aftermath of President Kennedy's assassination. Although his remarks were taken slightly out of context, his description of the incident as 'chickens coming home to roost' was likely to produce appalled astonishment from many Americans.

In April 1957 a Black Muslim was badly beaten by police in Harlem, the black district of New York. Malcolm used the threat of violence in the local black community to ensure that the police took the man to receive immediate medical treatment. This is a revealing insight into Malcolm X's tactics, as well as showing his degree of control over his supporters.

Malcolm X.

Malcolm X's comments about 'chickens coming home to roost' show that Malcolm X was now straying into the political field, despite instructions from Elijah Muhammad not to do so. As a punishment for his 'chickens coming home to roost' comments, Malcolm X was given a 90-day silence ban – a cruel punishment for one so articulate. He was on the road to a painful break-up of his strong spiritual relationship with Elijah Muhammad.

Split from the Nation of Islam and assassination

One of the things that the Nation of Islam had given Malcolm X was personal control. He had not merely given up his life of crime, but also abstained from alcohol, tobacco and sexual immorality. Now he found that Elijah had feet of clay, or rather fast cars and mistresses. The break-up that finally occurred in 1964 had immense potential significance. Martin Luther King was becoming more militant and more disillusioned with white attitudes, although still remaining strictly non-violent. King's greater awareness of the importance of publicising black racial pride meant that here was now a real possibility that his views and Malcolm X's, previously so far apart, could come closer together, if not actually coincide. Malcolm was more anxious to meet Martin than vice versa and began making less critical remarks about him. The two eventually met in 1964 and shook hands in front of the press. However, the chance meeting was never followed up. The split from the Nation of Islam was Malcolm X's undoing. In February 1965, members of the sect to which he had once belonged assassinated him.

THE RIOTS OF 1965–8

Los Angeles, August 1965

Not long after his death, the violence that Malcolm X had predicted broke out in northern and western towns and cities. The first of these was in the Watts district of Los Angeles in August 1965 – the first of three 'long hot summers' of rioting, as they became known. The local black community exploded in a great volume of anger after one of them was arrested on a drink-driving charge and then subjected to a brutal attack from police. This seemed to sum up the way black people were treated by the authorities and they had finally had enough. By the end of the night, 34 people were dead. Huge mobs, sometimes of several thousand people, rampaged through the streets attacking motorists and doing $40 million worth of damage. Some 14,000 troops were required to restore order and 4000 people were arrested.

The riots were very distressing to King. They started only five days after the 1965 Voting Rights Act had become law and seemed to undermine the non-violent policies of SCLC. The rioters showed both their ignorance of King and their

Protesters on the burned-out streets of Watts district in Los Angeles after the race riots in 1965.

determination to be noticed in their own way. It was rumoured that some rioters, on being told that 'Martin Luther King would be ashamed of you', replied 'Martin Luther who?'

As James Cone points out in *Martin, Malcolm and America* (1993), the black rioters could in theory ride on the same buses, eat in the same restaurants and even live in the same districts as the white people, but in many cases they did not have enough money to do so. For them, Malcolm X, even when dead, was a more realistic role model, with his problem-filled background, than the southern King from the 'black aristocracy'. There had been some local causes of the riots: a Fair Housing Act of 1964 had been repealed and the police chief of the time was particularly unpopular. But it had a much wider significance: it showed up graphically how economic and social issues were of more consequence to black people than formal desegregation or the right to vote.

Year	Riots	Killed	Injured	Arrested	Cost ($m)
1965	5	36	1206	10,245	40.1
1966	21	11	520	2298	10.2
1967	75	83	1827	16,389	664.5
Total	101	130	3553	28,932	714.8

The 'long hot summers', 1965–7.

The riots spread

As the table opposite shows, the total number of riots occurring increased over the next two years and spread to a large number of cities. The riots seemed to be spontaneous. Yet King was worried that their cause would be set back. But there seems to have been a lack of civil rights leadership in these places. It is significant that the Mexican minority in Los Angeles took no part in the rioting. They were better integrated and had developed a sense of their own racial pride, which Malcolm X had asserted was so lacking in the African-American.

Federal reaction

President Johnson's reaction was one of dismay, especially as the riots in Los Angeles came within a week of the passing of the Voting Rights Act. He sent a special agent, Ramsey Clark, to investigate the causes. What he found had nothing to do with voting: the grievances were social and economic. They lacked essential services in Watts; there were few jobs, poor schools and a lack of even basic sanitation. Even the food was bad and food poisoning was common. Some action was taken: the Firestone Rubber Company moved into the area to create 100 jobs and the Martin Luther King Hospital was built. But then Watts seemed to be forgotten. Things had improved little by the end of the century.

THE BLACK PANTHERS

Increasing militancy

During the early 1960s, Malcolm X and the Black Muslims were the best-known exponents of Black Power but, in the excitement of the late 1960s, other militant groups emerged. SNCC, as we have seen, became more radical, as did other groups such as CORE. Stokeley Carmichael of the SNCC made violent comments such as 'We're going to tear this country up'. In January 1966, Floyd McKissick had replaced James Farmer as executive director of CORE. Not as extreme as Carmichael, who used to answer the phone with the phrase 'ready for the revolution', McKissack was nonetheless a keen advocate of Black Power, demanding a better self-image for African-Americans and greater economic and political power.

More in the Carmichael mould was **H. Rap Brown**, who succeeded Carmichael as chairman of the SNCC. Helping to

---

KEY PERSON

H. Rap Brown was born in 1943 and joined SNCC in the early 1960s. He was shot and caught by New York City police in 1970, imprisoned, then paroled in 1976. In March 2000 he was arrested and accused of killing a sheriff's deputy in Atlanta. At the courthouse he told the reporters, 'It's a government conspiracy, man.'

---

organise a national conference on Black Power in Newark, New Jersey (in 1967, just after the riots), he made it clear that some white journalists would not be allowed in to report proceedings. Travelling to Cambridge, Massachusetts, he urged black people to repeat the actions of the Detroit rioters. They did. Charged with incitement, Brown evaded capture for some time.

The programme of the Black Panthers

The Black Panthers were led by **Huey Newton** and **Bobby Seale**. They wanted an end to white capitalist control in general and police brutality in particular; their positive demands were economic in emphasis. They developed a ten-point programme, which was clearly influenced by Black Power ideas and Malcolm X:

- freedom – power to determine the destiny of the black community
- full employment for all
- an end to 'robbery' of black people
- housing – fit for the shelter of human beings
- education – the truth about the 'decadent racist society'
- black exemption from military service
- an end to acts of brutality and murder by the police
- freedom for all black people held in jail
- fair juries – black juries for black people
- land entitlement as well as bread, clothing, housing, education, justice and peace.

They also developed the distinctive idea of armed patrols of black people in the ghettos to keep an eye on the white police. Firearm training was given and a uniform developed. But when the California state legislature proposed a ban on carrying firearms, the Panthers responded with an armed march to the building where the issue was to be debated. In October 1967, Huey Newton was shot when being arrested (two policeman were killed). Bobby Seale was imprisoned and, although **Eldridge Cleaver** continued to run the movement and its membership remained strong, it did not pose quite the same threat again.

Backlash

In 1968 the radical mood in the ghettos and on many student campuses gave the Panthers the favourable conditions they required for their policies. But their period of strength was short-lived. In 1969 came the backlash, when 27 Panthers were killed in shoot-outs with police. Informers completed the downfall of the group and Eldridge Cleaver emigrated in 1969. The movement had reached a membership of 2000 at its height during the late 1960s, but split badly in the 1970s and disbanded in 1982.

NATIVE AMERICANS

Affirmative action

During the mid-1960s, the advances of the Civil Rights Movement in general and the racial consciousness of Black Power in particular encouraged other racial groups to campaign more vigorously themselves. One of the last ideas of President Johnson, in 1968, was to launch a policy of affirmative action that would seek to ensure that any organisation receiving federal funds operated a satisfactory policy of inclusion towards racial minorities. This might mean, for instance, that educational applications from racial minorities would be more favourably received than those of their white counterparts. Affirmative action has proved a controversial policy both politically and legally, but it provided new opportunities not only for black people but also for smaller minority groups.

Legal action

Attempts by the National Congress of American Indians to bring legal actions against the federal government for taking so much of their reservation lands over the years had made only limited progress by the mid-1960s. As well as these reservation issues, fishing rights and the chance for an education were also discussed. Some of the younger members of the Native American tribes were critical of the slow progress of the National Congress – criticisms reminiscent of younger black peoples' impatience with the NAACP. In a move strikingly similar to the establishment of SNCC, a new body emerged in 1960 – the National Indian Youth Council. In 1968, the Indian equivalent of a sit-in – a fish-in – was held after the Washington **State Supreme Court** ruled against North American treaty rights to fish. Although this action was not successful, they did prevent President Eisenhower from ending their residential rights in 1958 by successful court action. Land was also recovered by legal action in New York and Massachusetts.

The Bureau of Indian Affairs

One Native American complaint was that they felt they had made little headway against the **Bureau of Indian Affairs**. One of the most notorious examples of this was in 1964, when Californian tribes were given compensation for the millions of acres taken from them during the previous 100 years: the price was a mere 47 cents an acre, the market value in 1861. President Kennedy's promises of action on Indian rights had not been fulfilled by the time he was assassinated in 1963.

Drift to the towns

Unlike the earlier period of black civil rights activity, Native Americans had little desire for integration into white society. Their chiefs were concerned that, with the Native American population nearly doubling to one million between 1945 and 1980, there had been a drift to the towns and away from the reservations by some of the younger generation. About 40 per cent were living in urban centres like Oakland, California, by the 1970s, assisted by government-sponsored relocation programmes. But the possibilities of a prosperous new life in these areas were not generally fulfilled. Unfamiliar patterns of work, coupled with the loneliness felt in what seemed an impersonal society, led to continued poverty and discrimination.

Living standards

The increase in the Native American population had not been matched by an increase in their living standards. Tuberculosis (where the death rate was three or four times as great as in the USA generally), trachoma (an infectious disease of the eyes), alcoholism and illiteracy were still all seen as major problems. Life expectancy, at 44 years, was 20 years lower than the US average. Suicide rates among the 16–25 age group were also well above the national average. On the reservations, the improvements of the New Deal period had not been maintained. Gerald Nagel's study on the condition of Native Americans, published in 1974, estimated that between 80 and 95 per cent of their housing was in a 'dilapidated, makeshift, unsanitary and crowded condition', the national average being 8 per cent. The majority had no running water.

Unemployment and low pay

These remained serious problems. In 1968, the Bureau of Indian Affairs estimated an average unemployment rate of 42 per cent, although in some cases it could be very much higher, such as 77 per cent among the Pueblo Indians of New Mexico and 72.5 per cent among the Blackfeet of Montana. A study of about 19,000 Oklahoma Indians found that almost half received no welfare benefits. Nearly two-thirds of all Native Americans who did work were employed in low-paid seasonal farm activities. Of those on the reservations in 1968, only about 3 per cent had industrial jobs. Not surprisingly, 300 Native Americans joined in the Poor People's Campaign in 1968.

The influence of Black Power

Black power influences became apparent by 1968 with the founding of the American Indian Movement (AIM), when 'Red Power' appeared as a new phrase and an increased militancy was shown. The rejection of racial integration by Black Power tuned in with existing Native American Indian feelings about maintaining their distinctive lifestyle. Similar sensitivity about language was also apparent: 'African-American' and 'Native American' were, by the 1960s, preferred to 'Negro' and 'Indian', which smacked of the colonial and slave past.

HISPANIC-AMERICANS

In contrast to the Native Americans, the period from the mid-1940s to the late 1960s had seen little activity on the civil rights front for Hispanic (usually Mexican) Americans. Victims of insulting comments just as much as black people (and for longer into the 1960s), they also experienced de facto separation in schools and public entertainments, such as cinemas and swimming pools.

Lack of political representation

Their lack of political representation and frequent brushes with the law were also reminiscent of the treatment meted out to black people. In towns like El Paso and San Diego, where they were the majority of the population, boundaries were **gerrymandered** to make it difficult for them to elect their own representatives. By 1968, a million Chicanos (see page 105) lived in Los Angeles, yet none was elected to the

KEY TERM

Gerrymandering is the drawing of electoral boundaries to give advantage to particular groups or parties. In this case, the boundaries would be arranged so that Hispanic-Americans would not be in the majority in any electoral district and so would probably be unable to elect their own representative. The term was named after Elbridge Gerry, who was allegedly the first US politician to make such an arrangement.

city council. At this time the total population of Chicanos in the USA was about five million. Of these, two million were in California, yet none served in the state government. They were more successful in Texas, where they had elected Henry Gonzales to Congress in 1961.

Police treatment

White police treatment of Mexicans, though not as systematically racist as against black people, was nonetheless prejudiced. A case where a white police officer was alleged to have shot and killed a Mexican was eventually abandoned on the grounds that a conviction in such a case was unlikely. This could be explained partly by the fact that few Mexicans were ever chosen as jurors. There were a few Mexican policemen and a handful of Mexican FBI agents, but only six out of a thousand working in the south-western USA in the late 1960s.

At this point, three important influences emerged.

The Immigration Act (1965)

Since the 1930s, immigration policy had been based on a **'national origins' system**. The Immigration Act abolished this effective preference for European immigrants. When it came into effect in 1968, it led to a substantial increase in Hispanic entry to the USA, not only from Mexico but also from Puerto Rico – a US territory – and from the states of Central and South America. The Mexican-American population in particular – no more then half a million in 1940 – now increased dramatically. However, this increased the scale of their economic plight, since the standard of living of Chicanos was much lower than that of Americans as a whole.

An effective trade union leader: Cesar Chavez

Cesar Chavez had a strong desire to achieve better conditions for the Chicanos of the west in general and California in particular. He founded the National Farm Workers' Association in 1962, which combined with other groups to form the Californian Farm Workers' Union three years later. This was the first really effective workers' grouping for many years. Soon, it was holding strikes and organising boycotts and other protests such as hunger strikes. In the San Joaquin valley area, he developed credit, insurance and shopping facilities.

Chavez was strongly influenced by the black Civil Rights Movement. 'We owe so much to Dr Martin Luther King,' he wrote to Coretta Scott King in 1968. In the same year Chavez went on a hunger strike in support of non-violent methods. With this emphasis, his denial of communist influence and his admiration for genuine American sympathisers like Robert Kennedy, he was very much in the King mould. By 1972, he had achieved his aim of union recognition.

The influence of Black Power

Black Power ideas were also starting to have an impact on Mexican-Americans, with the slogan 'Brown Power' matching the Native Americans' 'Red Power'. For instance, in the mid to late 1960s, **Reies Lopez Tijerina** was the militant leader of the Alianza (Federal de los Pueblos Libres). From 1966 onwards, 'camp-ins' of protest were held and Forest Service land was attacked and set on fire. Tijerina himself was arrested and charged with kidnapping and assault on a jail where some of his members were imprisoned. In a celebrated case held in Albuquerque, he was acquitted in December 1968, and militant activity continued.

DID BLACK POWER HELP OR HINDER THE CIVIL RIGHTS MOVEMENT?

- Black Power certainly influenced Martin Luther King, who became increasingly concerned with emphasising that black people had plenty to be proud of. He also stressed the importance of tackling social and economic questions, as well as voting and segregation issues. Black Power had helped to force these up the agenda.
- It gave the black community a greater sense of pride and confidence in their race and its culture. Black literature, music, theatre, fashion and food all flourished during the 1970s.
- It inspired other minority groups to follow the black example and campaign in a more militant fashion for their own rights: in particular, the Chicanos and Native Americans developed ideas of 'Brown Power' and 'Red Power'.

However:

- Black Power brought division to the movement, as some

campaigners developed increasingly militant policies and groups like SNCC were broken by the strain.

- By accepting violence, the supporters of Black Power undermined King's policy of maintaining the moral high ground and lost much of the white sympathy he had worked so hard to gain. Of course, many of them made clear they had no desire for this support.
- Despite one or two attempts, such as Stokeley Carmichael's book of 1969, it was never entirely clear exactly what Black Power's political aims were. Did they want a separate state? Did they wish to return to Africa, or stage a revolution and overthrow white rule altogether? This led to confusion in the ranks.

SUMMARY QUESTIONS

1 What influence did Malcolm X have on the Civil Rights Movement?

2 What do the race riots of 1965–8 tell us about the impact of civil rights in the northern states of the USA?

3 What did the Black Panthers aim to achieve and how did they go about it?

4 What were the main differences between the beliefs of Martin Luther King and Malcolm X?

CHAPTER 12

The achievements of the Civil Rights Movement

HOW MUCH HAD BEEN ACHIEVED BY 1963?

Why focus on 1963?

This was a year of crucial breakthrough for the Civil Rights Movement. Although many concrete achievements lay just ahead, a look at what had been achieved by this year shows us the progress already made. The position of black people in the USA in 1963 was very different from that in 1953. In 1953, 'Jim Crow' was still alive in the southern states. But, ten years later, there had been a major assault on the system of segregation and plans were afoot to introduce a major Civil Rights Bill into Congress.

In 1963, some of the leading US magazines which publicised and supported black civil rights included: *The Wall Street Journal* (financial), *Time* magazine (politics, science and arts), *Life* magazine (a wide range of contemporary issues), *The New Yorker* (literary) and *Newsweek* (current affairs).

Public opinion

There is no doubt that public opinion had changed dramatically outside the Deep South. Many ordinary people recognised the desirability of equality. Here, the media played a vital role. Books, magazines, television and radio were devoting a great deal of positive attention to the issue. In 1963, an average of nine books a week were published in the USA on problems regarding racial equality. There was attention and support from leading magazines.

These were bound to exert a great influence on people's thinking. In addition, despite King's complaint in his 'Letter from Birmingham Jail', white and mixed churches as well as black ones were lending the campaign support. The Roman Catholic Church was prominent: 65 Catholic organisations in 30 different states were actively opposed to racial prejudice. Public opinion is one thing: but was there concrete progress in achieving full civil rights for black people?

Progress on civil rights

On some issues, there had been more progress than on others.

- **Desegregation.** This was arguably the greatest change. The Supreme Court had ruled that segregation on public transport or in its terminals was unconstitutional. Moreover, no public facilities of any kind should be subject to a colour bar. By June 1963, desegregation of this kind had taken place in 161 cities. 'Public accommodation' was now largely desegregated, including buses, lunch counters, swimming pools, washing facilities, sports provision, and theatres and cinemas.

- **Justice.** In Mississippi in 1963, seven white men were found guilty of murdering an African-American. One of the guilty was the Imperial Wizard of the White Knights of the Ku Klux Klan. Just a few years before, it would have been impossible to imagine such a verdict being given in the Deep South. Many in the legal profession were anxious to see fair play for black people. Again in 1963, 200 lawyers volunteered to go on a special commission to investigate civil rights questions. However, police forces remained predominantly white and sometimes racist. This applied in Chicago, Illinois, as much as in Jackson, Mississippi.

- **Employment.** Gains in employment opportunities were more in theory than in practice. By 1963, 25 of the 31 states with a substantial African-American population had formally introduced Fair Employment Practices – the idea introduced by President Roosevelt for federal government employees back in the 1940s. The federal government had achieved a good deal in real terms. Blacks now held 39 per cent of upper-level federal jobs. But discrimination in this area was much harder to pin down. Moreover, black unemployment, at 11 per cent, was twice the national average.

In other fields, there was less advance:

- **Voting rights.** Despite court rulings, the proportion of black people registering to vote was rising only slowly. In 1963, only about 800,000 out of 20 million black people were on the voting rolls. In some places, such as the notorious Selma, Alabama, they made up over 50 per cent of the population but less than 1 per cent of the electorate.

- **Housing.** Housing patterns had seen little change. Black ghettos still existed in cities such as Chicago, Detroit and New York. In 1962, President Kennedy had finally signed an executive order to end discrimination in federal housing construction, two years after he had promised to do so.

- **Education.** In eleven southern states, only 31,000 out of about 3 million school pupils were in integrated schools. James Meredith (see page 134) remained in isolation at the University of Mississippi and school segregation was almost completely intact in that state as well as in Alabama, Louisiana, Georgia and South Carolina. Popular resistance was still strong and change would be expensive. Moreover, the lack of change in housing patterns made large-scale racial mixtures in schools unlikely without more prescriptive measures.

So who or what had been responsible for the progress that had been made? We can identify two major sources here.

Supreme Court rulings

Although the Brown case was the most celebrated, a number of other important decisions over the years had also made a difference, especially in the fields of transport, education and, to some extent, voting rights. As Chief Justice of the Supreme Court, Earl Warren brought a less cautious and more positive approach to the whole question of civil rights. It was clear that he regarded the *Plessy* v. *Ferguson* case of 1896 as belonging to another era and no longer appropriate for the mid-twentieth century.

The Court's decisions on transport had made the greatest difference in practice. Violations of the rulings could be seen relatively easily and enforcement was not particularly expensive. But the pronouncements on education often went unheeded, although a small number of African-American students, such as James Meredith, had entered previously all-white institutions of higher education.

The efforts of black people

The other factor that had been particularly significant in the achievements was the efforts of black people themselves.

- The NAACP had been a leading light in bringing many of the above cases to the Supreme Court in the first place.
- The more confrontational tactics of the SCLC and then CORE and SNCC between 1956 and 1963 had clearly been successful in keeping the whole issue of race relations in the forefront of political activity.
- Grass-roots efforts were responsible for many protests and campaigns in local areas, and achieved a great deal. It was

Year	Name of case	Issue	Decision
1944	*Smith* v. *Allright*	Voting rights	Whites-only primary in Texas illegal
1946	*Morgan* v. *Virginia*	Transport	No segregation during inter-state travel
1950	*Sweatt* v. *Painter*	Education	Black people must receive the same level of graduate education as white people
1954	*Brown* v. *Board of Education, Topeka*	Education	Desegregation of schools
1955	*'Brown 2'* ruling	Education	Desegregation 'with all deliberate speed'
1956	*Browder* v. *Gayle*	Transport	Montgomery's bus segregation unconstitutional
1960	*Boynton* v. *Virginia*	Transport	Ban on segregation in inter-state travel extended to terminal accommodation
1962	*Baker* v. *Carr*	Voting rights	One person, one vote confirmed in principle

Some of the more significant Supreme Court rulings with regard to civil rights that affected everyday lives, 1944–62.

not just the national organisations that began action. Places such as Albany, Georgia, and St Augustine, Florida, for instance, had well-supported civil rights activities before Martin Luther King and the SCLC were invited in to bolster their efforts. Places such as High Point and Portsmouth, Virginia, staged vigorous and ultimately successful sit-in protests against the segregation of public facilities without any outside assistance.

- The decision of the Kennedy administration to plan for a Civil Rights Act in 1963 – and for Johnson to persuade Congress to pass it in 1964 after Kennedy's assassination – owed much to the campaigning efforts of the dedicated and often extremely brave civil rights workers.
- One can see the period around 1963–5, between the March on Washington, the 1964 Civil Rights Act and the 1965 Voting Rights Act as the peak of the movement's success.

HAD MUCH FURTHER PROGRESS BEEN MADE BY 1968?

The Civil Rights Movement ran into difficulties after 1964. Further progress was made, but not always as far or as fast as many of its supporters had hoped for.

The impact of the 1964 Civil Rights Act
The 1964 Civil Rights Act was a powerful statement of the principle of equality. It meant the end for those areas of the USA where segregation of public facilities had still not

changed. By October 1965, a further 53 cities had formally desegregated to add to the 161 that had already done so. By this date, even in the Deep South, rapid progress was being made. Mississippi and Alabama now had almost two-thirds of their towns largely desegregated.

The 1964 Civil Rights Act also gave a much greater chance of a fair legal hearing and more guarantee of legal action being taken swiftly and effectively. Money was also provided to assist measures such as school desegregation. In this area, though, along with housing and equal opportunities in employment, change was still limited by 1968.

The percentage of black southerners in segregated schools was still as high as 58 per cent in 1968. This, however, represented a considerable drop on the early 1960s. As well as the 1964 Civil Rights Act, the Education Act of 1965 also helped. Moreover, in the next four years, progress became more rapid. By 1972, the proportion of black people in segregated schools had dropped to just under 10 per cent, aided by more favourable Supreme Court decisions.

Black unemployment rates remained persistently higher than the corresponding figures for white people. In the late 1960s, a time of relatively low unemployment rates, black figures stayed above 7 per cent when the national figure was under 5 per cent. But a prosperous black middle class was growing rapidly and gaining professional qualifications. The proportion of black families earning over $10,000 a year rose from 13 per cent in 1960 to 31 per cent in 1971. In the 1960s, black incomes went up over 100 per cent, although they still only earned 61 per cent of the average white family.

In 1968 the Fair Housing Act outlawed discrimination in renting or selling.

The impact of the 1965 Voting Rights Act

The black right to vote was another difficult area in which to make rapid progress. In spite of old constitutional amendments and recent court rulings, the Deep South was still using every available trick to prevent black registration. After the passing of the 1964 Civil Rights Act, the civil rights organisations planned to target voting rights as a separate issue that needed separate legislation. The 1965 Voting Rights Act had real teeth and made a major impact, as the tables below show.

Year	In the south	In the whole country
1965	Under 100	300
1970	500	1,400

Source: Figures are based on Howard Sitkoff, *The Struggle for Black Equality*, p. 229.

Number of black people elected to public office.

Year	Alabama	Georgia	Louisiana	Mississippi
1964	19.3	27.4	31.6	6.7
1968	61.3	60.4	60.8	67.5

Source: Figures are from Manning Marable, *Race, Reform and Rebellion*, p. 82.

Percentage of black adults registered to vote, by state.

The figures, though still lower than white people, represented a rapid change. In 1960, 4 million black people had voted; in 1964, 6 million did so. By 1968 the number of southern black registered voters had more than trebled from 1 million before the Act to 3.1 million. Many southern areas still had no black officials. Moreover, many black people had no involvement in the political process at all, not even voting. Nevertheless, both Acts had reinforced the changing climate of opinion about black participation in public life.

In the 1930s and 1940s, black people had been prominent in sport and music and literature but only very rarely in high political office. Now this was changing. With more black people voting, is it surprising that more would also hold public office? Some examples are:

- Richard Hatcher – Mayor of Gary, Indiana, 1967
- Carl Stokes – Mayor of Cleveland, 1967.

By 1980, Los Angeles, Detroit, Washington and Atlanta had all elected black mayors.

1968: A FATEFUL YEAR

Assassination of Martin Luther King

The year 1968 was a fateful year in the Civil Rights Movement. On 4 April, standing on a balcony of a hotel in Memphis, Tennessee, Martin Luther King was shot and killed. Thus, the town that figured in one of the first pieces of racial violence after the Civil War in 1866 was home to another violent act that was to end a chapter in civil rights campaigning.

Who King's assassin was is still disputed. James Earl Ray, a white racist, was convicted of the crime and spent his remaining years in prison. However, it is not clear whether he fired the fatal shot. Years later a televised reconstruction of the trial, with new evidence, found a representative jury 'acquitting' him. Even if he did commit the murder, were other people or organisations involved? Rumours persisted that the **Federal Bureau of Investigation** (FBI) and its boss, J. Edgar Hoover, might have been involved. Certainly they had King under surveillance for some time.

King and Hoover

Long-standing head of the FBI, Hoover had a particular dislike of Martin Luther King. He attempted to gain incriminating evidence against King in order to damage his career. For instance, from the autumn of 1963 onwards, he ordered the bugging of King's hotel rooms when he stayed away from home, campaigning. He was hoping to gain tapes

Mourners line the route of the funeral procession of Martin Luther King en route to Moorhouse College, Atlanta, Georgia, 11 April 1968.

that would prove that King entertained women friends in his room and that sexual activity had taken place.

Hoover acquired the evidence he wanted and sent some tapes to King's wife Coretta, who stood by her husband. There is no doubt that King was not faithful to his wife, but details of these sexual infidelities never became generally known in his lifetime. The grubby way in which the information had been obtained and his own sexuality seems to have prevented Hoover from making the information openly available. Even in liberal 1960s America, public revelations of this kind would have been very damaging to King. The policy seems to have been to get King's supporters to disown him as a result of the findings: it did not work. Under the threat of an inquiry by Congress, the bugging of King's hotel rooms stopped at the start of 1966.

Why did King visit Memphis?

King's visit to Memphis proved fatal. Why had he gone there? The answer is very revealing. He was supporting the black dustmen who were on strike for equal treatment with white dustmen. King led a protest march, which turned violent. Upset, he vowed to return to lead a better, more peaceful one. It was while preparing for this second effort that he was assassinated. This shows that by 1968:

- King was finding it more difficult to control civil rights demonstrators, as violence was becoming increasingly apparent
- social and economic issues, such as equal pay, were seen as increasingly important, but the problems had not been solved.

However:

- although his leadership was being challenged, many towns still wished to call him in to lead their protest
- King still held fast to non-violence as an absolute principle.

The year 1968 proved to be damaging for the Civil Rights Movement. After the assassination of King there was a whole swathe of rioting in many different parts of the USA. In over 100 cities, King's belief in non-violence was ignored, 46 people died and over 3000 were injured.

Richard Nixon.

The Poor People's Campaign

In the summer of 1968, the Poor People's March was
eventually led by King's deputy and successor as leader of the
SCLC, Ralph Abernathy. It was poorly organised and was
not a success. The camp set up at the foot of Capitol Hill,
within sight of the Capitol Building that housed the US
Congress in Washington, DC. It was called Resurrection
City, but it became a sea of mud when heavy rain descended
through most of June. The sight offended many who had
hitherto been sympathetic to the cause. Conditions were so
bad that many of the protesters left early before the local
police received orders to close it down. So, the Poor People's
Campaign dissolved in some disarray in the summer rains of
Washington. Without King's commanding presence, it
lacked bite and authority. Abernathy did not possess King's
dynamic personality and oratory. Not without abilities of his
own, he unwisely tried to imitate King's style, but without
success.

Further setbacks

There were more setbacks for the movement in 1968. Robert
Kennedy, a good friend to the Civil Rights Movement, was
also assassinated in that year. And President Johnson, borne
down by troubles in Vietnam, decided not to run again for
the White House. The Republican, **Richard Nixon**, replaced
him. Nixon felt that enough had been done on civil rights
and that it was now time to draw a line under the campaigns.
At the end of the 1960s, the atmosphere in the country
changed rapidly. It would be tempting to say that the end of
an era in civil rights had come. However, the changes that
had begun to affect the black community continued through
the 1970s and are still working themselves out today.

ACHIEVEMENTS OF THE MOVEMENT BY 1968

By 1968, black civil rights had progressed a long way in just a
quarter of a century:

- Segregation in public places had disappeared from all but
  the most resistant parts of the Deep South. This was a
  remarkable achievement in so short a space of time.
- Most transport facilities were now thoroughly integrated.
- Far more black people were now registered to vote.

- Racial integration of schools was now proceeding in many states. Where housing patterns discouraged this, the possibility of bussing students from one area to another to achieve a racial mix had just been suggested for the first time.
- Armed forces integration was well established and black people were starting to rise to high rank within them.
- Black people were rising to high office in many different walks of American life.
- The principle of equality was now thoroughly accepted by the great majority of the American public.

However:

- Black voter registration was still lower than white.
- Some parts of Mississippi, Alabama, Georgia and South Carolina maintained segregation in public areas, such as bus terminals.
- Major economic and social problems remained for black people in both the north and the south.
- The Civil Rights Movement itself was weakened and divided over tactics. Its two greatest spokesmen had been assassinated.

SUMMARY QUESTIONS

1 Why was Martin Luther King such a significant civil rights leader?

2 In what area of public life had the Civil Rights Movement made the greatest progress by 1968?

3 What major difficulties faced the Civil Rights Movement at the end of 1968?

AS ASSESSMENT

QUESTIONS IN THE STYLE OF EDEXCEL

Extended answers at this level that do not involve source material will require a piece of continuous writing, for which 30 minutes are allowed. This would mean an answer of approximately 500–600 words.

One of the questions (e.g. questions 1 and 3 below) will involve describing and explaining an important theme within the specification. Your answer must relate to the question and it must not be an unthinking narrative (story telling) of events. Nevertheless, it will need to demonstrate sound knowledge of the subject to illustrate the general points you are making.

The other question (e.g. questions 2 and 4 below) will ask you to explain the reasons for an event or development in the period. It thus involves analysis of the causes and/or consequences of an event or events.

When assessing answers to these questions, examiners will award them one of four levels of achievement (15 marks are available for each question):

- Level 1 will be simple statements and examples, but with little depth and limited organisation.
- Level 2 shows a little more development and a sense of context.
- Level 3 contains a more developed description of the relevant issues, in which candidates 'draw out the implications of the material they are selecting'.
- Level 4 has carefully selected and relevant material with a high level of accuracy and organisation. To reach this level candidates must show they can deal effectively with complex material. How can you achieve this level?

1 Describe the areas in which the Civil Rights Movement could be said to have achieved success by 1968.

Understanding the question. Pinpoint the key words in the question: 'areas' and 'success'.

What areas of civil rights activity should be included in your answer to this question?

Sort out these different categories. They might include:

- end of segregation in public places (e.g. transport facilities and in the armed services)

- equal voting opportunities
- integration of education
- adequate housing for black people
- equal employment opportunities
- the right to legal justice.

To attempt to assess success, you need to consider how far the aims of the movement were achieved. What were these aims? How easily can the success or otherwise of them be measured? Some figures would need to be given in order to show the greater number of black people who:

- had registered to vote and held public office
- were educated in mixed race schools
- were still unemployed at the end of the 1960s.

In addition, you could look at issues such as the attitude of the police and legal authorities towards black people, how far they could use public facilities on an equal basis to white people, and what their housing conditions were like.

How does the answer need to be organised? You might consider whether each area under discussion could form a paragraph in your essay. Could one or two be combined in a paragraph: for example, do employment and housing come under an economic and social section?

Having sorted out topics like these, you now have a framework for answering the question. Plan your answer in paragraphs. You need a short introduction and a conclusion. You also need to think about the degree of success in each area. This might help you to decide in what order to put the points.

Knowledge required. You could start off with areas where there seemed to be a high degree of success by 1968. Supposing you came up with the sentence 'Much of the segregation previously common in the southern states had been broken down by 1968.' This would be a sound assertion with which to start a paragraph. But supposing at this point someone were to say, 'I don't believe you.' What would be the best way to convince them? Some factual illustration of the point would be helpful. Now you are in a position to fill out the paragraph. You have followed the procedure – point followed by proof. Imagine the examiner is always whispering in your ear, 'I don't believe you.'

Now try the procedure above for each part of your answer. For example, if you are writing about voting, make a general assertion about the degree of success in this area and then look for some figures that tell you the proportion of black people that voted in the Deep South (perhaps some figures for one of its states). This might be contrasted with higher proportions from the north, and so you can make a distinction in your answer between north and south when it comes to degree of success. This difference could also be used when discussing education and the chances of a fair trial. This would show that you are dealing with the issues thoughtfully and would gain you extra credit.

If you follow this procedure, it should ensure that you do not just tell a story when faced with this type of question. The highest-grade answers will make judgements about the relative degree of success in different fields. As you write your answer, keep asking yourself two things: 'Am I answering the question?' and 'Am I proving my point?' If you can keep answering 'yes' to these two enquiries, you should be on the right track.

2 Why did the Civil Rights Movement run into difficulties in the mid-1960s?

Understanding the question. A 'Why' question demands an analytical approach – more so than you will have been used to at GCSE. You need to try to give reasons why a development or event occurred. In planning the answer, think of reasons for the difficulties. They might be:

- political (e.g. lack of sympathy from Congress or the President)
- social (e.g. it is hard to solve housing problems quickly)
- economic (e.g. problems in effectively monitoring discrimination in employment)
- personal (e.g. clashes between leaders)
- intellectual (e.g. Black Power challenging the philosophy of Martin Luther King).

How does the answer need to be organised? Approach the answer in the same spirit as question 1 and plan each paragraph carefully so that it focuses on a particular reason. It should begin with a general assertion in the form of a claim or an idea and then go on to illustrate it. In planning your answer, you may be thinking of a list of reasons, but in presentation you need to vary the style of approach. For example, don't write 'firstly' at the start of the first paragraph, then 'secondly' at the start of the next, 'thirdly' at the start of the next, and so on. Also, you need to ensure that you link the sections of the piece together. Linking words that reinforce the previous point are very useful. Here are some examples: 'Moreover . . .', 'In addition to . . .', 'As well as . . .', 'Not only was there progress in this field, but also . . .'.

For example, you could write: 'In addition to the Black Power challenge from Malcolm X, a new group, the Black Panthers, posed a severe challenge to a peaceful Civil Rights Movement.' This:

- provides a link with a previous sentence
- makes a clear and relevant assertion
- makes the reader want to continue reading, to see if you can give evidence to back up your point.

However, you may want to change direction rather than reinforce a point. In this case, a different range of words and phrases becomes appropriate: 'However . . .', 'Nevertheless . . .', 'Despite this . . .'. An example would be: 'However, despite the Supreme Court ruling, some states failed to take the necessary steps to integrate education.' This kind of sentence leads naturally to a specific illustration of the point in the next sentence.

You may simply want neutral linking phrases, such as 'In view of this . . .' and 'As result of that . . .'. An example would be: 'In view of the President's concern with Vietnam, his Great Society programmes ran into difficulties.'

Knowledge required. The exam boards ask for an 'extensive, accurate and precisely selected' range of material. Without a good factual base, you cannot use the range of skills that you have at your command effectively enough. You need to learn the material and there will be a lot more than at GCSE. It is no good leaving it until the last minute and then trying to drum too much into your skull at once. It may be that you have to learn a few statistics with which to illustrate your points. This may not always be the most exciting aspect of historical study for many, but sometimes it is necessary. Answers that lack factual detail cannot get high marks, however well written.

However, knowledge on its own is of limited value if it is not used effectively. Merely to pummel the examiner with facts is also ineffective. The best answers will achieve a good balance of general points and clear illustration. Some students who have revised hard get a little tense before the exam. They enter the exam room, open up the paper and see, for instance, the magic words 'Martin Luther King'. Then, without reading the question properly, they launch into a description of all they know about him. The result is a much lower mark than their efforts deserve. Try not writing for the first minute or so when you look at the exam paper, but think carefully about the nature of the question and work out what kind of answer you are required to produce.

> **3** Describe the extent of segregation of and discrimination against black people in the USA in the late 1940s and 1950s.

Putting your answer together. One important quality you need to show the examiner is your range of knowledge. With this question, one obvious way of doing this is to outline as many different ways as you can by which segregation showed itself. In an exam or in planning an assignment you may want to jot these down in rough in pencil at the top of the page and place a line through them when you have finished. This should ensure you don't forget anything. You can always add to your initial list when you suddenly think of another point whilst in the middle of writing the answer. Always give examples where you can. Possible areas of segregation to cover include:

- education – very few integrated schools, many of the top southern universities were all white

- transport – e.g. buses, trains, waiting room and toilet facilities in the southern states
- public places – e.g. restaurants, swimming pools, cinemas, and other places of leisure and entertainment, especially, though not exclusively, in the south
- churches and burial grounds – particularly but not exclusively in the south
- the workplace in many parts of the USA
- armed forces – though the navy was desegregated in 1946 and the army in 1948, it wasn't until the early fifties that segregation in the military was effectively ended
- housing – especially the ghettos in northern and western cities, as well as in the south.

By now, in working at this list, some other thoughts about how to approach this answer may have occurred to you. The word **extent** is crucial and means that not only do you need to think of different categories of segregation but also the extent to which they applied in different parts of the USA. While there was more segregation in the south, you need to point out that this was not the only area where this occurred. Some judgement is required as to how far other areas were affected.

When dealing with the armed forces, another point emerges. Segregation may not apply across the whole period and the lessening of segregation in this area needs pointing out. Moreover, there were one or two triumphs for desegregation before 1960 such as the buses in Montgomery at the end of 1956 and some schools outside the Deep South after the Brown verdict in 1954. If you are asked about a period of time always consider the possibility that the precise answer to the question could depend on which part of the period you are talking about.

So far we have only discussed segregation, but the question asks about discrimination as well, so balance your answer accordingly. Good candidates can sometimes lose out because their answer lacks balance over the whole question. The issues that might be discussed under discrimination include:

- voting – segregated voting would be pointless as it would not achieve the racist white aim of preventing black people from voting or rendering their votes null and void. Strenuous attempts were made to prevent black people from voting in the southern states
- employment opportunities – northern black people often fared as badly as southern black people despite the spreading during this period of fair employment practices and the more positive attitude to black employment of the federal government
- legal rights concerning arrest and trial – southern white people would not normally be convicted of offences against black people by all-white juries
- violent attacks – including lynching, though these were declining a little in the later 1950s.

By now you may have realised that there is a clear overlap between segregation and discrimination. Point out this overlap and make clear links between your arguments.

4 What were the main reasons for the continued discrimination against black people in the USA in the twenty years after 1945?

There is no doubt that discrimination continued in this period despite the changing mood of some parts of the country, support from the Supreme Court and the efforts of civil rights groups to produce a change. These might include:

- strong resistance of southern states to the implementation of Supreme Court verdicts
- a less committed response to removing discrimination from Presidents Truman and Eisenhower – especially the latter, who showed at Little Rock what he might have achieved if he had taken this kind of firm action more widely
- before 1960 successful campaigns by civil rights groups (the Montgomery bus boycott being the most famous) were limited in range and effect
- the entrenched nature of segregation in southern states and of housing and employment policies towards the black ghettos
- the change in attitude required from white Americans was coming but would inevitably take time to spread through the population
- the nature of the US political system that reserved power over internal affairs to the state governments, many of whom were reluctant to alter their policies.

To consider how to organise this answer look back at the advice given in the second paragraph of question two. Try to organise the points in the best possible order so that your argument flows well. For achievement at the highest level it is vital that you link these various points and show connections between them. You should also back your points up with evidence. For instance it should be possible to go from the southern opposition, to enforcing Supreme Court verdicts, to Eisenhower's relative lack of response. The start of the paragraph on Eisenhower could be phrased to make the vital connection. For example:

'This southern resistance could succeed partly because of Presidential reluctance to give the Supreme Court verdicts the necessary teeth.'

Clear links could also be made between the final three bullet points. One of the principal reasons for the limited effect of the efforts of civil rights groups (make sure you name them) was the kind of system that they faced. It might be possible to get a few more black voters on the rolls in the south but it would take time to change attitudes. Moreover, while a change in the area of voting – if it could be achieved – would come quickly and cheaply, the same could not be said of many economic and social changes. Getting all black people into decent housing is an aim that has still not been achieved in today's USA let alone in the 1950s.

QUESTIONS IN THE STYLE OF OCR

In the examination, questions on this paper come in two parts. The first is worth 30 marks and the second, 60 marks. These questions clearly ask for detailed and thoughtful answers. The examiner will be interested in the ability the candidate demonstrates to:

- consider the implications of the question
- identify the important elements of the answer
- recognise the potential complexities of the answer
- draw conclusions in response to the question and construct an argument
- select and deploy relevant information to support the argument.

With this in mind, look at the following question and consider how it might be answered.

1a Explain the aims of Reconstruction.

Understanding the question. Look carefully at the wording of the question. The key words here are 'explain' and 'aims'.

Health warning! To gain the highest marks, it is vital that you do not drift into giving a blow-by-blow account of Reconstruction. If you do this, you will be describing rather than explaining. You will not have clearly identified the aims and they will become lost in the detail of your description. You will get a mark, but it will be in the middle or lower band depending on the amount of detail you have included in your description.

Having avoided the pitfalls, the next stage in your thinking is to analyse what you have learnt about this period. In other words, you are asking yourself: 'What did the post-Civil War politicians actually want to achieve?' This is fundamentally different from asking yourself: 'What did they do?' An answer that is built around this kind of analysis will lead you into a higher mark band, provided that your identification of aims is supported by detailed explanation of them.

Once you have started on this train of thought, you might also begin to appreciate that not all of the individuals or groups involved had the same aims! Inevitably, considering these aims will also lead you into issues of motivation. What you are then on the way to doing is creating a more complex answer to the question, which will show the examiner that you have really appreciated and understood the problems of Reconstruction. Consequently, it will take you into the higher mark band.

Putting your answer together. Your response should:

- begin with a very brief introduction suggesting why Reconstruction was necessary (this might be just two or three sentences)
- consider those aims that were common to all parties involved (e.g. the need to restore the Union and ensure loyalty was common to all northern politicians, at least)
- move on to identify where different individuals or groups diverged in their aims (e.g. the aims of Johnson and his approach to the treatment of ex-Confederates; those of radical Republicans who wanted the south punished for secession and who were committed to securing the vote for freedmen; and those of moderate Republicans who were anxious to limit the rights given to former slaves).

1b Compare the importance of at least three reasons why Reconstruction did not produce a permanent improvement in the lives of southern black people.

Understanding the question. This is a more complex question and requires a more detailed analysis and answer than question 1a. The key aspects of the question are as follows:

- The identification of 'at least three reasons'. This suggests that you can consider more than three if you wish, but not fewer.
- The inclusion of the word 'permanent'. Reconstruction provided some gains (e.g. the vote in several states), but these were short-lived. You need to consider why these gains were not sustained.
- The instruction to 'compare the importance' of the different reasons. This is asking you to consider whether some of these reasons were more important than others and also to establish the links and connections between them.

Putting your answer together. The first stage is to identify the reasons for the failure of Reconstruction as far as southern black people were concerned. These might include:

- the lack of presidential commitment to equality for African-Americans (e.g. Johnson's views)
- the opportunity for some states to avoid the implementation of the Fourteenth and Fifteenth Amendments to the Constitution (e.g. the 'Black Codes')
- the actions of the Supreme Court in upholding states' rights over those of the federal government
- the failure to reform landholding and the subsequent development of sharecropping and the crop lien system
- the unchecked violence and intimidation meted out by anti-rights groups such as the Ku Klux Klan.

The next stage is to recognise the links and connections between these points in order to make decisions about their relative importance. For example:

- Sharecropping and poverty contributed to ensuring that blacks did not have the necessary income when it came to satisfying the property and literacy qualifications imposed by some state authorities to block the black vote.
- The fact that some states were able to challenge the federal government and assert their rights within the Constitution with the support of the Supreme Court meant that they could effectively ignore the terms of the Fourteenth and Fifteenth Amendments.
- The violent intimidation of African-Americans by anti-rights groups made many blacks reluctant to assert their rights.

Before you begin to answer the question, you must decide which of these factors are more important than the others. Then set out your answer, explaining your ideas in as much detail as possible in the time you have available. Make sure that you not only indicate why one or more factors might be more important than the others, but also explain why the others are of less significance. You might, of course, wish to challenge, albeit briefly, the assumption of the question. In many respects, Reconstruction did permanently improve the life of many freedmen, particularly those who could take advantage of the opportunity for education, even though it failed to guarantee them their civil rights.

A2 SECTION: CIVIL RIGHTS IN THE USA,1863–1980

INTRODUCTION

In this part of the book, we take up some of the key issues covered in the first section and examine them in greater depth, incorporating, where appropriate, the views and interpretations of historians of the subject. It is important, as you read this part of the book, to consider critically the interpretations of the authors and, from your own reading, research and reflection, arrive at your own views, supported by the evidence.

Section 1: The politics of freedom and equality explores the political implications of the extension of civil rights to all US citizens irrespective of race, religion and culture.

Section 2: The struggle for black civil rights, 1865–1968 examines in greater depth the extent of discrimination, segregation and violence endured by African-Americans in the north as well as the south.

Section 3: The rights of labour introduces new issues, not covered in the AS part of the book (specifically aimed at meeting the requirements of the OCR syllabus). It examines the significance of the labour movement to the evolution of black consciousness and organisation.

Section 4: The growing militancy of the Civil Rights Movement, 1950–80 examines the crucial period of the late 1960s in some depth, looking at the increase in violent revolt and the appeal of Black Power, and assessing the impact of these years on the course of events during the 1970s.

Section 5: America – the 'melting pot' investigates the obstacles to the evolution of a cohesive, multicultural society and, in the process, exposes the myth of the 'melting pot'.

SECTION 1

The politics of freedom and equality

DID THE US CONSTITUTION GUARANTEE THE RIGHTS AND FREEDOM OF ALL THE AMERICAN PEOPLE?

The struggle against racism.

In the preface to his book *A History of the American People* (1997), Paul Johnson is critical of the hyphenated terminology that is used to describe the different ethnic groups in the USA today. He sees only one race of people, whom he admires. It could be argued however, that this view is a luxury that only those looking at American society from the outside can reasonably hold. The relentless struggle against racism, both non-violent and violent, as well as the battle to overcome discrimination and prejudice have been described in the AS section of this book. The struggle has dominated domestic life in the USA, certainly since 1865. Moreover, the deeply entrenched intolerance of non-white people stands in stark contrast to the intention set out in the preamble to the Constitution of the United States.

The preamble to the Constitution of the United States: We the people of the United States, in order to form a more perfect union, establish justice, insure domestic tranquility, provide for the common defense, promote welfare, and secure the blessings of liberty to ourselves and our posterity . . .

The Constitution of the United States, together with the Bill of Rights, was undoubtedly intended to uphold the civil rights of all US citizens. This was done not only by defining these rights, but also by putting in place a series of checks and balances that would set limits to the exercise of power, avoid centralisation, safeguard democracy and protect the freedom of the individual. The result was a federal system of government. However, there can be little doubt that, when the USA was established, the 'individuals' who were entitled to protection and equal rights were white. In fact, the answer to the question posed above lies largely in the contemporary interpretation of the 'American people'.

Unequal rights. African-Americans – the vast majority of whom, in 1787, were still slaves and the property of their masters – were considered beyond the pale of politics, as were Native Americans and, indeed, all women. While white women were recognised as citizens, their right to vote was not granted until 1920. By the beginning of the nineteenth century, even free black people in the north, who had been briefly given their civil rights, including the right to vote, under the new Constitution, had lost them. White Americans clearly had no intention, even then, of recognising free black people as equal citizens.

There were divisions and contradictions among politicians in their thinking about the position of slaves. In the south, they were regarded as property, on the one hand, and their owners expected the protection that the Constitution offered. On the other hand, three-fifths of them were counted as men for the purposes of determining **proportional representation** of the states in Congress! For abolitionists and many Republicans in the north, it was repugnant to think of human beings as property, although those who supported the principle of equal citizenship were far fewer.

Indeed, the federal government ruled, in the late 1790s, that equal rights would not be extended to people of all races and that only white immigrants were eligible for **naturalisation**. They would be given voting rights after five years. At this stage, of course, the challenge that massive immigration was to present to the ideals that underpinned the Constitution still lay in the future. However, even before the War of Independence, there were overt signs of racism and prejudice not only towards African-Americans, but also towards those of immigrant stock, and these signs would manifest themselves further in the late nineteenth and early twentieth centuries.

The Bill of Rights. For those who qualified for its protection, the Bill of Rights was double edged. While on the one hand safeguarding the rights of individuals to freedom of speech, equality before the law and protection from government intrusion, on the other it left the poor destitute. Federal or state intervention to support the elderly and unemployed was perceived as a violation of the terms of the Bill of Rights, which upheld the right of all individuals to be responsible for themselves.

In the late nineteenth century, as the USA industrialised, the Bill of Rights provided at least some of the justification for the laissez-faire policy that condoned the exploitation of labour and allowed employers to outlaw trade unions and to respond repressively to industrial protests and disputes (see Section 4). Even in the 1930s it was still being invoked to oppose welfare benefits for the needy.

Federal versus state government. The Constitution also established the federal system of government and defined the power and responsibility of the federal and state governments. By this means, the rights of US citizens to be represented fairly, by men (initially) of their choice, were protected, at least theoretically. This placed the responsibility for virtually every aspect of daily life in the hands of the state authorities. It is probably true to say that, for most of the first half of the nineteenth century, power rested predominantly with state governments. They were even allowed to assemble their own militia. In any matter where the

KEY TERMS

Proportional representation
Seats in Congress were allocated on the basis of the number of male adults in the population of each state. In some southern states, therefore, where the African-Americans formed a significantly high proportion of the population, they had to be included if the state was to be well represented. In these instances, they were recognised as citizens of the community for convenience, even though they actually had no civil rights.

Naturalisation By the Naturalisation Act of 1800, white immigrants to the USA became US citizens after they had remained in the USA for five years. This gave them rights of citizenship, including the right to vote.

federal government chose to take the lead, legislation had to be ratified by a majority of the states before it passed into the law of the land. States could, and did, refuse to ratify federal legislative proposals.

The extent of the fragility of the relationship between the states, especially in the south, and the federal government, was clearly demonstrated in the secession of the south and the subsequent Civil War in 1861 (see Chapter 2). However, the emancipation of the slaves in 1863 and, more particularly, the issue of the extension of civil rights that ensued, presented the first really significant challenge to the Constitution and everything that it had come to represent by the second half of the nineteenth century. In many respects, the freedmen became pawns in a political power struggle in which they initially featured almost by accident, having gained their freedom as an expedient of the war. It was, however, a power struggle that put to the test the Constitution and the system of government that it had created, and one that ultimately gave birth to the Civil Rights Movement.

RECONSTRUCTION, CONSTITUTIONAL CONFLICT AND THE RIGHTS OF CITIZENSHIP

Reconstruction and civil rights. The period of Reconstruction (1865–77) that followed the end of the Civil War and also of slavery, represents a significant turning point in the history of the Civil Rights Movement. As such, it deserves particular attention. This was the result not simply of emancipation but, more importantly, of the ensuing struggle to gain full rights of citizenship for freedmen. Some see, in this period, the origins of civil rights and describe the campaign as the first Civil Rights Movement. In this respect, Reconstruction was to produce three significant pieces of legislation that were to influence the extension of civil rights in the longer term, not only to African-Americans, but also to other deprived groups. These were:

- the Civil Rights Act (1866)
- the Fourteenth Amendment to the Constitution (1868)
- the Fifteenth Amendment to the Constitution (1870).

It was the attempted ratification and implementation of this legislation, however, that brought the federal government into conflict with the states. Southern politicians claimed that the degree of centralisation that this legislation represented was an infringement not only of the authority of the state conventions, but also of the rights of the people whom they represented. Moreover, it threatened to frustrate the fundamental principles on which the Constitution was based. This was a view that gained support in the north from some moderate Republicans and certainly from Democrats and their supporters. On the other hand, there

Benjamin Franklin, for example, spoke out in 1775 against German immigrants settling in Pennsylvania:

Why should the Palatine boor be suffered to swarm into our settlements and, by herding together, establish their language and manners to the exclusion of ours? Why should Pennsylvania, founded by the English, become a colony of aliens, who will shortly be so numerous as to Germanise us, instead of us Anglicising them?

was a perceived need to re-establish the position and authority of Congress, following the defiance and secession of the Confederate south. Most unexpected, but nevertheless significant during this period, was the growth in political awareness and assertiveness of African-Americans.

Interpretations of Reconstruction. The complex background to this struggle has been described in Chapter 2. The rights of freedmen were inevitably caught up in the effort to re-establish the Union and punish the rebels in the south who had set up or supported the Confederacy. American historians have disagreed in their interpretations of this period of US history. Historians writing at the beginning of the twentieth century portrayed the defeated south as submissive and Presidents Lincoln and Johnson as the standard-bearers of reconciliation. Their efforts, it was claimed, were undermined by the radical Republicans, who harboured hatred towards the south and who, consequently, exploited the issue of black civil rights to punish the former Confederates and to keep themselves in power. This interpretation was upheld throughout much of the first half of the twentieth century. At the same time, black writers, such as W. E. B. Du Bois, interpreted Reconstruction as a brave effort to establish a truly democratic political order, but one that was perverted by the attitudes of white Americans to former slaves: 'One fact and one alone explains the attitude of most recent writers towards Reconstruction: they cannot conceive of Negroes as men.'

This view was not ill founded, even though it was largely ignored. It is clear that Lincoln himself had no clear policy for freed slaves after the Civil War. There are even suggestions that he hoped many would return to Africa! Certainly, with the exception of Radical Republicans who supported African-American advancement to equal citizenship, there was no vision of an interracial society based on equality.

It was only with the emergence of the modern Civil Rights Movement in the 1960s that revisionist historians recognised the remarkable features of this period. While it is true that the enfranchisement of black people was a political ploy to maintain Republican power in the south, to weaken the influence of the planter class and prevent the Democrats from re-establishing their southern power base, it nevertheless provided African-Americans with the opportunity to be involved in politics, albeit briefly, and to play a decisive role in some state conventions. This was an opportunity that, perhaps unexpectedly, many grasped enthusiastically. In this respect, it is seen as a time of remarkable progress. Eric Foner, in his *Short History of Reconstruction* (1990), certainly takes this view:

> Rather than passive victims of the actions of others or simply a 'problem' confronting white society, blacks were active agents in the making of Reconstruction whose quest for individual and community autonomy did much to establish the era's political and economic agenda . . . blacks seized the

opportunity created by the end of slavery to establish as much independence as possible in their working lives, consolidate their families and communities and stake a claim to equal citizenship.

WHY DID THE ADVANCEMENT OF CIVIL RIGHTS PRODUCE CONFLICT BETWEEN THE FEDERAL GOVERNMENT AND THE STATES BEFORE 1877?

The push for freedmen to receive full rights of citizenship came from the Radical Republicans. This cannot entirely be dismissed as exploitation and self-interest. Within their ranks, in the persons of dedicated white and black abolitionists such as Thaddeus Stevens, Frederick Douglass and numerous others, were those who genuinely believed that the extension of civil rights to such a significant proportion of the population would greatly strengthen the 'new' nation that was emerging from the destruction caused by civil conflict.

Certainly, freedmen benefited in the short term by the desire of the Republican-dominated Congress to punish Confederates while, at the same time, re-establishing national unity. In the process, however, one key issue became the exertion of the will of Congress over those rights and responsibilities of the states embodied in the Constitution. Another was the question of who should be responsible for the protection of individual rights promised by the Constitution when state authorities failed to take action.

Reconstruction Act (1867). The weapon that was initially used – disenfranchisement – was itself contentious where the protection of rights was concerned. Hundreds of white voters in the south lost the right to vote because they were either Confederates or their supporters. This left the way open for African-Americans not only to vote, but also to gain seats in the state conventions that assembled between 1865 and 1866. The black vote was confirmed in the Reconstruction Act of 1867, and black representatives soon formed the majority in southern state conventions such as South Carolina. The southern state conventions of 1867 and 1868 drew up new, progressive state constitutions that attempted to remove barriers to voting or holding office, such as property qualifications. The extension of the vote to all male residents, with the exception of former Confederates, benefited poorer white people as well as freedmen. Some states attempted to remove the restrictions on owning or inheriting property that specifically discriminated against African-Americans.

On the whole, these measures were more successful where there were large numbers of black representatives and less so where white representatives remained the dominant group, for example in Louisiana,

Alabama and Texas. Here, the state authorities introduced the 'Black Codes' that, while paying lip service to some civil liberties, rejected black suffrage, limited the rights of freedmen before the law and tolerated other forms of discrimination (see Chapter 2). Clearly, more decisive action was needed.

Freedmen's Bureau. Meanwhile, radical Republicans in Congress continued to push for the extension of civil rights for freedmen in spite of the fact that the President, Andrew Johnson, was moving towards a more conciliatory policy in his dealings with the south. To some extent, the legislation proposed by Congress was a reaction to this. First, in 1866, Lyman Turnbull, chairman of the Judiciary Committee, introduced a bill to extend the powers of the Freedmen's Bureau, set up in 1865, to support freed slaves in the transition period (see Chapter 2). Turnbull's bill aimed to expand the power of the Bureau's officers to enable them to act against state officials who withheld from freedmen those civil rights enjoyed by white Americans. It was, however, only intended as a temporary measure until the principle of equality had become established practice. This did not allay the concerns of those in Congress who believed that it was a misuse of federal resources.

1866 Civil Rights Act. The second measure proposed by Congress was the Civil Rights Bill. This was a landmark in the history of the Civil Rights Movement, in that it was the first attempt to define national citizenship in law. It defined all persons born in the USA, with the exception of

A racist poster from 1866 encouraging people to oppose Congress legislation to extend the powers of the Freedmen's Bureau.

Native Americans, as citizens. Its purpose was also to define the rights of citizens but, although it guaranteed equal rights in terms of justice without prejudice, the more contentious issue of the vote was omitted. The bill was a landmark, not only because it applied to the north as well as the south, but also because it changed the relationship between the states and the federal government. While responsibility for its enforcement would remain with the state, the federal courts would be empowered to intervene in the case of any state failing to enforce its terms. In this respect, also, it was controversial.

Johnson vetoed both the Freedmen's Bill and the Civil Rights Bill, claiming that they contravened the principles laid down in the Constitution and protected by the Bill of Rights. This represented a misuse of federal power, he argued, and threatened the rights of other citizens: 'the distinction of race and color is by the bill made to operate in favour of the colored and against the white race'. Congress, now in open conflict with the President, overrode the veto and the Civil Rights Bill became law.

The Fourteenth Amendment (1868). Enforcement of the 1866 Civil Rights Act remained a problem, as states continued to uphold their right to determine their own affairs. The only way to offset claims that the Act was unconstitutional was to secure an amendment to the Constitution. Consequently, the Fourteenth and Fifteenth Amendments were the most important ever to be added to the Constitution. The Fourteenth Amendment sought to uphold equality before the law and threatened to reduce the representation in Congress of those states that continued to discriminate. To its pro-reform critics, this was a serious weakness, since it offered those states for whom the concept of black equality was repugnant an opportunity to flaunt the law. If they were prepared to accept reduced representation, they could continue to discriminate. The amendment did nothing to address the issue of the franchise. This was addressed in the Fifteenth Amendment, two years later.

The Fifteenth Amendment (1870). Once again, this led to conflict and dissatisfaction. Its terms were, in fact, a balancing act to advance the cause of black enfranchisement in the south, without alienating the Republican support of states in the north and west. Many of these states already had their own voting qualifications that were deliberately discriminatory against certain groups. Western states, such as California, excluded the Chinese from voting. Rhode Island demanded that foreign-born immigrants should own property to the value of $134 in order to qualify for the vote. In others, voters had to be state taxpayers or pass literacy tests.

It was largely in order to placate the northern states that the Fifteenth Amendment allowed states to impose their own voting qualifications, while at the same time accepting the over-arching principle of the amendment. In the south, particularly, there was a wholesale imposition of voting qualifications in many states to exclude African-Americans from voting. Such qualifications inevitably deprived other groups of their rights, particularly poor white people who suffered as a result not only of low wages, but also of poor standards of literacy. By the end of the century, however, these were increasingly people of immigrant stock.

Feminist reaction. Women were enraged by this amendment, which promised, in principle at least, to extend the right to vote to all men irrespective of wealth or education, while at the same time continuing to exclude wealthy and highly educated women. Feminist activists who had strongly supported the cause of abolition now established their own organisation to galvanise the energy of women to demand the vote. Elizabeth Cady Stanton and Susan B. Anthony formed the National Woman's Suffrage Association to campaign for female suffrage, and abandoned the Equal Rights Association that had jointly campaigned for black and female suffrage.

Imperfect though they may have been at the time, the existence of the Fourteenth and Fifteenth Amendments were to form the necessary basis for future civil rights legislation. Indeed, even in 1870, many campaigners of the Abolition Movement hailed the Fifteenth Amendment as the climax of their campaign and began to disband. However, the immediate political impact of the amendments was to exacerbate the existing tensions between central and state government as well as to increase concerns within Congress that the Republicans were moving closer towards centralisation of government at the expense of the states.

Enforcement Acts of 1870 and 1871. Their fears were intensified by the Enforcement Acts, which came in the wake of the terror campaigns of racist organisations such as the Ku Klux Klan and the failure of some state authorities to punish the perpetrators of brutality, torture and murder. The 1866 Civil Rights Act had placed the responsibility for protecting threatened minorities in the hands of the state authorities. The activities of the Klan made it clear that some were not only failing in this duty, but actively condoning the violence and persecution. The Enforcement Acts encompassed a range of discriminatory actions and brought these under federal law. For infringement of others, federal attorneys could prosecute states if they did not take action and, in extreme cases, threaten them with the imposition of martial law.

The Acts sparked further constitutional conflict. On the one hand, a Republican argued that 'If the Federal Government cannot pass laws to protect the rights, liberty, and lives of citizens of the United States, why were guarantees of those fundamental rights put into the Constitution at

Some of the campaigning for female suffrage was overtly racist. Stanton herself wrote:

Think of Patrick and Sambo and Hans and Ung Tung who do not know the difference between a Monarchy and a Republic, who never read the Declaration of Independence . . . making laws for Lydia Maria Child, Lucretia Mott, or Fanny Kemble.

all?' On the other hand, opponents of the Acts in the south and the Democrats in Congress denounced them as 'Force' Acts and saw their existence as a threat to individual liberty. In spite of this, federal resources were put behind the campaign to use the new laws to terminate the activities of the Klan and bring the perpetrators to justice. In fact, few were tried, but the reign of the Klan in the south came to an end and more freedmen were able to access their rights unmolested and without intimidation.

1875 Civil Rights Act. By the mid-1870s, the Republicans were losing support, especially in the south, where the Democrats were beginning to regain lost ground. Certainly, the party's racial policy was a key feature of this demise. In particular, its tendencies to challenge the authority of the state were a factor. Many northern states did not want to admit the rights of minority groups either, so discrimination continued across the USA. The second Civil Rights Bill, introduced in 1875, was intended to end discrimination and segregation but, by the time it was introduced, the Republicans were already in irrevocable danger. Their weakened position is reflected partially in the removal of the clause relating to mixed schooling in order to ensure the passage of the bill into law. Although the 1875 Civil Rights Act was passed, the impetus for implementing its provisions rested with the persecuted themselves, who had to take responsibility for lodging complaints under the terms of the law. Few were brave enough to do this.

The Supreme Court supports states' rights to discriminate. With the demise of Republican support for Reconstruction by 1877, it was left to the Supreme Court to rule on the constitutional disputes that surrounded the legislation enacted by Congress during the period.

* The Slaughterhouse decision (1873) arose from a case that put to the test the assertion that the Fourteenth Amendment protected all US citizens. A group of butchers from New Orleans took a case to federal court complaining that they had been deprived of their livelihood as a result of the state authorities in Louisiana establishing a monopoly. They claimed that this was an infringement of their rights as safeguarded by the Amendment. In reaching their judgment, the judges discriminated between rights conferred by the federal government and those that derived from state citizenship, asserting finally that the rights of citizens remained under state control. The decision effectively removed the protection that the Fourteenth Amendment seemed to offer to African-Americans in particular.
* *US* v. *Cruikshank* (1876) undermined the effectiveness of the Enforcement Acts in protecting individuals from acts of violence. It related to a racist atrocity known as the Colfax Massacre that took place in Louisiana in 1873 following a disputed election. The fighting

left seventy African-Americans and two white people dead. Under the terms of the Enforcement Act (1870), federal officials arrested over a hundred white men, but they were freed when the Supreme Court ruled that this Enforcement Act was unconstitutional. The Court claimed that the Act empowered federal officers to take action only against states and not against individuals.

- In *US* v. *Reece* (1876), the Court recognised the right of states to exclude people from voting, irrespective of race, by the imposition of voting qualifications. In the years that followed, at least twelve states took the opportunity to exclude people from voting on the basis of literacy tests or payment of poll taxes.
- In 1883, the 1875 Civil Rights Act, which attempted to remove discrimination, was declared to be invalid.

These Supreme Court decisions effectively marked the triumph of state authority over that of the federal government, when it came to dealing with its own citizens. This gave predominantly white state governments *carte blanche* to pass discriminatory legislation that would control their former slaves or any other group that they wished to marginalise. Paul Johnson's summary of the situation in *A History of the American People* (1997) is cynical but apt:

> Thus the great Civil War, the central event of American history, having removed the evil of slavery, gave birth to a new South in which whites were first class citizens and blacks citizens in name only. And a great silence descended for many decades. America as a whole did not care . . .

Weakening of the cause. It is true that black civil rights became a politically contentious. The cause was severely weakened, if not obliterated as a political crusade, by racist attitudes in both the north and the south. No presidential candidate was likely to win an election campaigning on a civil rights ticket. The outcry that followed Theodore Roosevelt's casual invitation to Booker T. Washington to sit down to tea with him in the White House (1901) clearly indicated the prevailing racial climate.

Moreover, while voting qualifications discriminated against a large number of African-Americans, there was nothing to be gained politically by party factions supporting civil rights, although white support for civil rights continued among some members of Congress. Instead, presidents such as Theodore Roosevelt (1901–9) and Franklin D. Roosevelt (1932–45) paid lip service to the cause by appointing black advisers. Others, such as Woodrow Wilson (1913–21), himself hailing from the south, were clearly influenced by racist attitudes.

HOW HAD BLACK POLITICAL AWARENESS GROWN DURING THE RECONSTRUCTION PERIOD?

Growth of political involvement. The Compromise of 1877 (see Chapter 2), the decisions of the Supreme Court and the ascendancy of the Democrats in the south left freedmen there virtually unprotected. The gains they had made quickly disappeared. The result was the first of several large-scale migrations to the cities of the north that would take place by the end of the nineteenth century. In spite of this, the period of Reconstruction was a remarkable one for many African-Americans in the south, particularly for those living in urban areas. Some took the opportunity to gain an education, and a sense of community and self-reliance emerged. Particularly significant was the political awareness that developed, which expressed itself through mass meetings and the petitions drawn up to press for equality before the law and the right to vote.

An article in the *Charleston Daily News* reported:

Beyond all question, the best men in the convention are the colored members. Considering the influences under which they were called together, and their imperfect acquaintance with parliamentary law, they have displayed, for the most part, remarkable moderation and dignity . . . They have assembled . . . to legislate for the welfare of the race to which they belong.

In fact, involvement was patchy. In some rural areas especially, blacks were threatened and intimidated at election times and were often too afraid to vote. Where it existed, the political activity of freedmen was marked by moderation. They may have begun by being ignorant of politics and political processes, but they were more than willing to learn. This was particularly the case among those who became representatives in state conventions. Many came to be recognised for their intellectual abilities. They impressed people by their dignity and demeanour.

National Association for the Advancement of Colored People (NAACP). In the years following the end of Reconstruction, the political initiative passed largely to black people themselves to keep alive the campaign for civil rights. Handicapped by discrimination, violence and overt racism, this was not easy. In this respect, the formation of the National Association for the Advancement of Colored People by Oswald Garrison Villard (see page 68) in 1909 was significant, in conjunction with Du Bois' Niagara Movement (see Chapter 3). NAACP was well supported by white social and political reformers as well as by middle-class African-Americans in the cities. Through the pages of its newspaper, *The Crisis*, edited by W.E.B. Du Bois, the organisation drew attention to the evils of segregation and lynching, and campaigned for their removal.

NAACP was pledged to the enforcement of the terms of the Fourteenth and Fifteenth Amendments and to the achievement of voting rights and equal educational opportunities for African-Americans. It opposed discrimination in housing and won a number of important decisions from the Supreme Court on specific cases relating to discrimination. One of its most significant early successes was the Supreme Court decision of 1915, declaring the 'grandfather' clauses enforced in Maryland and Oklahoma to be unconstitutional. In 1917, residential segregation clauses in a Louisville by-law were declared to be invalid.

National Urban League. The cause of urban black people, whose numbers were increasing rapidly in the early decades of the twentieth century, was also represented by the National Urban League, founded in 1911 by African-Americans sympathetic to the ideas of Booker T. Washington. The League was especially concerned with social and economic injustices. Black organisations such as the National Urban League and particularly the NAACP were to assume an important role in the quest for political action to secure civil rights after the 1930s.

Indifference of successive presidents. The lack of political will to enforce the Fourteenth and Fifteenth Amendments was a significant factor in the persistence of *de jure* segregation in the south and *de facto* discrimination in the north (see page 102). Political careers were not built on such issues, even though white American reformers were in the front line of movements such as the NAACP and the National Urban League. Equal rights were not a vote-winning platform in a fundamentally racist white society. While some may have accepted 'separate but equal', the concept of assimilation was alien to significant sections of the electorate. Moreover, the potential power that the vote conferred on African-Americans, evident in areas with large black populations, appeared threatening. Although there was some support for civil rights on the radical wing of the Republican Party, as early as 1877 there had been clear moves towards the maintenance of the social and political status quo among the main body of the party, and this did not really change significantly.

Among key presidents of the pre-Second World War period, there was confusion, tacit but inactive recognition of the 'problem', overt racism or restrained reform.

Lincoln. It is clear that, following his tactical Emancipation Proclamation of 1863, Abraham Lincoln, apparent champion of freedom and equality, had no clear policy for the future of freedmen and almost certainly had not envisaged full political, social and economic assimilation (see Chapter 2). The passage of the Fourteenth and Fifteenth Amendments took place in a climate of conflict between Congress and his successor, Andrew Jackson, so their significance must be considered in the whole context of Reconstruction politics rather than of civil rights *per se*. Important though they were, the Amendments do not represent a total political commitment to civil rights. By 1877, threatened by the resurgence of Democratic support in the south and assertions in the north that freedom for black people had gone too far, all but the radical wing of the Republican Party had retrenched on the issue. Political expediency remained decisive.

Theodore Roosevelt. Clearly, the racial hostility that manifested itself in incidences of lynching and violent disruption was a fairly regular reminder of the depth and extent of the problem. Such incidences seemed only to harden the resolve of those who might have had the power to respond. Even so, the campaigns of the NAACP, Supreme Court rulings on discrimination and the emergence of a highly educated, articulate black elite in the late nineteenth century and early decades of the twentieth could not be easily ignored. Yet even a more reforming President such as Theodore Roosevelt paid only lip service to the fact that the situation of the African-American population was an issue that had to be addressed. His consultations with Booker T. Washington were a fairly empty gesture, producing no significant action other than the employment of black people in some government and civil service departments. Minor advances such as this could, however, be easily reversed.

Wilson and Hoover. Woodrow Wilson's overt racism was evident in his orders to segregate white and black civil service workers, in his praise for the 'work' of the Ku Klux Klan during the Reconstruction period and in his removal of African-Americans from government posts. Similar racist tendencies were evident during the presidency of Herbert Hoover, who wanted to purge the Republican Party of blacks in order to capture the votes of southern Democrats. His hostility was evident, for example, in his nomination of Judge John J. Parker to the Supreme Court in 1930. Parker had supported the disenfranchisement of blacks in North Carolina in 1920. That his election was prevented by pressure from the NAACP is, however, an interesting indication of the powerful influence that the latter could exert by this time.

The **National Council of Negro Women** and the National Association of Colored Women were founded in the early 1920s to campaign against lynching and against discrimination in employment. They are examples of the ways in which black women became organised to support the cause of civil rights.

Franklin D. Roosevelt. It was on the Democratic President, Franklin D. Roosevelt, that African-Americans pinned their hopes. During his first two terms of office, he consistently won the support of enfranchised black people in the north. Certainly, his appointment of the 'Black Cabinet' was an unprecedented innovation. It provided the opportunity for the nation to appreciate the intelligence and expertise of educated African-Americans. Particularly noteworthy was the appointment of Mary McLeod Bethune, a close friend of the First Lady, Eleanor Roosevelt, and president of the **National Council of Negro Women**. As Director of Negro Affairs of the National Youth Administration, she held a key position and was the highest-ranking black appointee in the Roosevelt administration.

It would be a mistake, however, to assume that Roosevelt was entirely sympathetic to the cause of black civil rights. Indeed, it could be argued that he did as much as was safely expedient to retain the black vote in the north, and no more. Reference has already been made to his refusal to support anti-lynching legislation. It is also clear that he was heavily committed to retaining the votes of southern white people. This is evident in his refusal to support a law to eliminate the poll tax. Such a law would have removed the obstacle to enfranchisement for a large number of African-Americans in the southern states.

Other aspects of his New Deal programme discriminated against blacks:

- Support for farmers under the Agricultural Adjustment Authority (AAA) deprived African-Americans of their land.
- The Civilian Conservation Corps (CCC), Roosevelt's own particular project, was racially segregated.
- The Federal Housing Administration (FHA) refused to guarantee mortgages on houses that were bought by black people in predominantly white neighbourhoods.
- Social security benefits and minimum wage guarantees promised by the Fair Labor Standards Act (1938) did not apply to those categories of unskilled occupations in which large numbers of African-Americans worked.

Only when Randolph organised the March on Washington Movement (see page 100) to demand equal access to jobs for African-Americans in defence industries did Roosevelt respond quickly with positive action. But then, the year was 1941 and war loomed.

WHAT DID AMERICAN GOVERNMENTS DO FOR CIVIL RIGHTS FROM THE SECOND WORLD WAR UNTIL 1961?

The American system of government. Because of the separation of powers in the US Constitution, the Civil Rights Movement needed three developments if it was to succeed: a Supreme Court prepared to rule in its favour, a sympathetic President and a Congress with a pro-civil rights majority. As we saw in Chapter 6, the Supreme Court began to change its outlook during the 1940s and was consistently supportive from 1954 onwards: the attitudes of the President and Congress, however, were less consistently positive. Even with the Supreme Court's decisions, southern courts and law enforcement officers could not always be relied upon to fulfil their legal obligations.

Roosevelt's approach. Franklin D. Roosevelt's response after his initial concession to Randolph in 1941 was not particularly positive. Wynn (1993) argues that Roosevelt was fighting off those who were less liberal, who wanted to prosecute black people for sedition in 1942. But the President's mildly friendly, if rather patronising attitude does not seem to have greatly changed. He suffered the difficulty of all Democratic presidents before Jimmy Carter: they needed to retain southern segregationist support. He needed little persuading that radical leaders had encouraged the troubles in places like Detroit and should not be listened to.

The period of Roosevelt's presidency did see the number of black federal government employees nearly quadruple from the 50,000 at the start of 1933; the government certainly provided employment for black people on a basis of equality of opportunity. However, the take-up of fair employment practices by individual states was slow. It was hardly encouraged by the fact that, in 1942, the Fair Employment Practices Commission lost its independent status when it was placed under the War Manpower Commission.

Truman's presidency. In 1946, Truman created a Higher Education Commission that sharply criticised segregation in this area. The President's Committee on Civil Rights (see page 112) had produced a report entitled *To Secure These Rights*, which called for a number of measures to end segregation. At this stage, it was congressional opposition to change that prevented progress on the civil rights front. Truman had hoped that Congress would pass a federal anti-lynching law and the abolition of the poll tax, which often prevented poor southern black people from voting. That they refused to do so showed up the President's impotence in domestic affairs when Congress was not sympathetic to his policy. Southern Democrats were strongly opposed to federal initiatives on civil rights. So alarmed were they that Strom Thurmond from South Carolina deserted the party to stand as a states' rights candidate in the 1948 election and obtained over a million votes.

However, the desegregation of the army in 1948 was a more concrete measure and showed that Truman was committed to civil rights. Congressional approval was not required for this measure: Truman, as Commander-in-Chief of the Armed Forces, could pass it himself using an executive order. The navy had already desegregated in 1946. Cynics would suggest that Truman was looking for the black vote in the 1948 presidential election and point out that A. Philip Randolph had again threatened a march on Washington if Truman did not take this step. Even after Truman's desegregation order there was, at first, less than full compliance: one or two segregated army units remained. It took the military necessities of the **Korean War** (1950–3) to complete the job in the army. All the same, there were now at least signs that segregation would no longer be positively supported from the White House.

One could go further. By addressing a meeting of the NAACP, appointing a black to the federal judiciary and regularly inviting black people to presidential functions, Truman was creating a climate of

KEY EVENT

Korean War (1950–3) US troops played a major part in assisting the anti-communist forces in a civil war in Korea and the last remnants of military desegregation in the US forces disappeared during the conflict. The war was inconclusive and resulted in the partition of the country into a communist North and an anti-communist South. It reinforced the Cold War atmosphere.

opinion that made the reception of the Brown decision and the Montgomery Bus Boycott much more positive than they would otherwise have been. Even the congressional rejection of civil rights reforms only made the NAACP and others even more determined to find the redress they wanted in the courts.

Eisenhower's presidency. Only a year after entering office in 1953, Eisenhower was faced with a different situation: the Supreme Court verdict in the Brown case. If this decision were dutifully enforced, the southern states would, at least, have to grant one concession for black people: an equal chance on the educational ladder. If it were ignored, would the federal executive put them under pressure to implement it? Eisenhower was generally reluctant to act. He suggested to the District of Columbia that its schools be integrated in advance of the court decision in order to set an example, but otherwise he did nothing.

Chafe (1999) sees Eisenhower's inaction as a major failing. Had Eisenhower insisted on desegregation and indicated his willingness to enforce it, he argues, compliance would have been more likely. Southern politicians, worried about their popularity, could have offered token resistance and then claimed that they had been forced to act by an overbearing federal government. This happened later with Governor Barnett's resistance to James Meredith entering the University of Mississippi in 1962 and similar resistance by Governor Wallace in Alabama to potential black university students at Tuscaloosa the following year.

In 1956, when Governor Daniel in Texas brought out his local troops, the Texas Rangers, to prevent integration, Eisenhower did not move. His intervention at Little Rock shows that, even when the federal government did flex its muscles, southern governors would fight back. This is what happened when Orval Faubus shut Little Rock Central High School to prevent integration. Faubus's decision was one with which the President was constitutionally unable to interfere. Nevertheless, in the long run, integration came to Little Rock, if not until 1959. By then, public opinion and the level of civil rights protest had moved on.

Compliance in the late 1950s. On examining the precise degree of compliance with the decision on the Brown case in the late 1950s, we find a complex position. More change occurred in law than in fact. In the first eighteen months after Brown, lower courts showed that they would uphold the Supreme Court's verdict and school segregation laws disappeared in a number of southern states. Federal district judges were certainly prepared to uphold Supreme Court verdicts. But would the state executives and their respective governors be prepared to enforce

White Citizens' Councils were organisations set up to maintain segregation. The earliest ones date from 1955 in reaction to the Brown verdict on segregated education. They began in Mississippi but soon spread to Alabama and other states in the Deep South. Aiming to maintain strict segregation in as many areas of life as possible, they waged economic warfare against anyone supporting integration and believed in defying Federal Court rulings if necessary. In short, they were much like the Ku Klux Klan without the costumes and the lynching.

Nullification theory was the idea that an individual state could render null and void an Act of the federal government which it believed to be unconstitutional as long as a special Convention agreed. It was first suggested by John C. Calhoun of South Carolina in 1828 to oppose the introduction of trade tariffs.

their rulings? In many cases the answer was no. Southern white public opinion would leave them little choice in reality.

White Citizens' Councils sprang up all over the south, showing that some white people were prepared to resist on this issue in particular and on segregation in general. In Alabama in 1958, John Patterson, a strong believer in the policies of racial segregation, defeated George Wallace, in the election for the governorship of the state. At that time Wallace was mildly liberal on racial matters. In normally more moderate Virginia, Senator Harry Byrd called upon the south to resist an enforced end to segregation. It was clear also that in the Deep South – Alabama, Mississippi, Georgia, Louisiana and South Carolina – state legislatures were moving in the opposite direction and passing pro-segregation measures. Those familiar with their history recalled the **nullification theory** of the nineteenth century. Mississippi and Louisiana even amended their constitutions. In the recent past, a few black students had entered predominantly white institutions of higher education. But in those universities that had not accepted black students, the doors would remain closed for a while yet. Black student Arthurine Lucy's attempt to enter the all-white University of Alabama in February 1956 was stalled at the last moment when other students rioted and the authorities suspended her for her own safety. Civil rights in these areas were clearly not going to be given willingly.

Resistance to desegregation in southern USA, 1962.

This southern resistance must also be seen in the context of the Montgomery Bus Boycott. The eventual outcome of this could be seen as a victory for another Supreme Court ruling and for the non-violent campaign of protest that had preceded it. There were signs that the resistance to the end of segregation was increasing as the possibility of real and (to many southern white people) unwanted change grew larger. In March 1956 the **Southern Manifesto**, promising to oppose integration, received wide support.

A pause in the action. Despite the great achievement of Montgomery and the subsequent formation of SCLC, the next three years did not produce any dramatic breakthroughs or government initiatives, either state or federal. Cook (1998) describes this time as 'treading water' and Fairclough (1987) calls it the 'fallow years'. Southern opposition to the implementation of Brown and the maintenance of segregation remained strong at this time. Eisenhower, President until early 1961, was clearly not prepared to go much further than he already had. The only area where he was prepared to look for change was in assisting black people to exercise their right to vote.

Civil Rights Acts of 1957 and 1960. Congress passed two Civil Rights Acts, in 1957 and 1960, though these were tame compared with later legislation. The first proposed:

- a bi-partisan Civil Rights Commission
- a new division in the Justice Department to investigate civil rights abuses in fields such as voting.

But even this moderate bill proved controversial and was vigorously opposed, especially in the Senate. Strom Thurmond, spoke for over 24 hours in a single-man filibuster. Senator Lyndon Johnson was able to steer the bill through only by watering down the provisions. The powers of the Justice Department to sue over school desegregation were removed, and jury trials remained for breaches of civil rights – white juries would rarely be likely to convict for this offence.

The Act of 1960:

- renewed the Civil Rights Commission
- allowed judges to make special appointments of those who would help blacks on to the voting register
- introduced federal criminal penalties for bombing and mob action.

Again, the enforcement aspects of the bill were weakened in debate. In truth the Acts gave little to civil rights save that the principle of federal action had been established. But public attitudes were changing. Both

Southern Manifesto This manifesto was a declaration of constitutional principles designed to oppose the implementation of the two Brown verdicts and increase the active level of southern opposition to integration. The idea was that all leading southern political figures would sign it. Of the few who did not, one was Senator Albert Gore of Tennessee (father of the Democratic Presidential candidate in 2000) and Senator Lyndon Johnson (Texas).

Democrats and Republicans at their party conventions in 1960 adopted an anti-segregationist position and praised the sit-in demonstrators.

King's hope that southerners would be shamed into removing Jim Crow was proving over-optimistic. But Aldon Morris (1984) regards this time as being important for developing organisations rather than taking new initiatives; and there were some isolated successes, such as one successful campaign of the NAACP to desegregate lunch counters in 1958. As a result, eating facilities in Wichita, Kansas, were integrated. There were also some significant moves in Nashville, Tennessee, where James Lawson attempted another non-violent protest; but there were no spectacular successes. Even the energetic and determined Fred Shuttlesworth in Birmingham, Alabama, made no lasting impact with a bus boycott in 1958. In fact, desegregation had not only slowed down, but gone into reverse. Vann Woodward (1974) notes that 712 school districts were desegregated between 1954 and 1957, but only 49 in the next three years. He also points out that by the end of 1956 over 100 pro-segregation measures had been introduced in eleven southern states.

DID THE COLD WAR ADVANCE THE CAUSE OF CIVIL RIGHTS?

Introduction. The generation after the Second World War saw the black Civil Rights Movement force a response from federal authorities. A significant proportion of Supreme Court business concerned equal rights, as the most eminent justices in the land mulled over exactly what was meant by, for example, that much-quoted equal protection clause of the Fourteenth Amendment to the Constitution. By the end of the 1960s, a good deal of civil rights legislation had been passed by the US Congress on issues first raised to national prominence in the Federal Supreme Court. Half a dozen presidents had issued numerous executive orders and used their powers to federalise state troopers in order to deal with local crises when Supreme Court rulings were not being enforced. On numerous occasions, civil rights had been number one or two on their domestic priority list. It became one of the most talked about issues in the US media during the early 1960s.

However, as we have seen, this progress would have been difficult to anticipate in the late 1940s: the anti-communist mood of these years seemed to militate against reform of any kind, and against civil rights reform in particular. Yet even in these early years there was an undercurrent of Supreme Court activity and the Cold War atmosphere was turned to the movement's advantage.

At state level, civil rights produced a flurry of activity on several occasions. During the late 1950s and early 1960s it was electorally popular to parade segregationist views in the Deep South. But the southern states were fighting an ultimately unsuccessful rearguard action against desegregation in public places. By the end of the 1960s it survived intact in only a few pockets, principally in Mississippi and Alabama. In these areas, change was hardly voluntary and was often imposed by the federal government, despite objections that it was exceeding its powers.

Post-war doldrums? After significant developments during the war itself, the post-war years appeared to bring a halt to some of the civil rights trends noted in the early 1940s. The NAACP continued with its legal cases and slowly made progress, culminating in the triumph of the Brown case in 1954. But the initiatives of the war years, which had involved more direct action, such as CORE's sit-ins, were not always followed up. Why was this? Did the Cold War atmosphere of the post-war period inhibit the cause of civil rights? In some ways it did, but the effects were not all negative.

Marable (1991) sees the Cold War atmosphere in the ten years after the end of the Second World War as an important factor in preventing a great deal of progress on civil rights. Very early signs had been promising. In the mid-1940s black people were appointed to state legislatures as far south as Kentucky and received senior judicial and academic appointments. In Harlem, Benjamin Davis was elected to the New York City Council. CORE continued to develop and, by 1947, had thirteen widely spread branches or 'Chapters'. Yet despite all this, and the rising number of black voters, more militant direct action did not occur.

Marable explains this by asserting that the strong anti-communist mood after the war made these more confrontational types of activity very difficult. He argues that, despite potentially favourable Supreme Court verdicts, such as *Smith* v. *Allright* in 1944, the atmosphere of the time meant that these were not followed up effectively. President Truman, he argues, was 'virtually silent' on civil rights after 1946. The following year, the President requested Congress to grant $400 million in aid, both military and civil, to Greece and Turkey to shore them up against communist infiltration. This, then, was the priority at the time. It is true that the anti-communist mood of the time was fearsome. Tennessee, in 1951, insisted on the death penalty for anyone putting forward revolutionary Marxist ideas. Not for nothing are the early 1950s known as the era of McCarthyism.

Effect of the Cold War atmosphere on civil rights supporters. The Cold War period had certain adverse effects on civil rights. Some civil rights supporters who showed communist sympathies or merely criticised the severe actions taken against them suffered at this time. The famous singer Paul Robeson lost his passport, his career suffered and he gained the title of 'Black Stalin'. Congress member Adam Clayton Powell found his influence much diminished and his friends gone, for criticising anti-communist witch-hunts. W. E. B. Du Bois, now over 80, was charged with being a foreign agent despite the lack of any evidence. Not surprisingly, other campaigners were anxious to distance themselves from any taint of communism. Socialist Philip Randolph was quick to denounce communism, although in his case the distaste went way back into the 1930s.

However, Randolph showed the other side of the effect of the Cold War. He argued that the lack of equality between the races in the USA was a propaganda gift for the Soviet Union. The Cold War atmosphere, not in itself conducive to radical movements for change, nonetheless contributed indirectly to the civil rights cause: the mismatch between the USA's championing of the free world and its treatment of a racial minority within its own country was causing increasing concern among many thinking people. The wartime period had seen a full-scale intellectual assault on the kind of racist views that underpinned the basis of white supremacy in the USA, and which the Nazis had now discredited.

Sitkoff (1993) identifies Gunnar Myrdal's *An American Dilemma* (1944) as particularly influential in this respect. Myrdal, a Swedish economist who had first visited the USA in 1929, pointed out the discrepancy between a country that proclaimed itself to be egalitarian and its unequal treatment of the Afro-American. He was very critical of the white American treatment of black people, admitting that he was 'shocked and scared to the bones' by all the evils he had witnessed. Yet he found much to praise in the American way of life as a whole. He believed that 'the moral pulse beats more strongly' in the USA than in much of Europe. His arguments appealed to black and white alike. The NAACP quoted him in the Brown case; the idea of the treatment of blacks being a major blot in an otherwise fine and free country was a theme taken up by Martin Luther King.

How much progress was being made? Not surprisingly, some historians do not take as pessimistic a view as Marable. Vann Woodward (1974) sees this as a period when a good deal was granted to the Civil Rights Movement, and not only by the Supreme Court (see below). Woodward also notes that modest but significant changes were taking place in the south. There were southern organisations such as the Southern Conference for Human Welfare: this had a radical agenda to assist *all* the poor and dispossessed. Campaigns to put an end to lynchings appeared to be bearing fruit, as their number steadily declined. No recorded lynching took place in 1952 or 1953. A few cities on the edge of the south began to desegregate public facilities. However, southern white attempts to give black people a better deal were supported by only a handful of the southern population as a whole. With northern politicians cautious and President Eisenhower largely inactive outside desegregating the District of Columbia, it seemed by the mid-1950s that the civil rights process was slowing down.

HOW FAR DID VERDICTS OF THE SUPREME COURT ADVANCE CIVIL RIGHTS UP TO 1964?

Supreme Court cases before 1954. Where historians Marable and Woodward are more likely to agree is that the Supreme Court was the branch of government doing most to take the initiative over civil rights, although the efforts of the NAACP also need to be acknowledged. The Supreme Court is not normally a **court of the first instance** and it needed to have cases brought to it on appeal. The black lawyer Thurgood Marshall certainly did this. After *Smith* v. *Allright* in 1944, the number of potential black voters that registered steadily increased. Subsequent rulings (see the table below) dealt with a variety of issues concerned with discrimination and segregation, not just voting.

The impact of these verdicts was variable. The most effective was *Terry* v. *Adams*, which showed that there could be no loophole for the 'white primary', but which also showed that white Texan Democrats had been trying to ignore *Smith* v. *Allright*. *Shelley* v. *Kraemer* had little impact on segregated housing patterns or on the estate agents who suddenly withdrew houses from the market in all-white areas if a potential black purchaser appeared. The judgments were significant but, before *Brown* v. *Board of Education, Topeka*, cautious. For instance, the decision in *Sweatt* v. *Painter* to allow a black law student into the all-white Texas Law School was based on the desirability of equal treatment rather than integrationist principles. The Court's verdict pointed out that the alternative black-only Law School had only five professors as opposed to fifteen in the White College, and 16,500 books instead of 65,000 – clearly separate but *un*equal. Nonetheless, these judgments were significant: they indicated the general direction of verdicts and set the tone for the momentous judgment of the Brown case in 1954.

KEY TERM

Court of the first instance A court that is first to hear a particular case. Apart from inter-state disputes and issues involving other countries, the Federal Supreme Court normally hears only cases on appeal that have previously been considered in lower courts.

Selected Supreme Court rulings, 1946–53.

Year	Name of case	Issue	Decision
1946	*Morgan* v. *Virginia*	Inter-state travel	Banned segregation on inter-state travel vehicles
1948	*Shelley* v. *Kraemer*	Land ownership in Missouri	No private housing agreements could exclude black people from residing in any area
1950	*Sweatt* v. *Painter*	Higher education	Black student must be admitted to white Texas Law School
1953	*Terry* v. *Adams*	Voting rights	An association of qualified white voters in Texas who chose Democratic candidates was ruled as a political organisation and so denying black people a vote

However, the Civil Rights Movement itself had also begun to lay the ground for future advances. Expectations were raised: tactics of protest had been devised that were to be used with great success later. There was a slow but steady increase of black people registering to vote. The painstaking legal tactics of the NAACP over education were about to pay off. It pressed for, and was granted, a major concession with the Brown case of 1954.

Why was Brown v. Board of Education, Topeka so important? The earlier rulings of the Supreme Court – such as *Plessy* v. *Ferguson* and *Cumming* v. *Board of Education* – had been disastrous for black well-being at the end of the nineteenth century, but we have seen that, during the 1940s and early 1950s, verdicts were increasingly helpful to the civil rights cause. The independent judiciary no longer had the political hang-ups that were still present in Congress and the presidency. Moreover, in the Brown case, they were prepared to overturn the ruling of *Plessy* v. *Ferguson* (1896), which had helped to entrench and even extend segregation. With the Brown decision in 1954, the Warren Court ended the vice-like grip of the Plessy precedent, which had dominated relations between black and white ever since. By going further than merely attacking inequalities, and insisting on the psychological need for integration of the black minority, it crossed the Rubicon in terms of race relations. The place of the mid-twentieth-century Supreme Court in the early achievements of the movement is secure.

Of course, the Court's rulings needed to be enforced and implemented and this did not always happen. Yet in landmark rulings such as Brown, it clearly played a major role in raising important civil rights issues. While, during the early 1950s, the system of segregation was prevalent in many states, over the next twenty years circumstances changed considerably. Without the authority of the Court and the respect in which it was held, it is hard to see how these changes could have been achieved. It gave many southern black people a belief in the American system that King was able to exploit effectively in the next few years. This undoubtedly changed the circumstances surrounding the Civil Rights Movement. It was a vindication of the legal strategy of the NAACP. Those who believed that the American way was the way of equality for all seem to have had their views confirmed. Historians are agreed that the Brown decision signalled the start of a new era, though not an era of straightforward progress. The dramatic success of the more militant, if still non-violent, Civil Rights Movement from the mid 1950s onward has slightly obscured the vital role of the NAACP. Yet without the efforts of the NAACP to bring cases to the Supreme Court in the first place, the legal foundations on which these later struggles were built would not have been laid. Indeed, the banning of the NAACP in Alabama and Louisiana in the mid-1950s – because of its legal successes – gave an opportunity for new organisations such as the SCLC to develop.

'Brown 2'. It was immediately clear that desegregation of schools was not going to happen at once. The Court promised to return to the question of the detailed implementation of its ruling and, for a year, the nation held its collective breath. In the Court judgment 'Brown 2', issued in 1955, the idea that integration should be done 'with all deliberate speed' suggested uncertainty about the precise timing of change. No deadline was given for the completion of the task.

Some historians have criticised the Court for not following up its original verdict with a more vigorous attempt at enforcement. Riches (1997) sees it as a 'serious error' based on Earl Warren's mistaken belief that authorities were already beginning to implement the initial court order on a wide scale. Sitkoff (1993) views Brown 2 as a backward step after the promise of the first judgment. The Court itself was anxious to preserve unanimity on the issue. The initiative should now pass to the states. Southerners opposed to desegregation pinned considerable hope on certain phrases in Brown 2. The 'proximity to local conditions' of district judges and the words 'reasonable time' gave them some hope that change would be long postponed.

Browder v. Gayle (1956). After the Brown case, the Federal Supreme Court continued to give favourable rulings on civil rights and racial questions. Earl Warren remained Chief Justice until 1969 and the Court's decisions in general wore a liberal air. The Supreme Court ruling in *Browder* v. *Gayle* (1956) that found Montgomery's bus segregation unconstitutional, played a vital part in the success of the black bus boycott of that year. Indeed, it could be said to have come in the nick of time. The boycott was, by November 1956, feeling the strain and was under legal attack locally. City leaders in Montgomery had petitioned a state court for an injunction against the Montgomery Improvement Association (MIA) car pool. King's insistence that this had been voluntary and spontaneous was being undermined by evidence that the MIA had $189,000 in a Montgomery bank. If it could be shown that the car pool was, legally, a private business, then the local authorities could ban it.

It was while attending this worrying case that King received the news of the Supreme Court verdict. The manner of judgment had been significant. The Court simply confirmed the earlier judgment of a panel of three that bus segregation was unconstitutional. It chose not to hear further evidence. This clear-cut decision meant the boycott could be called off. Unlike the rulings on education, there was little doubt that this decision would be implemented at once. On 8 December, King and white supporter Glenn Smiley rode on a bus side by side through the town. Whether the desegregation would last, however, and whether it would be effective in other southern towns was quite another matter.

Boynton v. Virginia (1960). The bold Freedom Rides were in part inspired by another Supreme Court decision, *Boynton* v. *Virginia*, which extended desegregation on inter-state travel. *Morgan* v. *Virginia* back in 1946 had outlawed segregation aboard buses: now, bus terminal facilities, such as waiting rooms and restaurants, were included. *Boynton* v. *Virginia* inspired the CORE Freedom Rides from which so many other developments came. Court decisions like this not only provided King with some substance for his argument that the American system was basically decent, but also made civil disobedience more acceptable. Taylor Branch recalls that, when the SNCC's John Lewis was directed to the black facilities in Alabama's waiting rooms, he always quoted the Boynton ruling and ignored the white thumb gesturing him in the other direction.

Now, the Bull Connors and Jim Clarks of this world seemed to be the ones defying authority rather than the demonstrators, largely because of the Court's rulings. But Connor and Clark were not unusual. As C. T. Vivian has remarked, 'the act of Jim Clark was the normal act of the south'. Resistance to Supreme Court verdicts was long and persistent. As late as 1959, Stenson Kennedy's *Jim Crow Guide to the USA* warned its readers that recent Supreme Court rulings on integrated transport since 1946 did not mean that these rulings applied in reality in the Deep South. Riches (1997) personally recalled that in Selma, Alabama, in 1966 he arrived at the bus station to find two things: the whites-only signs had been removed, yet the bus station was still rigidly segregated. Nor was this the only area where resistance continued. Fast-food stores in Birmingham continued to serve only white customers even after the excitement of 1963. Only the Supreme Court ruling *Katzenbach* v. *McClung* in the last month of 1964 put a stop to it. Significantly, the judgment cited the Civil Rights Act of 1964. Once this and the Voting Rights Act of 1965 had become law, the initiative seemed to pass away from the Supreme Court: it would return a few years later when whites were to complain that they were now the racial group subject to discrimination.

Other verdicts. Other Supreme Court decisions helped the civil rights cause indirectly.

- In *Shelton* v. *Tucker* (1960) it was established that states like Arkansas could not require teachers to list organisations to which they belonged before giving them a contract. While partly a reflection of fading post-war anti-communism, this would also make it easier for white sympathisers and black teachers alike to join civil rights organisations. A different climate of opinion was being created.
- The judgment in *Monroe* v. *Pape* (1961) may not have stopped police brutality, but it made turning a blind eye more difficult. The Chicago police were held liable for the treatment of a black man who had his

house broken into and ransacked without a warrant and was interrogated for over ten hours without benefit of legal assistance, before being released without charge.

- *Baker* v. *Carr* (1962) was a complicated case about voting boundaries in Tennessee, but it did confirm the principle of one person, one vote, which would be used in campaigning in the next few years. Moreover, it would prevent any future gerrymandering of election boundaries (see page 173). Once black people had got the vote in large numbers, there would be areas where they were in the majority.

The mood created by the Cold War atmosphere in post-war USA was not initially conducive to progress on the civil rights front. However, the stress on the USA as 'leader of the free world' was eventually turned to the movement's advantage. This title could hardly be claimed if there were no improvement in the pitiful condition and treatment of many black people. The increasingly favourable verdicts of the Supreme Court in the 1940s and 1950s were clearly of major importance in creating the climate for change in the 1960s that would attempt to bring black people within the compass of 'the American Dream'.

HOW DID KENNEDY'S 'NEW FRONTIER' AND JOHNSON'S 'GREAT SOCIETY' IMPACT ON CIVIL RIGHTS?

Kennedy's 'New Frontier'. The word 'frontier' would be a familiar one to American ears: it conjures up images of the pioneers moving westward in the USA in the nineteenth century, setting their frontier ever nearer the Pacific coast. John Kennedy first made reference to the 'New Frontier' in a speech in 1960 to accept the nomination of the Democratic Party as their candidate for President. This would involve tackling:

- 'uncharted areas of space and science'
- 'unsolved problems of peace and war'
- 'unanswered questions of poverty and surplus'
- 'unconquered pockets of ignorance and prejudice'.

These would require, he asserted, 'Invention, Innovation, and Imagination'.

From these very general statements developed a coherent policy. Scientific and space research proceeded apace through organisations such as NASA. The Soviet technical lead in space research, indicated by the launch of *Sputnik* in 1957, had to be ended. Moreover, Kennedy took a firm stand against the Soviet Union in the **Cuban Missile Crisis** of 1962. Trade agreements abroad, such as that with the Common Market, and tax changes at home indicated a determination to pull the USA out of

KEY TERM

Cuban Missile Crisis (1962) A dramatic moment in the Cold War between the USA and the Soviet Union. The Soviet Union was installing nuclear missile sites in Cuba within range of the US mainland. For a few tense days in October 1962, the world braced itself for conflict, but the Soviets backed down and thereby prevented a full-scale nuclear war.

temporary recession and back to rapid economic progress. Social plans included a programme for poor children and new housing projects.

Few hearing the 'New Frontier' speech could doubt that the main 'unconquered pocket' of prejudice to be tackled was the prejudice against black people. This was to be one of Kennedy's biggest challenges – all these policies required the assertion of federal authority, but the policy where this was most disputed was civil rights.

How committed was Kennedy to civil rights? In 1961 John F. Kennedy inherited the situation that the sit-ins had created and almost immediately faced the issue of the Freedom Rides. His election had produced a wave of political excitement and anticipation. The comparatively youthful Kennedy produced a new wave of interest in the political process on university campuses. In the midst of all this excitement, would there be initiatives on civil rights?

In the campaign in 1960 there had been a notable incident. Martin Luther King had been arrested in Atlanta, Georgia, for sitting-in at Rich's department store. He was then handed over to officials in the nearby Georgia county of De Kalb. He was already on a year's probation here and had broken its conditions by taking part in a sit-in. As a result, he was sentenced to four months' hard labour in jail. John Kennedy phoned King's wife, Coretta, and promised he would do what he could to help get King released. His brother, Robert Kennedy, meanwhile phoned the judge in the case to complain. King was released the next day. Some southern black Republicans, such as **Martin Luther King Senior** were, as strong Protestants, suspicious of the Roman Catholic Kennedy on religious grounds. As part of the long-running black tradition, King Senior had regarded southern Democrats as racist and had supported the Republicans until Kennedy in 1960. In a knife-edged presidential contest, Kennedy defeated the Republican Nixon by a whisker. Black votes had helped to swing things his way.

However, Kennedy's attitude to civil rights was complex. On the one hand, he personally had no objection to black equality and integration. But he was not committed to it heart and soul. He was to trying to get black support, but black people voted only in limited numbers. They may have helped him get elected in 1960, but only because the contest was so close. For Kennedy, the greater worry was losing the support of southern Democrats. This seemed likely if the federal government pushed for a vigorous civil rights policy, for this would mean riding roughshod over states' rights.

Pragmatism versus principle. In short, Kennedy's policy was based on pragmatism rather than principle. The crucial factor was law and order; if

KEY PERSON

Martin Luther King Senior (1899–1979)
Licensed as a preacher at the age of 16, he later arrived in Atlanta in 1919 and attended Morehouse College. He worked his way up to the black elite. He married Alberta Williams, daughter of the minister of the Ebenezer Baptist Church, Atlanta, in 1926 and succeeded Williams as minister in 1931. He had a daughter and two sons, including Michael Luther. In 1934 he went on a world tour and returned to announce he had changed his name to Martin Luther King Senior and that his son would change his name to Martin Luther King Junior. He urged Martin Jr. to quit when faced with danger at Montgomery, but went on to support his work. Became known as 'Daddy King' in the 1960s. On his son's death he remarked, 'He never hated anybody.'

the southern states could maintain order, Kennedy would not interfere too much. If they could not, then intervention could be justified. The argument of the Civil Rights Movement was that the continued existence of segregation laws that had been ruled illegal in the courts meant that law and order was *not* being maintained. But Kennedy believed that if southern authorities could protect the demonstrators from the mobs, the police could then arrest the protesters, as the Freedom Riders found out in Jackson, Mississippi, and as King and his supporters discovered in Albany, New York.

Ironically, one of Kennedy's actions made the problem worse. In order to curry favour with the south, his first judicial appointments were of pro-segregationists. This proved a problem when he came out more strongly for civil rights in 1963 and indeed well beyond. Less was done about issues such as voter registration than would have occurred with more sympathetic appointments. The appointments also impeded protests. For example, in July 1962, J. Robert Elliott, a US district judge, issued an injunction to prevent civil disobedience protests by King and others in Albany. Elliott was an out-and-out segregationist: Kennedy had appointed him.

Kennedy and the Freedom Rides. The attitude of Kennedy is well illustrated by the result of the Freedom Rides. Protesters were optimistic that Kennedy would be forced to intervene because of the appalling treatment they were receiving. However, Blum (1992) points out that federal intervention would have been rather more complex than this simple-sounding theory implied. Burke Marshall in the Civil Rights division of the Justice Department believed that federal intervention should be strictly limited and that too much use of the federal heavy hand would be against the spirit, if not the letter, of the Constitution. This was consistent with Kennedy's view that federal intervention was likely only if law and order seemed to be breaking down.

As with Eisenhower and Orval Faubus back in 1957, President Kennedy was annoyed that Alabama Governor John Patterson had at first claimed to have everything under control, and then subsequently reported that he could not guarantee the safety of the riders. Apparently the police in Montgomery could not cope with protecting 21 people, who were badly beaten up when they arrived in the town. This dereliction of duty resulted in a Justice Department regulation in September 1961, which clearly ordered the end of segregation in inter-state travel. The executive of President Kennedy had taken a firmer stand on this issue than Eisenhower's had over segregated education. But this did not automatically mean that the regulation would be enforced. There is evidence that Robert Kennedy was prepared to do a deal with southern authorities: avoid blood on the streets and control the howling mobs and

Klan agitators, and then you can arrest the demonstrators and prosecute them if you wish.

It is not surprising that John and Robert Kennedy wanted to avoid violence at any cost. This is because the other tactic behind the Freedom Rides was working only too well: violence was newsworthy. The outrageous treatment of the riders found its way into the northern press at once – in contrast with the Montgomery bus boycott, which had gone unnoticed for the first month. It went a long way to producing a climate of liberal white public opinion in the north and this was a major plank in the tactics of the civil rights demonstrators. But Kennedy's concern was with the international perspective. In the middle of delicate negotiations over the Cuban Missile Crisis, it hardly looked good for the supposed leader of the Free World to be receiving reports of the ill treatment of people who were clamouring for equality of treatment. More and more, the initiative seemed to be passing to the movement: more and more, the authorities seemed to be merely reacting.

The role of Kennedy in the 1964 Civil Rights Act. The Civil Rights Bill that passed in 1964 would have been an unlikely runner just twelve months before. Until late 1962 the Kennedy administration had not lived up to its rhetoric on civil rights. Kennedy's boast that he would be able to end segregation in federal housing projects 'at the stroke of a pen', with a presidential executive order, came to haunt him over the next two years. He eventually signed the relevant paper in November 1962. Apart from his brother Robert's work as Attorney-General, little else had been achieved. Robert had appointed more black people to the Justice Department and as judges. He initiated numerous court suits on voting rights and desegregated inter-state travel. But would the Kennedys pass a more effective measure than the tame Civil Rights Acts of 1957 and 1960? The events of Birmingham ensured that they would.

Birmingham, Alabama, 1963. By the middle of 1963, southern racist extremists were clearly infuriating President Kennedy. But the crucial factor in his more positive attitude to civil rights seems to have been 'Bull' Connor's treatment of the child demonstrators, and the fact that southern white business interests were now protesting about the disruption to normal commercial life that was being caused. Kennedy had sent Burke Marshall to negotiate a possible settlement. Desegregation and hiring of black workers was agreed with white business leaders, but Connor would not accept this and called for a boycott of any downtown shops that agreed to desegregate. Now pressured on two sides by both civil rights demonstrators and federal officials, the extremist white opposition showed its true colours. King's brother's house was firebombed and the Klan was nocturnally active.

It seems that these events pushed Kennedy into drawing up the comprehensive Civil Rights Bill that campaigners had been demanding. Bull Connor, for all his vigorous behaviour, had lost the initiative and played into the hands of his opponents. Kennedy, alarmed at the breakdown of law and order, had moved federal troops to within 30 miles of the town and was preparing to federalise the Alabama National Guard, just as Eisenhower had done in Little Rock, Arkansas back in 1957.

The occasion rather than the cause of President Kennedy nailing his colours to the mast was the action of Governor George Wallace in Alabama on 11 June 1963. Going even further than Governor Barnett in Mississippi over James Meredith, he stood personally at the entrance to the state's university at Tuscaloosa to ban black students from entering. Initially confronted by Robert Kennedy's deputy, Nicholas Katzenbach, Wallace seemed to be about to begin another major confrontation. But faced with Katzenbach's federal authority and the imminent federalisation of Alabama's National Guard he gave way, allowing the students to enter the building and later to register. The following day, Kennedy made by far his strongest speech in favour of civil rights. Identifying education, voting and restaurant facilities, in particular, Kennedy castigated those who would bar anyone from facilities simply because he or she had a black skin. In a King-like passage, he angrily referred to a '100 year delay' in dealing with these questions and said that it was now time to act. For the first time in years, the initiative in civil rights was to come from the White House.

Johnson's 'Great Society'. Just as President Kennedy had a catchphrase in 'New Frontier', so President Johnson was to have one with his 'Great Society'. As with Kennedy the concept ranged widely, but civil rights were a central part of the process. Johnson, nine years older than Kennedy, cut his political teeth in the Democratic Party at the time of Roosevelt's New Deal in the 1930s. The phrase 'Great Society' was not new, but was put into Johnson's mouth by his eloquent speechwriter Richard Goodwin.

Questions of poverty were tackled at federal level by bodies such as the Office of Economic Opportunity. Federal payment of goods and services to the poor were increased. A major Education Act of 1965 bypassed state governments and gave federal funds directly to the localities, while college scholarships subsidised students from low-income families. Community action programmes were developed. Medical care for the old (Medicare) and those unable to afford it (Medicaid) was introduced. Cultural facilities such as museums and dance companies were subsidised and measures were taken to attack water pollution. Restrictions were imposed on car emissions and misleading advertising. It was expected that the continued growth of the economy (and therefore of taxpayers) would help to fund all these projects.

Many of these moves benefited black people and other racial minorities indirectly. The war waged on poverty and attempts to raise American health standards would clearly help the black communities struggling with issues as varied as unemployment and food poisoning. Black culture's chances of sponsorship increased. The growth in federal housing projects held out hope that the most intractable of problems for black people would be seriously tackled. This, coupled with greater possibilities of equality of opportunity in education, would all have been enough to call Johnson a friend of black people. In 1965 and 1966 a flood of legislation poured through Congress and federal initiatives abounded. A Democratic Congress and a Democratic President committed to change proved, albeit briefly, a powerful combination for reform. But it is arguably in the area of civil rights that Johnson's greatest achievement is to be found.

The role of Johnson in the 1964 Civil Rights Act. There is no doubt that the greatest presidential contribution to civil rights during this period came from the early years of the Johnson presidency. Johnson's commitment to civil rights began as soon as he became President. Yet he had not always been so committed. A southerner from Texas, his track record on civil rights was not entirely unblemished. He had been criticised for being too willing to compromise when pushing through the Civil Rights Act of 1957. On the other hand, he had been more positive than most southerners. Johnson possessed certain advantages over Kennedy: having been a long-serving member of the Senate, he knew at first hand the wheeling and dealing that was necessary to get the Bill through; he could also use his southern background to appeal to those doubters; and he could use the death of Kennedy himself. He proceeded to exploit these factors to the full.

- He pushed the 1964 Civil Rights Act through with a vigour and skill lacking in previous times. He demonstrated that there was a majority in Congress for civil rights if the executive were sufficiently determined to find it. As a southerner, he could assert that the legislation was necessary without being accused of being an ignorant, interfering northern liberal. At its height, his identification with the movement was considerable. His use of the civil rights phrase 'We shall overcome' in announcing the 1965 Voting Rights Act was revealing.
- On the question of political persuasion, Johnson had the task of getting as many Republican votes as possible. He knew that many of his fellow southern Democrats would not vote for any Civil Rights Bill, however moderate. Johnson succeeded in persuading the Republican leader of the Senate, Everitt Dirksen, to give his support to

the bill and 'deliver' Republican votes. To emphasise the cross-party support for the bill, he pulled off a clever propaganda trick. All living ex-Presidents, Hoover, Truman and Eisenhower, agreed to sign a statement supporting the principle of civil rights. This made it easier for Johnson to assert that southerners were out of line and that this change was necessary to bring them into conformity with the rest of the USA.

- As for exploiting the death of Kennedy, we need look no further than Johnson's own words: 'No memorial oration or eulogy could more eloquently honour President Kennedy's memory than the earliest possible passage of the Civil Rights Bill for which he fought so long.' The last half-dozen words involved more than a little poetic licence.

Johnson's tactics paid off. The Bill went through Congress with substantial majorities. There was certainly stiff resistance, such as the filibuster from Senator Richard Russell from Georgia, but it was all to no avail.

The campaigners were heavily dependent on Johnson to see the Act successfully home, but they had continued to exert pressure by their own activities.

The Mississippi Freedom Summer. After the 1964 Civil Rights Act had passed, three civil rights organisations, SCLC, CORE and SNCC, were keen to test it by pushing for voter registration in the south, concentrating on difficult areas like Mississippi. The Mississippi Freedom Summer was one result. In view of Johnson's great efforts, the Democrats were the party to support, but the views of many other southern white Democrats were quite unacceptable. Alternative black political leaders were needed to represent the Democrats on the issues of the day.

The Mississippi Freedom Democratic Party was a bold and imaginative attempt to acquire this representation, but it fell foul of complex politics. Johnson felt he had to keep the southern Democrats on his side, so he would not accept the alternative delegation at the party conference in Atlantic City. Worse, he forced Senator Hubert Humphrey to do his dirty work for him. Humphrey was told that if he wanted the vice-presidential nomination to Johnson's presidential bid, he had to ensure that the Mississippi Freedom Democratic Party was not accepted. Senator John Connolly from Johnson's own state of Texas said the Democrats would walk out if 'those baboons' were allowed to vote at the conference. The liberal Humphrey was in a dilemma, but he put his career and loyalty to Johnson first, ensuring that the alternative party would have only token representation. SNCC angrily rejected his offer. The whole event clearly demonstrated the limited effect of the Civil Rights Movement on the President.

Passed in House of Representatives: 290–130

For:
Democrats 152
Republicans 138

Against:
Democrats 96
Republicans 34

Passed in Senate:
73 votes to 27

Congressional voting on the Civil Rights Bill.

1965 Voting Rights Act. It was clear that the 1964 Civil Rights Act alone was not sufficient to ensure universal black voter registration and that separate legislation was required. For SCLC, the focus was now to be on Alabama in general and Selma in particular. Once again a President would use language reminiscent of civil rights supporters. After the Selma protest, Johnson denounced any 'delay', 'hesitation' or 'compromise' and finished with the now traditional words of freedom, 'We shall overcome.'

Though it had by no means a straightforward passage, there was little doubt that Congress would accept the Voting Rights Bill. In many ways, this was an optimistic time for the movement. Johnson was 'on board' and social and economic reforms benefiting blacks seemed likely to follow in the Great Society programme. But from here on problems mounted. The unity, success and control of events that the movement had apparently achieved were all to be lost in a very short space of time.

Although there had been some action by earlier Presidents, it was from 1962 to 1965 that US presidents demonstrated their greatest commitment to civil rights. With the passing of the 1965 Voting Rights Act, the cooperation between the administration and the movement had reached its peak. A Congress prepared to enact two major pieces of legislation, a President and his administration committed to their cause, wholesale concessions on segregation in many, if not all, southern states, a strong and vigorous campaigning movement that, despite increasing stresses and strains, still held together: all suggested further advances. Yet it was not to be.

THE PRESIDENTIAL ELECTION, 1968

Democrats divided

By the time the American people went to the polls to elect a new President in November 1968, the Democrats were a seriously divided political party. There were several reasons for these divisions:

- The announcement in March 1968 by President Johnson that he would not seek re-election shocked many Democrats. While he could claim considerable success in the area of civil rights and social policy, Johnson had been worn down by the war in Vietnam. The war itself was escalating and the anti-war protest movement inside the USA was gaining more and more support. Many leading politicians and generals were beginning to realise that the Vietnam War was a war that the USA could not win.
- The assassination on 5 June 1968 of Robert Kennedy was a serious blow to those liberal Democrats who believed that there would have been a further advance in civil rights if he had been elected President. This killing, following so soon after the murder of Martin Luther King

in April, was seen as a major disaster by millions of liberal Americans, many of them Democrat supporters.

- The violence outside the Democratic National Convention in Chicago in August 1968, witnessed by millions on their television sets, tarnished the liberal image of the party in the eyes of many American voters. It also damaged the political fortunes of Senator **Eugene McCarthy**, whose campaign for the presidential nomination had become a moral crusade both against the war in Vietnam and against social injustice at home.
- The decision of the convention to select Vice-President **Hubert Humphrey** as presidential candidate increased divisions within the party, largely because he supported a continuation of the war and had not campaigned in a single primary.
- Divisions within the Democrats encouraged the political fortunes of an independent third-party candidate, George Wallace (see page 135), the right-wing Democratic governor of Alabama. His appeal to blue-collar workers and southern white people, fed up with anti-war protesters, militant black people, hippies and liberal intellectuals, was very strong. But its main effect was to split the Democrats even more as an electoral force and to increase the electoral prospects of the Republicans and their candidate, Richard Nixon.

The Republicans had no difficulty at all in portraying the Democrats as a hopelessly divided political fighting force. Although Humphrey ran Nixon fairly close in the popular vote, Nixon took the Electoral College (see page 46) very comfortably.

The Democratic candidate, Hubert Humphrey, received only 38 per cent of the white vote, which makes his achievement in polling almost as many votes as Nixon particularly remarkable.

THE PRESIDENCY OF RICHARD NIXON, 1969–1974

Foreign policy

Richard Nixon was elected President in 1968 partly because the Democrats were divided, but mainly because he convinced the majority of Americans that he could end the war in Vietnam. Indeed, foreign

Candidate	Electoral College vote	Popular vote	%
Richard Nixon	301	31,770,237	43.4
Hubert Humphrey	191	31,270,533	42.7
George Wallace	46	9,906,141	13.5
Minor parties	–	239,908	0.4

Results of the presidential election, 1968.

Eugene McCarthy (b. 1916) entered the House of Representatives in 1948, representing the Democratic Farm Labour Party. He was elected to the Senate in 1958. On 30 November 1967, he announced his intention to challenge Johnson for the presidency in 1968. He was outspoken against the Vietnam War and his massive victory in the New Hampshire primary was a major factor in Johnson's not seeking re-election. Amid the violence surrounding the Democratic Convention, McCarthy lost the nomination to Humphrey. He failed in two further attempts to run for presidency, in 1972 and 1976.

Hubert Humphrey (b. 1911) was elected Mayor of Minneapolis in 1945 and re-elected in 1947. At the Democratic National Convention in 1948, he made a strong stand on civil rights and in the same year was elected to the Senate. He failed to get the presidential nomination in

1960, but became Vice-President to Lyndon Johnson in 1964. He was defeated by Nixon for the presidency in 1968 and failed to get the Democratic nomination in 1972.

policy issues occupied much of his first presidency. Together with his Secretary of State, Henry Kissinger, he launched the policy of **'Vietnamisation'**. Until the Americans finally withdrew, the war would continue. At the end of April 1970, Nixon therefore ordered a joint US–South Vietnamese invasion of Cambodia, which led to US student protests and deaths at Kent State, Ohio, and Jackson State, Mississippi, universities. In February 1971, the South Vietnamese army, with US backing, invaded Laos. Nixon complemented his Vietnam policy with efforts to improve relations with communist China and achieved considerable success.

Domestic policy

Views of Nixon as President, particularly in domestic affairs, are rather confused. To many, he seemed a shadowy figure who rarely revealed his true character in public. In private, he appears to have been suspicious and insecure. Political enemies were seen as personal enemies and he always felt ill at ease among the Republican Party leaders of the East Coast. In terms of domestic policy, Nixon appears to have been inconsistent in his approach:

- On environmental and welfare issues, he appears to have been fairly liberal. The National Environmental Policy Act (1969), for example, required that every proposed federal project should include an analysis of its impact on the environment. The Family Assistance Plan, defeated in the Senate in the same year, aimed to provide all Americans with a guaranteed annual income.
- On other issues, such as law and order, drugs and left-wing movements within the USA, Nixon took a much more reactionary line. In 1969, he appointed the conservative Warren Burger as Chief Justice and, by 1972, he had appointed three more conservatives to be justices in the Supreme Court.
- During his first presidency, members of his government testified against expanding the 1965 Voting Rights Act and the 1968 Fair Housing Act.

Southern strategy

Initially, Nixon adopted a conservative approach to key domestic issues as part of what was known as the 'southern strategy'. This was the strategy followed by the Republicans at the time of the 1968 presidential election. Its aim was to attract white voters in the south to vote Republican by pledging to follow conservative policies, at the same time taking those same voters away from George Wallace, the right-wing Democratic Governor of Alabama, who was also standing for the presidency. The strategy was successful in defeating Wallace, but he remained a political threat in the south.

The Republicans continued to take a right-wing stance on a range of social issues, including civil rights:

- Writing in *Reader's Digest* in 1967, Nixon declared that the USA was 'far from being a great society but is becoming a lawless society'. He went on to declare that this lawlessness was due to the tolerance of civil rights groups.
- In the 1968 presidential election campaign, Nixon assured those Americans opposed to school integration that he would not withhold federal funds from school districts that were slow to follow Supreme Court rulings on school desegregation.
- After riots in Baltimore in 1968, Spiro Agnew, Nixon's Vice-President, attacked black leaders as 'Hanoi visiting . . . caterwauling, riot-inciting, burn-America-down type of leaders'. (Agnew later resigned in disgrace after income tax evasion and bribery charges.)

Such statements and policy stances on the issue of civil rights were bound to be popular with white southern voters and would persuade many of them to vote Republican in the 1968 election.

Richard Nixon and civil rights

There is considerable evidence to suggest that by the time Richard Nixon became President in 1969, the Civil Rights Movement had achieved notable advances since 1960 (see Chapter 12): However, problems remained, not least in the large cities where levels of poverty among black people remained high. The key issue is whether the progress achieved in the 1960s, particularly under Johnson, continued during the Nixon years or whether that progress was severely set back.

Although, on the civil rights issue, Nixon may have been fairly liberal in the 1950s, there are reasons to believe that by the time he became President in 1969, his opposition had grown:

- He had a rather low opinion of black people and their potential. This is well illustrated by his view that 'there has never in history been an adequate black nation and they are the only race of which this is true'.
- He personally opposed the idea of the birthday of Martin Luther King becoming a national holiday with the statement 'No, never!'
- He used the FBI to suppress black radical movements like the Black Panthers.
- He did not like meeting black leaders and when he did agree to meet them, the meetings achieved very little. His meetings with Ralph Abernathy, who succeeded Martin Luther King as leader of the SCLC, were particularly hostile and fruitless.
- He opposed expanding the 1965 Voting Rights Act, in order to ensure the support of white voters in the south.
- He nominated conservative justices to the Supreme Court who were generally opposed to the idea of desegregation. This was particularly true of his nomination, in 1970, of Judge Harold Carswell of Florida,

who was a strong supporter of segregation. The Supreme Court had overturned some of Carswell's rulings on the grounds that they were racist. Nixon refused to accept any criticism of Carswell and ignored the advice of leading lawyers and party leaders in nominating him.

- In the case of *Swann* v. *Charlotte-Mecklenburg* (1971), he refused to back the Supreme Court when it ruled in favour of desegregation.
- He was opposed to the idea of bussing to achieve racially mixed schools. He believed it to be harmful to children and local communities.

The programme of affirmative action

While Nixon and many Republicans may have opposed black civil rights as part of their southern strategy, they nevertheless followed policies intended to improve the lives of black Americans. Most important of these was the programme of **affirmative action**. During the Nixon presidency, the programme of affirmative action had several features:

KEY TERM

Affirmative action
This policy, introduced by the Democrats, was based on the idea that the way to improve the lives of black people and other minority groups was by discriminating in their favour – for example, in university selection and employment. This could mean that employers were forced by law to ensure that a certain percentage of their workforce was drawn from black and minority groups (the quota system).

- Nixon himself was not happy about the idea of quotas, but he thought that all federal contractors should hire more minority workers. Federally funded projects in Philadelphia were therefore targeted with a view to increasing workers from minority groups from 4 per cent to 26 per cent.
- Affirmative action was introduced in October 1969 at a federally funded hospital project. It was later extended to building trade unions in New York, Pittsburgh, Seattle, Los Angeles, St Louis, San Francisco, Boston, Chicago and Detroit.
- It was only to be expected that there would be opposition to affirmative action from within the Republican Party. It came from conservatives who believed that it was illegal under the 1964 Civil Rights Act. This stated that no one could be denied the benefits of federal financial assistance based on race, colour or national origin.
- There was also opposition from trade unions which believed that employment quotas were working to the disadvantage of white trade union workers.
- Perhaps surprisingly, there was opposition from black leaders themselves, who were convinced that quotas in particular had slowed down the pace of change.
- Such criticisms angered Nixon and made him more determined to continue this policy. By 1972, affirmative action policies had been extended beyond the construction industry to over 300,000 firms. In 1971, in the case of *Grigg* v. *Duke Power Company*, the Supreme Court supported the principle of affirmative action.

If affirmative action policies were unpopular, why did Nixon go to so much trouble to introduce them? After all, they were policies originally introduced by the Democrats, mainly under Johnson. This question can be answered in three ways:

- In a straightforward sense, Nixon believed that, if the lives of at least some black people could be improved, then this would reduce the possibility of black violence, particularly in the cities.
- More important, affirmative action policies, such as those dealing with employment quotas, broke the alliance between trade unions and civil rights leaders. This alliance, which had been so strong, had been a major factor in the success of the Civil Rights Movement up to this point.
- Nixon was an astute politician and realised that, while some black leaders may have opposed affirmative action, millions of individual black people saw it as a means of improving their lives – a way out of the ghetto. They would support attempts to break down racism in the workplace and might even become future Republican supporters.

Nixon and the idea of black capitalism

According to Daniel Patrick Moynihan, who advised the President on minority affairs, Nixon did not believe in programmes of welfare and handouts. Instead, he 'believed in government hand-ups, and was convinced that the best way to help disadvantaged groups was with capitalism rather than welfare which he believed was "creeping socialism"'.

In his memoirs, written in 1978, Nixon noted that, at the beginning of his presidency, minority enterprises were receiving only $8 million of business through government contracts. By 1972, largely through an office called the Minority Business Enterprise, they were receiving $242 million. He claimed that, in the same period, government grants, loans and guarantees directed towards helping minority business enterprises had increased from $200 million to $472 million. He also claimed that two-thirds of the top 100 black companies had been set up during his presidency and that tax receipts from businesses owned by blacks had increased from $4.5 billion in 1968 to $7.2 billion in 1972.

Although affirmative action policies and the idea of black capitalism received considerable criticism during the Nixon presidency, later Republican Presidents, Ronald Reagan and George Bush, continued to follow them. However, Nixon was mistaken in his view, certainly in the short term, that black capitalism policies would create a prosperous black middle class that would support the Republicans. In the 1972 presidential election, black American voters remained loyal to the Democrats. In the south, however, following the assassination attempt on George Wallace and his withdrawal from the presidential race, white voters voted overwhelmingly for the Republicans – the southern strategy had worked.

Nixon and school desegregation

Nixon opposed the desegregation of schools, if only to appeal to white voters in the south. He also opposed the bussing of children from one school district to another to achieve desegregation. In attempting to sustain this opposition, Nixon ran into a number of difficulties:

- Robert Finch, Secretary of Health, Education and Welfare, approved a scheme for the desegregation of schools in Mississippi and warned that, if the state failed to comply, federal funding would be withdrawn. When the state Senator, James Stennis, demanded a reversal of the policy, Nixon ordered Finch to go to the courts and ask for a delay. The Supreme Court ordered bussing to continue and the immediate end of the segregated system.
- To avoid further difficulty, Nixon decided to follow the advice of the Attorney-General, John Mitchell, which was to keep out of desegregation issues and leave them to the courts. So when, in 1970, a North Carolina federal judge supported the bussing of children to comply with previous rulings on bussing, the anger of southern white people was directed against the courts and not against Nixon.
- The Department of Health, Education and Welfare was responsible for enforcing rulings in favour of desegregation and bussing. Feeling angry and frustrated by the opposition of Nixon, 125 workers within the department resigned. In response, in March 1970, Nixon stated that he supported desegregation, but opposed bussing.
- He went to great lengths to assure conservative politicians, particularly from the south, that he would do all he could to limit the activities of the Health, Education and Welfare Department. He actually proposed a block on court orders requiring bussing until 1973.

What were the achievements of the Nixon presidency on civil rights?

On 9 August 1974, following the admission of his involvement in the Watergate 'cover-up', Nixon resigned as President. He was succeeded by the Vice-President, Gerald Ford. On the issue of civil rights, what had been achieved during the Nixon years?

- Despite opposition from Nixon himself, the desegregation of schools, particularly in the south, continued. At the beginning of his presidency in 1969, 68 per cent of African-American children were attending segregated schools in the south. When he left office in 1974, the figure was 8 per cent. Bussing had been a major factor in achieving this breakthrough, despite Nixon's funding of segregated private schools for white children.
- Many black leaders and liberal Americans believed that Nixon had done little or nothing to advance the cause of civil rights. In fact, his public pronouncements against civil rights and federal welfare programmes had threatened the progress already made. As the US economy faltered during the Nixon presidency, black people suffered

most. Unemployment among black people was twice the level of white people, and among black youths it exceeded 30 per cent.

- Former President, Lyndon Johnson, went further. He believed that Nixon had, in fact, destroyed his vision of the 'Great Society', not just by his opposition to civil rights, but also by his attack on all liberals, including consumer groups and environmentalists.
- There were those on the far right of the Republican Party who believed that Nixon had been too sympathetic to civil rights issues and had allowed too many concessions. Pat Buchanan was such a Republican. Together with the Governor of California, Ronald Reagan, Buchanan began a campaign to destroy the influence of liberals and any remaining communists in American political life.
- There was also a sense in which the progress of black people in the USA continued despite the actions of Nixon and the Republicans. Nixon himself would have argued that his support of black capitalism encouraged prosperity, but it had in fact been increasing for some years. In 1940, 87 per cent of black Americans were below the poverty line. In 1960 the figure was around 50 per cent, and by 1974 it was 30 per cent. Thus, whatever policies were being pursued, the overall trend apparently remained the same. In 1976, Ralph Abernathy was asked to resign from the leadership of the SCLC for suggesting that 'The civil rights movement was no longer as fashionable as it once had been.' Was he actually suggesting that the movement had achieved its aims despite the efforts of Nixon to prevent it?

THE PRESIDENCY OF JIMMY CARTER, 1977–81

Early political career

At the beginning of his political career in the 1950s and 1960s, **Jimmy Carter** had a rather poor record on civil rights:

- Between 1959 and 1961, as a member of the Americus and Sumter County Hospital Board and the Carnegie Library Board, he accepted segregation.
- As chairman of the Sumter County Board of Education in 1962, he did nothing to change the segregated system. He actively delayed the construction of a school for black children and never supported the equipping of schools that were supposedly equal.
- He failed to help a Christian interracial community in south-west Georgia, where there was evidence of its members being attacked by white vigilantes.
- As state Senator from 1963 to 1966, he opposed bussing to achieve racial integration and he visited a segregated private school.

Perhaps his reluctance to support civil rights issues at this time is

Jimmy Carter.

understandable. Clearly, Carter believed that, to advance his political career, he needed the support of southern white people and that a liberal stance on civil rights would deny him their votes.

By the time he became Governor of Georgia in 1971, there were signs of a more liberal approach. At his inauguration ceremony, he declared that the days of segregation were over. During his governorship, he increased the number of black state employees from 4850 to 6684, and his decision to hang a portrait of Martin Luther King in the state capital was an important symbolic gesture. By the time of the presidential election campaign in 1976, Carter was seen very much as a liberal Democrat. In the primaries, although opposed by the black leader **Jesse Jackson**, he won the majority of the black vote, even in states that he lost. His victory in the presidential election later that year shows that a southern white with a liberal record on racial issues could achieve the presidency, albeit against a Republican Party badly damaged by Watergate.

What were the achievements of the Carter presidency on civil rights?

There is considerable evidence to suggest that the Carter presidency saw a significant advance in the cause of civil rights:

- Carter appointed more blacks and Hispanics to be federal judges than any President before him. The number of black federal judges increased from four per cent in 1977 to nine per cent in 1981.
- The Carter administration made sure that minority-owned companies received their fair share of federal contracts and that a fair proportion of federal funds was deposited in minority-owned banks.
- The President increased the powers of the Justice Department over voting rights and strengthened the Equal Employment Opportunities Commission in its fight against job discrimination.
- Carter appointed two leading black women to his Cabinet. Juanita Kreps became Commerce Secretary and Patricia Harris, Secretary of Housing and Urban Development. Andrew Young, a Congressman from Atlanta and a former civil rights leader, became ambassador to the United Nations.
- The legal case *Bakke* v. *Regents of The University of California* was a major challenge to the policy of affirmative action. Former US marine, Allan Bakke, challenged the University of California because he had not been admitted to the medical school, although African-Americans and other minority candidates had gained places with lower scores. When he won his case in the California Supreme Court, the university appealed to the US Supreme Court. The Justice Department in Carter's government issued a brief strongly supporting affirmative action. Taking notice of this brief, the Supreme Court ruled in favour

of the policy, but declared the system of racial quotas to be unconstitutional.

It is clear that, as President, Carter took action to benefit minority groups, particularly blacks. But even among these groups, he was not always popular. His presidency was beset with economic difficulties and the need to control inflation led to cutbacks in social welfare programmes aimed at helping minority groups. In the 1980 presidential election, he lost heavily to Ronald Reagan partly because some black people were disappointed with his presidency but more significantly because a large number of black people in the south failed to register their right to vote.

WHAT PROGRESS HAD BEEN MADE ON CIVIL RIGHTS BY 1980?

In assessing the progress made on black civil rights by 1980, it is possible to recognise a number of positive advances:

- The 1965 Voting Rights Act made the USA, and particularly the south, more democratic. In the eleven southern states (the former Confederate states), the number of registered black voters rose from 1.5 million in 1960 to 4.3 million in 1980. This had the effect of opening up elections and of challenging the two main political parties, particularly the Republicans, to appeal more to black voters.
- Important court cases, such as *Gray* v. *Sanders* (1963) and *Gomillion* v. *Lightfoot* (1980), with their rulings against gerrymandering (see page 173) and fraudulent practices, made elections fairer. By 1980, the southern states had 2600 leading black elected officials. In the country as a whole, the figure was 4600.
- An increasing number of US cities were electing black mayors. In Tuskagee in Alabama, the first black mayor was elected in 1972. This was followed by such cities as Birmingham, Alabama (Richard Arrington), and Atlanta, Georgia (Maynard Jackson and Andrew Young). In the city of Charlotte, the election of a black mayor was made possible only by the support of white voters. In 1989, in Virginia, L. Douglas Wilder became the first black to be elected a state governor. In many cities across the USA, not just in the south, all branches of local government, including police forces, were becoming more racially integrated.
- A black Congresswoman, Barbara Jordan from Texas, was a leading member in the investigation of the Watergate scandal.
- In improving their economic and social position, black middle-class Americans made enormous gains in the years leading up to 1980. The proportion of black people below the poverty line – one-third in 1969 – continued to fall. Black family income as a proportion of white family

Speech made by Jesse Jackson on the occasion of the twentieth anniversary of the March on Washington in 1983.

Reagan won Alabama by 17,500 but there were 272,000 unregistered blacks. He won Arkansas by 5000 votes, with 85,000 unregistered blacks. He won Kentucky by 17,800 votes with 62,000 unregistered blacks … So the numbers show that Reagan won through a perverse coalition of the rich and the unregistered. But this is a new day. Hands that picked cotton in 1884 will pick the president in 1984.

income continued to rise. As black educational attainment continued to increase, so did the proportion of black people in the professions. A growing black middle class became evident, with a lifestyle similar to that of white people, and black people were seen more and more at work in banks, the civil service and in universities.

- There were, however, major problems remaining. In some large cities, many black people remained poor and were forced to live in the most run-down districts. As the economic climate became harsher in the 1970s, the income gap between black people and white people began to widen. Unemployment among black people rose to twice the level among white people, and among black youths it exceeded 30 per cent. Unemployment rates for black college graduates were higher than those for white high-school dropouts. As inflation rose, city welfare programmes were often cut and black people often suffered most. As economic conditions became harsher, the policy of affirmative action and racial quotas caused increasing bitterness.

Thus, the picture in 1980 was very mixed. Clearly, a great deal of progress had been made, not least through laws to extend legal rights. At the same time, however, millions of black Americans continued to live in poor conditions, very much at the mercy of the prevailing economic climate.

SECTION 2

The struggle for black civil rights, 1865–1968

INTRODUCTION

In 1918, a Tennessee newspaper announced the burning of a live negro. The advertisement drew a crowd of 3000 spectators to the 'event'. In February and March of the following year, African-American soldiers returning from active service in the First World War were welcomed back as heroes with parades through the streets of New York and other major cities. Very soon, however, many of them became the victims of lynching and racial violence. Several were hanged or burned alive still wearing their US army uniforms. In Illinois, in the same year, 40 black workers were killed in a riot because they had taken jobs in a factory with a government contract. During the fighting, a two-year-old black child was shot and its body thrown callously into the doorway of a burning building.

These examples represent only a small percentage of the incidences of racial violence that followed the end of slavery. In the last 16 years of the nineteenth century, 2500 men and women were victims of lynching, the majority of them African-Americans. During the first decade and a half of the twentieth century, a further 1100 cases can be added to the total. Nor

A sketch published in the *Illustrated London News*, 8 August 1863, showing a mob lynching a black person in New York's Clarkson Street.

did it end in the immediate post-war years. On 19 July 1935, a homeless tenant farmer, Rubin Stacy, was taken from the prison in Fort Lauderdale, Miami, and lynched. Stacy, whose only 'crime' had been to ask for food, was just one of 22 African-American men and women who were lynched between January and November of that year.

Such acts of violence and brutal injustice may represent the extremities of racial hatred and prejudice. Nevertheless, they are indicative of the depth of feeling that produced the determination, among white Americans, to segregate African-Americans and frustrate any attempt at racial integration. That, even in the 1930s, President Roosevelt refused to support a federal bill to outlaw lynching in his liberal 'New Deal' programme, sends out a powerful message about the political significance of the race issue.

DISCRIMINATION AND SEGREGATION

The right to vote. The lengths that white politicians in the south were prepared to go to in order to prevent freedmen from gaining their civil rights has been described in Chapter 2. Empowered by the Supreme Court ruling of 1876 (*United States* v. *Reece*), which asserted states' rights over those of the federal government, many southern states effectively excluded African-Americans, and any other 'undesirables' they might identify, from voting. Hence, the imposition of qualifications based on literacy or payment of the poll tax and 'grandfather' clauses all conspired to ensure that, following the short-lived political freedom of the Reconstruction period, the vast majority of African-Americans had been disenfranchised by the beginning of the twentieth century.

Jury service. This was compounded by the failure to reform landholding in the south, thus denying freedmen the opportunity to become landowners, except in a relatively small number of cases. Deprived, in consequence, of their right to serve on juries, it became virtually impossible for black people to receive fair justice in the southern states. The **Scottsboro Trials** of 1931 are a good example of this. This state of affairs remained until it was declared unconstitutional by the Supreme Court in 1944 (*Smith* v. *Allwright*) and 1953 (*Terry* v. *Adams*). By the eve of the Second World War, three-quarters of African-Americans still lived in the south, where, in spite of the Supreme Court decisions of 1915, 1917 and 1923, the majority continued to be prohibited from voting and from serving on juries. The majority also continued to experience discrimination in jobs and segregation in their access to hospitals, universities, public parks, theatres, swimming pools and public transport.

KEY EVENT

The Scottsboro Trials (1931) In March 1931, nine African-Americans travelling on a freight train near Scottsboro, Albama, were arrested and charged with assaulting some white men and throwing them off the train. Two white women, who were removed from the same train, said that they had been raped by the nine men. Medical evidence later showed that the women were lying. Within two weeks, the nine had been tried before an all-white jury and eight had been sentenced to death. The Supreme Court intervened on the grounds that African-Americans were barred from serving on juries in Alabama. The case dragged on until 1950 when four of the remaining 'Scottsboro Boys' were given parole from their life sentences and a fifth escaped.

Educational segregation in the south. Discrimination in education is of particular interest, as it was to prove a significant factor in the later Civil Rights Movement. The high priority that freedmen put on education has been discussed in Chapter 2. However, black children were denied the opportunities available for many white pupils as a result of forced attendance at segregated establishments. This in itself, though regrettable, would not necessarily have disadvantaged them, if the segregated schools had been equally funded. However, this was not the case. In spite of rising pupil numbers, funds were disproportionately allocated to white schools, and black students were consistently deprived of equal facilities and equipment and good-quality teachers, especially in rural areas.

In 1899, a case was brought before the Supreme Court demanding access to a white school for black students whose own school had closed down (*Cumming* v. *School Board of Richmond County*). The court refused to support the request. As time went by, the differential in expenditure widened. Between 1913 and 1932, 5000 schools were built for black children in fifteen southern states with money from a charitable trust. Yet in spite of this multimillion-dollar expenditure, facilities for black youngsters still lagged behind those for white people. Even in situations where all services were cut, black people still lost the most because they were always starting from a lower point of provision. This was the case when the Great Depression hit the USA in the 1930s. One positive development, however, was the equalisation of pay for black teachers, which, by 1945, was almost on a par with that of white teachers, thanks to the efforts of Thurgood Marshall and the NAACP (although this was achieved only after some legal wrangling).

	Spending per black student ($)	Spending per white student ($)
1900	2.00	3.00
1930	2.00	7.00
1935–6	13.09	37.87

1890	Mississippi
1895	South Carolina
1898	Louisiana
1900	North Carolina
1901	Alabama
1902	Virginia
1908	Georgia
1909	Oklahoma

States excluding African-Americans from voting.

1880	714,884
1910	1,426,102
1930	1,893,068

Black pupil numbers in school in Alabama, Arkansas, Florida, Georgia, Louisiana, Mississippi, North and South Carolina, Tennessee and Texas.

Disproportionate sums spent on the education of white and black students in the southern states.

Educational segregation in the north. During the First World War, increasing numbers of African-Americans moved north in response to the availability of work in wartime industries. There, the situation was little better. The growth of urban populations due to this influx meant that black people were forced to congregate in urban ghettos, thus avoiding the need for active policies of discrimination. African-American children inevitably attended schools in their communities that were predominantly black anyway. Northern states responded differently to this new challenge. New York State was unusual in that it prohibited forced

Supreme Court rulings

Guinn v. *US (1915).* 'Grandfather' clauses applied in Maryland and Oklahoma were declared unconstitutional on the grounds that they contravened the Fifteenth Amendment.

Buchanan v. *Warley (1917).* A Louisville law ordering negroes to live in a designated part of the city was declared illegal.

Moore v. *Dempsey (1923).* The trial of twelve African-American prisoners in Arkansas arrested because of their alleged role in a race riot in Elaine, Arkansas, in 1919, was declared to be unfair because there were no African-Americans on the jury. A retrial was ordered.

attendance in separate schools. Others pursued mixed policies where some but not all schools were racially segregated. In Kansas and Arizona, for example, elementary schools were separate by law. Communities then provided their own secondary schools, although these also were usually segregated. City administrations attempted to pursue 'separate but equal' policies. Ultimately, parental pressure dictated segregated education and students themselves supported it.

Education and the campaign for civil rights. In several respects, the experience of education is significant in the campaign for civil rights. On the one hand, the existence of segregated schools threatened to perpetuate white domination on the basis that the superior education available to white students increased the likelihood of their becoming leaders in all walks of life, but especially in politics. On the other hand, there were notable successes among African-Americans. The illiteracy rate was significantly reduced from 81 per cent in 1870 to 16 per cent by 1930. Admissions to black colleges of higher education also increased. By 1933, there were 38,000 African-Americans in higher education. This produced a recognisable middle-class elite who would emerge as leaders in politics, trade unions and the campaign for civil rights. Booker T. Washington and W. E. B. Du Bois are but two examples of these. By the time that Franklin Roosevelt formed his 'Black Cabinet' of advisers in the 1930s, there were black men and women with expertise in politics, economics, social work and the law. More significantly, perhaps, the wider effect of education was to create generations of African-Americans who were not prepared to accept injustice and discrimination.

WHY DID DISCRIMINATION AND SEGREGATION PERSIST BEFORE THE SECOND WORLD WAR?

The answer to this question lies partly in the efforts of the early Civil Rights Movement itself and partly in the reactions of the white, native-born population of the USA. A key factor was the fundamental racism of US citizens in the north as well as in the south, and the lengths that they were prepared to go to stop black Americans from obtaining their rights of citizenship. Of equal importance was the lack of support for black civil rights from politicians generally, and from successive presidents in particular. Also relevant were the divisions among African-Americans themselves about the way forward.

It is probably true to say that, in the period from 1865 until the end of the Second World War, the most optimistic time for African-Americans was during Reconstruction. For the former supporters of the abolition of slavery and for radical Republicans generally, the extension of the rights of citizenship to African-Americans, expressed in the Fourteenth and

Fifteenth Amendments, was the culmination of a long campaign for justice and freedom. That this political freedom was short-lived cannot be explained simply in terms of the assertion of states' rights in establishing discriminatory legislation. The answer lies partly in the dubious success of white supremacist organisations in the USA and partly in the divisions that developed on the subject of black aspirations for the future.

White Supremacist Organisations. Emancipation saw the emergence and rapid growth of societies such as the Order of the White Camelia, the Pale Faces, the White Brotherhood and the Knights of the Ku Klux Klan. Of these, the latter easily became the most notorious and successful in terrifying and intimidating the African-American population in the south. The emergence of groups seeking to uphold the purity of American society was not new. However, the first Ku Klux Klan was unprecedented not only in its violence and cruelty, but also in the way in which it declared war on the Republican Party and used terrorism to undermine its reforming policies in the south.

The Ku Klux Klan. The Klan began as a kind of club set up by ex-Confederate soldiers in Pulaski, Tennessee, in 1866. In their strange white, hooded clothing, they rode out in the night, their horses' hooves muffled, posing as the spirits of the Confederate dead returning as vigilantes to protect white communities from freed black people. Their calling card was a burning cross. The terror that the sight of them created was often sufficient to intimidate their so-called enemies, but this did not stop them resorting to beatings, whippings, brandings, mutilations and even murder. The Klan was particularly effective in preventing freedmen from using their vote in states where they had not been disenfranchised.

The Ku Klux Klan was, however, a fundamentally political organisation. The membership was fairly young, middle-class men, but in some areas its activities were dictated by older, powerful people in the Democratic Party, working to re-establish its traditional hold over the south. Republican **carpetbaggers** from the north and southern **scalawags** became a focus either of their intimidation (they left small wooden coffins on their doorsteps) or of their violence, as did educated black people who were active in the Republican cause. Freedmen trying to set up their own businesses in white areas or to own their own land were also persecuted, particularly if they were defiant or assertive. The Klan's reputation for lawlessness and terror sometimes threatens to mask this fundamental political purpose and probably helps to explain the necessity of the legislation of 1870 and 1871 that outlawed the organisation. Once started, the local branches and units of the organisation were difficult to control, even by its own leadership. Some branches undoubtedly attracted members who were motivated by racial hatred and who relished the torture and physical abuse in which they indulged.

KEY TERMS

Carpetbagger was a derisory term used to describe northern politicians who went to the south after the Civil War, supposedly to make money and then return to the north. In fact, they were not all politicians, but were people who wanted to promote the regeneration of the south and bring it closer to the north by developing industry, introducing free public education and encouraging enterprise.

Scalawag was a derisory term used to discredit native-born white southerners who supported the Republicans. Many were rich, but others were poorer farmers who saw the Republicans as their hope for future development and improvement.

HEINEMANN ADVANCED HISTORY

Dealing with the Klan. The difficulty faced by the authorities in rounding up Klan members for punishment under the Enforcement Act (or Ku Klux Klan Act, as it came to be known) of 1871 reveals two facets of this particularly sordid period of history. First, the fear and terror that the Klan had created made many victims as well as other potential informants reluctant to come forward to identify and give evidence against their tormentors. Second, there was significant passive support for the Klan and its 'crusade' in the south. Certainly Democrats in the north and south condemned the law, calling it a Force Act. When members were prosecuted, the wealth and influence of their backers was often evident in the quality of their lawyers, who were clever enough to overturn cases in court on technicalities.

Southern Republicans recognised that they would be unable to enforce the laws in the south without support. Consequently, federal troops were used in states such as North Carolina to round up and prosecute Klan members. Around 700 Klan members were successfully prosecuted in Mississippi, while in South Carolina it took a military campaign in October 1871 to purge some state counties. During this period, the Attorney-General, Amos T. Akerman, horrified by the evidence as it unfolded, made a point of publicising details of the atrocities committed by the Klan in the south and undertook lecture tours to spread the word in the north. 'I feel greatly saddened by this business,' he wrote. 'It has revealed a perversion of moral sentiment among the Southern whites which bodes ill to that part of the country for this generation.' Ultimately, while hundreds served prison sentences for their crimes, the punishments rarely matched the enormity of the crimes that had been committed and many more hundreds undoubtedly escaped punishment altogether. When the Ku Klux Klan re-emerged in 1915, it had a quite different focus and purpose. This is discussed in Section 5.

Conflicting views of progress. The activities of the Ku Klux Klan may have died down, but lynching, injustice and racial violence continued. Mass hysteria and hatred could easily be whipped up by fairly trivial incidents, sparking off full-scale riots, during which the most appalling atrocities were committed against African-Americans. It is not surprising that, against this background, they became divided about the way forward. There was no united black Civil Rights Movement before the outbreak of the Second World War, not at a national level, at least.

The concept of 'separate but equal' appeared attractive to many who lived in daily terror of reprisals or abuse. Discrimination and segregation appeared almost protective if economic security and advancement could be secured. Hence the attraction of the philosophy of Booker T. Washington (see Chapter 3). Those seeking integration were, at this time, ready to support the legal battle being waged by the NAACP while, for the mass of downtrodden, persecuted black people living in urban squalor by the 1920s, Marcus Garvey's proud assertion of self-awareness was comforting and hopeful (see Chapter 4). During this period the ground was prepared for future protest movements.

The situation in 1941. By the time of the USA's entry into the Second World War, almost three-quarters of the country's black population still lived in the south, in spite of the large-scale migrations that had taken place during the First World War and in response to the Great Depression of the 1930s. Here, they were almost all excluded from voting and from serving on juries. They were refused access to white hospitals, universities, public parks and swimming pools. In urban areas, they were condemned to work in lowly, unskilled occupations. In rural areas, they struggled to survive as sharecroppers, tenant farmers or labourers. Their life expectancy was at least ten years less than that of white people. In the north, they were subjected to racist violence and discrimination in the workplace and in housing. Unemployment rates, especially during the Depression, were significantly higher than those of white workers.

African-Americans had, however, taken advantage of opportunities for education and were developing the sense of solidarity that comes from shared adversity. This expressed itself in the formation of local self-help groups such as the Harlem Tenants League to fight rent increases and evictions. African-American consumers joined together to boycott white businesses that refused to employ black workers. The NAACP was emerging as a powerful pressure group, campaigning for the enforcement of the Fourteenth and Fifteenth Amendments and against lynching, as well as against forced segregation and discrimination in housing and jobs. It had gained some notable successes through its Legal Defence Fund. Admission of African-Americans to trade union organisations such as the Congress of Industrial Organisations and A. Philip Randolph's Brotherhood of Sleeping Car Porters provided another vehicle through which to assert rights and campaign for redress. The Second World War would provide the catalyst that would galvanise African-Americans into action, to win the rights to which they believed they were entitled.

HOW IMPORTANT WERE THE NEW CIVIL RIGHTS ORGANISATIONS TO THE SUCCESS OF THE CIVIL RIGHTS CAUSE?

Developments in the war years. Until 1942, the NAACP carried the banner for civil rights, campaigning at a federal level largely on its own.

The only other significant organisation to operate at this level, the **National Urban League,** had a more limited remit: it largely concerned itself with black social and economic welfare in the big cities. However, the next twenty years saw dramatic developments and new organisations that were to make an enormous impact on every conceivable aspect of civil rights.

Interpretations. Historians now see the modern Civil Rights Movement starting well before the Brown verdict or the dramatic events of Montgomery in the mid-1950s; moreover, 1968 cannot be seen as the finish either. Adam Fairclough (1987) calls the 'Montgomery to Memphis time bracket' too restrictive. Sitkoff (1993) sees the depression years of the 1930s, with its migration and New Deal measures, as the time when 'stirrings began', even though he concedes that the basic conditions of life for black people barely changed in the 1930s. Richard Dalfiume (1968), in a seminal article, viewed the war years as significant in beginning a change to a more militant black outlook. Recalling the way the Japanese fought back against the Americans, he refers to one African-American who said he wanted to get his eyes slanted: then, next time he was pushed, he too could fight back. And the issue of black people fighting a white man's war was all too apparent. Surely, as A. Philip Randolph himself had argued, they should fight as free men and not as 'Jim Crow' slaves.

A. Philip Randolph and the March on Washington Movement.

Even before the entry of the USA into the Second World War at the end of 1941, the need for additional workers in the country's defence industries became apparent. As in the First World War, blacks could frequently supply the need. But their manner of employment raised crucial questions of equality. This was the issue that concerned A. Philip Randolph when he organised the proposed march on Washington. At first sight, it may seem surprising that President Roosevelt apparently caved in so quickly to Randolph's threat. A week before the proposed demonstration he issued an Executive Order, 'reaffirming policy of full participation in the defense program by all persons regardless of race, creed, color or national origin'. This had been Randolph's precise demand. Moreover, the Fair Employees Practices Commission (FEPC), whose members were appointed by Roosevelt, investigated numerous complaints and addressed valid grievances. But Roosevelt felt, as he put it, that he was merely reaffirming existing policy: it was not altogether a new departure.

It seems that Roosevelt genuinely believed that Randolph would carry out his threat, since he had appeared to acquire an impressive degree of support. In his initial call for volunteers, Randolph mentioned a figure of 10,000. When he called off the march after Roosevelt had conceded to his demands, the figure of 100,000 was mentioned. Nor was the idea lost, as Randolph now organised the all-black March on Washington Movement (MOWM). In 1963, Randolph was involved with the famous actual March on Washington. Also in that decade, black-only movements developed again. However, Meier and Rudwick (1973) as well as Cook (1998) believe that in many ways Randolph's movement looked back as much as forward. They argue that his policies had much in common with the radical labour activism of the 1930s. Certainly, Randolph's movement had faded by the end of the war. Randolph felt that rights had to be taken rather than given: only power, he believed, could effect the enforcement or adoption of a certain policy. Even had he not lived to be involved with the 1963 Washington march (he did not die until 1979), he would still have to be seen as an early civil rights leader.

NAACP and CORE: variations in approach. The NAACP had a long tradition of protest and for a time during the war it became more militant. Before and after the war, it tended to concentrate on legal cases to try to undermine the system of segregation. But the executive secretary between 1928 and 1955, Walter White, demanded that black people be allowed to participate fully in the war effort. In the early days of the war in particular, the NAACP somewhat uncharacteristically gave its support to striking black workers in Detroit and demanded equality of treatment for them in the workplace. The circumstances of war helped to shape these demands for equality. For instance, Neil Wynn (1993) has pointed out that the rejections for military service on grounds of illiteracy brought the lack of black educational achievements into the forefront of public notice.

By 1942, a more militant atmosphere was in the air. The idea of the sit-in protest against Jim Crow and all it stood for was developing. The best-known example of this was the founding of CORE by James Farmer in 1942. Exempted from military draft by his well-documented pacifist views and impressed by the non-violent resistance of Gandhi in India, Farmer organised numerous non-violent protests in Chicago and other cities. He argued that black people must seize the initiative to demand reform. He was not the only one. Future Black Congress member Adam Clayton Powell had organised a protest in New York against segregation on the buses in the previous year. And, in another foreshadowing of future events, a group of black protesters demanded to be served at a segregated soda fountain in Washington in 1943. These actions were not without success. *De jure* segregation in public places in the north was far more restricted than in the south and declined still further after this type of campaigning.

With the serious race riots in 1943, however, some of these events were rather overshadowed. Moreover, the violence frightened the cautious leadership of the NAACP. They continued with their important legal work and scored a big success with *Smith* v. *Allright* in 1944, outlawing the white primary in Texas. But they withdrew support for more direct action. Sitkoff (1993) argues that the important black initiative was now lost, and even Wynn (1993), who takes a more moderate line, feels that the black press became more cautious. Therefore, Randolph's call for civil disobedience in 1943 came at an awkward time and received only limited support.

Other effects of the war. The irony of the USA fighting a racist group like the Nazis while oppressing blacks at home was not lost on black leaders. In October 1942 a group of black people met in Durham, North Carolina, pledged to fight for democracy at home as well as abroad. These included Martin Luther King's future teacher, Benjamin Mays. In the following year they met again in Richmond, Virginia, and this time issued a common statement on civil rights with sympathetic white support. Cook (1998) sees this as a modest but significant start to future post war cooperation between the **educated black elite** and liberal and radical white supporters. Seeds for future action were being sown.

In different areas, sometimes on a small scale, protest movements had been organised for a considerable time. When historian William H. Chafe (1980) researched the sit-ins at Greensboro, North Carolina in 1960, he discovered a whole previous generation of local protest in the area. In 1943, for example, Randolph Blackwell was inspired by a talk by Ella Baker and he set up a Youth Chapter of the NAACP in the town. In the same year, Robert Sharp, Secretary of the Colored Ministerial Alliance, received nearly a third of the electorate's vote with a pledge to attack segregation. Of course, Greensboro was well outside the Deep South, and the proportion of blacks able to register to vote without fear of attack was a lot greater. Soon after the war, a black voter registration drive produced 333 new voters. Positive ideas about civil rights could circulate more easily. There is no doubt that, in Greensboro at least, the 1940s was a significant decade for civil rights. It puts the sit-ins in the town in 1960 into clearer context.

The Montgomery Movement. Despite historical revision, the Montgomery Bus Boycott clearly remains significant in beginning the process of concrete achievement for civil rights and was an inspiration for more new organisations. It is true, as Cook (1998) points out, that few now see Rosa Parks' defiance, however significant, as a crucial starting point in the Civil Rights Movement. Nevertheless, during the event, we can see the raising of the horizons of the black protesters. No longer would they merely seek to gain a reasonable status for their race, separate from the white majority; the ultimate goal now became one of integration.

KEY TERM

Educated black elite This refers to the minority of blacks who had obtained a high standard of education and secure, well-paid employment, often in business or the professions, quite often in the Church and the law. In being able to provide valuable services for black people that white people were unwilling to, many of them found segregation to their advantage and were reluctant to support militant tactics that might disrupt it.

In this respect, the MIA played a crucial role. It mobilised grass-roots support among the black community and managed to avoid tension between the black elite, whose businesses could sometimes do quite well out of segregation, and the rest. In fact, the black elite provided the leadership that their experience and education qualified them to do. For all his great efforts in Birmingham, Fred Shuttlesworth found it hard to make the same progress, at least before 1963, because he lacked the support of the black elite, who did not want things stirred up. One of the great achievements of the SCLC was to mobilise these black elites in many southern towns.

The role of Martin Luther King and the SCLC. Not the least of Martin Luther King's crucial roles was to retain the respect and support of Montgomery's black elite while at the same time proving an inspiration for the working-class black community. They saw him as the person who could articulate their demands. The crucial moment came when King's house was firebombed and by force of example he prevented violent retaliation. Breaking the cycle of hatred and violence became a central plank not only in King's personal philosophy, but also in the formation of the SCLC in January 1957.

With CORE moribund, the NAACP committed to a different (if complementary) strategy and, with King's personal reputation so high, the SCLC was, from the start, a leading civil rights organisation. But it is easy to exaggerate its dominance in the early days. The initiatives of 1960 and 1961 did not come from the SCLC, although they certainly benefited from the more optimistic mood that was engendered. Moreover, the non-violent yet confrontational style of their protest fitted the SCLC philosophy very well.

So Montgomery should remain of central importance in the civil rights story. Marable (1991) plays it down by devoting only half a page to it in a book of 230 pages; yet even he acknowledges that 'this challenge to racism blossomed into an international event'. From now on the world watched the struggle with interest. One factor that would in future influence US policy-makers was the frequent criticism from abroad, not least the Soviet Union. The USA, supposedly the champion of the free world, was busy oppressing large numbers of its own people. The Cold War situation could once again be turned to the movement's advantage.

From the start of February 1960, dramatic developments in civil rights activity raised the tempo of the movement and brought one new group (SNCC) and one revived group (CORE) into the forefront of demands. With the aid of a change of president and of mood in the federal government, the new protesters were to force a response to their vigorously put demands.

Sit-ins and the SNCC. The student sit-ins that began at Greensboro in February 1960 were a striking case of an initiative being suddenly taken. They started as an entirely spontaneous movement. Branch (1990) points out that having no plan was an advantage, since this meant there were no limitations on their actions and no thoughts about the problems they might find. In fact, the initiative surprisingly remained with them as the shop management became confused about what to do. If this had been Mississippi or Alabama, we can guess what would have happened to them. Moreover, the students served as an inspiration for many other places, firstly in other parts of North Carolina and then all over the south. The generation of black students that got so involved in these activities was one that was less conscious of black life before the war. As the 1960s wore on, some could not even remember life before the Brown verdict.

Some of the students were not unaware of black liberation movements in Africa, where a number of countries were gaining their independence at about this time. Tom Mboya, the Kenyan fighter for independence from Britain, had spoken at W. E. B. Du Bois' old university, Fisk, in the late 1950s. But domestic factors were more significant. Here was the first generation of schoolchildren since the Brown verdict, yet they had now reached college and still there was no real racial integration. Their hopes of change had been dashed and they decided to protest in their own way.

The very fact that they were students distinguished many of them from their parents, who had rarely had higher educational opportunities. In this respect things had changed, but what the students still demanded was equality of opportunity and treatment. It was an old demand. On hearing of the sit-ins, Eleanor Roosevelt, now 77 years old, thoroughly approved. And they joined in demonstrations and sit-ins so widely that they now provided opportunities for organisations like SCLC to run more campaigns. The result was the formation of the Student Non-violent Cordinating Committee (SNCC, pronounced 'Snick'), an organisation independent from SCLC, although one with which it was to have close, if sometimes explosive, links. King's supporters from the SCLC, James Lawson and Ella Baker, played a major role in setting up the organisation.

Freedom Rides and CORE. This renewal of action was not just confined to the south. Indeed, the next significant initiative after the sit-ins, the Freedom Rides, presented an opportunity for north and south, black and white, to work together. CORE had been declining since James Farmer had left in 1950 and had now been inactive for some years. Its revival reminds us of the links between the new style of protest and the old wartime activity. Now, having been Campaign Director for a short time for the NAACP, Farmer returned to his old organisation in 1961 and immediately set about organising the Rides.

These bold trips did not come out of nothing. They were in part inspired by the Boynton case in the Federal Supreme Court (see Section 1), extending desegregation on inter-travel services to bus terminals. The plan was simple and the tactics were revealing. Black and white passengers would board a bus together in the north and stay together even when it reached the south. If they remained unmolested, they had scored a great victory; but if, as was likely in the Deep South, they were arrested, then pressure could be put on the federal authorities to get the state officials to enforce the law. In this way, the federal authorities would be made to intervene to ensure the law was kept.

Mobilising the black community. The vigour of all these protests, and the commitment and courage of the sit-in demonstrators and Freedom Riders, again succeeded in mobilising important elements of the black community. This time it was not so much the older members, tired of the injustices of segregation, but the younger ones, who became involved. Their expectations were beginning to be raised, but they still found their race a bar to their progress in US society. Again, CORE was to be prominent in this development along with SNCC, which had also organised some of the Freedom Rides.

In the next few years, SNCC played a crucial part in removing segregation from many states outside the Deep South, such as Virginia, Tennessee, Texas and parts of Florida. In addition, during the early 1960s they worked at voter registration campaigns in some of the most difficult and dangerous areas of the Deep South, especially Mississippi. While these efforts were not immediately successful in statistical terms, they raised civil rights issues in the remotest corners of the land and provided an organisational base for later progress.

SCLC. The SCLC, with all its resources, commitment, enthusiasm and charismatic leadership, could clearly play a larger role here. Only after the sit-ins and Freedom Rides did it become more active. King and SCLC tended to run campaigns only when they were invited to do so, such as at Savannah, Georgia, and Gadsden, Alabama. This was certainly true of the campaign in Albany, where local leader John Anderson asked King and Abernathy to join the protest. Some leaders, such as James Forman of SNCC, felt they should not have intruded into what were local affairs.

The relative failure of the Albany campaign showed the SCLC how dependent the movement was on having southern officials who would play into their hands. If, like Albany police chief Laurie Pritchett, they ensured no police brutality, there would be less unfavourable publicity to feed on and no likelihood of federal interference. But Albany and other campaigns did show how the grass-roots nature of the movement was growing, with sit-ins and protests in a wide variety of places. When deciding to join the campaigners at Saint Augustine in 1964, the SCLC had been faced with a choice of several towns where King had been invited to go. This is a testimony to his popularity and reputation: it is also a testimony to the vibrant nature of local protest in places such as Danville, Virginia, and Jackson, Mississippi.

At the start of 1963, all the civil rights organisations had made clear progress both in the strength of their campaigning and in the more favourable attitude of the federal authorities towards them. But concrete achievements were still limited. In the next two years, vast strides were made, both in the scale of protest and in the degree of federal response. Also, unconsciously, opponents of civil rights played into the movement's hands. Nowhere was this clearer than in Birmingham, Alabama.

The role of the main organisations in Birmingham, 1963. The need to ensure favourable publicity was clearly a key factor in selecting Birmingham for a major civil rights campaign in 1963. The choice also owed a good deal to the reputation of its police chief and erstwhile mayor, Bull Connor. Historians are agreed that one factor in choosing Birmingham was that, if Birmingham's tough nut could be cracked, segregation in the south could be broken down. But there were others. The strength of Shuttlesworth's supporters – over 600 dedicated men and women – was important and made possible the length of the protest, despite the severity of the treatment they received. Perhaps even more significant was the well-known short fuse of Connor, which, it was hoped, would bring him unfavourable publicity. At first, Connor did not oblige, but then he lost his temper and exceeded all their expectations.

The effects of Birmingham were considerable. It gave a great boost to civil rights protesters in many different states. Flushed with the success of Birmingham, they continued campaigning. The logic of the Birmingham campaign was that other places would succumb quickly and, indeed, desegregation proceeded apace. In October 1963, Danville, Virginia, where there had been strong resistance to desegregation, appointed its first black policeman. In Greensboro, home of the 1960 sit-ins, full-scale integration now became the policy after further demonstrations. Cook (1998) has pointed out that segregated towns on the fringes of the south, such as Louisville, Kentucky, voluntarily desegregated in late 1963 without any direct campaign.

Washington and after. The March on Washington in the summer of 1963 was designed to show the strength and unity of the movement.

Kennedy had been wary of the original plans, which seemed more like a demonstration for jobs than a march for freedom. However, he was persuaded of the value of the march. If black protesters were to be out on the streets already – and after Birmingham they were hungry for more – then it was best that their enthusiasm be channelled in a respectable and peaceful direction. The appearance of a calm, smartly dressed, multiracial crowd, apparently united in their desire for peaceful constitutional change, would, it was hoped, impress the waverers in Congress who were still deciding on their course of action. It was clear that the 1964 Civil Rights Act alone was not sufficient to ensure universal black voter registration, and that separate legislation was required.

For the SCLC, the focus was now to be on Alabama in general and Selma in particular. Early in 1965 the voter registration campaign began there. Its rationale, tactics and ultimate effects were not dissimilar to Birmingham. Once again, the television cameras faithfully recorded the full horrors of southern racism. They also recorded Sheriff Clark's crude attempt at censorship by putting his hand in front of the camera. Once again the initiative lay with the campaigners. Their efforts at Selma would ensure that a voting rights act, with teeth, would become law. The 1964 Civil Rights Act had clauses that should have made a subsequent Voting Rights Bill unnecessary. After the Act had passed, the main organisations, the SCLC, CORE and SNCC, were keen to test it by pushing for voter registration in the south, concentrating on difficult areas like Mississippi. But the civil rights organisations were now entering rougher waters.

SCLC, NAACP and SNCC: the organisations compared. The different successes of Birmingham and Washington owed much to the campaigning skills of the SCLC. So they must take considerable credit for the success of the movement in bringing about desegregation. The organisation provided a platform for the greatest orator of the movement, Martin Luther King, and inspired many important figures in the Civil Rights Movement to join its ranks, such as Shuttlesworth, C. T. Vivian, Andrew Young and Jesse Jackson (see page 237). It has been criticised on several counts. It was not run democratically and King had to take some flak for imposing his wishes on it in deciding where the next campaign would be and exactly what tactics would be followed. Its detailed organisation often left much to be desired and, unlike the other groups, it had no provision for individual membership. But Adam Fairclough (1987), in his sympathetic if not uncritical history of the movement, argues that its lack of organisation enabled the SCLC to adapt with the minimum of bureaucratic delay to a new situation.

Here, the SCLC was a contrast to the NAACP, which was criticised for being too bound up with organisation and slow to respond to events. The

President Kennedy poses with Whitney Young, Martin Luther King, John Lewis, Rabbi Joachim Prinz, Dr Eugene Donnaly, Philip Randolph, Walker Reuther, Vice-President Johnson and Roy Wilkins, 28 August 1963, at the White House.

NAACP and its leader Roy Wilkins have also been accused of lacking commitment to the militant but non-violent action developed by the other groups. It is true that Wilkins seemed embarrassed by the success of tactics that he had thought would fail. However, the NAACP provided a different kind of service after the Brown decision. In continuing to focus on legal cases that would bring benefit, such as *Boynton* v. *Virginia* (1960), it could claim achievements of its own. For years it had kept going when other groups had foundered and Brown must be seen as one of its greatest triumphs. Its top-down structure may not have produced as much excitement as the other groups, but it provided a certain amount of stability and it still keeps going today.

In contrast, the lively SNCC, while making a much bigger impact during the early 1960s, fell victim to internal disputes as the decade went on and the divisions between Black Power and the traditional movement became apparent. It ceased to exist in the early 1970s. It was clear that divisions in the movement had already begun to appear.

Conclusion. A. Philip Randolph's effort during the Second World War with the March on Washington Movement is now seen as setting out issues that would be at the forefront of debate for some time. Moreover, the efforts of CORE and other groups and individuals to set in train non-violent protests in the war years played their part. They set an agenda for a later time when circumstances would be more favourable for greater progress to be made. The NAACP, too, made significant progress on the legal front. Though we must also look to earlier developments for the origins of the modern Civil Rights Movement, Montgomery did produce a fighting spirit and a great leader. New organisations were spawned and the nature of campaigning became more confrontational and dynamic. At this stage:

- unity was more noticeable than differences
- outside the Deep South, segregation was breaking down under the pressure that the organisations exerted
- the federal government was becoming more responsive to the demands made.

The dramatic scale of the protest in Birmingham and the impressive size of the multiracial March on Washington bear witness to the crucial role of the main organisations in the progress of the Civil Rights Movement.

HOW UNITED WAS THE CIVIL RIGHTS MOVEMENT UP TO 1965?

Introduction. As is perhaps inevitable in any large and wide-ranging movement, stresses and strains over principles, aims, ideas and tactics were always present in the Civil Rights Movement. Disagreements would surface over the morality of the non-violent principle, whether integration of black and white was the ultimate aim, the validity of the idea of Black Supremacy and whether political and legal or social and economic concerns should be the chief priority of the movement. The worst of these divisions did not appear until the mid-1960s, but how far were they foreshadowed in the years before?

Wartime contrasts: NAACP and CORE. The NAACP had a cautious, not to say conservative, image and has perhaps suffered in comparison with the other organisations in not having a single volume history of the organisation, though Mark Tushnet has written extensively on their legal campaigns for educational equality between 1925 and 1961. The SCLC has had Adam Fairclough; SNCC, Claybourne Carson; and CORE, August Meier and Elliott Rudwick. More radical historians have sometimes been scathing about NAACP leadership. Marable (1991) – following the views of W. E. B. Du Bois – sees its executive secretary, Walter White, as totally self-centred and intolerant of any questioning of his policies. Yet White was an effective NAACP chief from 1928 until 1955. He used his pale skin to pass himself off, when occasion demanded, as 'white' in skin as well as name. His shrewd and detailed analysis of the causes of the Detroit riots in 1943 showed his grasp of the important issues, such as the complexity of housing patterns, employment problems and violent attacks on black people.

However, there were always those who felt that direct protest action would be more effective than White appeared to acknowledge. Philip Randolph's approach, emphasising labour questions rather than schools and the franchise, clearly brought a new perspective. His success in getting a response from President Roosevelt on the question of fair employment contrasted with the slow and painstaking legal complexities that the NAACP was undertaking on questions such as education and the vote.

As we have seen, during the war years, the Civil Rights Movement spawned new organisations such as CORE. Its direct action style, involving sit-ins, was far more confrontational than anything the NAACP was doing. But at this stage the differences between the organisations tended to be merely tactical. The broad aims of desegregation, voting registration and fair treatment at work were uniformly apparent. The move north of many blacks had changed the priorities somewhat, but essentially the objectives were similar. The source of future divisions and different philosophies, however, was developing with the rapid population movements, the closed nature of the ghettos, the hostility of many white people and rapidly developing social problems. Civil rights campaigns, especially those led by southern black people from the black elite, did not touch the minds of many working-class northern black people. Later on, the allegiance of some of these groups was to be given to Black Power. But it was not that the mainstream Civil Rights Movement had lost the support of these northern black people; it had never really had it in any significant numbers.

How good were relations between the SCLC and the NAACP? During the early Cold War years, when CORE faded from the scene, the NAACP was again the main banner carrier for black civil rights. However, the dramatic events of Montgomery and the subsequent formation of the SCLC in 1957 produced tensions within the movement as a whole. Nonetheless, the divisions between the SCLC and the NAACP can be exaggerated. Both essentially had faith in the American system. The legal campaigns of the NAACP were designed to show that the Constitution had already made provision for black equality and that the modern Supreme Court would give it to them in time. Similarly, King's 'dream' was, he argued, deeply rooted in 'the American Dream'. At his famous Washington address, King quoted directly from the Declaration of Independence: 'We hold these truths to be self-evident, that all men are created equal.' The problem was that the original Constitution did not make any direct references to equality, and it was the Constitution and not the Independence Declaration against which the Supreme Court would be making its judgment. The best hope was the 'equal protection' clause from the Fourteenth Amendment to the Constitution: 'Nor to deny to any person within its jurisdiction the equal protection of the laws'.

In the 1950s, all civil rights organisations had to steer clear of any association with communism but, in the case of men like Wilkins and King, this distance was quite genuine. Indeed, King, like others, tried to turn the anti-communist feeling to his advantage. As he remarked, 'Nothing provides the communists with a better climate for expansion and infiltration than the continued alliance of our nation with racism.'

King went out of his way to try to avoid hurting the feelings of men like Wilkins. The SCLC made it clear that it wanted to cooperate with the NAACP over issues of common interest, such as voter registration. The SCLC's structure was also very different from that of the NAACP, and it avoided having individual membership, so that the NAACP would not feel that its members were being poached. The Prayer Pilgrimage to Washington in 1957 demonstrated the relative unity of the movement at this stage. It was organised to protest against the fact that the Eisenhower administration had done little to implement Supreme Court decisions such as the Brown case and had refused Philip Randolph's request to discuss the issue with black leaders. The Brown verdict saw King, Wilkins and Randolph on the same platform. In fact, Randolph had been instrumental in getting Wilkins to agree to join with King. Although the occasion was much less celebrated and clearly had far fewer people than the march of 1963, the 25,000 who joined it were an impressive enough number at the time, although disappointing to its leaders.

The SCLC and SNCC in the early 1960s. The NAACP remained sceptical of the value of direct action and the student sit-ins and Freedom Rides of 1961–2, the latter indicating the revival of the almost defunct CORE. It was too militant for the NAACP leaders' taste. King, however, thoroughly approved, and saw the non-violent principles with which the protests were run as consistent with his own philosophy. Relations between the SCLC and SNCC, however, could produce tension from time to time. SNCC was a separate organisation, but its leaders complained that King and the SCLC saw it as a kind of youth wing of their own organisation. The SCLC retaliated by pointing out that SNCC was happy to take its money to help run its own campaigns. SNCC was doubtful about the idea of local movements importing big names like King and Abernathy to assist them. James Forman of SNCC, for example, did not feel that King and Abernathy should have accepted the invitation to go to Albany in December 1961: he felt their presence complicated the situation and interfered with SNCC's own efforts there. It might discourage local workers from making the major effort themselves.

The decision to make SNCC an independent organisation was a significant one. It would be, as Cook (1998) puts it, more of a grass-roots movement than the SCLC, where King, despite consulting his leading colleagues, exerted somewhat dictatorial powers as leader. Within SNCC there were vigorous debates. After the Freedom Rides, should non-violent direct action continue or should they focus on voter registration? In the end a compromise was reached. They would do both: Diane Nash would lead direct action projects and Charles Jones would organise voter registration projects. These were both seen as vital since, if they were successful, additional pressure could be placed on politicians who would then see an electoral advantage in courting black interests.

After the Freedom Rides, SNCC spent a good deal of time on voter registration and school integration campaigns. This latter subject was an area where all the civil rights groups felt they could cooperate. So, in 1963, to work together better, they formed the Co-ordinating Council of Community Organisations (CCCO). In some areas, this helped provide a sense of unity for a while.

Women in the movement. Personality differences could cause tensions. Ella Baker – a key figure in the SCLC and SNCC– felt that she was patronised in what we would now call a sexist way by Martin Luther King. She claimed that he was pompous and poor at genuine dialogue, and that he treated women condescendingly. Other members of these organisations were awed at the way she stood up to King and answered back when she did not agree. She was one of a number of women who felt that the movement was too male dominated, and who were annoyed that men's perception of women was that they should act in a merely supportive role, like Coretta Scott King. Many women followed Ella Baker into an active role in the movement, and all this before the 1960s feminist movement in the USA had got fully under way. Oates (1982), in his biography of King, discounts much of the criticism, but Fairclough (1987), who is by no means hostile to King overall, admits that, in common with many men at the time, 'he found it difficult to treat women as intellectual equals'.

In fact, women had been prominent in the Civil Rights Movement from the start. Rosa Parks and Jo Ann Robinson had played the crucial opening roles in the Montgomery bus boycott of 1955. The respectability of Rosa Parks made her a suitable sufferer for the cause. Her brave refusal to move down the bus and Jo Ann Robinson's initial suggestion of a boycott had made it all possible. A number of women were to play other significant roles in a variety of guises. Fannie-Lou Hamer was instrumental in the Mississippi Freedom Summer in 1964 and Septima Clark was prominent in the Citizen Education programme of SCLC, which trained people for non-violent direct action. She had been sacked as a teacher for insisting on maintaining her NAACP membership. Diane Nash – married to co-worker James Bevel – was a significant figure in SCLC organisation.

There was also more grass-roots female assistance for the movement. A group called Women Power Unlimited assisted the Freedom Riders and helped to organise joint SNCC/SCLC rallies.

First signs of division. It could be seen as ironic that, at the time of the movement's greatest successes in 1963, the earliest signs of really serious division in the movement became apparent. But the nature of the success at Birmingham, for example, was to mobilise far more black supporters committed to direct action than had ever been previously apparent. Sitkoff (1993) argues that 'Birmingham . . . induced the . . . very poorest blacks to participate in the racial struggle'. They were comparatively uninterested in the chances of a place at the University of Mississippi or a discussion of the finer points of Gandhi's non-violence theories. They were concerned with more bread-and-butter issues concerning housing, employment chances and police brutality. This meant that the different civil rights organisations became more radical (even the law-abiding Roy Wilkins suffered arrest), increasing the level of demonstrations and the nature and breadth of their demands. In the north, CORE organised rent strikes and school boycotts and also protests concerning equal employment opportunities. In the south, SNCC was active in voter registration activity, but also in getting ordinary black people to join in the political process. Their emphasis was on a bottom-up approach rather than the top-down style of the SCLC. The movement's degree of success, moreover, meant that a little division was affordable and some began to question the need to maintain a strictly non-violent stance.

In 1963, the Birmingham protests also put a strain on non-violence. The black community erupted into violence when, after an agreement had been reached, white racists would not accept it and firebombed both King's brother's house and the SCLC headquarters. At the time of the Montgomery bus boycott, King had prevented violent black retaliation: now it was barely possible to do this. Not surprisingly, the violent protesters wondered if Birmingham's white people would ever grant them real equality. From this time on, it was clear that many black people, even in the south, would not accept non-violence. The northern riots of the mid-1960s should not really have been a surprise.

March on Washington, 1963. None of this was apparent on the surface during the March on Washington. This displayed the movement's orderliness, unity of purpose and white support more effectively than anything that had taken place before. Yet, behind the scenes, there had been considerable wrangling. The original format of the march, as conceived by A. Philip Randolph and Bayard Rustin, was to have demonstrations in the capital demanding equal job rights for black people. They met opposition. King, as well as Roy Wilkins and

Whitney Young of the Urban League, insisted the event become more respectable, and their arguments won the day. It would be a peaceful assembly on one day only and would be for both jobs and freedom. Chafe (1999) sees the change from the original idea as a major one and Cook (1998) argues that in the end it was a rally for the Civil Rights Bill rather than a march for jobs and freedom. Fairclough (1987), however, argues that King persuaded Randolph of the need for a change of emphasis and then supplied much of the effort required to realise the ideas.

The march did not improve relations between the SCLC and SNCC. The speech of SNCC chairman John Lewis had been planned as a radical and uncompromising one, in particular attacking the Kennedy administration for lack of action and claiming that racism was still at the heart of American society. These controversial passages were left out on the insistence of King, as it was felt they would offend some of the labour and church leaders in the march. For the sake of unity, Lewis reluctantly agreed. But the change rankled with him and he felt he had been censored. It did show that tactical unity was still seen as important, but this view would not last much longer in a number of quarters.

Nonetheless, the march was a triumphant occasion and gave the impression of a united, responsible movement. It widened the nature of American support for its demands: they became acceptable, even desirable, and, for some, morally essential. It had been necessary to keep the representatives of the church and of labour on their side, as they were now major supporting forces to be reckoned with in the campaign. However, the unity was not to last.

Further tension in Mississippi. The Democratic rejection of the Mississippi Freedom Democratic Party group showed up some of the tensions in the movement. For a time, the civil rights groups had worked together in Mississippi under another umbrella group, the Council of Federated Organisations (COFO). But King and others in the SCLC, such as Bayard Rustin, had tried to persuade SNCC to accept the Humphrey (see page 228) deal over black representation. SNCC, however, regarded it as an insult and a number of its members began to believe they would never get justice from white people. The seeds of Black Power ideas were being sown in their minds.

Tensions at Selma. The circumstances of the twice postponed but eventually triumphant civil rights march from Selma to Montgomery in 1965 produced a good deal of ill feeling in the movement. This stemmed from the murder of Jimmie Lee Jackson as a result of an SCLC march, and the savage treatment handed out by Sheriff Jim Clark to a large number of the protesters. After these events, an 87-km trek was planned, to protest to Alabama Governor George Wallace about police brutality and racism. King was criticised later for not joining the march, which was led by Hosea Williams of the SCLC and John Lewis of SNCC. King did not want another spell in jail, which might well have been the result. The subsequent police violence to stop the first march was certainly of value to the movement, although the injured protesters could be forgiven for thinking that it had been a disaster. It became known as 'Bloody Sunday'. The television pictures identified quite clearly the cause of the violence and it shocked the rest of the USA.

However, for King, it posed a dilemma. Rushing to Selma from his Atlanta base after 'Bloody Sunday', he was consistent in his view that federal court orders should be obeyed, so he was reluctant to agree to a second march until it had been ruled legal. But the prevailing mood was that, if the march were cancelled, the frustrated protesters might lose their discipline. So King came to a secret agreement with Leroy Collins, a special emissary whom President Johnson had sent to sort out the difficulty. The marchers would go as far as the Edmund Pettus Bridge on the outskirts of Selma and then obey police instructions to stop. It was an unsatisfactory arrangement and made King's embarrassment worse. The marchers reached the bridge and met the police, and King asked if they could pray, which was agreed. The police then moved out of the way, daring King to go on with the march or look timid. But King stuck to his side of the bargain and ordered the marchers to turn round and go home.

Not surprisingly, King's own supporters expressed a good deal of dissatisfaction at the outcome. Not only had King appeared timid, but also he was accused of negotiating behind people's backs. In a sense the problem was remedied: once federal permission had been given, the third and this time triumphant march wound its way over the bridge to the accompaniment of freedom songs. Wallace and the police did not this time attempt to prevent it. In Montgomery the marchers were protected by the Alabama National Guard, federalised by the President. King addressed the marchers and promised that freedom would not now be long delayed.

Divisions grow, 1965–6. With stirring words like these, the movement still looked impressive and united at the time of the Selma campaign, especially knowing that President Johnson was committed to the Voting Rights Bill for which they had all campaigned. The Civil Rights Movement had fulfilled one of King's aims: to gain the support of all men and women of good will. Black and white, worker and boss, male and female, young and old – they all seemed united in their desire to see justice prevail. But damage had been done. In particular, SNCC felt deceived and let down, and King's rather feeble explanations for the delay

Part of King's Montgomery Speech:

How long? Not long because no lie can live for ever.

How long? Not long because you will reap what you sow.

How long? Not long because the arm of the moral universe is long but it bends towards justice.

How long? Not long because mine eyes have seen the glory of the coming of the Lord.

in marching did not convince them. Most SNCC supporters now withdrew from the Selma campaign and relations with the SCLC deteriorated steadily. Selma was the trigger for division, but underlying differences had already begun to show. King's close connections with the federal government and his general insistence on obeying federal court orders had made him an object of suspicion among some of the black militants.

It was now clear that the Civil Rights Movement was running into major difficulties. Harry McPherson – aide to President Johnson – remarked in 1966: 'The civil rights movement is obviously in a mess . . . the Negro community is fragmented.' In some ways, these were the problems of success. By this time segregation was fading fast in all but the Deep South, and even here it was under attack. The Civil Rights Act of 1964 and the Voting Rights Act of the following year produced major gains for the movement. But an air of dissatisfaction hung over the more militant campaigners. In particular, many members of SNCC were becoming increasingly restless.

The 'N' in SNCC stood for 'Non-violent', but the letter became less than appropriate in 1966. When James Meredith was shot on his one-man Freedom March in 1966, the civil rights groups at first acted together. The enormity of the crime against Meredith united them all. The meeting of the major groups suggested unity. In fact, King postponed another visit to Chicago to be present. But tensions were apparent on the march, as when Stokeley Carmichael requested armed protection from the Deacons of Defense, a paramilitary black group. Of course, this was unacceptable to King, but it raised tensions further. It was on this march, after Carmichael had been arrested in Greenwood, Mississippi, that he used the phrase 'Black Power'. Vowing not to be arrested for a twenty-eighth time, Carmichael proclaimed: 'What we gonna start saying now is Black Power'. It became an alternative chant to the SCLC's 'Freedom Now' – a clear difference that would be appreciated even by those with little knowledge of the tactical or ideological differences between the organisations.

The more militant philosophy that was to challenge the dominant hold of Martin Luther King and the SCLC in the mid-1960s, goes back a long way to some of the divisions in the earlier part of the century. While King controlled violent retaliation in Montgomery in 1956, it was apparent in Birmingham in 1963. Even the apparently united march on Washington had a powerful undercurrent of tension. Impatience with the lack of federal action in economic and social affairs, and what was seen as King's excessive willingness to obey the federal authorities, surfaced in Selma in 1965 and then in violence in the north and west. The relative unity of the early 1960s was never to be repeated.

The year 1968 was of crucial importance in the political life of the USA. Abroad, the war in Vietnam was escalating and was turning the USA into an increasingly divided society. The assassinations of Martin Luther King and Robert Kennedy cast a dark cloud across the whole political spectrum, but particularly over the hopes of liberal Americans that civil rights and social justice would be extended. In the presidential elections of that year, the Republican Richard Nixon became President, and he was re-elected in 1972.

SECTION 3

The rights of labour

INTRODUCTION

Throughout the twentieth century, running parallel to the struggle for civil rights in politics and education was the fight for rights in labour and labour relations.

The Pullman strike (1894). On 10 May 1894, workers at the Pullman Palace Car Company went on strike. The company, owned by George Pullman, made sleeping and 'parlour' cars that were then leased to virtually all of the railway companies in the USA. Pullman prided himself on being a 'model' employer. His workers lived in a company-owned town, where the manufacturing plants were situated, on the outskirts of Chicago. Pullman made much of his claim that his workers were well paid and contented. However, in 1893, when the USA was in the grip of an economic depression, he suddenly cut wages by 25 per cent and laid off over a third of his workforce. The reduction in wages was not matched by a reduction in living costs in his supposedly ideal industrial town and, consequently, the workforce was angry. An attempt to negotiate at least a reduction in rents was rejected by management. The three representatives at the meeting were subsequently sacked. The sackings precipitated the strike. On 11 May, the Pullman works closed.

Two years earlier, the American Railway Union (ARU) had been formed by **Eugene Debs** in an attempt to unite railway workers all over the country. This was a militant organisation that quickly seized on the case of the Pullman workers. The workers joined the union and Debs took over the leadership of the strike. After a refusal by the company to discuss **arbitration** procedures, all members of the ARU were asked to refuse to operate trains using the Pullman carriages. The action soon brought much of the railroad network to a standstill, especially trains leaving Chicago. The union told railroad companies that they would operate their services without the Pullman cars, but the companies claimed that they were unable to do this because their contract with the Pullman Company required them to haul the sleeping cars on all journeys. Company managers agreed that they would resist union action.

The strike is broken. Passenger trains also pulled the mail cars and, as the conflict deepened, this proved to be a crucial factor. When the railroad companies appealed to the federal government for help, claiming that violence was being used to stop the movement of trains, the Attorney-General responded by issuing an order restraining anyone from interfering with the movement of the mail or inciting other railroad workers to do so. Strikers agreed to operate trains pulling the mail carriages, but the railroad bosses refused to allow their trains to move without the Pullman sleepers. Finally, on 3 July 1894, President Grover Cleveland sent in federal troops ostensibly to ensure the movement of the mail, but actually to break the strike. Debs and the officers of the ARU were arrested and later imprisoned for breaking the order.

The ARU offered to end the strike at the Pullman works, provided that the workers were all reinstated. However, when the company resumed production on 2 August 1894, leaders of the strike from within the company were not given back their jobs.

The significance of the Pullman strike. Of the many late-nineteenth-century examples of labour protest, the Pullman strike is particularly interesting. Its several strands reveal much about the rights of labour in the USA at the end of the nineteenth century, and the lengths to which employers and the authorities were prepared to go in order to curtail or deny them:

- The strike arose as a result of the refusal of the management to recognise the right of the workers to engage in **collective bargaining** to protect their standard of living or to improve their working conditions. The reaction of management in this case is typical of the anti-union attitude of the owners of major companies at the time. Any attempt to exert these rights was regarded as potentially subversive and was consequently resisted, often violently.
- It exemplifies the power and influence of employers who resisted the organisation of labour in their plants and factories.
- It reveals how far federal authority was prepared to go to suppress any assertion of the rights of labour. In this instance, it superseded that of the state, whose duty it was to restore and maintain order. Federal intervention of this kind was resented, particularly by state officials. For example, John Altgeld, the State Governor of Illinois, was sympathetic towards the workers and wished to use the state militia to resolve the situation rather than invoke federal authority.
- This was the first time that the law had been invoked in an effort to break a strike. Employers continued to use court injunctions against strikers until 1932 when their use was prohibited by federal legislation.

KEY TERM

Collective bargaining is when employees' representatives join together to discuss issues (e.g. wages, working conditions).

Andrew Carnegie (1835–1919) moved from Scotland to the USA in 1848 and grew wealthy through careful investment and involvement in the steel industry. In 1899 he founded the Carnegie Steel Company and controlled 25 per cent of the nation's iron and steel production. He retired in 1901, having sold his company for $250 million. During his lifetime, he gave over $350 million to educational, cultural and peace organisations.

John D. Rockefeller (1839–1937) controlled 90 per cent of US oil refineries. He formed the Standard Oil Trust in 1882, which was declared an illegal monopoly and dissolved in 1899. It was replaced by the Standard Oil Company of New Jersey. He remained its president until 1911, when he retired. He amassed a personal fortune of $1 billion, and gave $550 million away to philanthropic projects.

WHY WAS THERE LITTLE RECOGNITION OF LABOUR RIGHTS IN THE LATE NINETEENTH AND EARLY TEWENTIETH CENTURIES?

Laissez-faire capitalism. The USA's industrial revolution was under way in the 1830s, but gained real momentum in the second half of the century. The process was characterised by all the worst features of the British experience – exploitation of labour, particularly that of women and children, long hours, low wages and poor working conditions. A key factor in explaining this was the government's laissez-faire policy. This effectively empowered capitalists to form powerful business corporations and to make huge fortunes. The scale of this was far greater in the USA than in Britain, partly as a result of the formation of business corporations. This made it possible for a small number of highly successful capitalists to control several key industries and, in the process, come to monopolise them: for example, **Andrew Carnegie** (steel) and **John D. Rockefeller** (oil).

Although there were moves by the end of the century to curtail monopolies, such as the **Sherman Anti-trust Act** (1890), unfettered by restrictive legislation, manufacturers could and did cut wages without warning, lay off workers and change working hours. In these circumstances, the workers themselves had no right of redress and certainly no mechanism for expressing their dissatisfaction. Strikes and protests were organised from time to time, but employers resisted any kind of union organisation in their works. In many cases, they employed labour spies to operate under cover among the workforce and root out potential disruptive elements. The use of armed force in the event of attempted strikes, as in the Pullman strike, was not unusual, although strike breaking was more often carried out by local rather than federal militia.

A divided workforce. The nature and composition of the workforce was itself significant. From the 1830s, many industries depended on unskilled immigrant labour. This was cheap and plentiful, and became even more so as the century wore on. Following the end of slavery in 1863, African-Americans began to enter the industrial workforce in increasing numbers, at first in urban areas in the south and, after 1877, increasingly in the north. This multicultural mix was crucial. Immigrants from Europe were divided by language and religion, and were treated with hostility and suspicion by white, native-born Americans. Both the immigrant and white American workforce refused to work with African-Americans.

These divisions impeded the development of the kind of unity and solidarity that labour needed in order to assert its rights and be recognised. Instead, employers were able not only to reject any concept of labour rights, but also to exploit the divisions. Hence, in times of unrest, white American and immigrant workers were laid off and replaced by black labour. The ability of the workforce to protest was also fundamentally weakened by poverty and the need to work to survive. Troublemakers were dismissed and labelled as such, making it hard for them to find other employment. This did much to impede the emergence of the kind of assertive leadership necessary to unite the labour force and win change and reform.

The impact of violent protest.

In the late nineteenth and early twentieth centuries, association with radicalism, violence and anarchy tainted organised labour protest. The activities of the **Molly Maguires** in the anthracite mining districts of Pennsylvania, the violence and bloodshed that characterised the Haymarket Affair (1886) in Chicago (see page 58) and the **Carnegie's Homestead steel plant strike** (1892) are some of the most notorious examples of strikes that went terribly wrong during this period. This produced reactionary attitudes not only on the part of employers and the general public, but also among the labouring classes themselves. Workers were reluctant to join unions either from a sense of disapproval of their methods or as a result of intimidation by employers.

The partiality of the law.

The fact that not only the authorities, but also the courts, supported the employers further limited the development of labour representation. Reference has already been made to the use of court injunctions to break strikes. In the first decade of the twentieth century, a series of Supreme Court decisions further impeded attempts to give workers their rights. One in particular, *Lochner* v. *New York* (1905), actually invoked the Fourteenth Amendment to declare as unconstitutional a law imposing a ten-hour day, claiming that it violated the rights of workers to determine their hours of work. Others placed federal injunctions on unions that organised strikes, attempted to boycott unfair employers or encouraged others to do so.

The growth of trade unions.

In spite of this, unions were established. At first, these were groups of skilled workers operating a **closed shop** at a local level. Early attempts at the formation of national unions – joining together skilled unions – were fairly ineffective, partly for the reasons mentioned above.

- William H. Sylvis's National Labour Union lasted only six years, largely due to poor leadership and a lack of clear principles and policies.
- The Knights of Labour, founded in 1869, was one of the first attempts not only to unite skilled and unskilled labour, but also to remove the barriers of racial and cultural origin imposed by existing local labour associations. In many ways, it was ahead of its time, demanding an

KEY TERM

The Sherman Anti-trust Act (1890) outlawed business trusts. These were huge companies that came to monopolise trade in a particular commodity. The Act also declared illegal any contract or combination that attempted to stop trade.

KEY EVENT

The Molly Maguires were a group of Irish immigrant miners who formed a secret association to fight for better conditions in the anthracite mines of north-eastern Pennsylvania. During a series of strikes in 1873 resulting from wage cuts, railroad cars were derailed, coal tips set on fire and a superintendent murdered. Pinkerton detectives infiltrated the organisation and 19 men were arrested, convicted and hanged.

HEINEMANN ADVANCED HISTORY

Carnegie's Homestead steel plant strike (1892) arose due to wage cuts and developed into a dispute about the right to collective bargaining. Three hundred Pinkerton detectives were employed to break the strike. The state militia eventually removed the strikers who had public support until the plant manager, Henry Clay Frick, was murdered. This ended union organisation at the plant.

Closed shop
A term used to describe a factory or workplace that is dominated by one trade union and where all workers are obliged to belong to that union. In contrast to the closed shop is an open shop, where it was agreed that employees were free to join a union or not, as they pleased.

eight-hour day, equal pay for women and the abolition of child labour. Moreover, it rejected strikes as a means of achieving its ends, preferring instead to seek reforming legislation. By 1886, its membership had grown to around 70,000, but after the violence of the Haymarket Affair its reputation was destroyed and its influence and support dwindled.

- Perhaps more significant was the American Federation of Labor (AFL) that effectively took its place. Again, this was a national union linking all unions. Its leader, **Samuel Gompers**, while seeking reform by legislation, supported the use of strikes and boycotts. Nevertheless, some of the USA's most influential businessmen, including **Mark Hanna** and **J. P. Morgan**, were prepared to work with him in an attempt to establish the machinery for giving workers the right to mediation and conciliation. By 1914, the Federation had over two million members, although these were just a small percentage of the national industrial workforce.
- Less effective but still interesting was a union set up in Chicago in 1905, calling itself the Industrial Workers of the World (or the 'Wobblies'). This was a more militant organisation with a reputation for violence. Employers therefore regarded it with suspicion. However, it stood out at the time for its defence of the rights of poor, and of illiterate workers such as immigrants.

African-Americans and the rights of labour. The development of union membership and representation for black labour represents a landmark in the movement for black civil rights. It was slow to come, but the struggle for labour rights contributed to the wider struggle in two significant ways:

- The rejection of black workers, initially, by white unions forced them into forming their own labour associations. This contributed to their emerging self-awareness and solidarity. It also enabled some to develop leadership skills and abilities.
- African-American historians such as John Hope Franklin and Alfred A. Moss Jr (*From Slavery to Freedom*, 1994) see the final admittance of black people to national unions as significant. It helped to create a sense of belonging among African-Americans and of national identity. This provided further impetus to the demand for equal rights in every aspect of their lives. Ultimately, trade unions would become a powerful pressure group. In the meantime, membership gained political significance for some, particularly for the black leadership that emerged.

The situation of freedmen in the south, bound by sharecropping and the crop lien system, has been discussed in Chapter 2 of this book. Many enslaved African-Americans had acquired skills. Hence, blacksmiths, carpenters and other craftsmen, wishing to throw off plantation life, went in search of work in urban areas. Inspired by the work of Booker T. Washington (see Chapter 3), many set up their own businesses in spite of experiencing discrimination and, often, violent intimidation.

Rejection by the union movement. Initially, the mass of black labour, both skilled and unskilled, was treated with hostility and remained excluded from the union movement in the late nineteenth and early twentieth centuries. Apart from the inherent racial prejudice, black workers were perceived as posing a threat. Not only were they used as 'scab' labour to thwart strike action, but they were also seen as responsible for pinning down wages. They did, however, represent a significant section of the workforce, particularly during and after the First World War when thousands moved to the heavily industrialised north in response to the wartime demand for labour. It could only be a matter of time before white union leadership recognised and accepted that the movement for labour rights could succeed only if labour were totally united. This would mean admitting African-Americans and other rejected ethnic minorities into the unions.

This latter point was not entirely lost on those attempting to establish a national labour movement in the late nineteenth century. The Knights of Labor had certainly wanted to admit African-American members as well as members from other ethnic groups, and around 60,000 black workers joined. The American Federation of Labor similarly rejected discrimination. Unions were allowed to affiliate only if they admitted all workers as members. However, many circumvented this rule by establishing separate branches of the same union at local level. The Federation tolerated this when its white membership began to dwindle as a result of its inclusive policy. As white unions operated a closed shop in many firms, this effectively excluded African-American workers from entering those industries and so further polarised the total workforce.

Black unions. As early as 1869, African-Americans had begun to form their own unions. The National Negro Labor Union was founded in that year and attempted, unsuccessfully, to affiliate with white skilled unions. Ongoing discussions about unity with the American Federation of Labor during the First World War produced nothing. In 1925, when Philip Randolph formed the Brotherhood of Sleeping Car Porters and Maids (BSCP), the Pullman Company refused to work with it. Randolph, himself, held radical views and even many black workers regarded the 'Brotherhood' as suspicious. Nevertheless, it gained the support of the American Federation of Labor as well as of the National Association for the Advancement of Colored People and was finally recognised by the Pullman Company in 1935.

John Pierpont Morgan was the son of a rich international banker. He became a co-founder of the New York banking house of Drexel, Morgan and Co. This became J. P. Morgan and Co. in 1895. He became a great financier, rescuing rival business corporations from financial difficulty and restructuring them. In 1901, he formed United States Steel by bringing together a number of companies. Morgan dominated the world of high finance until his death in 1913.

In his book *The Crisis of the Negro and the Constitution* (1937), Randolph wrote:

> True liberation can be acquired and maintained only when the Negro people possess power, and power is the product and flower of organization – organization of the masses, the masses in the mills and the mines, on the farms, in the factories, in churches, in fraternal organizations, in homes, colleges, women's clubs, student groups, trade unions, tenants' leagues, in cooperative guilds, political organizations and civil rights associations.

Congress of Industrial Organizations (CIO). The CIO, formed in 1935, was actively committed to organising labour, regardless of race. Randolph's BSCP became affiliated, as did many other black union organisations. Above all, the CIO aimed to break down racial barriers to uniting labour, especially in the mass production industries that had begun to proliferate during the 1920s.

Shipbuilding	26,648
Coal mines	75,000
Railroads	150,000
Black women in industry	21,547

The black workforce during the First World War.

HOW WAS LABOUR AFFECTED BY THE YEARS OF PROSPERITY?

Economic prosperity. The years of the First World War saw a slight improvement in the position of trade unions. In spite of the racial tensions caused by the influx of immigrant and African-American labour into northern industrial areas, the needs of the war and the opportunities it offered to industrialists encouraged a more conciliatory policy towards unions. Employers agreed to some collective bargaining in order to ensure that essential services were not disrupted by strike action. These gains were, however, short-lived.

Between 1920 and 1929, Americans enjoyed an unprecedented level of economic prosperity. During these years, wage levels rose steadily and a whole range of consumer goods became available, largely due to the new techniques of mass production. These, together with the availability of credit, led to a huge increase in demand for such things as cars, refrigerators, washing machines, vacuum cleaners and cookers. High tariffs protected US industry from foreign competition. There was a widely held belief, especially in political circles, that this economic progress was unstoppable. However, this illusion was shattered in 1929, when the Wall Street Crash and its aftermath plunged the USA into the depths of the Great Depression. What happened to the labour force during these years?

Welfare capitalism. The rise in real wages and the dramatic fall in unemployment during the 1920s reduced many of the causes of the industrial unrest during the first decade of the twentieth century. Moreover, what appeared on the surface to be conciliatory action by employers – improved working conditions, a reduction in working hours, benefits including insurance and pension plans, profit-sharing schemes and recreational facilities – were, in effect, a ruse on their part to avert strikes and industrial unrest that might disrupt production. This 'welfare capitalism', as it came to be called, included the setting up of 'company unions'. Representatives could meet with employers to discuss such things as grievances, production levels and plant safety. However, they were not allowed to call strikes and did not have the power to negotiate wages. Behind the scenes, management spies and private police worked for employers to suppress any attempt at unionisation.

Henry Ford is a good example of 'welfare capitalism' at work. Ford owned the biggest factory complex in the world at River Rouge, his birthplace in Dearborn, Michigan. Here he employed 80,000 workers who endured the monotony of the car production line. In 1914 he had reduced the length of the working day to eight hours, doubled the daily wage to $5 and introduced a scheme of profit sharing. By 1927, when the new factory opened, the workforce remained tightly controlled and closely supervised. Archie Accicea, a worker at one of the Ford plants, described his working conditions thus:

> Once you start the production going . . . you have just got to think, I have got to keep up with this line, because if you don't keep up with the line, you're in trouble.

Ford's Protection Department employed strong-armed security men who watched over potential union organisers, intimidating and assaulting them. It was not until 1941 that any labour union was recognised by the Ford Company for the purposes of collective bargaining.

THE WALL STREET CRASH AND THE NEW DEAL

The Wall Street Crash. The prosperity bubble soon burst. On 24 October 1929, share prices on the New York Stock Exchange on Wall Street fell faster and lower than ever before. Millions of dollars were lost as the Wall Street Crash brought the USA's golden age of prosperity to a sudden end. The total collapse of the economy that ensued led to factory closures and bankruptcy for large numbers of businesses. More disastrously for the labour force, unemployment soared from 3 per cent in 1929 to 25 per cent by 1933. In terms of numbers, these figures represent a daily increase of 12,000, reaching a total of 13 million by 1933. Unemployment made individuals and families destitute. African-Americans were particularly badly affected, since unemployment among them was double that of white Americans. Industrial cities such as Chicago were badly affected, and voluntary relief organisations were unable to cope with the huge tide of destitution.

In these circumstances, people who were in work were pleased to have a job at all. However, there was greater conflict between employers and workers. Incidences of strikes, sit-ins and the occupation of factories by desperate workers increased. Employers called in the police or, in some cases, employed their own strike-breakers. Consequently, by 1933, only ten per cent of the workforce was unionised, for, although workers had the right to join unions, employers had the right to sack them if they belonged to a union and went on strike.

A 'New Deal' for labour? In among all of the misery, the Republican President, Herbert Hoover, lost the confidence of the people when he failed to respond positively to the effects of the Depression. In 1932, therefore, US voters elected a new President, Franklin D. Roosevelt, a Democrat. Roosevelt was given unprecedented powers by Congress, for 100 days, to implement a programme of reform that would get the American people back to work. A further challenge was to settle the industrial unrest that existed when he took office.

National Industry Recovery Act (1933). On 16 June 1933, Congress passed the National Industry Recovery Act (NIRA), which established the National Recovery Administration (NRA). The aim of the NRA was to foster co-operation between the different sides of industry by developing agreed codes of practice about issues such as production levels, wage rates, working hours, prices and trade union rights. Of these, perhaps the most significant was a law giving workers the right to organise trade unions and take part in collective bargaining. Companies who joined the NRA were allowed to display a blue eagle symbol. By 1934, 557 codes had been agreed by joining companies, covering 23 million workers. However, its positive effects were limited. Employers such as Henry Ford refused to sign the NRA code and those codes that were agreed generally favoured employers more than employees. The NIRA also came under the scrutiny of the Supreme Court, which once again raised the issue of states' rights over those of the federal government when it declared the NRA unconstitutional in 1935.

The Wagner Act (1935). In 1935 the cause of trade unionism was taken a step further by the passage of the National Labor Relations Act. This is also known as the Wagner Act after **Robert Wagner**. Roosevelt, himself, was very nervous of empowering organised labour. While it had potential political advantages in increasing Democratic support, it also involved an implicit reduction in the control of industrialists over their workforce.

However, Wagner's intention was to regulate and reduce labour disputes by providing a structure for collective bargaining. This would reduce picket line violence and avoid the disruption to production that was caused by strikes. Only legislation would reduce the ability of powerful industrialists to subvert attempts to give any rights to their workers.

The Act gave workers the right to join trade unions and to bargain collectively through their own chosen representatives. It also set up a three-man National Labor Relations Board that had the power to bargain on behalf of the workers and to stop companies from using blacklists and company unions. Having established and protected the rights of labour, the Act facilitated the expansion of trade union membership. This rose from 3.7 million members in 1933 to 9 million in 1938.

How successful was the Wagner Act in extending labour rights to all workers? The rise in union membership is clearly an indication of some success. However, disputes between employers and their employees continued to be acrimonious. Moreover, divisions within the trade union movement itself continued to deprive the mass of unskilled workers of their rights. This was especially true of labour in mass-production industries. The American Federation of Labor was predominantly interested in amalgamating craft unions to the exclusion of unskilled labour. Consequently, in 1935, a breakaway group of leaders formed the Committee on Industrial Organisation (CIO), which by 1937 was known as the Congress of Industrial Organisations.

The CIO set about the task of organising labour in the mass-production industries – steel, automobile and glass, for example – gathering 3.7 million members in the process. Employers resisted with every means at their disposal the closed shop that the CIO established. By the end of the 1930s, strikers were using a new form of protest – the 'sit-in' or 'sit-down' strikes. This was used effectively in 1937 to gain recognition from car manufacturers of the right of their workers to join a union. Only Henry Ford held out until 1941. Black workers and other ethnic groups benefited from the opportunity to join the CIO, as did many women's unions. The CIO's consistent support for equality of labour gave African-Americans the confidence to take part in strikes. It also began the process of black integration into US society.

What did the New Deal do for disadvantaged groups?

- African-Americans and Mexican-Americans continued to face discrimination in the workplace. This was exacerbated by the agricultural policies of the New Deal, which resulted in the eviction of large numbers of African- and Mexican-Americans who had migrated to the cities in search of work. There was no opportunity at all for Native Americans.

- The position of women in the workplace was not improved. Although a number of women's unions had been formed and, although the NIRA and the Fair Labour Standards Act (1938) had established a minimum wage, it upheld differentials in pay between men and women.

- As described in Chapter 4, welfare reforms helped some of the poorer paid. However, attempts by federal government to help those in need were constantly thwarted by the conflict between states' rights and federal government. Discrimination was particularly felt by African-American women.

Therefore, the extension of the rights of labour to all workers was by no means complete when the USA entered the Second World War in 1941.

The Rights of Labour: Legislation, Development and Progress after 1935

Date	Event/Development	Significance
1935	**The Wagner Act** (National Labor Relations Act)	The first national legislation that recognised the right of workers to elect their own representatives to take part in collective bargaining with employers. The Act is a landmark in the development of labour rights in the USA.
	Committee of Industrial Organization (CIO) within the American Federation of Labor (AFL)	Its purpose was to encourage industrial workers to unionise. Unions became affiliated to the CIO.
1937	The Supreme Court declared the Wagner Act constitutional	Following sit-down strikes, a number of unions in major industries were recognised by employers, i.e. union membership was accepted and the union representatives were accepted as bargaining agents e.g. General Motors recognised the Union of Auto Workers; US Steel recognised the Steel Workers Organising Committee.
1938	Fair Labour Standards Act	Created a $25 minimum wage and payment of time and a half for hours worked in excess of 40 per week. **Committee of Industrial Organisation** left the AFL and became the **Congress of Industrial Organisations**.

1941–5	Wartime measures to recognise and safeguard the rights of labour but also to prevent disruption of essential wartime industries	• United Auto Workers recognised by the Ford Motor Company **(1941)** • Organised labour was strengthened by needs of wartime industry. Union membership grew (9 million to 14.8 million between 1941 and 1945) partly due to the wartime increase in the size of the labour force. Strikes were kept to a minimum but union leaders were able to exploit the wartime situation to gain fringe benefits for members (e.g. paid holidays, health insurance schemes). The **National War Labor Board (1942)** was set up to limit wage increases in order to keep inflation rates low. • Creation of *Fair Employment Practices Commission* set up by Roosevelt to eliminate racial and ethnic discrimination in war industries **(1943)** • **1944** – 18,600,000 union members in the US (3,500,000 of these were women. Generally, however, women regarded unionism as a male preserve!)
1946–50	Post-war Labour Problems and Truman's 'New Deal' Restraints on Union power	• End of wartime controls unleashed a massive wave of strikes. There was a growing belief that the unions were becoming too strong and powerful. They had to be controlled. **(1946)** • *1947 Taft-Hartley Act* (otherwise known as the **Labour Management Relations Act**) passed to restrict union activities. This made it illegal for unions to operate a closed shop and affirmed the right of states to pass 'right to work' laws. These measures were welcomed in the southern states where more conservative politicians were less sympathetic to union organisation. The president could order a 60-day cooling off period prior to strike action under the terms of this act. (President Harry Truman attempted to veto this act in order to court the labour vote but was overruled by Congress.) • Pay code linked to standard of living costs introduced by *General Motors.* **(1948)** • **1949 'New Deal'** – Truman persuaded Congress to pass legislation raising the minimum wage and extending access to social security benefits. This was designed, in part, to reduce the propensity to take strike action and so control the unions. • Progress in car industry – *General Motors* agreed 5-year contract giving pensions and cost of living increases to employees **(1950)**
1950–60	New technology and its impact on labour	• Transition from manual labour to computer technology changed the nature and composition of the workforce

	Labour rights in danger	Decline in number of blue-collar workers; increase in white-collar workers by 1960. This reduction weakened the unions (by 1980, TU membership was a smaller percentage of the total workforce than in 1953). • White-collar workers often in federal, state or local government occupations. They signed no-strike agreements and were often barred from joining a trade union. These restraints made white-collar workers difficult to organise. • Created awareness among trade unions that there was a need for labour solidarity. **1955 AFL and CIO united**.
1961–3	JFK's 'New Frontier'	*John Kennedy was a liberal president. He began with an ambitious programme of social reform.* **1961** he introduced a bill to increase the minimum wage. Like his other reforms, this failed to be accepted by Congress. In his attempts to address the problem of inflation, he succeeded in persuading the steelworkers' union to accept a non-inflationary contract with employers that included acceptance of minimal raises in wages. **1963 Equal Pay Act** prohibited wage differentiation on the basis of gender.
1963–8	Lyndon Johnson's 'Great Society'	Johnson's prime target was to reduce the number of people who were living below the poverty line. Hence his **War on Poverty** became the most significant aspect of his domestic policy. Between 1963 and 1973, numbers classified as living below the poverty line fell from 25% to 11%. This was achieved by the creation of millions of new jobs and increased spending on social security benefits. **Civil Rights Act 1964** prohibited discrimination in jobs based on race, colour, religion, sex or national origin. **1968 Age Discrimination in Employment Act** made it illegal to discriminate in hiring or firing an individual between 40 and 65 on the basis of age.
1970	**Occupational Safety and Health Act**	Federal law establishing health and safety regulations in the workplace. **The state of Hawaii** became the first to give state and local officials the right to strike.
1974–5	Development of unionism among women and public sector employees	**Coalition of Labour Union Women** formed in Chicago. **AFL/CIO** created a public service department in response to growth of unionism among public employees. **1975 American Federation of State, County and Municipal Employees** organised a strike of 80,000 members. This was the first large-scale, legal strike of public employees.

1977	**Minimum Wage**	**President Jimmy Carter** and Congress established the minimum wage at $2.65.
1981	**The Reagan Administration**	Basis of Ronald Reagan's economic policy was the privatisation of publicly owned industries and businesses. Restrictive regulations on these businesses were lifted. Independence given to owners was not in the interests of the workers. **Air Traffic Controllers' Strike.** Reagan sacked most of the nation's air traffic controllers and de-certified their union in response to an illegal strike. The union was destroyed.

CONCLUSION

Clearly, after 1945 successive governments went a long way towards establishing a framework of entitlement to rights in the workplace and towards identifying the criteria within which negotiation and collective bargaining could take place. The right to join a trade union was accepted and established in law. Advances towards equal opportunity and status were certainly made by women. Many facets of discrimination were confronted in the context of the civil rights legislation of the 1960s. However, while unions in traditional industries may have gained power and influence, they remained tightly controlled by legislation that established the parameters of acceptable union activity. Organized labour was vulnerable to political swings and fortunes as well as economic change. From the 1960s, trade unions were in decline, initially as a result of the advent of new industries that ultimately reduced the numbers of workers in traditional industries and consequently, in their unions. The right wing policies of Ronald Reagan after 1981 strengthened the position of employers and further weakened the unions. Almost certainly, those who remained unprotected were ethnic minority workers – African-Americans and Hispanics – in low paid, service occupations. By 1990, trade union membership had fallen to only 16.1 per cent. It seemed that the wheel had almost, though not completely, turned full circle. The USA's new breed of workers either chose or were persuaded to reject organized labour.

SECTION 4

The growing militancy of the Civil Rights Movement, 1950–80

HOW IMPORTANT WAS THE LACK OF EMPLOYMENT OPPORTUNITY TO THE SUCCESS OF BLACK POWER?

The post-war boom. Post-war USA enjoyed an economic boom. An increasing population, abundant supplies of energy and delayed consumer spending from the war all contributed to the general prosperity. Employment opportunities were as many and varied as the reasons for the economic well-being. Fears that recession would set in once wartime needs had ended proved to be groundless. Government spending continued to contribute to economic progress: 60 per cent went on defence spending in the Cold War era, but large sums were also spent on increasing federal welfare payments, space research, a substantial highways programme and water projects (which flooded Native American land on occasions). The Korean War, 1950–3, gave a further boost to the armaments industry and technical innovations added to the speed of progress: the digital computer was developed in 1944 and the transistor in 1948.

Credit to aid consumer spending became more and more freely available with the development of the credit card from 1950 onwards. The rapid production of television sets, motor cars, central heating systems, new types of informal clothing and acre upon acre of suburban housing all contributed to people's well-being and gave good employment prospects to millions. The middle-class standard of living made immense strides in terms of consumer goods purchases. Domestic appliances of all kinds – fridges, stoves, vacuum cleaners and washing machines – abounded in many American homes. Employment prospects in chemicals, electronics and information processing were all good. The USA took an increasing share of the international trade market as firms with a US base expanded in western Europe. By 1975 US exports were 45 times the value of 1945.

The economic plight of black people. Only a small minority of the USA's black population shared in the resulting prosperity. At a time when black people from the south were pouring into northern and western cities, such as Chicago, Detroit and Los Angeles, the unskilled jobs – the only ones for which many of them were qualified – were actually declining in number. In the 1950s, about one and a half million jobs disappeared as automation took over many factories. Black people had held many of these jobs and a good number of them had only recently arrived in the north, yet they still continued to come. By 1970 half of the USA's black population was were living outside the southern states, compared with barely a third in 1950. But their hopes of finding employment opportunities were now often short-lived. There was an irony in the way that automation made many of them redundant in the 1950s, often soon after they had arrived. The very causes of prosperity for others, such as technical advances, actually worked against the black minority.

Many of the opportunities were for skilled workers with formal educational qualifications, and thus were not open to African-Americans who had frequently left school with minimum attainments. In 1964 in Chicago, over 85 per cent of all black pupils were in largely (over 90 per cent) segregated schools, as were 78 per cent of white pupils, and the figures were increasing rather than decreasing. In 1950 black workers formed 8 per cent of the labour force but 22 per cent of the unemployed. In the late 1950s and early 1960s, black people formed a disproportionate percentage of the long-term unemployed (variably defined, but usually over about 20 weeks). In 1964, the black unemployment figure stood at 12.4 per cent, with the corresponding white figure being 4.9 per cent. The disparity was also widening: in 1948 black unemployment was 1.6 times that of white people; in 1960, 2.25 times as much. Many other immigrant groups to the USA had started in poverty but over two or three generations had improved, yet northern black people seemed to be going backwards.

When in work, four out of five black workers were in unskilled or semi-skilled jobs. Moreover, areas where black people traditionally worked, such as mining, iron and steel, and the textile industry, were lowering their manpower requirements. When in work, low pay produced relative poverty: in 1960, black people were 15 per cent of the US population, but produced 32 per cent of the families with the lowest category of annual earnings, under $5000. In 1962, the black male worker earned on average 55 per cent of the wages of his white counterpart. Although the situation was marginally less acute for black women, in the early 1960s, they generally earned only two-thirds of white women's earnings, except where the latter, in child-bearing and family-raising years, chose to stay at home or work very restricted hours.

Trade union attitudes. Trade unions (known as 'labor unions' in the USA) did not provide the help that might have been expected. Two large union organisations, the American Federation of Labor (AFL) and the Congress of Industrial Organisations (CIO) had amalgamated in 1953 and officially pursued a non-racial policy. A. Philip Randolph was on their executive committee for many years. But in practice, many of their affiliated branches operated a near-complete colour bar. Black people would often be rejected on the convenient grounds of lack of experience or educational qualifications. Some of this might have been genuine, but there was clearly a good deal of racism. Paper, chemicals, oil, metal, printing and tobacco trades all saw discriminatory practices; the seafarers' union allowed black people to work only in the galley and steward's department. The 'G plan technique' for dealing with black applicants was a well-known procedure: 'G' stood for garbage (rubbish), and many black applications were simply binned.

The NAACP Labour Secretary, Herbert Hill, complained of racism in the building trades – a boom industry with great employment opportunities. Here, black apprenticeships were severely restricted: as late as 1970, black people held only three per cent of them. Hill also pointed out that, whereas the unions had been ruthlessly efficient at expelling communists, they had not done the same when confronted with evidence of racist practices. Potential black plumbers, elevator constructors or sheet metal workers found their way to apprenticeships barred. The NAACP took many cases of individual prejudice to the courts with increasing success. Indeed, so common had these cases become by the 1960s that one can see here the origin of the affirmative action of the 1970s and 1980s. Rather than be overwhelmed with masses of individual cases, the authorities eventually decided that it would be easier to set guidelines and quotas as to how many black workers should be employed.

Discrimination in employment. While affirmative action has been controversial and seen as racist by some white people, a look at the statistics shows the need for some sort of action. The increasing dominance of chunks of the US economy by a few large firms proved disastrous for black employment when these firms simply did not recruit them. While the colour bar was not absolute, the figures are revealing. Ford, one of three dominant firms in the motorcar industry, employed a total of 74 black workers in 4 of their main plants that had a total of 7665 workers – less than 1 per cent. By contrast, the federal government had been employing black people in considerable numbers since the 1940s. In the mid-1960s, for instance, nearly one in five of federal civil service employees in the Chicago region was black, although many were employed in the lower ranks.

Many black people lacked the educational qualifications to attain even these lower positions. In fact, there is a significant parallel between discrimination in education and employment. In both cases, integration came at a snail's pace. The more extreme policies of bussing in education and affirmative action in employment were reactions against the lack of progress in these areas by the mid-1960s. Yet before these developments occurred, many black people had decided on their own 'remedy': violence.

Disaffection and frustration. It is not difficult to trace the poverty and disaffection that this lack of employment opportunities caused in the black community, especially when so many (though by no means all) whites seemed to be grabbing a slice of the cake. To see the white prosperity and to compare it with their own condition must have been intensely frustrating for black people. The employment prospects of young black men were the bleakest and they became the most disaffected group, since domestic service proved a more fruitful area for women. Teenage rates of unemployment were always higher than the overall figures, and by the mid-1960s one young black male teenager in three was often unemployed. Not surprisingly, this group also proved to have the highest crime rate. The Moynihan Report (see page 155) revealed that almost 50 per cent of black males between the ages of 16 and 23 had some sort of criminal record.

These young, frustrated black people would hardly begin to connect with the prosperous King family and were unlikely to feel affection for the American values and principles that it supported. Excluded from proper economic participation in American society, many now rejected any kind of cooperation with it at all. They would agree with Martin Luther King's comment about 'an island of poverty in a sea of affluence' but, unlike him, they showed no sign of wanting to push out the boat and attempt to take to the water. Non-violence had not produced a decent education or a job for them, and they felt trapped in a system that seemed to be working against them. As NAACP's Herbert Hill put it: 'when the building Trade Unions prevent Negroes from working on highly visible public construction projects . . . they are directly contributing to the racial crisis in the cities'.

Efforts to deal with the problem met with limited success. The National Urban League helped individual blacks, but hardly tackled the underlying problems: Roy Wilkins, executive secretary of the NAACP, spoke to the newly elected President Kennedy in 1961 and urged him to organise training in industrial skills and literacy. A mobilisation for youth training scheme was set up to prepare youngsters for the employment opportunities that might come their way, and there was further aid for families with dependent children.

Housing and education. It was not just the inadequate employment opportunities that provided the fertile ground for Black Power activists. In many ways, housing could be seen as even more of a root cause of the problem. Trapped in the ghetto in Chicago's south or west side, there seemed no escape for the young. They would be prevented from moving by a segregation that might have been *de facto* rather than *de jure*, but was no less rigorous for all that. Estate agents' agreements effectively prevented black people from moving, since complex legal restrictive covenants were placed on property. Only occasionally was this drawn to public attention, as when black baseball star Willie Mays tried unsuccessfully to buy a house in a white area of San Francisco.

The fact that black people were trapped in one area of housing meant that education was *de facto* segregated. Black schools in the great US cities rarely provided the equivalent educational opportunities to their white counterparts, so their pupils became caught in a poverty cycle, leaving school with few formal qualifications and thus ill-equipped to compete in the job market.

Once again, moves that benefited others in American society rebounded on the black community. During the 1950s, many slums were demolished but, instead of replacing them with low-cost public housing, many builders opted for the more lucrative areas of luxury apartments or an impressive new stadium. With the population increasing by both natural means and immigration from other parts of the USA, this resulted in extreme overcrowding. In Chicago in 1960, 23 per cent of the population was black, but they occupied just 4 per cent of the physical space available.

The growth of Black Power. As in the south, a small proportion of black people were much more prosperous than this general pattern suggests. Polenberg (1982) notes that by the early 1970s the top 7 per cent were earning over $25,000 a year – a substantial sum that placed them in the upper middle class. Moreover, things continued to improve as more and more black people reached professional status later in the decade. But much of this had come too late. In the late 1960s, just as their overall condition was starting to improve, northern blacks seem to have decided collectively that they could take no more.

The regional contrast that had existed for so long between northern and southern black people in their overall approach to the question of civil rights had become a stark one by 1966. As Martin Luther King pointed out in a television interview at the time of his Chicago protest in 1966, non-violent activity, such as a march, gave black people an outlet for their pent-up frustrations. But in the north, no Martin Luther King had emerged: there was no non-violent leader to turn to. It was Malcolm X in the early 1960s who most accurately articulated the feelings, frustrations and desires of the northern black community. The outlet they turned to was violence, and for their philosophy of action they chose Black Power. All this came just as President Johnson's 'Great Society' programme was taking measures to effect improvements in the overall condition of black people. But it was too late: the rioting had begun. Johnson's reaction was, not surprisingly, to feel that black people were ungrateful. As the situation in Vietnam began to take priority, further civil rights measures were postponed or watered down.

WHAT WAS THE IMPACT OF BLACK POWER ON CIVIL RIGHTS IN THE 1960S?

The radicalism of SNCC and CORE. The relative unity of the Civil Rights Movement was broken by Black Power. In 1966, its ideas began to infiltrate the main civil rights organisations. In that year, Floyd McKissick replaced James Farmer as CORE leader and Stokeley Carmichael had, within the previous two weeks, become the chairman of SNCC. Both these men, especially Carmichael, were rapidly losing faith in the non-violent philosophy of the SCLC, as were many other activists. Another leading SNCC figure was James Forman, who was not alone in feeling that federal politics was essentially corrupt and that politicians did not really care 'about people down here'. But Carmichael was probably the most extreme. It was rumoured that when he answered the phone, he always said 'Ready for the revolution'. He co-wrote a much-discussed book entitled *Black Power* in 1967, which further helped to popularise the phrase. In that year he broke with SNCC and joined the revolutionary Black Panthers, but criticised them for being too prepared to work with radical white people. To Carmichael, 'black' meant 'black only'. This eventually proved an issue that divided even Black Power.

In 1966, SNCC and CORE, now more radical, began to remove white people from their organisations; black people could control their own destiny. Ironically, this process appears to have started in King's hometown of Atlanta during a campaign to involve southern urban black people.

Black Power: the balance sheet. Did Black Power add anything positive to the Civil Rights Movement? It certainly brought greater pride and confidence in being black. King himself acknowledged its contribution to raising black people's self-esteem and willingness to take action. Black people were not prepared to be treated as second-class citizens. Moreover, it brought a greater awareness of black culture and black achievements, from the study of African history and the development of departments of black studies at universities, to the sporting of an Afro-hairstyle and the wearing of dashikis (traditional African dress).

But Black Power brought pride at a cost. It brought a more serious and fundamental division than had been seen before in the movement. Cook (1998) sees the early divisions of the Civil Rights Movement as not necessarily harmful: the battle for resources brought a variety of fundraising strategies. By organising separate campaigns in different areas, the different groups were able to campaign and have an impact in many different parts of the USA. But the division that emerged in the mid-1960s was of a different order. The whole thrust of the movement up to this point had been to win white allies, and differences had often been tactical: over speed, method, style and location. Now, however, there seemed to be a return to the Garveyite-type separatism of the pre-war years, but with an added degree of venom towards whites that seemed in the more extreme cases to exhibit racism. This was certainly the view of Roy Wilkins of the NAACP, who described Black Power as Hitler or the Ku Klux Klan in reverse.

The followers of King and the SCLC, let alone the NAACP and the Urban League, could never accept a philosophy that would undermine all they had been doing to achieve improvement through the system. Above all, Black Power rejected the cherished ideal of non-violence and all the underlying philosophy that went with it. When Floyd McKissick said that non-violence was a strategy that had outlived its usefulness, he revealed what many had thought previously: that non-violent methods were merely tactical and not a fundamental principle of the movement. Of course, this was not a view shared by King and his closest followers, such as Ralph Abernathy and C. T. Vivian.

Interpretations. It was not as if supporters of Black Power managed to bring a united strategy of their own into the movement. Cook (1998) sees them as 'more slogan than concept', and their precise aims remain uncertain. Carmichael's book on Black Power suggested that integration should be abandoned and that black people should form a conscious racial grouping within the USA, developing their own agenda for change. Others seemed less certain. The speed of changing thought and the pace of political upheaval in the eventful years of 1965–8 were bewildering for everyone. In 1966, Carmichael voted in the minority in a close decision not to expel all white members from the SNCC, yet within a year he had changed his views completely.

How far a white backlash was produced is open to question. Sitkoff (1993) asserts that this was so, though Cook (1998) argues that white reaction was well under way before Black Power really developed. King himself certainly warned white people, as in his speech at Soldier's Field, Chicago in 1966, that many black people would take matters into their own hands unless their overall condition was quickly improved. At times during the early 1960s, a figure like King could use the bogey of someone more extreme such as Malcolm X to frighten the authorities into granting concessions, as Malcolm X himself recognised. But it is generally argued that, at the very least, Black Power fanned the flames of division.

Riots in 1965–7. The reaction to the riots of 1965, 1966 and 1967 emphasised the increasing division in the movement. The young man who called out to King amid the rubble of Watts, 'We won', said so because he felt that attention was now going to be paid to the plight of inner-city black people. He was not impressed with King's argument that destroying the community in which you live and losing lives in the process cannot possibly be a victory. For these rioters, civil disobedience was not the appropriate response; for they were not usually protesting against specific laws, but against a whole social and economic system. The riots gave a boost to those in the movement who had argued that something like this was bound to happen sooner or later in the black communities, such was their feeling of alienation. Analysis of the causes of the riots varied. For some liberals, they were social and economic and indicated the urgency of reform in these fields. But for others, such as previously sympathetic white people, they indicated the need for a halt to change and the re-establishment of law and order.

Black Panthers. A 'legacy of hatred', as J. M. Blum (1992) puts it, was inevitably left over after the riots. In 1967, the Black Power Conference called for the USA to be partitioned into two independent homelands, one for black people and one for white people. The previous year, a number of young black California militants, led by Huey Newton and Bobby Seale, organised the Black Panther Party for Self-Defense. Eldridge Cleaver, who became one of its leading spokesmen, declared that the country had to choose between 'total liberty for black people or the total destruction of America'. When Newton was convicted of the manslaughter of an Oakland policeman, Black Panther groups began to appear in most of the major US cities. They demanded full employment, decent housing and an end to repression and brutality. Many soon clashed with the police. Some were sent to prison, charged with murder or attempted murder.

The movement became a target of the FBI, which set out to eliminate it – with considerable success. By 1980, it was a much smaller and less effective group. Huey Newton began to concentrate more on writing than on direct action; Cleaver became a born-again Christian. Although relatively short-lived, however, the Black Panther Movement illustrates the way in which many black people, particularly the young, saw violence as the only way to achieve their aims. The fact that the Black Panthers attracted Carmichael and Rapp Brown from SNCC showed just how broken the Civil Rights Movement had become.

Conclusion. Northern ghetto blacks did not share in the general prosperity of post-war USA and this deprivation was important in building up the tension that spilled over into violence from 1965 onwards. Largely segregated education, lack of stable and well-paid employment opportunities and a low standard of housing all played their part in this process. The legacy of hatred that resulted produced a mood among northern black people that would be much more receptive to the philosophy of Black Power protest than to the accommodating views of the well-off Martin Luther King.

HOW SIGNIFICANT WAS THE ROLE OF MARTIN LUTHER KING TO THE SUCCESS OF THE MOVEMENT?

The divisions in the Civil Rights Movement are often personalised by contrasting the approaches and views of two of the leading personalities of the late 1950s and 1960s: Martin Luther King and Malcolm X. While this can be a simplistic approach that ignores subtle divisions and underlying economic and social forces, the impact of these two men is sufficiently profound to justify a look at their huge personal impact on civil rights. Though barely separated in age, their very differing social backgrounds and contrasting outlook make them clear representatives of two different approaches to the major civil rights issues.

The appeal of Martin Luther King. From 1957 to the mid-1960s, King had no major rival for overall leadership of the Civil Rights Movement. His achievement was to articulate the feelings of the ordinary black person in words that were both memorable and easily understood by all the communities in the USA. He was equally at home and equally popular with southern black and northern white audiences. His argument that waiting was no longer appropriate struck home to its target. He managed to inject a sense of urgency into the attitudes of the federal authorities. His bravery and clear living out of his Christian faith were an inspiration to millions. Above all, he could not be ignored. In keeping to the moral high ground and insisting that his demands should already be a reality because of the US Constitution, he made them seem reasonable and overdue. 'Justice, fair play and democracy' were words he used frequently and effectively.

King's awards and recognitions, of which the Nobel Peace Prize in 1964 was merely the most renowned, gave him status and respectability, which were essential if the demands of the movement were to be generally accepted. The civil rights campaigners were not in the same position as those struggling for liberation in Africa. They were in the minority in the country and were not, save for the most extreme Black Power advocates, attempting to take it over altogether, but rather to have an established, respected and equal place within it.

The effect of the Montgomery Bus Boycott. King led by example, such as in his reaction to the bomb threats to his house, which only made him the more determined to carry on with campaigning. Once the initial euphoria of the magnificent success at Montgomery had died away, it was clear that much more of this campaigning was going to be required if black people were to gain their full civil rights. Montgomery indicated not so much a completely new method, but more a very effective revival of the sit-in protests of the war years. However, this time there was far greater support, superior organisation, charismatic leadership and a coherent philosophy.

Victory at Montgomery meant that King became a well-known civil rights leader almost overnight. The boycott had been well timed. Fairclough (1987) argues that the American left wing was at an especially low ebb after suffering for a decade in the unfriendly and virulently anti-communist Cold War climate of post-war America. Delighted with what happened in Alabama, they saw the possibility of similar action in many other parts of the USA. Moreover, King recognised the need for the assistance of experienced organisers to guide him along the next step of what he now realised was to be a long, eventful and dangerous road. He rejected his father's argument that it was God's will that he return to Atlanta for his own safety.

The Southern Christian Leadership Conference (SCLC). On the day his house was fired upon, King spoke to Bayard Rustin, and not long afterwards he met **Stanley Levison**. These men were experienced campaigners who could give him valuable strategic advice and help him to maintain the initiative. Rustin, who had assisted James Farmer to set up CORE back in 1942, now turned his attention to creating a new organisation that could build on the success of Montgomery. It would extend his influence all over the USA.

The result was the establishment of the SCLC, which would be more of a direct campaigning organisation than the legalistic and bureaucratic NAACP. The word 'Christian' was not in the original proposal for a name, but it was soon decided to include it. This reminds us of the crucial role that King's Christian beliefs had on his campaigning.

Activities of King and the SCLC, 1960–4. King and the SCLC did not initiate the important phase of the movement that began in 1960–1: the Sit-Ins and the Freedom Rides. But King's reputation was such that he was soon contacted about them and addressed gatherings of students. King and the SCLC were able to exploit the more favourable conditions that now existed for civil rights protests. He was prominent in the maintenance of non-violent yet vigorous protest, which maintained the moral high ground and thus won over sympathetic white people, especially in the north. Even more significantly, his tactics forced a federal response, as happened after Birmingham.

King maintained the oratorical reputation he had acquired in Montgomery with speeches that both raised the movement's morale and continued to articulate the feelings of ordinary black people, especially those in the south. It is significant that King was asked to give the closing speech after the march on Washington in 1963. King's great oratory on this occasion hit just the right note. It was essentially a speech designed for a wide and largely white audience. Some of the words and phrases had been delivered before, little was new and nothing original, but it revealed the great orator to an even wider audience.

KEY PERSON

Stanley Levison (1912–81) a white New York lawyer and businessman, and then an NAACP member and communist sympathiser in the 1950s. He helped with the formation of the SCLC and was an adviser to King, who held his abilities in high regard. However, his communist background meant that, like Bayard Rustin, he would never play a leading public part in the movement.

Martin Luther
King at Albany,
1962.

The Civil Rights Act (1964). By the time of the Washington march,
leaders like King were certainly dependent on the President and Congress
to see a Civil Rights Bill pass successfully, but he continued to put
pressure on the authorities with more demonstrations. This was now a
crucial time, as the Civil Rights Bill was undergoing its final preparation,
and then being discussed, in the early months of 1964. King hesitated
before proceeding with a new campaign in St Augustine, Florida, in
January 1964, but decided to go ahead as he felt the pressure on Congress
needed to be maintained. White's (1990) view of the St Augustine
campaign – undertaken in traditional SCLC style – was that, although it
did not completely succeed in gaining desegregation in the town itself, it
kept the civil rights protesters in the forefront of the news.

HOW SIGNIFICANT WAS THE ROLE OF MALCOLM X TO THE SUCCESS OF THE MOVEMENT?

The ideas of Malcolm X

By 1963, the King approach was subject to serious criticism. For example,
not all sections of society favoured the aims and ideals of the Washington
march. One prominent black critic of the whole strategy was Malcolm X.
He saw the white supporters of the movement as hypocrites and the black

leaders as deceived men. Malcolm X provided the main critique of the direction of the Civil Rights Movement up to 1963. In fact, he went a lot further and questioned the validity of the movement altogether.

The demand for civil rights, Malcolm X asserted, was based on the false assumption that it was desirable for black people to integrate with white people. From his northern perspective, Malcolm X saw nothing but white hostility to the black people in the ghettos, and their treatment was little better than in the south. He saw the unemployment, crime, filth, disease, prostitution and drugs of the ghetto as dehumanising those who lived there. The solution was not legal equality, desegregation or voting rights; it was an opportunity for these people to shape their own destiny. This would certainly not be done by 'turning the other cheek' – black people had the right to defend themselves. He was sceptical of King receiving the Nobel Peace Prize in 1964. To Malcolm X, this was a reward from an enemy general before the end of the war.

Broader horizons. Malcolm X's horizons widened considerably in 1964. In April and May he went on a tour of Muslim countries and moved towards orthodox Islam and away from the sectarian views of Elijah Muhammad. He was surprised to find many white Muslims, a point not appreciated by many in the west until the Bosnian crisis of the 1990s. Even more significant, he discovered a powerful Muslim philosophy of racial harmony and brotherhood. As James Cone (1993) puts it, 'Orthodox Islam challenged his theology of race.' Now he was clearly becoming less sweeping in his statements about white hostility. Given Malcolm X's reputation and popularity in the black ghettos, would this mean that this group could now embrace the wider Civil Rights Movement?

Malcolm X's speech 'The ballot or the bullet?', given at various venues in 1964, gave some indication that this might be possible. He talked about the need to 'submerge our differences' and talked about Martin Luther King as a civil rights leader without criticising him. The common feature of blackness was now more significant to Malcolm X than any differences between Muslims and Christians. Uninvited, Malcolm X joined both a school boycott and a rent strike rally in 1964 organised by militant but non-violent civil rights activists. Also, he urged black people to join voter registration campaigns. Malcolm X's opportunities to criticise the mainstream Civil Rights Movement, however, were limited: his spiritual leader, Elijah Muhammad, would still not allow him to make direct political comment and he got into trouble with Elijah over his 'chickens coming home to roost' remarks about the death of President Kennedy.

By 1963, though, there were signs of alternative organisations that would adopt a different strategy. Just before Kennedy's assassination in

November, the Northern Grass Roots Leadership Conference was held in Detroit, after black nationalists had been excluded from a Civil Rights Leadership Conference. About 2000 people heard Malcolm X give what was for him, at that time, a relatively political talk. It showed his increasing interest in the worldwide movement for black liberation in Africa and Asia, and urged black people in the USA to take up the same strategy. In making a distinction between a worldwide black revolution and an American Negro revolution, Malcolm X played an important part in the change of language from 'Negro' to 'black' or 'African-American' that took hold in the late 1960s and early 1970s.

The influence of Malcolm X. The impact of Malcolm X was clearly greater after his death. His view in the 1950s was that God would punish the wicked white man and that all black people had to do was to live a virtuous life. James Cone points out that Malcolm X's achievement at this stage was to make clear the depth of anti-black feeling in many parts of the USA and not just in the Deep South. Malcolm X, though not personally violent, was scornful of the idea that black people should simply accept discrimination without complaint or attempting to retaliate. In this way, he certainly had an important influence on emerging Black Power thought; but he was not to live to see its results.

There is no doubting the impact of Malcolm X on the more militant wing of SNCC and CORE in the mid-1960s, and on individuals like Stokeley Carmichael and James Forman. One can also see it in the demands of the Black Panthers when asking for the power to determine the destiny of the black community and wanting separate treatment for blacks in the fields of education, the law and economic justice.

HOW DO KING AND MALCOLM X COMPARE AS LEADERS OF THE CIVIL RIGHTS MOVEMENT?

Aims and tactics. Martin Luther King did not appeal to all the nation's African-Americans. He was a southerner and, as a Baptist Minister, was seen as someone from the black elite. Malcolm X, by contrast, could be viewed as a role model. Many northern black people could identify with him and did so. He served as an inspiration for the Black Power movement and certainly had an indirect impact on the development of CORE, SNCC and groups like the Black Panthers. But these developments, as we have seen, brought tension and division to the movement. Moreover, these divisions were not merely tactical. In rejecting the idea of integration, Malcolm X and his followers were rejecting the central aim of the original Civil Rights Movement. This does not mean, however, that his ideas were necessarily disastrous for the achievement of civil rights. The pride and confidence he gave to African-

Americans made many committed to work for change and an improvement in the black condition. Many were prepared to work with traditional civil rights followers, as Malcolm X himself did at the end of his life. One can only speculate about what he might have achieved for the movement had he lived.

Unlike Malcolm X, Martin Luther King became a convinced advocate of the moral power of non-violence, but here there was some limitation to his achievement. First, many of his followers, such as Hosea Williams, accepted it more for tactical reasons than because of their absolute belief in it. Later in the 1960s, when it seemed tactically less appropriate, they would drop the principle. Also, King himself came to the view that many of his racist opponents would not be converted by his shining moral example. The nature of the resistance in Birmingham and Selma, but also in Chicago, made him feel this way.

Changing views. The bombing of the church in Birmingham (see page 146), shortly after the protests there in 1963, affected King deeply. Four young black girls attending Sunday school died and no one was arrested for it. Could people prepared to do this ever be impressed with non-violence? Therefore, the best hope of success was to create a situation from which the protesters would be ill treated and then hope that the resulting publicity would bring in more support. When he was criticised for supporting the decision to bring children on to the streets in Birmingham and allowing demonstrations that would inevitably end in severe suffering for some of the participants, King had an answer. All he was doing was to ensure that the violence that had already occurred, but behind the police station out of view, was brought out in the open for all to see.

King's campaigns in Birmingham and Selma, while not a total success in local terms, had been crucial in getting the federal authorities to act. This tactic was extremely effective in the south until the mid-1960s. But the centre of gravity in black protest now moved to the north: here Malcolm X's ideas were to have more impact, ironically just after he died. As James Cone (1993) has pointed out, King did not quite appreciate the depth of the problem of racism in the north that Malcolm X had absorbed at first hand. King did not realise, for instance, just how virulently racist working-class northern white people could be until his campaign moved north. When he too experienced this, King's own views moved nearer to those of the now deceased Malcolm X.

How much did King and Malcolm X learn from each other? In the early days of his leadership, King was suspicious of having any connection with Malcolm X. He criticised the Black Muslims as early as 1959 and disliked the idea of Black Supremacy. To King, God was interested in the well-being of the whole human race. Moreover, King's commitment to non-violence was so strong that he found Black Muslim talk of 'self-defence' unacceptable. Non-violence was not disempowering. On the contrary, it could easily disarm the oppressor who did not know how to react to it. It could also impress the white sympathisers whom King wanted and welcomed, but who, for so long, Malcolm X despised as hypocrites. King's 'American Dream' was that black and white people could live in harmony, but Malcolm saw only a 'nightmare'.

Whereas Malcolm X was free with his criticism of King as a black leader popular with white people, King avoided too much comment about Malcolm. This was because, at first, he took a low view of his opinions. But in 1964, as Malcolm X moderated his views, King also became increasingly aware of the extent of the black plight in the northern ghettos. He began to develop some respect for Malcolm X. King's speeches began to include more regular references to being proud of being black – a point he first made forcefully in the north in a speech in Detroit in 1963. After Malcolm X's assassination in February 1965 and the serious race riots in the summer of the same year, King came to appreciate even more the seriousness of the black condition in many of the larger US cities.

By the end of his life, Malcolm X had learned from King the value of non-violent but militant protest. Malcolm X's analysis of the plight of many black people was in some ways better informed than King's. On the other hand, King's analysis of the solution seemed more level-headed: he realised that, however badly they had been treated, a violent response from black people, as a minority, would merely play into the hands of those white people who wished to suppress them.

HOW FAR DID KING LOSE HIS AUTHORITY AFTER 1965?

Chicago. In 1966, King moved his own attention to the north and turned his energies towards protests concerning employment and housing. His lack of experience of black life in northern ghettos and his much lower personal reputation in these areas were always going to make King's campaign in Chicago a tricky one. To the black nationalists, King's difficulties in Chicago emphasised the innate racism of northern whites and, to some of them, the need for more than a non-violent protest. The decision of King and the SCLC to target Chicago was ambitious but understandable. It gave the organisation a chance to focus on the north and fitted with the idea of tackling a tough area like Birmingham or Selma. In focusing on segregated housing, it also combined a traditional issue with the newer focus on social questions.

King and SNCC's Floyd McKissick addressed the opening gathering, although the show of unity was a tense one. The march into a white housing area at the end of July 1966 provided a lesson for King. The last thing these white people wanted was a black influx into their carefully preserved neighbourhood. The result was the pelting of the marchers with bottles, stones and rocks in a display of naked racial hatred that King admitted he had not encountered to the same degree before, even in Mississippi. In Chicago, white racists had come out on the streets to attack black demonstrators in larger numbers than southern white people ever did.

The way that Mayor Daley was seen to have outmanoeuvred King suggested to many that white party bosses still had many tricks to play to avoid conceding power. Daley seemed to have little interest in tackling the issue of the black ghetto or attempting to soften white racist feelings, and King was made to look slightly naïve in his dealings with him.

Vietnam. In January 1967, King's denunciation of the Vietnam War brought still more difficulties for his leadership. A brave move on his part, it brought some tension to the SCLC, which was divided on whether King should denounce it quite so clearly. Vietnam showed up King's difficulty in holding together an increasingly fragmented Civil Rights Movement. Roy Wilkins felt that King was being disloyal to his country, and even Andrew Young of the SCLC thought King was unwise to make the comments he did. On the other hand, it kept his credibility intact with some of his more militant supporters, such as Hosea Williams.

There is no question that King's criticism of the war was on principle and without too much thought of the precise consequences for the SCLC. In some ways, it may have helped his standing with the Civil Rights Movement as a whole, if not with all of his own supporters. While causing some division in SNCC, it did signify King's gradual move in a more radical direction. He was concerned with the social questions of the black ghettos and anxious to focus protests on economic questions now that voting rights had been achieved and segregation was proceeding apace. Expenditure on the Vietnam War brought him some useful propaganda: $0.5 million was being spent on killing a Vietnamese soldier, but only $35 to help each poor person back home.

On balance, however, Vietnam was clearly not helpful for the movement. Feelings of despair that Johnson's Great Society programme would never be fully achieved became common; the legislation of the President's last year, such as the Civil Rights Act of 1968, which dealt with housing, was not greeted with great enthusiasm or optimism by many civil rights supporters. The idea was developing in Black Power circles that black people would have to build up their own independent institutions. Only by doing this would they have the ability to introduce the social change they wanted. Not before time was the 'N' in SNCC changed to

'National': officially it happened in 1969, but the change had effectively taken place two or even three years earlier.

The Poor People's March (1968). The planning for the Poor People's March indicated King's continued trend towards an even greater emphasis on social concerns. First suggested by NAACP lawyer Marian Wright, it was envisaged as a militant protest to force some response from the federal government. It was not anticipated that the government would react like southern authorities and attack the protesters brutally, but some sort of confrontation was predicted. In this sense, it was hoped that it could be a campaign that would unite rather than divide. King envisaged that it would bring together other minority races with a high proportion of deprived citizens, such as Mexican-Americans and Puerto Ricans, as well as poor white people. It would be non-violent and would seek to attract those who wished to avoid yet another summer of rioting.

Yet King was also anxious for a vigorous campaign to show that non-violence was not dull and passive. Partly out of conviction and partly to keep the movement together, he was striking an increasingly radical tone in his last months. Adam Fairclough (1987) points out that King now asserted that racial integration was desirable only if the 'value system' of capitalism was changed. The prospect of widespread civil disobedience loomed. But King's assassination ended these plans: what would have happened on the Poor People's March if he had lived to lead it remains in the realm of speculation.

TO WHAT EXTENT WAS THERE A 'BLACK REVOLUTION' IN THE USA, 1968–80?

The election of Nixon. The election of Richard Nixon to the presidency in 1968 and his inauguration in 1969 represented a move to the right in US politics. The liberalism of the early and mid-1960s was rejected in favour of a more conservative approach. Liberal causes, however, remained. Environmental concerns, the anti-nuclear movement and consumer rights would continue to be at the forefront of US political life. Perhaps most important of all, the left had made the continuation of the Vietnam War increasingly difficult. The protest movement against the war, centred very often on university campuses, had been a major factor in the decision of Johnson not to seek re-election to the presidency, while Nixon's pledge to end the war had been a major reason for his election in 1968.

Nixon's domestic policy. Of great significance was a traditionally held Republican view that federal government was wasteful. Taxes were too high and money spent on assistance for minorities and those on welfare was a waste of resources. Republicans in the election campaign of 1968 poured scorn on students and left-wing activists protesting against the war, often labelling them as pro-communist anarchists. In the area of civil rights, Republicans opposed the forced bussing of schoolchildren to achieve desegregation. These at least appeared to be the main features of Nixon's presidency. The reality may have been slightly different. To many, it was seen as the beginning of a new era, a period of stability after the chaos and violence of the preceding years. Environmental issues did not die. Laws limited the use of pesticides, protected endangered species and established maximum levels for pollutant emissions. The National Environmental Policy Act (1969) required proposed federal projects to include an analysis of their impact on the environment. In other areas too, the Republicans could claim considerable progress. Nixon signed bills to increase social security benefits, to build subsidised housing, and to grant the vote to eighteen-year-olds.

But the extent of this progress must not be exaggerated. Nixon was personally suspicious of liberals and he regarded those who opposed him as personal enemies. He took a tough stand against domestic radicalism. The Justice Department and FBI worked with local officials to arrest Black Panther members on dubious charges, while the CIA illegally investigated the dossiers on thousands of US dissidents. The Department of Justice was authorised to prosecute anti-war activists and militant black people. Unspent 1968 campaign money was used to create a secret task force in 1969 to spy on liberals and government critics, while the Huston Plan to use the CIA and FBI in illegal wire-tapping and surveillance missions was a forerunner to the scandal of Watergate. It could well be argued that the personal liberties and civil rights of millions of Americans were considerably curtailed by these actions.

The response of the Civil Rights Movement. The more that black Americans saw of Nixon as President, the more they felt justified in their view, widely held in 1968, that he would do nothing to advance significantly the cause of black Americans. Not that they regarded their situation in 1968 as anything like acceptable. Although the 1960s had seen some advances, overall progress on civil rights had been slow. Indeed, in 1968, the National Advisory Commission on Civil Disorders declared that 'our nation is moving towards two societies, one black, one white – separate and unequal'. The election of Nixon in 1968 made many black people feel increasingly vulnerable.

The result was an increased feeling of black consciousness, which took various forms. Many decided to abandon the word 'Negro' as a racial designation in favour of the term 'black' or 'Afro-American'. It became increasingly common to adopt African or even Arabic-style names or to wear African or Arabic dress or hairstyles. In areas with a high proportion of black people, school boards often introduced courses on black studies, including important elements on black history and literature. All these strategies were intended to increase the feeling of black identity and to link blacks in the USA, emotionally and spiritually, with their brothers and sisters in Africa and throughout the world. After all, many felt a greater affinity with these people than with many white Americans, who, some felt, were out to destroy them.

Educational segregation. The 'southern strategy' was central to the election of Nixon in 1968 and his re-election in 1972. It was based on the view that a Republican victory in the country as a whole depended on victory in the southern states. To achieve this, it was necessary for Nixon to appear to southern white voters as more right wing than George Wallace, the Governor of Alabama, who was standing as an independent candidate. This explains the strong Republican stand against desegregation and the use of bussing to achieve it. In the south, there was some evidence of resegregation. White and black students were racially separated in different classes, or black students were excluded from extra-curricular activities. Black school officials and teachers either lost their positions or were assigned to inferior ones.

In other areas of the country, desegregation continued without interruption. In 1968, the city of Berkeley in California achieved it fully by bussing pupils across the city. However, in 1971, Nixon warned federal officials to stop pressing for the desegregation of southern schools by forced bussing. In his view, efforts to force integration in the suburbs were 'counterproductive and not in the interest of better race relations'. He also threatened to seek legislation to prevent courts from promoting racial integration through the bussing of students. In 1973, the Supreme Court permitted a circuit court decision to stand that barred the bussing of schoolchildren across city lines. Thus by 1978, in some large US cities, there was hardly any racial mix in the schools.

Whenever federal government appeared to be pressing for desegregation, many white families moved to the suburbs or placed their children in private schools. Black children were often left in a majority with an insufficient number of whites to achieve a balance. But despite Republican opposition, desegregation of schools, often by bussing, continued. In 1974, a smaller percentage of American children were attending segregated schools than had been attending them when Nixon first became President in 1969.

Affirmative action and black capitalism. Nixon and the Republicans supported programmes of affirmative action and encouraged black capitalism, partly for party political reasons. Nixon clearly believed that affirmative action policies would break the strong links between the trade unions who opposed them and the civil rights leaders who, with some reservations, supported them. He also believed that capitalism was the best way to improve the lives not just of black people, but of other minorities as well. A prosperous and growing economy would lead to an improvement in the standard of living of all Americans and particularly minorities.

Unfortunately, the US economy during the Nixon years was neither prosperous nor growing. The Republicans had inherited serious economic problems from the Democrats. Massive expenditure by Johnson on the Vietnam War and on schemes to create a 'Great Society' had left Nixon facing a budget deficit of $25 billion and an inflation rate of 5 per cent. A tax cut of $2.5 billion made the problem worse and led the Federal Reserve Board to raise interest rates and reduce the money supply. As inflation continued to rise, economic growth declined throughout 1971 and unemployment soared. The dollar was devalued and inflation remained a serious problem throughout the Nixon years. In this difficult period for the US economy, all Americans suffered to a greater or lesser extent, but it was black people and other minorities who suffered most. In the 1972 election, black voters and those from other minority groups stayed loyal to the Democrats and were not attracted by Republican promises of a better life under capitalism – so far, there were no signs that it was about to happen.

A Black Revolution? Some historians do take the view that, broadly between 1968 and 1980, there was a 'Black Revolution' in the USA. But this was not a violent revolution with bloodshed and assassinations. During the period, there was a steady increase in black political power and this helped to reverse the sense of powerlessness and hopelessness felt by many black people when Nixon assumed the presidency in 1968. Intense drives to increase the number of black people registered to vote gave much more meaning to the 1965 Voting Rights Act and encouraged a growing awareness among African-Americans of their power to improve their lives through the ballot. This increasing awareness became evident in different ways.

Democratic participation. In 1966, there were 97 black members of state legislatures in the USA and 6 members of Congress. There were no black mayors in any US city. In 1973, more than 200 black people sat in 37 state legislatures and there were 16 black people in the US Congress. This figure included one Senator and the only Republican, Edward Brooke of Massachusetts. There were also four women: Shirley Chisholm (New York), Barbara Jordan (Texas), Yvonne Burke (California) and Cardiss Collins (Illinois). By 1979, although Jordan and Burke had retired and Brooke had lost his seat, black representation remained strong, with 17 members in the House of Representatives. During the decade ending in 1973, black people had served as mayors in Cleveland, Los Angeles and Newark, plus many small towns. By 1979, there were black mayors in Atlanta, New Orleans, Los Angeles and Detroit. By the same year, more than 600 black people were serving as members of city councils and increasing numbers were working on school boards or as judges, aldermen, constables and marshals. The overall trend was very clear: black participation in the US democratic process was increasing.

The realisation that black Americans had the potential to exert enormous political power was nothing new. In 1960 the black vote had been crucial in the victory of John Kennedy in Illinois and South Carolina – vital states for him to win in his attempt to become President. The re-election of Robert Wagner as New York mayor in 1961 was due mainly to the large black and Puerto Rican vote. Aware of this enormous potential, many black people demanded greater participation in the Democratic Party. After all, in the 1968 presidential election, 85 per cent of black voters voted for Hubert Humphrey – 20 per cent of the total Democrat vote. In many ways, these demands were met and at the Democratic Party Convention in 1972 there was a significant increase in black delegates. The difficulty was that black people were not always united in their demands and the National Black Political Agenda of May 1972 reflected deep divisions on policy.

Limitations on participation. There was, however, a significant percentage of black Americans who believed that increased participation was mere 'tokenism'. According to this view, those black people who involved themselves in the democratic process were simply being 'bought' off in accepting the existing political system, which had already failed millions of their brothers and sisters. A Gallup Poll taken in 1971 reinforced this view: 25 per cent of employed black people expressed themselves as being dissatisfied with their jobs compared to 9 per cent of employed white people. More worrying still was the statistic that 44 per cent of black people expressed themselves dissatisfied with community life compared to 18 per cent of white people.

Although, by the mid-1970s, there was a heightened sense of power among many African-Americans, there was also a feeling that this power and influence should have been greater. By the time of the 1976 presidential election, only 58.5 per cent of all eligible black voters were registered and only 48.7 per cent actually voted. This problem of lack of involvement was particularly acute among black people aged between 18 and 24. So great was the apathy among this group that, in 1976, only 38 per cent were registered and only 26 per cent voted.

Participation under Carter. In the 1976 presidential election, 90 per cent of all black voters voted for Jimmy Carter. He swept the entire south except for Virginia, where voters favoured the Republican Gerald Ford by 55 to 45 per cent. While southern white people rejected Carter, black people rightly claimed credit for his election. Carter responded by appointing Patricia Harris as Secretary for Housing and Urban Development and Andrew Young to be Ambassador to the United Nations. Wade McCree became Solicitor-General and blacks were appointed to be under-secretaries and assistant secretaries throughout the government. Nine blacks were appointed to be US ambassadors and John Reinhardt became head of the International Communications Agency.

Carter was criticised for not doing enough to advance black people in his government and of being too obsessed with balancing the budget. Certainly, there was no African-American influence in the government until Louis Martin became Special Assistant to the President in 1978, but, throughout the Carter years, black delegations and pressure groups were regular visitors to the White House and enjoyed regular access to the President.

How widespread were the economic and political gains? On the question of a 'Black Revolution', the key issue is whether the economic and political gains of the period were enjoyed by all black people or limited to those of the middle class. Considerable evidence has already been presented to suggest that, over the period, more black people than ever before were participating in the American political process and exerting considerable power and influence. But this was not true of them all. Millions of African-Americans still felt a deep sense of alienation from the political process because they had not enjoyed the fruits of the economic system.

Although there had been an overall increase in the levels of prosperity of black people, in 1976, 31 per cent still lived below the poverty line. While this represented a reduction from the figure of 42 per cent in 1966, it meant that many black Americans were still living in considerable poverty. Between 1966 and 1976, unemployment rates for black workers were consistently higher than those for white workers. In 1977, the jobless rate for white people was 6.3 per cent, but for black people it was 13.2 per cent. For white teenagers, the figure was 15 per cent, but for black teenagers the figure ranged from 40 to 55 per cent.

Perhaps the Chicago University sociologist William J. Wilson best summed up the situation in his book, *The Declining Significance of Race* (1978). He spoke of the way in which 'Trained and educated blacks, especially the younger ones who have recently entered the labor market, are experiencing unprecedented job opportunities that are at least comparable to those of whites with equivalent qualifications.' But he also spoke of how discrimination and oppression had created 'a huge black underclass and the technological and economic revolution threatens to solidify its position in society'.

Thus it is possible to see the growth of an African-American middle class, with occupations such as civil servants, bankers and publishers being added to well-established black occupations such as lawyers, teachers and ministers. Most serious of all, however, was the widening gap between this rising middle class and millions of poor blacks who were falling further behind the more privileged. For the more prosperous, a 'Black Revolution' was a reality; for the poor, it simply didn't exist.

SECTION 5

America – 'the melting pot'

INTRODUCTION

> America is God's crucible, the great Melting Pot where all the races of Europe are melting and reforming! Here you stand, good folk, think I, when I see them at Ellis Island, here you stand in your fifty groups with your fifty languages and histories, and your fifty blood hatreds and rivalries, but you won't be long like that, brothers, for these are the fires of God you've come to . . . A fig for your feuds and vendettas! German and Frenchman, Irishman and Englishman, Jews and Russians – into the Crucible with you all! God is making the American.

These words, spoken by the character David Qixano in a play, *The Melting Pot*, echo the assertions of J. Hector St John de Crèvecoeur, in his *Letters from an American Farmer* back in the eighteenth century, that the USA was the place where people of different backgrounds and cultures would miraculously be joined into one nationality.

The Melting Pot, however, written by **Israel Zangwill** in 1908, sounds a warning note: 'The real American has not yet arrived. He is only in the Crucible. I tell you – he will be the fusion of all races, the coming superman.' The history of the USA in the late nineteenth and twentieth centuries suggests that the advent of the 'true American' was still awaited. In 1998, the *Washington Post* published a series of articles exploring the racial divisions still prevalent in contemporary US society under the title, 'The Myth of the Melting Pot'. Certainly, the evidence of the period before the Second World War is indicative of a society deeply divided along lines of culture and origin as well as colour.

The origins of the USA's multiracial society have been described in Chapter 3 of this book. This section looks a little more deeply into the challenge that mass immigration presented to the USA in terms of the acceptance and assimilation of groups of people with differing cultures and lifestyles.

KEY PERSON

Israel Zangwill (1864–1926) His writings give insight into Jewish life at the end of the nineteenth century. The concept of the USA as the birthplace of a new race, forged in a crucible, owes its origin to Zangwill's successful Broadway play.

WHY DID IMMIGRANTS TO THE USA EXPERIENCE PREJUDICE AND DISCRIMINATION?

Nativism. The influx of immigrants from northern Europe in the nineteenth century and from southern Europe increasingly in the first decades of the twentieth century produced a right-wing reaction in the form of 'nativist' organisations. These grew up among sections of the white, native-born ancestors of the original Protestant settlers in North America. They were pledged to protect the purity of the American ideal. Moreover, their reactionary beliefs also found expression in political circles. In 1850, for example, a House of Representatives committee reported on 'vicious foreigners . . . the dregs and off-scourings of alien peoples'.

At this time, the 'vicious foreigners' were German and Irish, who brought with them not only their poverty, but also Roman Catholicism. Hostility to Catholicism had characterised relationships with foreigners throughout the eighteenth century. As immigration accelerated during the nineteenth century, these hostilities were revived and augmented, leading to the formation of secret societies such as the Order of the Star Spangled Banner, or the 'Know Nothings' as they were rather disparagingly known. Even so, in some parts of the USA, they had popular appeal. By the end of the century, a plethora of nativist, protective societies had sprung up all over the country.

The beliefs and propaganda of the Know Nothing Party were unashamedly purist and anti-alien. The USA was held up as an ideal state approaching an unequalled level of perfection that nothing must be allowed to taint. Foreign immigration threatened to destroy the ideal:

> America has done and is doing the world's work, establishing the only true principles of liberty the world has ever known . . . The hand that guides this light is a Divine one. It is the hand of God . . . America has a mission to teach the world.

Interpretations of nativism. Historians have disagreed in their interpretations of these nativist organisations. Some see them as bigots who terrorised the weak and vulnerable, or explain their extremism in the context of an inability to respond to a rapidly changing and more complex society, within which they sensed a loss of power or control. Others explain their attitudes as arising from the fear created by economic uncertainty at times of slump and depression. David H. Bennett, in his book *The Party of Fear* (1988), presents the Know Nothing Party as people who perceived the USA as the perfect state, a Garden of Eden, and for whom this fantasy had become a faith that had to be protected. Hence, they blamed the arrival of immigrants during the mid-nineteenth century for rising crime, poverty, city slums and epidemic diseases, all of which threatened to destroy their fantasy.

Immigration from southern Europe. The Civil War years saw some acceptance of aliens in the north. Catholics and Protestants, Germans, the Irish and native-born Americans became united in a common cause. Besides, during the closing decades of the nineteenth century, a new wave of immigrants, this time from southern Europe, became the focus of nativist hostility. This hostility was exacerbated by the huge numbers involved. Between 1880 and 1915, 20 million immigrants arrived in the USA, representing a quarter of the total population. The majority of these were from Italy, Russia and the Austro-Hungarian Empire.

At first, many of the new arrivals travelled west to make a new life in the sparsely populated areas of the Great Plains. However, the closure of the frontier in 1890 resulted in a heavy concentration of the immigrant population in the major eastern cities. Here, the increasing labour unrest and acts of anarchist violence (see Section 4) were blamed on aliens, especially Italians.

Racist response. The English, Irish and German immigrants of northern Europe were contrasted positively with those from southern Europe. In his *History of the American People* (1902), for example, Woodrow Wilson compared 'men of the sturdy stock of the north of Europe' with 'the more sordid and hopeless elements'. He went on to say that the countries of southern Europe were 'disburdening . . . men out of the ranks where there was neither skill nor energy nor quick intelligence'. A sociologist at the University of Wisconsin, contemplating the inevitability of inter-marriage, wrote that it was 'unthinkable that so many persons with crooked faces, coarse mouths, bad noses, heavy jaws and low foreheads can mingle their heredity with ours without making personal beauty yet more rare among us than it actually is'.

In the closing years of the nineteenth century and the early decades of the twentieth, Italians were particularly singled out for discrimination, being described by many white Americans as 'undesirable . . . largely composed of the most vicious, ignorant, degraded and filthy paupers with an admixture of the criminal element'. This hostility manifested itself in the dubious trial of Sacco and Vanzetti. The imposition of Prohibition was also aimed at cities such as Chicago that were dominated by the more financially successful Italians (see Chapter 4), besides being an assertion of the white, Anglo-Saxon, Protestant (WASP) elements that dominated small-town America. The ultimate triumph of anti-alienism were the laws limiting immigration – the **Quota Act** (1921) and the **National Origins Act** (1924).

KEY TERMS

The **Quota Act** (1921) drastically reduced immigration from eastern and southern Europe by establishing a quota system to regulate entry into the USA. The limit was fixed at 3 per cent per year of the foreign-born people of the same nationality who already lived in the USA in 1910. This applied to Italians and Poles (Catholics) and Russian Jews. It targeted the unskilled and illiterate. Professional people, artists, actors, singers, nurses, etc. were allowed to enter the country without restriction.

The **National Origins Act** (1924) went a stage further by reducing immigration from eastern Europe to 2 per cent of the existing population of the same country of origin. It excluded Asian immigrants (Chinese and Japanese) completely.

Much hostility was also directed against Jewish immigrants, particularly those who, once they had settled, became successful and prosperous. This was especially evident during the 1920s. Anti-Semitism manifested itself in a variety of ways during these years. Henry Ford, for example, bought a local newspaper and used it as a vehicle for attacking Jews. Jews suffered discrimination in employment. They, along with Catholics and other immigrant groups, became targets for the second Ku Klux Klan.

The second Klan. Re-formed in Georgia in 1915, the Klan had several thousand members by 1920. This growth may well have been due to some clever but corrupt marketing of membership by its founder, William J. Simmons. But once Hiram Wesley Evans had replaced him, the Klan took on a more overtly nativist image. Unlike the first Klan, it was not a vigilante organisation. In true nativist tradition, it focused on the evils of Catholicism and, added to this, anti-Semitic propaganda. Evans spoke out against 'the vast horde of immigrants who have reached our shores . . . Italian anarchists, Irish Catholic malcontents, Russian Jews, Finns, Letts, Lithuanians of the lowest class'. It naturally appealed to the WASPs who believed that their dream of America was about to be shattered. By 1924, even allowing for exaggerated membership figures, it was clearly a mass movement, openly parading through the streets of Washington, DC – in itself, a reflection of the extent of anti-alienism in the USA at that time.

The culture and ambitions of immigrants. The position of immigrants from Europe was not helped by their tendency to live in culturally distinct ghettos in the big cities. As described in Chapter 2, they retained their language and culture from choice. Ultimately, their adoption of hyphenated titles was not forced upon them by racially prejudiced native-born Americans, but was something they chose to do because these titles described them accurately and appropriately. European-Americans may have faced discrimination in the workplace because, for a long time, immigrants of whatever nationality were seen as a huge reservoir of cheap labour. This was a situation that they were prepared to tolerate because it, at worst, enabled them to survive and, at best, set them eventually on the path to greater prosperity.

Once naturalised, they received full rights of citizenship even though they still sometimes experienced prejudice at times of stress or economic hardship. Italian businessmen became influential in the city politics of Chicago, for example, as did the Irish in New York. German brewers came to dominate what was a lucrative industry, at least until the outbreak of the First World War in 1914 and the imposition of prohibition in the 1920s.

While it is easy, with hindsight, to regard European immigrants as a vulnerable and exploited group, it must also be remembered that not all of them wanted assimilation. They had no wish to be placed in the cauldron and to be melted into Americans. Many Italian and Russian Jewish immigrants had been driven by poverty or persecution to leave their homelands. Many equally regarded the move as temporary. For example, of the 604,000 Italian immigrants who entered the USA in the 1890s, only 484,000 remained by 1900. In 1900 a further 2.1 million immigrants arrived in the USA but only 1.4 million remained in 1910.

WHICH ETHNIC GROUPS SUFFERED MOST FROM DISCRIMINATION IN THE PERIOD BEFORE THE SECOND WORLD WAR?

While the situation of European immigrants might have been bad enough, with the exception of African-Americans, those who suffered most from racial prejudice, discrimination and segregation were Hispanic/Mexican-Americans and those of Asian origin. The position of these groups has been described in Chapter 3. Like African-Americans, they were denied full rights of citizenship, including the right to vote.

Mexican-Americans. It must be remembered that a significant proportion of Mexican-Americans were not within the borders of the USA from choice, but rather as a result of the acquisition by the USA of territory from Mexico. Others migrated north during the nineteenth century to work as agricultural labourers, but with the consumer boom of the 1920s they moved into the cities of the west – Denver, Los Angeles, San Antonio, Tucson – in search of better-paid work. There they found themselves the victims of prejudice, segregated in public places and forced by discrimination and poverty into low-rent accommodation in ghetto areas or *barrios*. Here, deprived of much of their dignity, they at least maintained their language, culture and traditions. Immigrants from Puerto Rico, surplus labour in their own country, encountered similar difficulties in New York, where they tended to congregate. Like other ethnic groups, Mexicans suffered most at times of economic depression. During the Great Depression of the 1930s there were wholesale deportations.

Chinese-Americans. The treatment of the Chinese and Japanese was significantly worse than that of the Mexicans. The Chinese had arrived in San Francisco in 1849 to labour for gold prospectors and work in the mines. Almost immediately, they became victims of racist violence, being derisively referred to as 'coolies' or 'mongol peons'. By 1852, the Governor of California was crying out for federal action to stop Chinese immigration. The reasons for this cannot be rationally explained.

Compared with other immigrant groups, the rate of Chinese immigration was relatively slow. By 1865 there were only 60,000 Chinese in the whole country. By 1880, of the 300,000 that had arrived, two-thirds had returned to China, driven out by violence, intimidation and discrimination. The census of 1880 revealed that there were only 105,465 Chinese in the country (i.e. 0.21 per cent of the total population of the USA).

Yet in the 1880s, the Chinese, always enterprising and industrious, were handicapped in their attempts to establish laundries by prohibitions. School boards tried to enforce segregation on Chinese and Japanese children, obliging them to attend Chinatown schools. Here, white American teachers insisted on teaching in English, even though their Chinese pupils clearly did not understand anything that they said!

Everything about the Chinese was despised – their food, dress, language. When unemployment was high, white workers blamed the Chinese. Outbreaks of anti-Chinese violence in Los Angeles, Seattle, Denver, Tacona and in the Rocky Mountain mining areas where they worked resulted in the Chinese Exclusion Act (1882). Determination to keep the Chinese out resulted in renewals of the Act in 1892, 1893 and 1902.

Japanese-Americans. Similar kinds of discrimination and abuse were meted out to the Japanese. The Mayor of San Francisco declared at one point that 'the Chinese and Japanese are not bone fide citizens. They are not the stuff of which Americans . . . can be made.' Labour leaders organised themselves against both by forming the Asiatic Exclusion League, and Japanese children shared the same fate as the Chinese by being excluded from white schools. By 1907, such incidences of racism were clearly causing the President, Theodore Roosevelt, so much embarrassment that he reached a gentleman's agreement with the Japanese whereby the government of Japan agreed not to issue passports to labourers seeking to emigrate to the USA. In return, the US government agreed to try to end discrimination against Japanese who were already in the USA. This agreement effectively blocked immigration from Japan.

Native Americans. Of all the ethnic groups, the Native Americans (whose fate has been described in Chapter 3) were distinctively different, because they had no desire to become assimilated. Instead, they wished to retain their traditional culture and way of life. In so far as they wished to lay claim to their rights, it was their right to their tribal lands and integrity that concerned them most. In the closing decade of the nineteenth century, the tribes struggled to survive. The Dawes Severalty Act (1887) had broken up the reservation lands in an attempt to destroy tribal culture, but condemned Native American families who took advantage of the opportunity to own their own property, to live on barren land that was beyond cultivation. Ultimately, they had no choice but to abandon their holdings. This disadvantaged them during the Depression as, being landless, they did not qualify for federal aid.

Some Native Americans did have the opportunity to become educated and for them the dilemma became a conflict between maintaining their tribal loyalties and seeking assimilation into white American society. In 1911, these educated men and women formed the Society of American Indians (SAI). They campaigned for better education and health facilities and for civil rights. However, a lack of mass support from Native Americans and a lack of money to challenge discrimination in the courts limited their success. Consequently, by the 1920s, the SAI had collapsed.

Nevertheless, by 1941, the position of Native Americans had improved as a result of the supportive policies of Franklin D. Roosevelt. Under John Collier, founder of the American Indian Defense Association, Indian lands were restored and the division of tribal lands was prohibited. Loans were made available to Native Americans for economic development and they were encouraged to develop systems of self-government. This period saw a revival and a celebration of their traditional arts and culture. However, by the 1940s, there were Native Americans who were attracted by the opportunities of mainstream American life and who wanted assimilation. When they tried to enter this world, they faced the same degree of discrimination as that endured by African-Americans and Hispanics. The movement for black civil rights would eventually provide them also with an opportunity for protest.

HOW DID JAPANESE AND CHINESE COMMUNITIES FARE FROM THE SECOND WORLD WAR TO BLACK POWER?

Effect of the Second World War on Japanese-Americans. Once the USA had joined the Second World War, the discrimination against Japanese appeared to be immediate and intense. Their civil rights soon disappeared. Some distinction was made between the Nisei (young Japanese born in the USA and generally US citizens) and the Issei (an older generation of immigrants who, for legal reasons, were unable to become US citizens). The Issei, with an average age of 52, were accused of having a 'sentimental attachment' to their mother country and their 'oriental' habits of life. In the camps to which the Japanese were sent, the Nisei were given some authority, although this caused tension with the older generation, who were used to exercising authority. Both groups were treated with suspicion until 1943, when they were all asked to swear unqualified allegiance to the US government: the 15 per cent who refused were placed in separate camps.

There seemed little sympathy for the Japanese plight. Normally liberal journals such as the *Nation* and the *New Republic* approved the measures taken against them. It was even asserted that Earl Warren's unsympathetic attitude was born of political calculation: he wished to follow popular policies to improve his chances of being elected Governor of California. Unfriendly publications such as the *Grizzly Bear*, the paper of the 'Native Sons of the Golden West' questioned the Japanese right to citizenship at all. In truth, there had been a prevailingly racist attitude to Japanese settlers ever since they came in large numbers after 1868. Way back in 1908, presidential candidate, William Jennings Bryan, had described them as 'essentially different' and incapable of assimilation.

The theory of many Japanese was that it was wisest to cooperate with the authorities, no matter how badly they were treated. In this way, they could show their loyalty and meet accusations of their unreliability and sympathy with the Japanese war cause. Many Japanese-Americans fought for their country, such as those in the 442nd regimental combat team in Italy. However, this approach did not bring an immediate improvement in their conditions. General John L. De Witt remarked 'a Jap's a Jap' and insisted that they were a 'dangerous element' whether or not they were loyal. But their forbearance in the war produced an improvement afterwards. In 1945, the Supreme Court case of *Endo* v. *US* established that forcible retention of citizens of Japanese ancestry who were of proven loyalty was unauthorised. In 1948, President Truman signed the American Evacuation Claims Act, which reimbursed Japanese who had lost their property during the war. An official apology from Congress, however, was not forthcoming until 1988.

Progress for Japanese-Americans after the war. The Japanese recovery was most evident in their economic progress. When relocated to the west coast, many went back to their traditional agricultural occupations, especially growing fruit and vegetables. Others, however, saw wider opportunities in the expanding post-war US economy, training as engineers, lawyers, managers and doctors. In 1950, the proportion employed in agriculture was 20 per cent; in 1960, 10 per cent. A sign that the Japanese were moving up in US society was that, despite this fall, the percentage who were farm *managers* increased in the same period from 17 per cent to 21 per cent. Still others moved into small businesses, such as grocers and launderers. After the McCarran-Walter Immigration Act (1952), Japanese again began to enter the USA in substantial numbers: 3800 in 1952 and 6000 in 1960.

Discrimination, though still apparent, was decreasing. In 1945, Takao Arantani's parents challenged California's separate school provision and a Los Angeles Court agreed that it violated the Fourteenth Amendment equal protection clause. Educational segregation in California was ended the following year. But, despite great advances, it remained difficult for Japanese-Americans to get the very top business positions which, into the 1960s, remained largely reserved for white people. In Hawaii, however, perhaps because Asiatics outnumbered Caucasians, there was no apparent discrimination in any walk of life.

Chinese-Americans during and after the war. Unlike the Japanese, Americans of Chinese extraction found war circumstances to their favour. In 1943, Madame Chaing, wife of the Chinese leader, visited Eleanor Roosevelt at the White House. In the same year, the laws excluding further immigration of Chinese were repealed. The political friendship towards China created by the war triumphed over any racist feelings – not that these were absent entirely: the *Grizzly Bear* argued for continued exclusion on the revealing grounds that the USA already had one racial problem that had not been solved (black people). But the Chinese were now better treated than at any other time. Gone were the days of the 1930s in San Francisco when banks openly refused to employ Chinese.

The new generation of immigrants that arrived during the war years soon became tired of living in the ghetto-like conditions of San Francisco, with its sub-standard housing and low-pay employment prospects. After the war, New York became a more significant place for settlement than the west coast. Chinese-Americans managed to escape their stereotyped Chinese restaurant image and furnished a financial base for the next generation to prosper still further. Like the Japanese, they were particularly well integrated in Hawaii.

One significant development was in 1962 when President Kennedy allowed Hong Kong refugees fleeing from communist China to enter the USA: 6000 came in the first year and over 30,000 by the end of the 1960s. This did create some difficulties. In 1970, unemployment in this group ran at nearly 13 per cent, double the other residents of San Francisco, and two-thirds were in sub-standard housing compared with under one-fifth of the rest of San Francisco's inhabitants. As with other ethnic groups that were relatively economically deprived, this produced youth militancy at the end of the 1960s. A movement calling itself the New Yellow Peril developed and student activists at San Francisco State College formed the Free University of Chinatown Kids Unincorporated.

HOW DID WAR AND POST-WAR DEVELOPMENTS CHANGE THE NATURE AND EFFECTS OF MEXICAN IMMIGRATION?

Effect of the Second World War on Mexican-Americans. As with other ethnic minorities, the wider effects of the war impinged upon the Mexican community quite considerably. Their fighting record was distinguished. Although forming around 10 per cent of the population of the Los Angeles area, they achieved 20 per cent of the region's awards, including 39 Congressional Medals of Honour. Not surprisingly, some of these were posthumous, since 20 per cent was also the Mexican casualty figure.

But these men hardly came home to a hero's welcome. They were more likely to encounter a swimming pool or a restaurant that continued to discriminate against their presence in the same area as white Americans. This prejudice was not new. Many white Californians refused to work with Mexican-Americans, and they were excluded from certain industries such as the fruit-canning factories. Terms such as 'Coyote' were intended to be insulting, and their schools remained segregated on the grounds that language problems prevented effective integration. Yet in the past Mexican-Americans had had a good work record and a comparatively low crime rate.

Aside from the existing prejudice that many white Californians seem to have had against the Mexican-Americans, a small number of young Mexicans may have contributed to the maintenance of these feelings. The gang warfare in Los Angeles during the war years was ascribed to the presence of 'zoot suiters', wearing generously cut, oversized clothes, and 'jivers', who danced to highly charged music with a strong beat. Their aggressive forms of behaviour did not endear them to other inhabitants of the area.

Progress in the 1940s and early 1950s. As with black people, the late 1940s and early 1950s, though not a time of spectacular advance, saw the groundwork laid for further progress towards full civil rights for Hispanics, especially in the field of legal judgments. There had already been some recognition by the federal government of the difficulties faced by the Hispanic immigrants. In 1943, President Roosevelt had set up a Spanish-speaking department to help them to integrate more fully into American life and to be on the lookout for discriminatory practices, which were to be discouraged. Towards the end of the war, community service clubs were set up with similar ends, and these continued until the early 1950s.

In 1944, the first favourable decision came in the form of equal access to the public swimming pool at San Bernardino, thanks largely to the work of Ignacio Lopez. In 1945, a Californian judge ruled segregation in education illegal – a significant judgment. The grounds given for the verdict were the rejection of the argument about language difficulties preventing integrated classes. Although this particular point would not apply to black education, the judgment certainly encouraged NAACP lawyers to continue their efforts in a similar field.

During the 1950s, two organisations took up the civil rights banner for the Mexican-Americans:

- Alianza Hispano-Americana was originally a late-nineteenth-century Friendly Society, which had come to represent the interests of its people in a wider sense. During the 1950s, it adopted a more campaigning tone than previously. In NAACP style, it proved – for instance, in Tolleson, Arizona – that Mexican schools were separate but *un*equal. It would take the Brown case in 1954 to go a step further and outlaw segregation for racial minorities on principle.
- In 1950, the American Council of Spanish-speaking people was formed, with a more coherent programme for reform. It demanded desegregation not only of schools, but also of housing and all public facilities. An end to discrimination in employment and jury selection was also demanded. There were some successes here. For example, in 1954 a Spanish-American had his murder conviction quashed on the grounds that the selection of an all-white jury had prejudiced his case and denied him his constitutional rights under the Fourteenth Amendment equal protection clause.

The American Council worked in co-operation with the NAACP and strove to improve police–community relations. However, this was not an easy task. The McCarran Act (1952) actually resulted in some Mexicans being denaturalised, and police were always on the lookout for illegal immigrants. In 1953, one million were deported under 'Operation Wetback', wetbacks being another demeaning name for Mexican-Americans who had supposedly swum from Mexico to enter the USA illegally.

Developments in the 1960s. By 1960, civil rights progress had been limited, but Kennedy's Roman Catholicism, relatively youthful image and somewhat liberal reputation provided hope from a new and powerful quarter. 'Viva Kennedy!' clubs were set up to campaign for his election to the presidency. The generally more optimistic civil rights climate of the early 1960s provided renewed hope, although no measures were introduced that were aimed specifically at the Mexican-American community.

Cesar Chavez's union campaign, from 1965 onwards, provided a change of emphasis towards economic and social questions that mirrored developments in the black Civil Rights Movement. Guaranteed wages, improved working conditions, proper collective bargaining, union contracts and closed shops were all on the agenda, as were demands for legislation to protect agricultural workers. In addition, there was an appeal to the public to end social discrimination against Mexican immigrants. Vigorous campaigner that he was, however, Chavez continued to follow Martin Luther King's non-violent philosophy. He advocated 'turning the other cheek' and saying a prayer for his oppressors.

The more militant Brown Power movement, modelled on Black Power, is best shown in the Red Berets. This group first developed in Los Angeles in 1967, from some of the leaders of Young Citizens for Community Action. When their efforts to improve relationships between the Mexican community and police failed, they formed the Berets and turned to militancy with leader David Sanchez as 'Prime Minister'. Disturbances in Los Angeles high schools and on the streets in March 1968 saw the Berets take a confrontational line with police, and these protests went on into the 1970s before the police broke them up with gunfire.

HOW DID WAR AND POST-WAR DEVELOPMENTS IN THE USA CHANGE THE STATUS OF NATIVE AMERICANS?

Effects of the Second World War. War developments did little to benefit the Native American (or Indian-American) community. John Collier's Bureau of Indian Affairs (see Chapter 4) was largely removed from Washington to Chicago, and cuts were made in its budget. Colorado River Indians showed considerable resentment when Japanese-Americans were 'relocated' on to their reservation land. Many able-bodied Native Americans were lost to military service. But the greater educational opportunities that had been provided by Collier before the war were coupled with an increased number of Native American employees in the Indian Bureau. This resulted in a greater confidence to push for wider recognition of Native American needs and priorities, hence the formation of the National Congress of American Indians (NCAI) in 1944.

Assimilation. After the war, as with attitudes towards blacks, President Truman's approach held out brief hopes of a sustained policy of improvement. A Special Education Council was set up in 1946 to aid the Navajos and Hopi tribes. Rehabilitation programmes were developed, and respect for religious and social customs increased. But, with Collier gone, there was a revival of the old assimilationist policy in the form of 'termination'. The idea was gradually to end federal control by the Bureau for Indian Affairs and make Native Americans subject to the same laws, and entitled to the same privileges, as other Americans. They would be seen more as individuals than as tribal members.

In 1953, firearm purchase was allowed and alcohol restrictions could be removed subject to local decision making. The wisdom of this last move might be questioned with evidence that at this time cirrhosis of the liver was 300 per cent higher among Native American communities than in the rest of the USA. Some distinctions remained: leaders could still be selected according to kinship and religious factors, and traditional clothing and long hair were formally protected. Gradually, with greater speed during the early 1960s, increasing numbers of Native American children attended mainstream public schools – about 90 per cent by 1965. But with little account frequently taken of their cultural background and special needs, they often dropped out early with little in the way of formal qualifications.

Relocation. White prejudice was generally not as overt towards Native Americans as towards black people. Bolt (1990) argues that this was because Native American problems were 'less rooted in the social prejudices of the whites'. Nonetheless, there was some tension when Native Americans moved to urban areas, as they did in increasing numbers after 1945. Indeed, the authorities frequently encouraged relocation. Bureaux were established to aid this process in cities such as Chicago, San Francisco, Oakland and Oklahoma City, all near substantial Native American reservations.

The Indian Vocational Training Act (1956) was designed to help improve their employment prospects in their new environment. But on a lesser scale, the new urban dwellers encountered the kind of social problems that faced so many more northern black people, particularly poverty and unemployment. Around 25 per cent were officially accounted for as 'poor' and almost 20 per cent lived in sub-standard housing. Not surprisingly, Native American life expectancy was only two-thirds of white peoples'. Unemployment varied. Less of a problem in Chicago (4.3 per cent), it was very high in other areas, such as Seattle (18 per cent).

Lobbying. The NCAI remained the main lobbying group for Native Americans. It was comprehensive in that it recruited members from all tribes, and women were well represented too, taking 50 per cent of executive board positions by the mid-1950s. The organisation looked to getting a commission established to hear and settle Native American land ownership claims against the federal government and improved administration from the Bureau for Indian Affairs, which, it was argued, should employ more Native Americans. It wished to monitor congressional legislation affecting Native American territory. By 1960, it had succeeded in getting both major parties to drop further termination policies. Many of its demands were peculiar to the needs and situation of the Native American community. Nonetheless, some comparisons could be made with black civil rights organisations: their concerns with voter registration and better health and educational services, for instance.

Increasing militancy. By the start of the 1960s, as with black people, the younger generation of Native Americans was becoming impatient. The NCAI was now accused of being largely dominated by the more prosperous and acculturated Native Americans: the views of the young had been neglected. The result was the setting up of the National Indian Youth Council in 1961. Comparisons with SNCC the previous year are clear, although at this stage there were no Native American sit-ins. However, more militant tactics could be found with the development of the American Indian Movement in 1968, and the 1970s were to see a series of protests that reflected dissatisfaction with both the previous approach of the NCAI and the Native American policies of the federal government.

WHAT WAS THE SITUATION BY THE LATE 1960s?

Each of the ethnic minorities surveyed had its own distinctive issues and problems in the post-war generation and they all reacted in different ways.

- The Japanese and Chinese made the greatest economic progress.
- Native Americans continued to hold long-standing grievances against the federal government and found their culture and traditions frequently jarring with the mid-twentieth-century mores of much of the rest of the USA.
- Mexican-Americans suffered similar, if less intense, prejudice to black people, and struggled to become accepted as equal partners in the American Dream.
- Both the Hispanics and the Native Americans developed pressure groups to claim their equal place in society, and both were becoming increasingly militant at the time of Black Power in the later 1960s.

Gerstle, Rosenberg and Rosenberg (1999) note that, by the end of the 1960s, all groups were 'moving away from individual advancement and towards ethnic group interests': this was another factor that hastened the coming of affirmative action in the 1970s.

What was the situation for Native Americans in this period?

Between 1945 and 1980, the population of Native Americans more than doubled to reach nearly one million. The majority lived west of the Mississippi river, most in Oklahoma, Arizona and California. Even by 1980, roughly half the total number of Native Americans lived on reservations, where life was hard and beset with difficulties. Unemployment levels ranged from 20 to 80 per cent and the average life expectancy was 44 years compared with a national average of 64 years. Diseases continued to kill thousands and there were high suicide rates, particularly in the 16–25 age group.

Over the period, many Native Americans left their reservations and moved to the cities in large numbers. They were encouraged by government programmes to relocate them. These programmes were based on the belief that, if Native Americans could be integrated into white society, problems such as alcoholism and high mortality rates could be tackled more effectively. By 1980, therefore, those Native Americans who had left the reservations had become urban dwellers, some in small towns but many more in large cities like San Francisco and Los Angeles. Congregating together in large numbers made many increasingly aware of their own economic and social inferiority compared to white people and many black people. It also increased the possibility of the emergence of new protest movements.

Traditionally, Native Americans had tried to extend their civil rights through the courts. The National Congress of American Indians (NCAI) (see page 313), formed in 1944, was the first pan-Indian movement and used the courts to obtain justice in the same way that the NAACP had done. It sued state and federal governments over employment discrimination, schooling and the breaking of treaty rights. Most Native Americans agreed that this was the only way to make progress.

But, unlike most African-Americans, it was never the intention of Native Americans to seek integration into American society. They certainly demanded the same rights as all Americans, but they were equally concerned to preserve their own cultural identity. In pursuing this objective, the NCAI achieved modest success when they gained a pledge from Kennedy to develop the human and natural resources of the reservations. But working through the courts was slow and frustrating and, as more and more Native Americans fell further into poverty, their anger grew. The attitude of many white people towards Native Americans did nothing to help progress. To many white people they were inferior people whose role was to act as servants and whose eventual destiny would be destruction.

Increasing militancy

During the 1960s and 1970s, the growing anger of the Native Americans was directed against the Bureau of Indian Affairs (BIA), which exercised power over the reservations (see page 172). By 1968, protest was growing stronger, particularly among younger Native Americans. The song 'As Long as the Grass shall Grow', recorded in 1968 by Peter La Farge, was one of a number protesting at the abuse of Native Americans by white people. In 1969, Vine Deloria Jr published the book *Custer Died For Your Sins*. It was followed a year later by *Bury My Heart at Wounded Knee: An Indian History of the American West*. This book, by Dee Brown, raised the awareness of millions about the history of the Native Americans and their plight. Native American protest at this time gained great momentum and inspiration from other protest movements, such as those demanding black civil rights or an end to the war in Vietnam.

The occupation of Alcatraz

In 1969, encouraged by the idea of protest and direct action, fourteen Native American men and women occupied the island of Alcatraz, which had been abandoned as a prison six years before. They offered to buy the island for $24 in glass beads and cloth – the same price paid by the white settlers for Manhattan. When their proposal to turn the prison into a Native American museum and institute was rejected, 80 Native Americans returned and occupied the island. They were supported by San Francisco students and hundreds became involved. Eventually, over 10,000 Native Americans visited the island, which had its own radio station 'Radio Free Alcatraz', named after the US propaganda station 'Radio Free Europe'. The occupation of Alcatraz received wide media coverage throughout the world and millions became aware of it, although in itself the occupation achieved little.

The Alcatraz incident showed what could be achieved by direct action and encouraged many Native Americans to call for 'Red Power' – a militant approach to achieve separation from whites. Native Americans occupied federal lands and disobeyed state and federal fishing regulations. In Maine, members of the Passamaquoddy tribe even collected tolls on busy highways crossing their land.

The American Indian Movement

The most militant group was the American Indian Movement (AIM), which began in Minneapolis–St Paul in 1968. Faced with police harassment and what they considered racial discrimination, young Native Americans, dressed in red berets and jackets, patrolled the streets monitoring the police. As a result, there was a decline in the arrest of Native Americans and their numbers in local jails fell by 60 per cent. AIM also sought to improve the housing, education and employment of Native Americans in the cities and to project a more positive image. Between 1969 and 1970, they set up 18 branches and held their first national convention in 1971.

In 1972, together with other organisations, AIM took part in the Trail of Broken Treaties to the BIA in Washington, DC. This march took its name from the removal by Andrew Jackson of Cherokee Indians from the Georgia–North Carolina border to Oklahoma – known as The Trail of Tears. When they arrived in Washington, AIM members took over the Bureau's offices. They examined the files and concluded that each Indian family could receive a further $4000 per year if the bureaucracy of the BIA was removed.

They published a list of twenty demands, but these were ignored by the Nixon government. In 1973, militant members of AIM staged an armed confrontation with government officials at Wounded Knee, South

Dakota, where the US cavalry had massacred the Sioux in 1890. However, only about 300 members of AIM supported the confrontation and it achieved very little.

What had the Native Americans achieved by 1980?

- In 1969, the Nixon administration appointed a Mohawk-Sioux, Louis R. Bruce, as Commissioner for Indian Affairs. The government later returned 48,000 acres of sacred land to the Taos Pueblos Indians.
- In 1970, Nixon assured the tribes that they would be given greater autonomy 'without being cut off from federal concern or support'. The intention was to free the Native Americans from federal supervision and to transfer the cost of their support to the states – it failed.
- The Indian Self-Determination Act (1975) attempted to give Native Americans more control of their reservations.
- The American Indian Religious Freedom Act (1978) granted to Native Americans the right 'to believe, express and exercise traditional religions including access to sites, use and possession of sacred objects and freedom to worship through ceremonials and traditional rites'.
- However, many problems and difficulties remained. Many Native Americans disliked the approach of militant groups like AIM. They felt it was not in keeping with traditional Native American ways and led to many divisions.
- Poverty and deprivation continued, both in the reservations and in the cities. When the US economy hit difficulties, it was often minority groups who were hit most, and Native Americans were no exception.

What was the situation for Hispanic-Americans in this period?

By 1978 the Hispanic-American population of the USA had reached 7.2 million, largely as a result of immigration and high birth rates. Most Hispanics lived in Arizona, California, Colorado, New Mexico and Texas. In these five states they made up one-sixth of the population. Beginning in the 1960s, many Hispanics moved to the cities, attracted by jobs in industry and by the prospect of a better life – much better, they hoped, than the poverty they had suffered in the countryside. By 1970, 85 per cent of Hispanic-Americans lived in cities. There were 1 million in Los Angeles, comprising approximately one-third of the city's population, and Hispanics made up half the population of San Antonio and El Paso. For many, their hopes of a better life in the cities were soon shattered. Unemployment rates among Hispanic-Americans remained very high. Housing standards were low and children attended segregated schools. Many also felt strongly that the police were discriminating against them in administering the law.

In response to these problems, many Hispanic-Americans launched their own Civil Rights Movement. To emphasise their Mexican identity, they began calling themselves Chicanos rather than Hispanic-Americans (see page 105). They soon discovered what could be achieved by acting together when voter registration drives in 1974 resulted in the election of Chicano governors in New Mexico and Arizona. They found a leader of great stature in Cesar Chavez, who became the first president of the United Farm Workers' Organising Committee and began organising strikes and boycotts to improve workers' conditions. In 1997, President Clinton described him as 'the Ghandi of the fields, who rose to become one of America's greatest forces in the labor and civil rights movement'.

What had the Hispanic-Americans achieved by 1980?

As a result of the work of Chavez and others, there were improvements in the life of many Chicanos:

* In many areas, trade union recognition led to better working conditions.
* The process of school desegregation was speeded up, and there was a rise in the number of Chicano teachers and administrators.

But in most other ways the general picture remained unchanged:

* The bulk of Mexican immigrants were poor, illiterate peasants who remained unskilled.
* They continued to suffer from low levels of education, high unemployment and low-paid, dead-end jobs.

Chicanos were the second largest minority group in the country. Should they not, therefore, have achieved greater advances? Perhaps they suffered from the way in which they saw themselves not as permanent US residents, but as temporary workers. Strong family and language ties with their homeland made them reluctant to put down roots, and this seriously damaged their economic and political progress.

CONCLUSION

In conclusion, the 'melting pot' is a myth. It can be argued that the experience of deprivation and discrimination and the subsequent struggle for civil rights served only to increase self-awareness amongst the USA's ethnic groups and a determination to retain and assert their separate cultural identities. Clearly, assimilation occurred successfully amongst those descended from white, European immigrants. But, irrespective of civil rights legislation, white US society remained fundamentally racist and fostered the sense of alienation and rejection that produced the determination to celebrate diversity. Consequently, from the crucible emerged, not one, but a variety of US citizens who continue to assert their peculiar differences within the context of that single nationality that all technically possess.

QUESTION IN THE STYLE OF AQA

Consult the following sources and answer the questions that follow.

Source A

Denied the vote, legally impotent, rigidly segregated, in constant danger from individual or collective white violence . . . Blacks remained a cruelly – indeed a uniquely – deprived minority. Fifty years after Emancipation . . . those who had moved to cities and towns . . . found themselves increasingly restricted to the more menial and less well-paid occupations.

From Maldwyn Jones, *The Limits of Liberty* (1983).

Source B

This . . . mine in Lexington was where the Jim-Crow system first hit me. The Negroes and the Whites very seldom came in contact with each other. Of course there were separate company patches for living quarters. But even in the mine the Negroes and the whites worked in different places. The Negroes worked on the north side of the mine and the Whites on the south. The Negroes never got a look-in on most of the better-paying jobs. They couldn't be section foreman or electricians or surveyors . . . They could only load the coal . . . be mule-boys . . . The Negro miners got the worst places to work. We worked in the low coal, only three or four feet high.

From Angelo Herdon, *You Cannot Kill the Working Class* (1934); quoted in Thomas Frazier (ed.), *Afro-American History: Primary Sources* (1970).

Source C

We come then to the question presented. Does segregation of children in public schools solely on the basis of race, even though the physical facilities and other 'tangible' factors may be equal, deprive the children of the minority group of equal educational opportunities? We believe that it does . . . We conclude that in the field of public education the doctrine of separate but equal has no place. Separate educational facilities are inherently unequal. Therefore we hold that [those] for whom the actions have been brought are, by reason of the segregation complained of, deprived of the equal protection of the laws guaranteed by the Fourteenth Amendment.

From the Supreme Court verdict on *Brown* v. *Board of Education, Topeka* (1954).

Source D

I was in jail when Medgar Evers was murdered and nothing, I mean nothing, has been done about it. You know what really made me sick? I was in Washington DC at another time reading a paper where the US gives Byron de Beckwith – the man who is charged with murdering Medgar Evers [a black civil rights leader] – . . . so much money for some land and I ask, is this America? We can no longer ignore the fact that America is NOT the 'land of the free and the home of the brave'. I used to question this for years, what did our kids actually fight for? They would go in the service and go through all of that and come right out to be drowned in a river in Mississippi. I found this hypocrisy is all over America.

From *Life in Mississippi: An Interview with Fanny Lou Hamer* (1965); quoted in Thomas Frazier (ed.), *Afro-American History: Primary Sources* (1970).

Questions

> **a)** Study Source B.
> Explain the meaning of the term 'Jim Crow' as applied to African-Americans from the 1880s to the 1960s. (5 marks)

How you should answer this question. Marking of this question will be based on two levels of response. To achieve the higher, Level 2, standard you need more than a basic definition with limited development.

When explaining the meaning of terms, think of three Xs and an I: E**x**plain, E**x**ample, Conte**x**t and **I**mplications:

- Explain what the term 'Jim Crow' means.
- Give an example of a Jim Crow law in action.
- Context is particularly important. Try to make a direct reference to the source with the key word or phrase, but use your own knowledge to widen your comments about the term. If appropriate, ensure you cover the whole of the period, distinguish between north and south, and try to give some specific illustration of your points.
- Finally, look at the implications of the system's wavering fortunes as Jim Crow declined during the twentieth century.

Possible answer

Jim Crow became the term given to the system of segregation that developed in the southern states towards the end of the nineteenth century. Discrimination spread to all facets of life and quite often affected the north as well, though here Jim Crowism was de facto rather than de jure. In the north, it was particularly common in housing and also in employment, as indicated in Source B. But in the south it was officially sanctioned by state governments, which passed laws enforcing segregation in public places, especially towards the end of the nineteenth century. They ensured that black and white pupils did not mix in schools and on public transport. The system remained largely intact until well after the Second World War, but was undermined during the 1950s and

1960s. Legal verdicts such as the Brown case of 1954 and the growth of the Civil Rights Movement, as shown in the Sit-Ins and Freedom Rides of the early 1960s, meant that Jim Crowism was already in decline before the Civil Rights Act of 1964. After this, it only remained in a few pockets of the Deep South.

> **b)** Consult Sources A, B and D and use your own knowledge.
> How useful are Sources B and D in confirming the assertions about the legal and economic inequality of black people in Source A?. (10 marks)

How you should answer this question. Of the four levels of marks here, the highest, Level 4, expects you to select material that is relevant from all three sources and reach a carefully considered judgement in your answer.

To achieve this standard, you need to refer both to the extracts and to your own knowledge. It is best to start by looking at the assertions in Source A and then seeing how you can use Sources B and D.

Source A covers a good deal of ground in revealing the wide range of discrimination against black people: political, legal, in public places, and economically in the north. Source B confirms that the Jim Crow system was operating in areas outside the Deep South when it came to employment and gives precise details of the nature of the inequality to which you could refer in your answer. Source D confirms that there were cases where white people would not be tried for crimes against black people, despite evidence of their guilt. The later date of this extract shows that, in Mississippi at least, legal inequalities still remained in the mid-1960s. So, these two extracts are very useful when examining the degree of economic and legal inequality respectively. However, these are specific examples, which means that they might not necessarily be typical. So, your own evidence for discrimination in these fields needs to be added.

Reference could also be made to Hamer's remark in Source D that hypocrisy about the system was present all over the USA. This is an opportunity to show that little was done by the federal government to end the Jim Crow system until the legal verdicts of the Supreme Court in the 1940s and 1950s brought the subject to the forefront of the political agenda. Even in the 1960s there was a reluctance to interfere too much with areas that were seen to come under the heading of states' rights.

So the guidelines for this question are:

- Make reference to the source (A) upon which the other sources (B and D) will shed some light. Indicate what it is dealing with, but don't merely summarise the contents.
- Point out the ways in which the other two sources (B and D) are helpful. Remember to use linking words.
- Refer to any limitations of the sources in number, personality or location, and use your own knowledge to develop further illustration for your answer.

c) Discuss the view that African-Americans gained little in the way of effective equality with white people in the USA in the period 1877–1980. **(15 marks)**

How you should answer this question. To achieve the standard required for the higher levels of assessment, Levels 4 and 5, you will need to show that you can effectively and relevantly select material both from the extracts and from your own knowledge, remain analytical in your approach and attempt to reach a conclusion of your own.

Remember that this a synoptic question. It covers the entire period of 100 years. While specific knowledge is clearly essential to illustrate your argument, the examiner will be particularly looking for an overall grasp of the subject. Different good answers will probably use different material with which to illustrate their points. It is the way you handle and present the evidence that you have which is so important. Whatever the answer, you need to cover the whole of the period. You must not, for instance, concentrate on just one section, such as the 1945–68 period. This will lead to an unbalanced piece of writing. If appropriate, make sure you include references to both north and south, and if talking about inequality and segregation, a variety of issues within these fields. You may also need to look for a balance between the agitation for change from civil rights organisations and the response from the legal and political authorities, both federal and state.

The balance between your own knowledge and the documents is important. Too often, students will make one of two mistakes. On the one hand, they will fail to refer to the documents at all. This is to reject a valuable source of help. You are being asked a question and have been given some free information that will help you answer it, so use it! On the other hand, the extracts can dominate too much. Do not start a paragraph: 'In Source B . . .' Remember that the information in the sources is to be used to illustrate your points. So it is better to make your own point first, and then use the extract to illustrate it. Unlike people, sources are there to be exploited entirely for your own benefit. Try to work brief quotations from the extracts naturally into your answer. For instance one sentence might read:

In theory, the Constitution protected the black right to the franchise. In practice, however, as Source A reminds us, black people were 'denied the vote' in the south by artificial restrictions on registering, and also by the presence of a climate of fear.

Make particularly sure, in the case of this question, that you refer to Source C in your answer. It does not feature specifically in either of the other questions, so why has it been included? Clearly, it must be particularly useful when trying to illustrate points in question c).

You will have 45 minutes in total to answer this question, so you need to distribute your time sensibly, bearing in mind the different marks for each sub-section.

Part of the content of the specification includes the phrase 'The concept of Civil Rights, in particular in relation to the American Constitution'. With this in mind, we will look at the following question:

> How significant was the interpretation of the US Constitution in helping or hindering the cause of civil rights in the period 1877–1980?

How you should answer this question. This is the synoptic part of the assessment and you will need to look at a theme or trend over at least 100 years. While a good deal of specific knowledge is clearly essential to illustrate your answer, the examiner will also be looking for an underlying understanding of the topic. Different good answers will use contrasting yet equally appropriate illustrations to get their points across. When answering, try to cover as wide a range of points as possible. For example, don't just concentrate on a narrow period such as 1945–68: this would lead to an unbalanced essay.

A 'significance' question calls for a particular technique. It is not like the list-type assignments you will have encountered at AS level. In these you were asked 'why' something occurred and then you could develop your answer with a list of arguments. The overall theme will be 'the cause of civil rights'. But the question is angled to a particular aspect of that theme and you have to respond. You need to show that you can adapt your knowledge and understanding to the question set. In this case, you are asked to assess the role of the Constitution and its interpretation.

What equipment do you require? You will need to know about the important amendments to the Constitution after the abolition of slavery, and why they might be thought to assist the cause of civil rights. For instance, there is the famous 'equal protection clause' of the Fourteenth Amendment. But to see whether these amendments were helpful in practice will require you to look at the institutions that could influence or actually give interpretations of the Constitution:

- civil rights groups willing to assert their constitutional rights
- a Supreme Court able to give positive or negative judgments
- state governments prepared to enforce the relevant clauses of the Constitution
- a presidential executive with the will to enforce the decisions if no action is forthcoming elsewhere.

You will have to decide how much time you will devote to 'hinder' and how much to 'help'.

Hinder:

- Supreme Court judgments such as *Plessy* v. *Ferguson* (1896).
- State governments passing 'Jim Crow' laws during the late nineteenth century.
- Federal governments allowing states to develop their own state constitutional laws on segregation.

- The general reluctance of presidents to take action to enforce constitutional rights before the late 1950s.

Help:

- More positive judgments by the Supreme Court in the 1930s and 1940s, culminating in the *Brown* v. *Board of Education, Topeka* decision in 1954.
- The reaction of civil rights groups, which became willing to test Court decisions. Examples are the Montgomery Bus Boycott after the Brown verdict (1954) and the Freedom Rides after the *Boynton* v. *Virginia* case (1960).
- The increased willingness of presidents to act, such as Kennedy and Johnson in the 1960s. An example is the desegregation of inter-state travel in 1962.
- Legislation passed by Congress. Early legislation such as the Civil Rights Act (1875) had been struck down by the Supreme Court and thereafter Congress was more reluctant to act. But in the 1960s it was persuaded to pass the Civil Rights Act (1964) and the Voting Rights Act (1965).

When preparing your material, a theme may come to mind. For instance, you may feel you want to argue as follows:

For much of the century under discussion, the potentially helpful clauses in the Federal Constitution lay dormant. When the Supreme Court did make a judgment, it was usually negative. However, in the later part of the period, a combination of a more sympathetic Court and active civil rights organisations forced presidents and Congress to act.

Look at the above paragraph. It could form the basis of an introduction to your essay. You should try to develop a clear general theme that relates directly to the question and gives you a basic structure for further progress.

Some of the good habits you should have picked up at AS will help you here. Careful structuring paragraph by paragraph, the point-proof approach, and the use of general assertions followed by specific illustration could all be invaluable. The analysis you will be expected to do at this level will be more sophisticated then merely 'why' questions, which you can plan with a list of reasons. 'To what extent' and 'how far' involve more complex planning. You have to adapt your knowledge to the particular angle of the question that the examiner has given you.

To reach the top band on this question, you will need to define your terms carefully, produce a balanced answer across the whole period and introduce a sense of comparison between the different factors. Remember that you have just 45 minutes to answer the question. Your points need to range widely and bring in specific illustration. So, how do you avoid running out of time? By making sure that, while giving each point its due weight, you do not linger excessively in any one area. The top-grade candidates will show good control of their material throughout and will be rewarded accordingly.

BIBLIOGRAPHY

AS SECTION

These books are also suitable as introductions to A2.

General texts
The following books are good for overall context and contain useful material on civil rights.
J. M. Blum, *Years of Discord: American Politics and Society 1961–74* (Norton, 1992)
W. H. Chafe, *The Unfinished Journey: America since World War Two* (Oxford University Press, 4th edn, 1999)
G. Gerstle, E. Rosenberg and N. Rosenberg, *America Transformed: A History of the US since 1900* (Harcourt Brace, 1999)
M. Jones, *The Limits of Liberty: American History 1607–1980* (Oxford University Press, 1983)

Surveys of civil rights, 1941–80
C. Patterson, *The Civil Rights Movement* (Facts on File, 1995)
H. Sitkoff, *The Struggle for Black Equality 1954–92* (Wang, 1993)
J. White, *Martin Luther King, Jr, and the Civil Rights Movement in America* (British Association for American Studies, 1981)
J. White, *Black Leadership in America* (Longman, 2nd edn, 1990)

Biographies
C. Carson (ed.), *The Autobiography of Martin Luther King,* (Warner Books, 1998)
R. Jakoubek, *Martin Luther King, Jr: Civil Rights Leader* (Chelsea House, 1989)
N. Shuker, *Martin Luther King* (Burke, 1988)

Source books
Coretta Scott King (ed.), *The Words of Martin Luther King* (Collins, 1986)

A2 SECTION
General texts on civil rights
D. H. Bennett, *The Party of Fear: From Nativist Movements to the New Right* (University of North Carolina Press, 1988)
J. M. Blum, *Years of Discord: American Politics and Society 1961–1974* (New Norton, 1992)
C. Bolt, *American Indian Policy and American Reform* (Unwin, 1990)
P. S. Boyer et al, *The Enduring Vision: A History of the American People* (Houghton Mifflin Company, 1998)
T. Branch, *Parting the Waters* (Macmillan, 1990)
T. Branch, *Pillar of Fire: America in the King Years 1963–4* (Simon and Schuster, 1999)
D. Brown, *Bury My Heart at Wounded Knee* (Vintage, 1970)
W. H. Chafe, *Civilities and Civil Rights* (Oxford University Press, 1980)

J. H. Cone, *Martin and Malcolm and America* (Harper Collins, British edn, 1993)

R. Cook, *Sweet Land of Liberty?* (Longman, 1998)

A. Fairclough, *To Redeem the Soul of America: The Southern Christian Leadership Conference and Martin Luther King Jr* (University of Georgia Press, 1987)

E. Foner, *A Short History of Reconstruction 1863–1877* (Harper Perennial, 1990)

J. H. Franklin and A. Moss Jr, *From Slavery to Freedom: A History of African Americans Vol. 2* (McGraw Hill, 1994)

D. Garrow, *Bearing the Cross: America in the King Years 1954–63* (Vintage, 1988)

D. Garrow, *Protest at Selma* (Yale University Press, 1978)

P. Johnson, *A History of the American People* (Pheonix Giant Paperback, 1997)

S. Lawson, *Running for freedom: Civil Rights and Black Politics in America since 1941* (Columbia University Press, 1985)

J. Mandle, *Not Slave, Not Free* (Duke University Press, 1992)

M. Marable, *Race, Reform, and Rebellion* (University Press of Mississippi, 2nd edn, 1991)

A. Meier and E. Rudwick Cure, *A Study in the Civil Rights Movement 1947–68* (Oxford University Press, 1973)

Aldon Morris, *The Origins of the Civil Rights Movement* (Macmillan, 1984)

M. B. Norton et al, *The People and the Nation: A History of the United States* (Houghton Mifflin Company, 1996)

B. Perry, *Malcolm* (Station Hill, 1991)

R. Polenberg, *One Nation Divisible* (Penguin, 1982)

W. T. M. Riches, *The Civil Rights Movement: Struggle and Resistance* (Macmillan, 1997)

S. Rowbotham, *A Century of Women: The History of Women in Britain and the United States* (Penguin Books, 1999)

M. P. Servin, *An Awakened Minority: The Mexican-Americans* (Glencoe Press, 1974)

C. Vann Woodward, *The Strange Career of Jim Crow* (Oxford University Press, 1974)

W. J. Wilson, *The Declining Significance of Race* (Chicago University Press, 1978)

N. A. Wynn, *The Afro-American and the Second World War* (Holmes and Meier, 2nd edn, 1993)

Useful article

Richard Dalfiume, 'The Forgotten Years of the Negro Revolution', *Journal of American History* (1968)

Source books

T. R. Frazier (ed.), *Afro American History: Primary Sources* (Harcourt Brace and World, 1970)

T. Hampton, *Voices of Freedom: An Oral History of the Civil Rights Movement* (Bantam, 1990)

Biographies

J. Coliaco, *Martin Luther King Jr.: Apostle of Militant Non-violence* (Macmillan, 1993)

A. Fairclough, *Martin Luther King Jr.* (University of Georgia Press, 1990)

S. B. Oates, *Let the Trumpet Sound: A Biography of Martin Luther King* (Search Press, 1982)

B. Perry, *Malcolm* (Station Hill, 1991)

INDEX